ALL THE FREQUENT TROUBLES OF OUR DAYS

Also by Rebecca Donner

Sunset Terrace

Burnout

ALL THE FREQUENT TROUBLES OF OUR DAYS

The True Story of the Woman at the Heart of the German Resistance to Hitler

REBECCA DONNER

CANONGATE

This paperback edition published in Great Britain in 2022
by Canongate Books

First published in Great Britain in 2021
by Canongate Books Ltd, 14 High Street, Edinburgh EH1 1TE

canongate.co.uk

First published in the USA in 2021
by Little, Brown and Company, an imprint of Hachette Book Group,
1290 Avenue of the Americas, New York, NY 10104

1

Excerpt from *Ravensbruck: Life and Death in Hitler's Concentration Camp for Women*
by Sarah Helm, copyright © 2015 by Sarah Helm. Used by permission of Nan A.
Talese, an imprint of the Knopf Doubleday Publishing Group, a division of
Penguin Random House LLC. All rights reserved. Excerpt from *The Notebooks of
Thomas Wolfe* by Richard S. Kennedy and Paschal Reeves, copyright © 1970 by the
University of North Carolina Press. Used by permission of the publisher. www.
uncpress.org. Excerpt from *The 'House Prison' at Gestapo Headquarters in Berlin:
Terror and Resistance* is reprinted with the kind permission of Stiftung Topographie
des Terrors. Excerpts from *Two Thousand and Ten Days of Hitler*, copyright © 1940
by Patsy Ziemer. Reprinted with the kind permission of Barbara Eadie Myer of the
Estate of Patsy Ziemer.

Illustration credits begin on p. 545.

British Library Cataloguing-in-Publication Data
A catalogue record for this book is available on
request from the British Library

ISBN 978 1 78689 221 8

Printed and bound in Great Britain by Clays Ltd, Elcograf S.p.A.

For Mildred and Don

Contents

THE BOY
III (1938–1939)

MILDRED
IV (1933–1935)

THE BOY
V (1939)

MILDRED
VI (1935–1937)

VII (1937–1939)

THE BOY

VIII (1937–1940)

MILDRED

IX (1940–1942)

X (1942–1945)

XI (1942–1952)

THE BOY

XII (1946)

Author's Note

This is a work of nonfiction.

Any words that appear between quotation marks are from a letter, a postcard, a memoir, a diary, a handwritten note, a declassified intelligence report, or other document that I discovered in an archive.

In books, newspaper articles, and archival documents, Mildred appears variously as Mildred Harnack, Mildred Fish-Harnack, and Mildred Harnack-Fish. The confusion stems from Mildred herself. In the United States, she called herself Mildred Fish-Harnack; in Germany, she called herself Mildred Harnack-Fish. For the sake of simplicity, I refer to her in these pages as Mildred Harnack.

Mildred was known to many as a woman who chose her words carefully. "Her utterances were sparse," a German woman remembered, "often with a surprising clarity." "She listened quietly," an American woman recalled. "When she did speak, she commanded attention." If you flip to the end of the book you'll see the sources for these quotations. Throughout this book I use endnotes, not footnotes, to cite my sources.

This book follows two narratives: one chronicles Mildred, and one chronicles a boy named Don. In Don's chapters, I use italics instead of quotation marks to indicate the thoughts and conversations he remembered having during that time. During the Second World War, at the age of eleven, Don became Mildred's courier.

The title of this book comes from a poem by Johann Wolfgang von Goethe that Mildred translated in her prison cell. There is some debate about whether an "s" can be discerned at the end of the word "trouble" in Mildred's original handwritten translation. We must bear in mind that translation is an art, not a science; Mildred's translations were often looser, and less literal, than the academic renditions of Goethe poems that we may encounter. We must also bear in mind that Mildred wrote with a pencil stub in a damp prison cell.

Harald Poelchau remembered seeing Mildred bent over the book of Goethe poems, the pencil stub in her hand, when he visited her prison cell. Poelchau worked as a chaplain of the prison and was a member of an underground resistance group founded in the rural town of Kreisau in Silesia. It is because of Poelchau that we have Mildred's translations of Goethe. On February 16, 1943, he slipped the book into the folds of his robe and smuggled it out.

ALL THE FREQUENT
TROUBLES OF OUR DAYS

Fragment

Questionnaire
Plötzensee Prison, Berlin
February 16, 1943

Last name	Harnack
First name	Mildred
Date of birth	9/16/02
Place of birth	Milwaukee, Wisconsin, USA
Do you have assets? How much and what do they include?	8.47 (?) in my pocket 1 ship ticket United States Lines $127 (paid in Reichsmark) in my purse some money in Deutsche Bank Apartment furnishings, especially in the two front rooms, Woyrschstr. 16, Berlin, with two Oriental carpets; a light and a dark one with uneven stars and colors
Why are you punished now? Do you admit committing the crime you are charged with? In which circumstances and for what reason did you commit the crime?	Accomplice in treason

Introduction

HER AIM WAS SELF-ERASURE. THE more invisible she was, the better her chances of survival. In her journal she noted what she ate, read, thought. The first was uncontroversial. The second and third were not. For this reason, she hid the journal. When she suspected the Gestapo was closing in on her, she destroyed it. Burned it, most likely.

She was at the harrowing center of the German resistance, but she wasn't German, nor was she Polish or French. She was American—conspicuously so. The men she recruited acquired code names: Armless, Beamer, Worker. She operated under no code name. Still, she was elusive. The nature of her work required absolute secrecy. She didn't dare tell her family, who were scattered across the towns and dairy farms of the Midwest. They remained bewildered that she, at twenty-six, had jumped aboard a steamer ship and crossed the Atlantic, leaving behind everyone she loved.

Her family is my family. Three generations separate us. She preferred anonymity, so I will whisper her name: *Mildred Harnack.*

In 1932, she held her first clandestine meeting in her apartment—a small band of political activists that grew into the largest underground resistance group in Berlin by the end of the decade. During the Second World War, her group collaborated with a Soviet espionage network that conspired to defeat Hitler, employing agents and operatives in Paris, Geneva, Brussels, and Berlin. In the fall of 1942, the Gestapo pounced. She was thrown in prison. So were her coconspirators. During a hastily convened trial at the Reichskriegsgericht—the Reich Court-Martial—a prosecutor who'd earned the moniker "Hitler's Bloodhound" hammered them with questions.

She sat on a wooden chair in the back of the courtroom. Other chairs held high-ranking Nazi officers. At the center of the room sat a panel of five judges. Everyone there was German except her.

When it was her turn, she approached the stand. She was emaciated, her lungs ravaged by tuberculosis she'd contracted in prison. How long she stood there remains unknown; surviving documents don't note the time the prosecutor began questioning her or the time he stopped. What is known is this: the answers she gave him were lies, real whoppers.

The judges believed her. The sentence she received was considered mild: six years of hard labor in a prison camp. Two days later, Hitler overrode the verdict and ordered her execution. On February 16, 1943, she was strapped to a guillotine and beheaded.

AFTER THE WAR, THE U.S. Army's Counter Intelligence Corps opened an investigation. "Mildred Harnack's actions are laudable," one CIC official observed in 1946, noting the "rather extensive file" they had on her. "It is quite possible that investigation will disclose the commission of a war crime," wrote another. Their higher-ranking colleague later reprimanded them in a terse memo: "This case is classified S/R [secret/restricted] and should *not have been* referred for investigation. Withdraw case from Detachment 'D' and *do not* continue the investigation."

So the CIC buried her case. The reason for this would not come to light for over fifty years.

Still, news leaked out. On December 1, 1947, the *New York Times* ran a story under the headline HITLER BEHEADED AMERICAN WOMAN AS A PERSONAL REPRISAL IN 1943. "With comprehensive knowledge of the German underground movement, Mildred Harnack stood up courageously under Gestapo torture and revealed nothing," it noted. Later that week, the *Washington Post* praised her as "one of the leaders in the underground against the Nazis." Readers of the *New York*

Times and the *Washington Post* were probably surprised to learn that an active underground resistance in Germany had even existed.

A central problem for anyone who wanted to write about her group was a lack of documentary evidence. It wasn't until 1989, when the Berlin Wall came crashing down, that a trove of documents stashed in an East German archive came to light. Several years later, Russia permitted historians a peek at foreign intelligence files, and in 1998, under the Nazi War Crimes Disclosure Act, the CIA, FBI, and U.S. Army began to release records once classified as top secret, a process that continues to this day. We now have a more nuanced understanding of the underground resistance in Germany, but factual inaccuracies persist. Details about Mildred Harnack are scant and frequently incorrect. The ashes of the journal she kept can't serve as a corrective.

Despite her wish to remain invisible, she left a trail for us to follow.

Along the trail are official documents—British, U.S., and Soviet-era intelligence files, thick as your wrist. Then there are the unofficial documents, which reveal deeper truths: The letters she wrote. The letters other people wrote to her and about her. Family and friends left behind notes, datebooks, diaries, photographs, testimonials. It can't be said that there was a consensus about the woman they knew, or thought they knew. To many, she was an enigma, inspiring a range of contradictory conclusions about who she was and why she did what she did.

Nearly all the people who knew her are lost to history. Those who are still alive are well into their nineties. One I hoped to find more than any other.

He was just a boy when he met Mildred, young enough to be her son. I tracked him down, and implored him: *What did she tell you? How did she enter a room? Did you hear her weep? Sing? Did she trust you?*

The Boy with the Blue Knapsack

1939

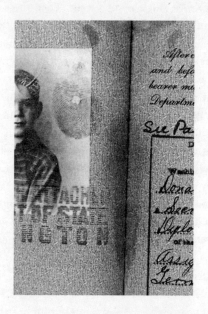

That night I saw a movie of soldiers. There was a little speech of Hitler, which I didn't _____ there was a dance.

SNOW. FEAR. LIGHT. One morning in December 1939, an eleven-year-old boy bursts out of the arched front door of an apartment building in Berlin, wondering whether he'll get caught. On his back he carries a blue knapsack. Before him, the wide expanse of Schöneberg Park is blanketed in white. He shivers. He wears a wool coat, a black cap. The cap makes him look like a German boy.

Four steps and he's down the stairs; four more and he's crossing the street. The boy heads for the U-Bahn station. He's not traveling far. A ten-minute ride to Nollendorfplatz, a short walk to Woyrschstrasse 16. His father showed him how. His father said: *Pay attention.* And: *Talk to no one.*

The boy sees a tall man with a handlebar mustache, a woman wearing a fur hat, two boys with red mittens, and a goose-stepping girl. Christmas is soon. Along the sidewalk, merchants stand behind carts, ringing bells. In one cart, charred chestnuts. In another, wilted cabbages. In another, crockery. In another, squadrons of marzipan soldiers. Somewhere, buildings are in flames, bombs exploding. The boy knows the fighting is far away, but he imagines he can smell the war.

Burnt. Like the charred chestnuts.

Headlines blackening the pages of Berlin newspapers that month report ALL BRITISH AIR ATTACKS ARE DOOMED TO FAIL, denounce THE PLAGUE OF JEWS, and promise VICTORY IS CERTAIN! The newspapers are loaded with lies. The boy knows this from his father, who spends most of his waking hours at his desk writing intelligence reports, sending them to Washington by telegram if they are confidential and by diplomatic pouch if they are highly confidential. On several occasions, the boy accompanies his father to Bremerhaven, a port on the North Sea coast, where his father hands the diplomatic pouch to a man in the foreign service, who then boards a steamer ship. Sometimes, the report inside is addressed to Secretary of the Treasury Henry Morgenthau, sometimes to Secretary of State Cordell Hull.

The boy lifts his chin, searches the sky. German bombers. He doesn't see them but he knows they're up there. Their rumbling rattles his teeth, or maybe he's just jittery, thinking about the job he's got to do.

An important job, said his father.

Like yours? asked the boy.

Like mine, yessiree, said his father, a Kansas native who holds two positions, one at the U.S. embassy in Berlin and one in the ranks of a department that has no official name or organizational structure, although soon it will come under the auspices of a hastily cobbled-together wartime intelligence group called the Office of the Coordinator of Information, the precursor to what will eventually become — after several iterations, upheavals, shake-ups, and shakedowns — the Central Intelligence Agency.

At the U-Bahn station, the boy waits on the platform. The train comes; its doors gasp open.

He jumps in, finds a seat. Nollendorfplatz. Only ten minutes away.

THREE AND A HALF months earlier, shortly before the German Luftwaffe dropped five hundred sixty tons of explosive bombs onto Poland, the State Department urged all the men at the U.S. embassy in Berlin to send their wives and children back home to America. The boy and his mother went to Norway instead. They checked into a hotel in Oslo, where they waited for the boy's father to send a message.

The message came in November, early in the morning. They packed quickly.

Where are we going? the boy asked.

Back to Berlin, his mother said.

Why? the boy asked. A war was under way. It didn't make sense to return to Berlin.

We need to help some people was his mother's response.

They boarded a coal-powered train that swept them past farms and fields and ice-caked lakes. Snowcapped mountains lay bunched together, as if huddling for warmth. The boy rested his forehead on the window, watching it all whiz by, wondering, *Help how?*

NOLLENDORFPLATZ.

The boy shoulders his knapsack and exits the train, jumping nimbly over the gap between track and platform. He walks up a flight of stairs and out a glass door. Once past the U-Bahn station, he counts his steps in German: *eins, zwei, drei.* At *zwanzig* he squats down. His shoelaces are tied, but he fakes that they're loose and ties them again, stealing a glance over his shoulder. Two men. One is bald; one wears wire-framed glasses. He remembers what his father told him: *Make sure no one follows you.*

He crosses the street. At the corner is an enormous department store, the Kaufhaus des Westens. Berliners call it the KaDeWe. He walks in.

The KaDeWe smells of perfume and doughnuts. There are seven stories. It won't be long before an American bomber crashes into the building during an air raid, making a spectacular explosion, but right now the building is as intact as it is inviting. The perfect place, the boy knows, to give someone the slip. He skips every other stair to the second floor, walks past a carousel of winter coats, ducks into an elevator that takes him up to the top and back down to the ground floor, where he exits through a side door. Once outside he breaks into a run, the knapsack banging against his back.

No one follows him that day.

But suppose you did. You would have seen an eleven-year-old boy with a blue knapsack run all the way to Woyrschstrasse 16, a few blocks south of the Tiergarten. If you'd asked him why he was visiting Woyrschstrasse 16, he would have told you that his tutor was giving him lessons there. This is only half true.

He enters the building and races up the stairs, his knapsack heavy with books. At the top floor, a young woman wearing a modest dress typical of Nazi Berliner *Frauen* opens the door. Her honey-colored hair is pulled back into a bun.

You would not guess that she, too, is American. Nor would you suspect that when the boy leaves the apartment an hour later, his knapsack will contain something more valuable than books.

THE BOY IS HER courier, in the language of espionage. An eleven-year-old spy. Twice a week he visits her apartment, where they sit side by side on a sofa with wooden armrests and talk about the books she assigns him. The books are various and unpredictable: classics and potboilers, Shakespeare and cowboy Westerns. She questions him about the plot, the characters, the themes. She has a low, kind voice. She says, *Tell me what this book is about.* She says, *Tell me what you think, not what you think you should think.* She is unlike any teacher he has ever had.

Their lesson lasts an hour, sometimes two. When it's over, she asks, *Which way are you going home today?*

Every time he takes a different route—she makes sure of it. Looking into his eyes, her gaze steady and solemn, she asks the boy to repeat the street names. If his attention wanders, she will cup his cheeks with her hands, the way his mother does, and ask him to say the names again.

At the door, she helps him with his coat and slips a piece of paper into his knapsack. Sometimes the paper looks like a reading list. Sometimes it looks like a recipe. Sometimes it looks like a letter, which she signs *Mildred* or, simply, *M.*

Mildred

I

We Must Change This Situation as Soon as Possible

1932

rring only Nazis to get through with little slits in it for shooter back and forth taking range at ployed + workers, Communists + nd down the streets on the limit to the police and Fascists. of having been bled white by (they were forbidden) gathered near

1.

On July 29, 1932, Mildred exits the U–Bahn station and heads north on Friedrichstrasse, a leather satchel in her grip. It's Friday. She's on her way to the University of Berlin, where she lectures twice a week.

Her pace is brisk. Berlin is bustling; the sidewalks are clogged with pedestrians, the streets swarm with cars, trams, buses, bicyclists. Everywhere she looks, she sees people, young and old, rich and poor. Mainly poor. Begging, sleeping, fighting, selling shoelaces, scraps of newspaper, passing between them cigarette butts scrounged from a gutter.

Two years ago, the University of Berlin hired her to teach a course called American Literary History. The department head may have expected her to lecture about authors of the previous century—Herman Melville or Nathaniel Hawthorne or James Fenimore Cooper—but Mildred doesn't want to discuss books about sailors or adulteresses or frontiersmen. She wants to talk about books written by people living *now,* especially those who write about what it's like to be poor. Facing a roomful of German undergraduates, she wants to deepen their understanding of the downtrodden at a time when so many in their own country are caught in a daily struggle to put bread on their tables. And so for four semesters she has lectured about American farmers and factory workers and immigrants, about William Faulkner and John Dos Passos and Theodore Dreiser. She doesn't hide her political views. Her lectures move fluidly from American novels to the prevalence of the poor in Germany and the troubling ascent of the Nazi Party.

"Germany is going through such very dark hours," she wrote in a recent letter to her mother. "All feel the menace but many hide their heads in the sand."

She reaches a wide boulevard: Unter den Linden. She turns right.

The boulevard takes its name from the profusion of linden trees flanking it, trees that are in full bloom now, cascades of tiny white blossoms perfuming the air she breathes. But all this beauty can't mask the ugliness here. Swastikas are cropping up like daisies everywhere: on posters pasted to the walls of U-Bahn stations, on flags and banners and pamphlets. A white-haired, walrus-mustached man is leading the country right now, but just barely. President Paul von Hindenburg is eighty-four, tottering into senility. A politician half his age is growing in popularity, a high-school dropout named Adolf Hitler who, Mildred predicts, will bring "a great increase of misery and oppression."

She turns left. Before her is the University of Berlin.

She enters the building. The hallways swarm with students. She approaches the door of her classroom knowing that today's lecture will be her last. An administrator has already informed her that she will not be invited back to teach in the fall.

Mildred can hardly believe it. All along, she has taken for granted that she can speak her mind.

2.

In letters to her mother, Mildred writes plainly and simply, knowing that Georgina Fish's tenth-grade education hasn't prepared her for the complexities of German politics.

> *There is a large group of people here which, feeling the wrongness of the situation — their own poverty or danger of poverty — leaps to the conclusion that, since things were better before, it would be a good idea to have a more absolute government again.*

The official name of the Nazi Party is the Nationalsozialistische Deutsche Arbeiterpartei (NSDAP), Mildred explains, or the National Socialist German Workers' Party, "although it has nothing to do with socialism and the name itself is a lie. It thinks itself highly moral and like the Ku Klux Klan makes a campaign of hatred against the Jews."

Mildred writes most of these letters with a black-ink pen. Sometimes she writes part of the letter while she's on the U-Bahn, on her way to teach a class, and finishes it on the typewriter at home. Sometimes it's the reverse; she types the letter first and finishes it on the U-Bahn, apologizing for her messy handwriting.

ater A and I were in the Lustgarten and saw all together a mighty crowd. But not yet so mighty as those with the re National Socialists. who in their ignorance support the fascists

Mildred doesn't tell her mother right away about losing her job at the University of Berlin. She will wait awhile. Maybe a week. Maybe two. She doesn't want to worry Georgina Fish, who lives in a small, brown-wallpapered room across the Atlantic and is prone to worrying.

3.

Fired. Booted. Axed.

Whatever word you choose, the outcome is the same. The officious administrator refused to articulate a reason. Contracts are not renewed for various individuals for various reasons at various times.

Mildred is twenty-nine, still a graduate student, halfway through her dissertation. She had planned to teach American Literary History until she got her PhD. What now? She can take classes at the University of Berlin, but she's not permitted to teach them anymore. A group of students have circulated a petition urging the university to reconsider its decision. It's no use, though. The bustling hallway, the shuffle of footsteps, the doorknob in her hand, the cold metal feel of it—they're all tokens of her time here, conspiring to remind her that she can't return.

She opens the classroom door and strides in.

Her students, seated in rows before her, rise to their feet. This is the custom in German universities, a gesture of respect. When she sees what they've done to her desk, she's overcome with emotion. They have covered it with flowers, a profusion of lavender and golden blooms, a big, beautiful pile. Eyes brimming, she makes a clumsy joke.

It's so high I can't see your faces!

4.

Within spitting distance of the University of Berlin is Opernplatz, a large public square. Students carrying satchels of books mingle here between classes, strolling past the grand butterscotch columns of the State Opera. In the evening, wealthy operagoers spill out onto the square, and beggars trail raggedly alongside them, stretching out open palms. Opernplatz is the whole of German society, condensed.

Next year, students in a Nazi fraternity will burn twenty-five thousand books here, throwing them into a massive bonfire at the center of the square. The fraternity will stage similar bonfires in universities across Germany, circulating a list of authors deemed deviant, impure, "un-German." The list will include Nobel Prize winners and obscure writers, philosophers and playwrights, novelists and physicists. Books by Jews and Christians and atheists will be condemned alongside books by Communists, socialists, and anarchists. Nearly every book Mildred assigned in the two years she taught at the University of Berlin will be burned.

5.

The Reichstag—Germany's parliament—is a cornerstone of democracy, acting as a check and balance to the executive authority of President Paul von Hindenburg. Seats in the Reichstag are open to a dizzying array of political parties, from the well established to the lunatic fringe.

In 1928, the Nazi Party got less than 3 percent of the vote in a Reichstag election.

In 1930, it got 18 percent.

And in 1932? Fascism is on the rise in Germany, but it still seems possible to defeat it. Left-wing politicians outnumber Nazis by a wide margin.

On July 31, 1932—two days after Mildred is ousted from the University of Berlin—there will be another election. Walking around Berlin, Mildred sees Nazi propaganda wherever the poor and unemployed congregate: parks, plazas, train stations, public urinals. Posters stamped with swastikas promise "Work! Freedom! Bread!" Hitler used the same slogan when he ran for president in March, and lost. President Hindenburg has just started his second seven-year term. What Hitler will do next is unclear.

Mildred waits for the Reichstag election results with mounting anxiety. Her neighbors wait, too, clustering around the newspaper kiosks dotting the block.

6.

The Nazi Party gets 37 percent of the vote. For the first time in history, it's the largest party in the Reichstag. The Social Democratic Party trails behind, with 22 percent. The Communist Party trails even further, with 15 percent. The remaining 26 percent is divided among a squabbling hodgepodge of parties. Every imaginable point of view is represented. They have names like "Radical Middle Party" and "Reich Party of the German Middle Class" and "National Middle Party Against Fascism and Socialism" and "German Farmers Party" and "Christian Social People's Service Party" and "Justice Movement Against All Parties and Wage Cuts and for Provision for Unemployment" and "Highest Salary for Civil Servants, 5,000 Marks for the Unemployed and Victims of the War, Hitherto Trodden Underfoot."

On the heels of the Nazi Party's victory, Hitler commands President Hindenburg to name him chancellor of Germany. President Hindenburg refuses.

7.

Mildred reads *Mein Kampf.* Hitler's book has been published in two volumes, the first in 1925, the second in 1926. In 1932, it isn't read widely in Germany—not yet. An English translation hasn't been published yet either. Mildred worries that Americans don't understand how dangerous Hitler is.

Germans don't understand either. Too many are dismissive. Most major German newspapers declined to run reviews of *Mein Kampf* when the book was published. One newspaper predicted that Hitler's political career would be "completely finished" after people read his ramblings. Another mocked Hitler's "fuzzy mind." Even Nazis and right-wing nationalists took potshots. The pro-Nazi newspaper *Deutsche Zeitung* sneered at Hitler's "illogical ranting." The nationalist newspaper *Neue Preussliche Zeitung* fumed: "One seeks ingenuity and finds only arrogance, one seeks stimulation and reaps boredom, one seeks love and enthusiasm and finds platitudes, one seeks healthy hatred and finds insults....Is this the book for the German people? That would be dreadful!" When Hitler bragged that all of Germany was eagerly anticipating his book, the anti-Semitic newspaper *Das Bayerische Vaterland* scoffed at Hitler's egomania. "O how modest! Why not the entire universe?"

Cartoons gleefully mocked Hitler. The popular magazine *Simplicissimus* ran a derisive front-page caricature of Hitler peddling *Mein Kampf* to uninterested customers in a beer hall.

It was at a beer hall in Munich, the Hofbräuhaus, where Hitler, age thirty, delivered one of his first significant speeches. The occasion was a meeting held on February 24, 1920, by the German Workers' Party, an obscure political party with only 190 members, Hitler among them. Hitler had fought in the First World War and was still in the army, working in the intelligence department of the Reichswehr. He had a dim view of the German Workers' Party steering committee, a bickering bunch of drones who chose a priggish doctor to deliver the first speech.

When the doctor was done, Hitler leaped onto a long table positioned smack in the middle of the crowd. His oratorical style was provocative, his language colloquial and at times coarse. He hollered insults at politicians, capitalists, and Jews. He castigated the Reich finance minister for supporting the Treaty of Versailles, a humiliating concession to the victors of the war that would bring Germans to their knees, he warned, unless they fought back. "Our motto is only struggle!" Hitler cried. The beer-hall crowd, a fizzy mix of working-class and middle-class men, erupted—some cheering, some jeering. His controversial speeches fueled attendance at future meetings of the German Workers' Party, which grew to 3,300 members by the end of 1921, at which point it had a new name, the National Socialist German Workers' Party, nicknamed the Nazi Party. It also had a new chairman, Hitler, who gave himself a new title: Führer (Leader).

Simplicissimus skewered the Führer as a minor player on the stage of German politics. From 1921 through 1932, Hitler appeared in the magazine as a harmless imbecile. A cartoon in 1930 lampooned Hitler as a doltish schoolboy copying passages from *Das Kapital* while the ghost of Karl Marx scolds him ("Adolf, Adolf! Give my theories back to the Socialists!"). Another showed two policemen raiding the cavernous interior of Hitler's empty head and finding a brain so small they needed tweezers to lift it out.

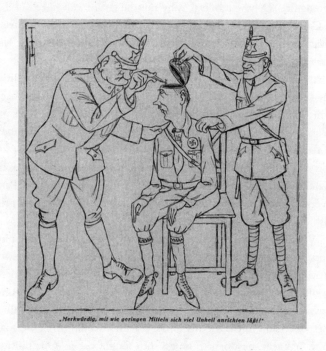

„Merkwürdig, mit wie geringen Mitteln sich viel Unheil anrichten läßt!"

For over a decade, the *Münchener Post* published mocking screeds against Hitler and his band of bootlicking cronies, linking them to sex scandals and binges at luxury hotels. "Hitler," the paper gloated, "has no secrets from us." Hitler claimed to enjoy the publicity ("It makes no difference whatever whether they laugh at us or revile us," he wrote in *Mein Kampf*, "whether they represent us as clowns or criminals; the main thing is that they mention us"), but the paper's ridicule irked him so much that he dispatched a group of thugs to raid the offices of the *Münchener Post* in 1923 and smash everything in sight. The thugs were Hitler's personal bodyguards, the Stosstrupp Adolf Hitler—the Adolf Hitler Assault Squad.

As Hitler's popularity increased, the *Münchener Post* sounded an alarm about his murderous agenda. Under the headline THE JEWS IN THE THIRD REICH, a 1931 article reported a "secret plan" for "the solution of the Jewish question." An unnamed Nazi source had leaked a detailed list of restrictions that would be imposed on Jews if the Nazi Party got its way; there was also a plan "to use the Jews in Germany for slave labor." Now, in 1932, the paper runs a story about "Cell G," a secret death squad within the ranks of the Nazi Party that murders Hitler's opponents. The journalists at the *Münchener Post,* known to readers as a mouthpiece of the Social Democratic Party, take Hitler seriously, even as many others don't.

8.

In Alexanderplatz, Mildred sees a bloody confrontation. A ragged procession of unemployed factory workers march in the public square shouting, "We are hungry!" as police officers bludgeon them with batons. A military tank appears—a monster of a vehicle, Mildred recounts later, "with little slits in it for shooting and an automatic gun which swung back and forth taking range at the crowd."

The tank is driven by men known as Schutzstaffel—or simply the SS. They wear black uniforms and are not members of the German police or in any way affiliated with the German government. They're an elite corps of officers in a private paramilitary force run by the Nazi Party. The size of this private army—which includes a number of the bodyguards in the assault squad who protected Hitler when he was hollering speeches in beer halls—has been building steadily since the mid-1920s. So has another private paramilitary army of men, in brown uniforms, known colloquially as Brownshirts and more formally as Sturmabteilung—Storm Troopers—or simply the SA. In 1932, the number of Storm Troopers is a staggering 400,000. Both paramilitary forces stand armed and ready to carry out orders issued by the Nazi Party, which, to all appearances, is preparing for a violent right-wing revolution in Germany.

9.

Everywhere Mildred looks, she sees signs of brutality and suffering. She writes:

Many of the unemployed have the look of having been bled white by hunger and cold.

And

They eat potatoes day after day and nothing else.

And

The situation grows steadily worse.

While walking to the U–Bahn, she spots a German woman who looks about the same age as her own mother

standing on the street-corner in the bitter wind. She had no coat on, and her clothes were thin and threadbare, and she was trying pitifully to sell papers. Whenever I see such a sight, and there are many such to be seen, I think We must change this situation as soon as possible.

Yankee Doodle Dandy

1902–1919

—Thomas J h 37 28th
—William C horse-dlr h 2102 Grand av
—William H yardmaster h 429 19th av
                        John K Fish)

down the other day and
now he can't walk.
Well I'm getting sleepy
Good-by
        Mildred
P.S. I love's 'oo.

1.

Mildred entered the world on September 16, 1902. She was born at home, on the first floor of a boardinghouse in Milwaukee with a leaky roof and no indoor plumbing. She was her mother's fourth child. Georgina Fish hadn't planned on getting pregnant. Three children were enough, more than enough.

More often than not, Mildred's father was flat broke. William Fish found employment as a butcher. He rang up lettuce and sacks of flour at the local grocery. He persuaded a man in town to hire him as a life insurance salesman. He never held a job for long. When the novelty wore off, William quit on short notice and returned to the only occupation that held his interest: horse-trading.

I'd better go check on Rustler, he'd tell Georgina before disappearing for days, sometimes weeks. William stabled Rustler and his other horses in affluent neighborhoods far from the boardinghouses of Milwaukee, making arrangements to rent empty barns the well-heeled owners of mansions no longer used, having abandoned their horses for motorcars. William kept as many as six horses at a time, trading and selling them to pay off debts. When times were lean, he'd sell all but Rustler, the swaybacked stallion he doted on.

Whenever William couldn't scrape together the rent, he moved his family to another boardinghouse. In the decade before Mildred was born, William, Georgina, and their three children—Harriette, born 1893; and the twins, Marion and Marbeau, born 1895— moved nearly every year.

Georgina, fed up, taught herself shorthand. Her tenth-grade education was plenty preparation, she figured, for a secretary. She strode out the door in a no-nonsense, high-necked dress and rode the streetcar into town, where she took dictation and typed letters for various businessmen.

When she returned home after a long day of work, she alerted her children by letting out a whistle. Sometimes William was home; sometimes he wasn't.

As the youngest, Mildred was often left alone. She roamed the macadam streets of her neighborhood, dodging streetcars. She climbed to the top branches of an enormous elm tree whose roots buckled the front yard. Straddling a branch, she'd sing songs—*I'm the kid that's all the candy, I'm a Yankee Doodle Dandy*—swinging her legs in time. In the winter she went ice-skating alone, borrowing skates from a neighbor whose daughter had died of scarlet fever.

She was seven when her older sister left home. When the acceptance letter from the University of Wisconsin arrived, no one in the family could believe it, least of all sixteen-year-old Harriette, a trash-talking bookworm whose considerable intelligence escaped the notice of nearly everyone she met. Harriette told whoever was within earshot that she didn't have scholarly ambitions; it was a decent husband she was after, one who wasn't a horse-trading boozer.

2.

The next year William Fish moved his family to a red-brick boardinghouse that smelled of mice.

Two years later, they moved to a boardinghouse on Chestnut Street.

A year later, they moved to Twentieth Street.

A year later, they moved to Twenty-First Street.

A year later they moved back to Twentieth Street.

One raw morning when Mildred was fourteen, Georgina packed a suitcase. She'd had enough; she was leaving William. Mildred's other siblings had moved out by now: Marbeau had gone off to work on a farm, Marion had married a man from Evanston, Illinois, and Harriette had obtained both a bachelor's degree and a husband at the University of Wisconsin. Georgina and Mildred moved to Madison, where Georgina's sister had a spare bed big enough for a mother and daughter to share. William begged his wife to return to Milwaukee, saying he'd changed his ways and had a good job now. Georgina steeled herself for a final attempt at reconciliation and moved back. She found a boardinghouse on Prairie Street that had a few rooms for rent and enrolled Mildred at the local high school. Within a few months William lost interest in the new job, once more running up debts.

He disappeared, this time for good.

William sold all his horses, even Rustler, the swaybacked stallion he adored. A few weeks later, on January 7, 1918, he died alone in an empty barn during the heaviest blizzard of the winter. A neighbor found William slumped in a chair, the coal stove stone-cold.

3.

Georgina and Mildred moved again, this time to Chevy Chase, Maryland, where Harriette lived in a comfortable two-story house on Brookville Road. Her husband was a gentle, civic-minded law-yer named Fred—an odd match for a trash-talking bookworm, but Harriette didn't give a damn. She'd come up in the world.

Harriette had children of her own now, two little girls. In the front yard, Harriette planted an elm tree for them, a tribute to the enormous elm in Milwaukee that Mildred loved to climb.

Mildred was sixteen. All the moves during her childhood had disrupted her schooling. Harriette declared she didn't have a chance in hell of getting into college, not unless she got the best possible education now. So it was decided: Fred would pull some strings.

The first day of school, Mildred woke up at dawn, swallowed a hasty breakfast, and hustled out the door to catch a streetcar bound for Washington, DC. Western High was in Georgetown, her class-mates the children of senators and diplomats. The cafeteria was a foreign country: china plates, linen napkins, polished silver. Mildred did her best to fit in. She joined the French club, though her French was terrible. She tried out for the swim team and nearly drowned. She signed up for basketball and hated the uniform, a blousy smock with a big bow noosing the neck and knee-length knickers that bal-looned out from a cinched waist. She tried her hand at homemaking, but sewing was a bloody endeavor, and she burned everything she cooked. It wasn't until she joined the school newspaper that she discovered where she belonged.

When Mildred got home from school, Harriette's little girls cir-cled around her, curious as cats. The youngest took a liking to her. Everywhere Mildred went, Janey wanted to go too. Once, on a winter afternoon, Mildred took her ice-skating. As they neared the middle of the lake they heard a tremendous crack and a woman's scream. A boy had fallen through the ice. The ice around the hole split. Another child fell through. Then another, and another. The woman wasn't the only one screaming now—everyone skating on the lake was, a shrill chorus of terror.

Janey began to cry.

Don't move, Mildred commanded. She unlaced Janey's skates, then her own. *Now hold my hand.* They inched toward the shore, sliding over the ice in their socks, feeling it crack and buckle.

Good Morning, Sunshine

1932

ID: 3879384 ~~TOP SECRET~~

DF 232

HARNACK, Mildred

    Wife of Arwid HARNACK. American by birth. Maiden name
Carried on illegal training of workers and Marxist propagand
of the German group of the "Rote Kapelle". was called on by
Fetched her husband from the office. Was present during the
tion with KENT. Helped her husband with cipher work. Procur
information by pumping GOLLNOW. Did liaison work. Was execu

1.

It is September 1, 1932.

In exactly seven years, the Second World War will begin.

This morning, by comparison, is not noteworthy. For Mildred it
begins, we may imagine, like any other morning as she rises from a
simple, wood-frame bed to draw back the curtains, letting in the
light. Because the apartment has wide windows there is plenty of it,
even in the dead of winter, when the air in Berlin seems grainy, the
texture and hue of chalk. A narrow hallway leads to the main room,
where Mildred drifts from window to window, drawing back curtains. Bookcases crammed with well-loved books line the walls. Oil
paintings of dense forests bring rich splashes of gold and emerald to
an otherwise modestly furnished room. Here is a sofa with wooden
armrests. Here are two tattered rugs. A sturdy round table, two
sturdy chairs. Floor planks show their wear, pitted in places, and

creak under Mildred's feet as she moves to the far corner of the room, where a white porcelain stove stands, its thick pipe stretching to the ceiling. Sometimes there's coal, sometimes there's not. Today, perhaps, there is. Mildred stokes the coal lumps with an iron rod, bringing up fresh sparks. The water in the kettle she sets on the stove is enough for two cups of coffee, one for her, one for Arvid.

It's by force of habit that she does this. She is alone, though not for long. Arvid will return from his trip to Russia soon, in time for her birthday. She will be thirty—*Is it possible?*—in just over two weeks.

Breakfast is simple, usually nothing more than a hunk of bread swiped with whatever's on hand—jam, butter, mustard, she's not particular. At the center of the table she likes to put a flower or two in a glass of water. Tulips in spring, lilacs in summer, alpine roses in the fall, honeysuckle in winter. Sometimes the flowers are from her students. Sometimes they're from Arvid.

Arvid is a romantic. It's a side others don't see. Others see a man who wears round, owlish spectacles and rarely leaves the house without a necktie. (Behind closed doors, he happily yanks it off.) Others see a man who spends hours on end at his desk. (But Arvid loves nothing more than to amble around a mountain on a Sunday afternoon, letting his thoughts wander, inhaling the tart, bracing air.) And though it's true that Arvid is a man who loves the certitude of cold, hard facts, his head is stuffed with poetry. He was made to read Goethe as a boy and can now, at thirty-one, recite long verses from memory, murmuring them into her ear.

They met at the University of Wisconsin, when Arvid wandered into the wrong lecture hall. He'd wanted to watch Professor John Commons deliver a lecture on American labor unions, but the person at the lectern wasn't Commons. It was Mildred, then a twenty-five-year-old graduate student. The topic of her lecture was American literature, and he stayed until the end. Then he approached the lectern and introduced himself.

She'd gotten a BA in humanities and started her master's. He had a law degree and was on his way to getting a PhD in philosophy. After these preliminaries were out of the way, Arvid told her—with a sweet, tenderhearted formality that pierced her to her core—that his family home was in Jena, a small university town along the Saale River in Germany. He spoke English awkwardly, though earnestly. How different he was from the Midwestern boys at UW, boys who tackled each other in cornfields and on football fields, boys who bragged about all the money they'd make with their degrees, boys who vied for Mildred's attention with boisterous jokes — *Har-dee-har-har!*—that weren't at all funny, at least not to her, although you were supposed to smile anyway, smile and blush and flip your hand and say, *Oh, you're such an egg.*

The second time they saw each other, Arvid brought her a fistful of wildflowers. He'd picked them himself. "A great bunch of thick, white odorous flowers mingled with purple bells," Mildred wrote later, remembering every detail.

It was morning—a "beautiful" one. Arvid stood on the porch of the two-story house where Mildred rented a room. The house was near campus, owned by a professor who lived there with his wife and their two children. The wife peeked through the curtains, absorbing the sight of blue-eyed Arvid and his wildflowers. She'd taken a keen interest in Mildred's private life. As Mildred worked doggedly on her master's degree, the professor's wife may have believed the younger woman could benefit from a little motherly guidance, mindful that the wrong man could lead her astray. Or maybe she was just nosy. At last she closed the curtains and nodded her frank approval. "Men from the North Sea," she said, "make very good husbands."

A husband—good or otherwise—was *not* what Mildred was

looking for. Not now. She was still reeling from a heart-wrenching breakup with an anthropology major from Kansas City named Harry, but she stepped onto the porch anyway, shutting the door behind her. Arvid gave her the wildflowers and expressed his hope that Mildred was having a good morning. He labored to soften his German accent, and she realized he'd practiced what he was about to say many times before coming to her door. He wanted to take her canoeing—on Lake Mendota, he said, "the greatest of all the lakes."

His shy gallantry.

All right, she told him, with a shy smile of her own. She would join him in a canoe.

Six months later, on a Saturday, they said their vows under an improvised bower on a ramshackle dairy farm.

Arvid returned to Germany to finish his PhD. Mildred would join him soon; Goucher College in Baltimore had hired her to teach English literature for the 1928–29 term. While they were apart, they wrote long letters. They described the books they were reading, their plans for the future. They would both become professors and teach in German universities, and perhaps American universities too. Mildred ended her letters with a drawing of a sun. Arvid ended his letters with the same sun.

Finally, on June 2, 1929, Mildred boarded the SS *Berlin* with two thousand other travelers and crossed the Atlantic. It was a long, windswept journey. The Atlantic gave way to the North Sea, cold and fathomless. Mildred stood on deck, shivering under her coat. On the horizon, between sky and sea, she saw Germany, thin as a pencil line.

Mildred enrolled in a PhD program at the Justus Liebig University in Giessen while Arvid put the finishing touches on his dissertation. On weekends they went hiking in the Harz Mountains, their rucksacks stuffed with sandwiches and books. Arvid read aloud his favorite verses from Goethe, and Mildred read aloud her favorite Whitman poems. Under a lush canopy of evergreens, they followed well-trodden trails and made their own. Fir, spruce, pine; Arvid knew the difference between the trees by their needles, long or short, spindly on a branch or dense as brush bristles.

"We were so happy to be together," Mildred wrote. "He is a kind of Christmas tree with all the candles lighted."

THERE ARE MOMENTS—this morning may be one of them—when she misses Arvid with a force that takes her breath away. Right now, he's probably eating breakfast too, seated at a table in Moscow with a group whose very name is a mouthful: Arbeitsgemeinschaft zum Studium der sowjetischen Planwirtschaft, or Working Group for the Study of the Soviet Planned Economy. (Mildred prefers to refer to the group by its less cumbersome acronym, ARPLAN.) Its members include economists, political scientists, literary critics, politicians, and playwrights, among them self-avowed right-wing ultranationalists and die-hard Communists. In other circumstances, these strange bedfellows might not have shaken hands, much less sat around a breakfast table, but Arvid is optimistic; they may disagree about methodology, but they are united in their aim.

Germany is in crisis. Something must be done. By studying what appears to be a novel economic solution to the Soviet Union's woes, Arvid hopes to discover a remedy for the crisis in his own country. Arvid is secretary of ARPLAN. He receives no pay for this work, but his compassion for the poor in Germany and his desire to devise a new economic model to address this problem drive him to his desk day and night.

There are two desks in the apartment. Arvid's is a great expanse of carved wood that once belonged to his father. The other desk, equally imposing, was once his maternal grandfather's—Arvid calls him Grossvater Reichau. This is Mildred's desk now. A big slab of mahogany. Lectures, articles, translations—she writes them all in longhand, filling page after page before turning to the typewriter.

It's here, at Grossvater Reichau's great slab of a desk, that Mildred stokes her own outsize dreams. One day she will be a great literary scholar; she will write magnificent books. The desk imparts heft and weight and stability, qualities that are entirely foreign to Mildred. She has no family heirlooms of her own. Whatever slim sticks of furniture had cluttered the small, drafty rooms of her childhood she has long since left behind.

MILDRED DOESN'T LINGER LONG over breakfast. A final swallow of coffee and she's on her feet again, setting the cup and saucer in the sink, brushing crumbs from her lips. Dirty dishes will accumulate there for days before she notices them, a teetering tower of plates and cups and cutlery. There are always better things to do than the dishes.

She's still wearing a bathrobe over her nightgown and long, boiled-wool stockings knit by her mother, who bundled them up in a trim package that took two months to make its way from a transatlantic steamer ship to her front door. Her feet skim the creaking floorboards—the heel of one stocking is wearing thin—as she walks to a wide window and opens it. The air, crisp as a cold apple, invigorates her. She flings off her bathrobe.

She begins a series of exercises now, following directions from a book she bought for a few pfennigs. "Most of the exercises aim to strengthen the muscles of the abdomen," she wrote to her mother last year, scribbling a hasty assurance that she and Arvid will have children "as soon as we can." The routine—leg lifts and sit-ups and backbends—takes twenty minutes. She's slender as a dancer, but she's more earnest than graceful as she flails her arms, kicks her legs. Her nightgown bunches. Her stockinged feet on the wood floor skid and slip.

After exercising, she bathes quickly, using lard soap, and gets dressed.

Though today isn't significant in the grand stretch of history, to Mildred it's an important milestone. Today she begins a new teaching job at the Berliner Städtisches Abendgymnasium für Erwachsene—the Berlin Night School for Adults—nicknamed the BAG. There, she'll come into contact with a fresh crop of German students, and she's energized by the possibilities. They will be different from the students she taught at the University of Berlin—poorer, predominantly working-class, mostly unemployed. Precisely the type of person the Nazi Party has been relentlessly targeting with propaganda.

See her now, striding out the front door with her leather satchel, descending four flights of stairs to the sidewalk. See her walking toward the U-Bahn station, swinging the satchel. In the eyes of her neighbors, she's an American graduate student, nothing more.

2.

Once, Mildred adored the wide-open prairies of the American Midwest, but she has grown to love the hustle and bustle of Berlin.

Living here is like living at the crossroads of Europe. Every day two hundred fifty trains speed into the city's five train stations from cities near and far. Walking on cobblestone streets, Mildred hears a symphony of languages—Russian, Polish, Dutch, Italian, French. The boulevards are dense with bicycles, double-decker buses, electric trams, taxis, and automobiles jockeying for position. Alongside and between the boulevards flows an intricate webbing of waterways and canals that stretch past the city's borders to the Baltic Sea, the North Sea, and the Rhine. Berlin, it is said, has more bridges than Venice, more statues than Rome, and more theaters than Athens. The very first traffic light in Europe appeared here, at the five-cornered intersection at Potsdamer Platz. Berlin is generous in its lateral dimensions, nine times larger than Paris, yet it has more space devoted to parks and forests than any other European metropolis. At its center is the Tiergarten, a heavily forested expanse that's nearly twice the size of London's Hyde Park.

Mildred has never visited Italy or Greece or France, and until very recently she hadn't been to London. In Milwaukee, she never visited an art museum or attended a concert, and the only plays she had seen were staged on the thickly varnished floor of her high-school gymnasium.

Now she lives in an apartment above a café that's jam-packed with artists claiming passionate allegiance to the tenets of Expressionism or Dada or Constructivism or the Bauhaus or any number of other movements that have been colliding here over the past decade. If she wants to see a play by Bertolt Brecht or a musical by Kurt Weill or a symphony by Arnold Schoenberg or a painting by Marc Chagall, it's simply a matter of walking out her apartment door and down four flights of stairs to the street below, where a taxi or a tram or a train can spirit her to the theater or concert hall or gallery of her choice.

Censorship is forbidden in Germany. After Germany lost the First World War, a radical group of twenty-five men including historians, sociologists, and theologians (Arvid's uncle Adolf von Harnack among them) met in the small town of Weimar to produce the Weimar Constitution, granting both men and women the right to vote, the right to religious freedom, and the right "to express opinions freely in word, writing, print, image, or otherwise." An explosion of intellectual and artistic achievement followed, one that encompassed the sciences as well as architecture, painting, sculpture, music, film, theater, and literature.

The U-Bahn and S-Bahn trains that Mildred takes to get around Berlin are crammed with Germans reading books—classics and dime-store novels and thick tomes on history and philosophy. A broad range of newspapers too, from tabloids to pamphlets, representing a spectrum of political opinions. Communist newspapers like *Die Rote Fahne* intermingle with newspapers for Social Democrats (*Vorwärts*), conservative German Nationalists (*Die Deutsche Allgemeine Zeitung*), and Nazis (*Völkischer Beobachter*).

Germany publishes more newspapers than any other industrialized nation right now. Among them are four thousand seven hundred weeklies and dailies, many with morning, midday, and evening editions. The *Berliner Morgenpost* has the largest circulation and is produced by Ullstein, the largest publishing house in Europe. A prominent Jewish family owns this Berlin-based company, which employs ten thousand people and presides over dozens of publications, including *Berliner Allgemeine Zeitung,* a daily newspaper for blue-collar workers; *Blatt der Hausfrau,* a magazine for housewives; *Die Koralle,* a science magazine; *Siehen Tage,* a newspaper about the radio; and *Der Querschnitt,* an arts magazine that features contributions from Ernest Hemingway and James Joyce.

In Berlin alone, there are ninety daily newspapers to choose from. They fill the kiosks stationed on sidewalks, their pages flapping like flags when the wind picks up.

1932 ballot, Berlin

Germany's vigorous free press reflects the multiparty system in the Weimar Republic. During an election, a staggering number of political parties—as many as sixty-two—appear on a ballot.

Now, for the first time in history, a range of voices is heard in the Reichstag. Some of these voices belong to women, as article 109 of the Weimar Constitution grants them the same fundamental rights and duties as men, including the right to hold office. Members of the Reichstag are elected, as is the president.

Gone is Emperor Wilhelm II, whose family had ruled Germany since the eleventh century and who was related to an assortment of other monarchs scattered across Europe, including his grandmother Queen Victoria of England. Like many a sovereign, Wilhelm II lived in an enormous castle, though unlike that of his royal predecessors his throne was a stool shaped like a cavalry saddle, where he sat in full uniform wearing a spiked helmet and hiding a paralyzed and withered left arm in the folds of his cloak. Wilhelm II suffered from Erb's palsy, a neurological injury that also caused his head to loll to the side, and he'd endured during childhood a series of treatments involving electric shocks and rabbit-blood baths, as ineffective as they were bizarre. In spite of his physical impediments, the emperor developed a militaristic swagger, insisted on the title "supreme war lord," and launched Germany into the horrendously bloody First World War.

But the old order is gone now, and in its place, knock-kneed as a foal, stands a fragile democracy.

"Life seemed more free, more modern, more exciting than in any place I had ever seen. . . . The old oppressive Prussian spirit seemed to be dead and buried," wrote the American journalist William Shirer, remembering the days when he was a young foreign correspondent in Berlin. Scores of American and European expats felt exactly as he did. A group of British writers, among them W. H. Auden and Christopher Isherwood, poured out poems and plays and thinly veiled autobiographical novels about their adventures in Berlin. "For many of my friends and for myself," the poet Stephen Spender wrote, "Germany seemed a paradise where there was no censorship and young Germans enjoyed extraordinary freedom in their lives." Still, some harbored a sneaking suspicion that these "extraordinary freedoms" wouldn't last. "In the streets of Berlin," a young German writer noted, "one is often struck by the momentary insight that someday all this will suddenly burst apart."

There's a lively friction in the air here, a chafing of the avant-garde against the establishment. And there's another sort of friction too. Mildred senses it every time she watches women in mink coats stroll past bone-thin beggars on the Kurfürstendamm, a boulevard with a long, glittering string of brightly lit shops that resembles nothing so much as a tawdry necklace of jewels.

3.

It's late in the day now. Outside, the sun slants toward the horizon, lengthening shadows, though Mildred can't see them; the U–Bahn runs underground. She's heading west, to a station called Wittenbergplatz. Inside her leather satchel are her books and lecture notes. In November there will be another election, just four months after the last one. The composition of the Reichstag will shift again. Communists will clash with Social Democrats, Nazis will brawl with both. It can't go on like this much longer.

Wittenbergplatz. Mildred has reached her destination.

She rises from her seat and exits the train. She strides up a staircase and out the door.

To the west of the station, the KaDeWe department store commands the street corner. Well-heeled shoppers stroll past the black-hatted porter minding the entrance and disappear inside.

She heads away from the KaDeWe, walking south. The wide boulevard before her is Lietzenburger Strasse. She turns left, then left again, following the narrowing road to Wormser Strasse 11. Gripping her leather satchel, she opens the door and walks inside.

The BAG

1932–1933

HANDBUCH
DES
BERLINER
ABEND
GYMNASIUMS

ZWEITE AUSGABE

BERLIN W 62
WORMSER STR. 11
FERNSPRECHER: BARBAROSSA B 5 2471

MILDRED HARNACK-
Lektorin:
Einer seit langem in d
Staaten ansässigen Fan
mend, wurde ich am 16. S
in Milwaukee geboren.
ich die Vorschule und d
High School. Später sied
Washington, D. C. über,
Universität an der ,,West
Danach studierte ich
englische Philologie, Phil
Jahre 1925 bestand ich
Master-Prüfung. Meine D
lische Homerübersetzung
Von 1924 bis 1928 lehrte

1.

The BAG opened its doors at Wormser Strasse 11 three years ago, on September 2, 1929. It's the first school of its kind in Berlin. The traditional view in Germany held that education for the middle to lower strata of society should be limited to vocational training, which meant laborers and office clerks knew little of mathematics, philosophy, science, history, and literature, subjects that aristocrats and other upper-class elites could claim as their own. The BAG flouts tradition. Its mission is to educate the working class.

Books are free at the BAG, as are hot meals. Some of the students who crowd into the classrooms are so destitute that Mildred wonders whether the school will make any difference in helping them escape poverty. They "have come hoping to win more freedom and breadth in life," Mildred writes, and

> to a very large extent they are doomed to fail on the social scale rather than rise. There is little work to be had; they lose their positions; their unemployment insurance gives out after a time and they are thrown into the lap of charity, which means, when they have no other help, slow ruin and starvation by degrees.

A ragtag bunch of factory workers, electricians, construction workers, and clerks are at their desks when Mildred enters the classroom. There is a sudden commotion, the scraping of chairs against the floor, as the students rise to their feet. She strides to the lectern. They take their seats. They'd already seen, and perhaps scrutinized, the photograph in the BAG handbook of their twenty-nine-year-old professor—the only American and the only woman on the faculty.

"You never heard her coming," one of them would reminisce years later. "Suddenly, there she was in the middle of the room. Her walk like all her motions was light and deliberate."

Mildred's class is called, simply, English. But its parameters extend far beyond grammar and sentence structure. The books she assigns are a mix of literature, philosophy, and political theory, now and then leavened by a limerick or fable. Standing at the lectern, she wants to inspire her students, to show them a different way of seeing the world; she wants to *reach* these men and women in a way they haven't been reached before. And so she lectures about Ralph Waldo Emerson and the tenets of transcendentalism, emphasizing the importance of self-reliance and courageous independence in thought and action; she discusses Mahatma Gandhi's heroism and the treacheries of monarchy as dramatized by Charles Dickens's novels and William Shakespeare's tragedies; she talks about the tyranny of the majority as presented in the philosophical writings of John Stuart Mill, highlighting how a small group may be victimized by a larger group and encouraging her students to think about present-day parallels in Germany. Again and again, Mildred returns to her core themes: the plight of the poor, the urgent need for political change.

On the last day of November, she begins class by asking a question. Usually she speaks to her class in English, but today she wants to make sure her students understand perfectly.

"Hitler soll Kanzler werden?" Should Hitler be chancellor?

The question is provocative. One of her students, a thirty-one-year-old man named Samson Knoll, is so struck by her question and the discussion it prompts that he notes it in his diary that night.

Montag, 31. November 1932: "10 Uhr B.A.G. Mrs. Harnack. Hitler soll Kanzler werden?"

2.

Mildred's neighborhood straddles two areas of Berlin, Kreuzberg and Neukölln, and is a mix of the working-class and the bohemian. The streets are lined with shops and restaurants and newspaper kiosks. A lively café on the block blasts jazz from morning to night, when the street is—in Mildred's words—"a stream of little lights." Now that it is autumn, the leaves of trees in a park near the apartment building have begun to turn burgundy and gold, lemon and pumpkin orange. Her wide window offers a commanding view of it all, which is one of the reasons she likes this apartment. She can observe nature and its glories from her fourth-floor perch while taking in the city's jazzy clamor. She can also get a sense of things, see clearly who's coming and who's going.

Mildred has begun to hold meetings in her apartment. She invites her students from the BAG, including Samson Knoll. After class, they all take the U-Bahn together and get off at Südstern. From there, it's a five-minute walk to Hasenheide 61, where they sit in her living room and discuss Germany's political climate. Soon, they will be driven underground. Already, they're exercising caution. The meetings, they agree, must be kept secret.

In 1932 the resistance in Germany is a fledgling thing, still in its infancy. No: it's not even that. It's embryonic, barely a speck.

3.

Mildred also runs what she calls an English club. Any student can join. She holds meetings at a café nearby and invites guest speakers to deliver informal talks.

The focus of the English club is political, not linguistic.

An American journalist speaks about "America and World Politics." Another American journalist discusses "American Foreign Policy and the Manchurian Crisis." A professor from the University of Berlin examines "India at Present" and shares his thoughts about British colonialism and the caste system. Arvid's cousin Elisabeth von Harnack talks about her doctoral dissertation and presents her research on "The Hull House and Chicago Social Work."

On January 23, 1933, Consul General George Messersmith is the guest speaker. It's a Monday evening, and it's so cold in Berlin that Mildred and her students can see their breath, cloudy puffs of white, as they approach the café. Once inside, they take their seats. Mildred introduces Messersmith, who sits at the head of the table. In six months, he will mince no words in describing Hitler to a colleague at the White House:

With few exceptions, the men who are running the government are of a mentality that you and I cannot understand.

Some of them are psychopathic cases and would ordinarily be receiving treatment somewhere.

But tonight, speaking to the English club, Messersmith doesn't mention Hitler. He sticks strictly to the topic at hand, his job at the U.S. embassy. He might have put it to them as plainly as this: *If you're an American who wants to come to Germany, I'm in charge of getting you in, and if you're an American who wants to leave Germany, I'm in charge of getting you out*. The English club members listen respectfully. Not one of them is American. What about Germans who want to leave Germany? Samson Knoll doesn't ask this question, but perhaps someone else at the table does. Samson was born in a small town in Poland. He loves the BAG, and he doesn't want to leave Germany. Lately, though, he has begun to wonder about his safety. He is a foreigner, and a Jew.

Sometimes Mildred takes her BAG students to see a play. Sometimes she persuades them to put on costumes and perform their own play. And sometimes Mildred sings to them.

Yes, *sings*.

They are seated at their desks, exhausted after a long day toiling on a construction site or working on the lower floors of an office building or wielding a hot welding torch inside a factory.

She stands at the lectern. She clears her throat, takes a breath, and sings "Clementine":

> In a cavern, in a canyon,
> Excavating for a mine
> Dwelt a miner forty-niner,
> And his daughter Clementine

and "John Brown":

> John Brown died that the slaves might be free,
> John Brown died that the slaves might be free,
> John Brown died that the slaves might be free,
> His soul goes marching on.

At first, what her students feel most of all, listening to her solitary, warbling voice fill the room, is "embarrassed." They've never heard a professor sing.

They're melancholy, these songs, and she sings them in English. Now and then she translates the trickier words and idioms into German so her students will understand them. The first song, she tells her students, is about the death of an American laborer during the 1849 California gold rush—a "miner forty-niner"—and his daughter. The second song is also about the death of a working-class American, an abolitionist.

She goes on to recount the story of John Brown, a white man who tried to instigate a slave rebellion in 1859. He recruited a small group of twenty-one people to join him, among them college students, farmhands, and fugitive slaves. John Brown's plan—to raid a federal armory in Virginia, seize all the muskets and rifles they could get their hands on, and distribute the weapons to slaves—was thwarted by local white militias and a company of U.S. Marines. John Brown was led to the gallows and hanged for treason.

Mildred sings "Clementine" and "John Brown" many times during the winter of 1932. Each time, she stands at the lectern and looks out at a roomful of Germans weary from work or demoralized by unemployment. She is entirely unselfconscious, singing so "freely" and "naturally," a student would recall years later, that their embarrassment gives way to relief and, eventually, "to tender respect."

4.

One morning Mildred and Arvid pack a small suitcase, take a train south to Baden, and check into an inn on the edge of the Black Forest.

Arvid used to hike here with his father.

Otto Harnack had been a professor of German literature at a university nearby, in Stuttgart. He was exacting, dutiful, and severe, a model of Prussian rectitude, but he also had a tender side and fostered in Arvid a love of nature and Goethe's poetry. When Arvid was twelve, Otto Harnack walked into the Neckar River. His suicide bewildered Arvid. Did he walk into the river at night or in the bright light of morning? Did he fill his pockets with stones first? Arvid didn't know, or say.

Mildred knew her father had been nothing like Otto Harnack. Still, the horse trader and the professor had something in common. Both had felt a deep sadness run through them like a cold fluid. *The blues* was how William Fish would have put it.

And Otto? He was *Mutterseelenallein*. The literal translation is "mother-soul-alone." A man suffering from this type of sadness is so lonely he feels as if his mother's soul has been ripped out of his own. When Mildred speaks the German word, it is so much richer and more wretched than any English word for "sad."

The Black Forest is enchanting, dusted with snow. Rucksacks on their backs, Mildred and Arvid follow a narrow trail that cuts through dark, dense woods. Arvid's sense of direction is excellent, not in spite of his poor vision, but because of it. Arvid is nearly blind in one eye. When he was a teenager, a bully bludgeoned him with a stick, shattering his glasses. Arvid walked to the town hospital, where a surgeon removed nine splinters of glass from his left eye, a delicate procedure that Arvid endured without anesthesia.

Now, Arvid notes his surroundings meticulously; it's the only reliable way he has of navigating the world.

The woods they explore are known to have inspired the Grimm brothers' fairy tales. They hike for hours, inhaling the cold, pine-scented air. On Sunday evening they return to Berlin, invigorated.

5.

It's January 1933. Mildred has lived in Hasenheide 61 for six months. She loves this apartment. The rent is the equivalent of seventeen dollars a month—more than she and Arvid wanted to pay, but they're adept at getting by on little. So many others in Germany get by on far less. While Arvid puts the finishing touches on his first book—it is slated for publication next year—Mildred translates a German book on sports, five hundred single-spaced pages. It's an enormous project, and she is paid nearly nothing for her labors. To supplement her income she teaches a class at the Commercial University, an uninspired institution that shares nothing of the vision of the BAG.

On January 29, 1933, Mildred sits down at Grossvater Reichau's great slab of a desk to write a letter to her mother.

There's so much to work for in the world nowadays. Never have there been more glorious prospects . . .

She rests her pen on the page. What passes through her mind then? A flutter of insecurity, a twinge of self-doubt? She has been unfocused at times. She hasn't always planned ahead. In previous letters, she has admitted that she daydreams. "I'm trying to get rid of old habits," she writes now. To "see my main path ever more clearly."

If she felt self-doubt, it's purged now. She continues the letter, resolute:

I'm thirty years old and a free woman. I have the work I want, there are no insurmountable obstacles to advancing in it . . . life is good.

The next evening, Mildred strides into the classroom at the BAG clutching her leather satchel. Tonight the class will not be singing songs or discussing literature, she tells them. Instead, they will discuss a historic event.

It is January 30, 1933. Hitler has just been appointed chancellor of Germany.

[Montag, 30. Januar 1933:   "Hitler Kanzler."]

II

Fragment

Questionnaire
Plötzensee Prison, Berlin
February 16, 1943

Mother's name	Georgina Hesketh Fish
Father's name	William Cooke Fish
Position, Occupation, Profession	Lecturer and Translator
How much was your income at the time you committed your crime?	100 Reichsmark a month
Did you go to a school for mentally retarded children?	No

Chancellor Hitler

1933

1.

Berlin is burning. Flames curl and lick and leap into the air, but the conflagration isn't an act of vandalism or war—not yet. No buildings or houses have been set on fire, though the air is thick with smoke. What's burning the night of January 30, 1933, are torches—twenty thousand of them.

It's a Nazi victory parade. The celebration begins at seven p.m. and lasts six hours.

A relentless procession of men holding their torches skyward march in lockstep through the streets of Berlin, the SA in brown uniforms, the SS in black. Military bands march alongside them, brass instruments gleaming in the torchlight. Baby-faced boys march too, wearing the brown uniforms of the Hitlerjugend—Hitler Youth. Man or boy, SA or SS or Hitlerjugend—each wears a strip of fabric encircling his upper arm that bears a hooked cross, a sacred symbol of good fortune in ancient civilizations. The Nazis have appropriated it, perverted it, transformed it into a symbol of German nationalism and racial supremacy. It's an instrument of propaganda now, an emblem emblazoned not only on armbands but also on medallions, caps, badges, posters, flags, and banners. It's a *Haken-kreuz,* otherwise known as a swastika.

See them marching, stomping their boots. Hear the shrieking of trumpets, the crashing of cymbals, the pounding of drums, brash as artillery fire, rat-a-tat-tat.

They march the tree-lined paths of the Tiergarten to the grand

Brandenburg Gate west of Pariser Platz, on past four stately embassies—American, French, Russian, and British—and down the Wilhelmstrasse to the Reich Chancellery. There, President Hindenburg can be seen standing behind a closed window, a stooped figure gazing out at the thunderous procession. Hindenburg's face is rigid, "like cast bronze," observes a German journalist jotting down her impressions. The old man's expression strikes her as "bewildered and somewhat startled." Fifty yards south, before another window—this one flung wide open—stands Hitler.

For years, Hitler has been dismissed as an amateur, a crackpot, a buffoon, a semiliterate fool with a Charlie Chaplin mustache. He's a high-school dropout who was twice rejected from the Academy of Fine Arts Vienna; who in his twenties suffered a series of humiliations, living as a struggling artist and sleeping in a homeless shelter; who in his thirties became the leader of the Nazi Party after discovering he could mesmerize first a room, then a hall, then a stadium with his populist rhetoric; and who, at forty-three, has just been appointed by President Hindenburg to serve as chancellor of Germany.

Gazing out at the torchlight parade held in his honor, Hitler is "beside himself with excitement," notes an American journalist who stands near the Chancellery window. The pale blue eyes that could convey fury and stone-cold cruelty are joyful tonight, "full of tears." Now and then Hitler thrusts a stiff right arm into the smoke-filled air. The thousands who surround the Chancellery cheer and raise their right arms, returning his salute.

2.

Arvid Harnack is there, watching. He has positioned himself on the street near the Chancellery window.

The crowd bursts into song: *Deutschland, Deutschland über Alles!* Arvid does not salute, nor does he cheer or sing.

Arvid isn't alone. He has brought along his nineteen-year-old nephew, Wolfgang. The torch smoke stings their eyes, making them water. An acrid smell hangs in the air. The jostling crowd is deafening, everyone chanting and hollering and singing, a gleeful chorus. The song is different now — *Raise the flag, stand in ranks, ready! Storm Troopers march, their steps calm and steady!* — and as columns of Nazis march past, Arvid murmurs, "Butchers. They're capable of anything."

Wolfgang is thirteen years younger than Arvid and still in school. Tall, with a thick, adolescent tousle of brown hair, he bears a superficial resemblance to his father, a fairly well-known violinist and conductor named Gustav Havemann who has recently remarried, taking as his third wife Arvid's younger sister Inge. The resemblance stops there. Wolfgang is shy; his father is domineering. Wolfgang speaks softly; his father's voice fills the room. Wolfgang is uncertain about his career; his father has pursued music since boyhood, becoming a concertmaster at nineteen. Most significant is the difference in their political views. Wolfgang finds himself veering toward antifascism; his father ingratiates himself with the Nazis. Gustav Havemann is a member of the Kampfbund für deutsche Kultur — the Militant League for German Culture — a Nazi lobby group founded four years ago that agitates against aspects of Weimar culture it deems corrupt, including anything produced by Jews. Last May, Gustav refused to conduct an orchestra unless the Jewish musicians in it were removed. A violin tone produced by a Jew, he insisted, was "too soft and sensuous."

Arvid detests Gustav Havemann. How can his sister stand him? The deterioration of Inge's first marriage pains Arvid. He always liked Johannes Auerbach, who fled Germany and is living in Paris. Now, whenever Arvid visits Inge, he gets into heated, red-faced arguments with Gustav, who refuses to reconsider his views even when confronted with the fact that Inge's first husband is a Jew and their two little boys — now Gustav's stepchildren — are half Jewish.

This is why Arvid has taken Wolfgang to the torchlight parade tonight. He's determined to rescue him from his father's malevolent influence.

WOLFGANG GAZES AT THE men Arvid calls butchers marching past, row after row.

The lenses of Arvid's eyeglasses flash with fire.

"With their torches they'll set Germany ablaze, then Europe," he says. "Just wait, Wolfgang, soon they'll have you in uniform."

Wolfgang wonders if Arvid is right. Will Germany go to war? Will he be forced to fight?

Killing. He loathes the idea.

When he returns home that night, and for many days and nights afterward, Wolfgang thinks about what he should do. His home country is collapsing before his very eyes.

His father sees things differently, of course. Gustav Havemann believes Germany is on the ascent now that Hitler is in power. Finally, after so much undignified stumbling and struggling, after ignominious defeat in the First World War—known then as the Great War—Germans will get on their feet. Germany will be strong again.

3.

"An ominous night," the German journalist Bella Fromm writes in her diary. "A night of deadly menace. A nightmare."

"Germany has awakened!" Nazi propagandist Joseph Goebbels writes in his diary. "The German revolution has begun."

4.

Two days later, on February 1, 1933, Mildred sits at her desk to write a letter.

> *The steep roofs and wide streets starred with light are gleaming softly with snow tonight as I see them from my window—a big arched lookout.*

Behind the apartment building is a church surrounded by trees, and beyond that is an open field where the police practice shooting. Now and then she can hear the firecracker-pop of their bullets. The thought of the police so near is unsettling, but she doesn't tell her mother this. She wants to begin with beauty. With serenity. With steep, snowy roofs and lights like stars.

What she wants to say—*needs* to say—will be difficult. How to find the words? She writes,

> *Arvid and I have just eaten supper. He is tired. I am going to put him to bed and read John Dos Passos's new novel to him— 1919 it's called.*

Dos Passos is a socialist, scorned by Nazis, but she doesn't tell her mother this.

> *We are safe, very well and happy.*

This is a version of the truth. She is happy, and so is Arvid. Happy in the sense that they love each other and awaken every morning with the sweet knowledge that they are together. They're lucky— they're alive and well and working toward a common goal. But this truth is pierced with a lie, sharp as a splinter. She isn't safe, and neither is Arvid.

> *Thinking about my last letter, I feel I may have frightened you. . . . Don't worry about us at all.*

She said too much the last time. Her letter was too political— she'd been too candid about her hatred of the Nazi Party.

> *We are not active politically.*

Entirely untrue. She is deceiving her mother now, blatantly.

> *Who would bother himself about two students sitting off in a corner, thinking thoughts about the future of the world? So don't worry about us at all. And best keep still. If anyone asks you about us, we are not interested in the world from a political but from a scientific standpoint. That's all you need to say.*

5.

The same day Mildred writes the letter, a fair-haired young man enters a building on Potsdamerstrasse. Inside the building is a radio station that has invited him to be a guest on a popular program. He walks up the stairs to the fifth floor.

He is Arvid's cousin Dietrich Bonhoeffer, a rebellious twenty-six-year-old Lutheran pastor in Berlin. Today, he speaks into the microphone with the grave authority of a man twice his age. Historians will come to recognize his speech as one of the first public acts of defiance against Hitler.

Midway through the speech, his voice gathers force. It is critical, Dietrich Bonhoeffer says, to distinguish between a "leader" and a "misleader"—

Abruptly, his microphone is cut off. Across Germany, all people hear from their radios is a thick band of static.

Two Nazi Ministers

1933

1.

Within five hours of being sworn in as chancellor, Hitler convenes his first cabinet meeting.

Over a dozen men in dark suits, including the minister of justice, the minister of defense, the minister of labor, the minister of finance, and the minister of foreign affairs, file into the Reich Chancellery. Nearly all belong to the nationalist conservative party, Deutschnationale Volkspartei (DNVP), whose leader is Alfred Hugenberg, minister of the economy and of food and agriculture, a rotund, mustachioed, filthy-rich film and newspaper mogul who detests parliamentary democracy and longs for the days when a monarchy ruled Germany. Hugenberg is backed by aristocrats and wealthy businessmen who cringe at the Nazi Party's populist rhetoric. Hugenberg thinks he can control Hitler. So do Vice-Chancellor Franz von Papen and President Hindenburg.

Vice-Chancellor Papen belongs to a right-wing Catholic party known as the Zentrum. He has convinced President Hindenburg, an independent, that a cabinet chock-full of conservatives who, to varying degrees, distrust and even disdain the Nazi Party will surely keep Hitler in check.

The minutes of this cabinet meeting will remain under lock and key for over twelve years, inaccessible to the German public and the rest of the world until after the Second World War, when an international tribunal that holds a series of war crimes trials in the German city of Nuremberg will reveal that Hugenberg, Papen, and Hindenburg were wildly wrong.

2.

Hitler begins by cordially greeting the men seated around the table. In the discussion that follows, he is mindful not to alienate the ministers whose confidence he needs to win, soliciting their viewpoints on the current political climate in a manner that is gently inquisitive and respectful. The minister of finance, a nonpartisan conservative, is pleased, noting that Chancellor Hitler is "polite and calm" and receptive to others' opinions, even when they conflict with his own. Other ministers observe that the rabble-rousing leader of the Nazi Party seems, strikingly, to have mellowed now that he has been granted a position of authority in the German government.

As the men warm to the discussion, Hitler mentions that the Reichstag is due to meet tomorrow after a two-month holiday and tosses out the suggestion that the Nazi Party form a coalition with the DNVP and the Zentrum. By banding together, they can crowd out the left wing.

"We might," Hitler ventures, "consider suppressing the Communist Party to eliminate its votes in the Reichstag."

To nearly all the ministers in the room, this seems a reasonable suggestion. Squabbling about how Hitler's agenda differs from that of other right-wing parties appears pointless.

But DNVP leader Hugenberg smells a rat. He has already tried several times to form a coalition with Hitler, first in 1929 and again in 1931—fragile alliances that fractured under the pressure of relentless power struggles. He listens as Hitler nimbly steers them toward another idea that also seems, to many ministers in the room, reasonable: they could call off tomorrow's meeting of the Reichstag and hold a new election.

Hugenberg objects.

Hitler presses his case. The election will surely give their right-wing coalition a parliamentary majority, enabling them to pass a law that will effectively crush their left-wing opponents.

Hugenberg considers Hitler's proposal. He made a fortune during the economic collapse of the 1920s, buying up a slew of provincial newspapers and building a media empire that includes Scherl-Haus, one of the largest publishing firms in Berlin; Allgemeine Anzeigen, an advertising agency; Telegraphen Union, a news agency; and UFA, Germany's largest film company, which has a joint-distribution contract with the lavishly successful Hollywood studios Paramount and Metro-Goldwyn-Mayer. The DNVP leader may enjoy a near monopoly in the German media, but his efforts to achieve power in the political sphere have been continually thwarted, mainly due to the Nazi upstart who has now inexplicably risen to chancellor. If Hugenberg lets Hitler have his way in the cabinet meeting, just this once, he can handily manipulate the lowborn Nazi leader and position himself for his own power grab.

Hugenberg withdraws his objection.

Later, he will remark, "I've just committed the greatest stupidity of my life."

3.

Chancellor Hitler is a tool in the hands of the nationalist conservatives. This is what many believe, including both liberal and conservative politicians in the Reichstag and editors of major German newspapers and the international press. Hitler may run the cabinet meetings, but he's not the man in charge.

"The cabinet is really Alfred Hugenberg's," remarks a prominent Social Democrat in the Reichstag. A member of the DNVP writes in his diary, "If Hitler sits in the saddle, Hugenberg gets the whip."

The *Berliner Tageblatt* has no confidence in Hitler's ability to outwit "the foxy capitalist Hugenberg."

The French newspaper *Le Temps* points out that President Hindenburg "has never concealed his feelings about Hitler, which amount to veritable aversion," and predicts that Hitler "will be quickly exhausted."

The *New York Times* reminds readers that Hitler was "twice rejected last year" for the position he now occupies. "The composition of the cabinet leaves Herr Hitler no scope for gratification of any dictatorial ambition."

4.

Two days after his first cabinet meeting, Hitler convenes a second. He greets the dark-suited ministers seated around the table, his manner as cordial as ever. He informs them that the current Reichstag has been dissolved and the next election will be held in March.

Hitler aims to destroy the parliamentary democracy, abolish the Reichstag, and grant himself dictatorial powers, but he doesn't tell the ministers this. He says that their right-wing coalition will strengthen Germany and restore their great country to its former glory.

The nationalist conservative ministers need only glance around the table to reassure themselves that they hold the reins of power. President Hindenburg and Vice-Chancellor Papen have appointed them to ensure that the nationalist conservatives will hold the most influential and powerful posts, with responsibilities that include the economy, the law, and the military.

There are just two Nazis among them, the only ministers Hitler was permitted to appoint. They are Wilhelm Frick, the minister of the interior, and Hermann Göring, who is currently the president of the Reichstag. Göring doesn't yet have a specific role in Hitler's cabinet and is known by the somewhat dismissive title "Minister Without Portfolio."

5.

That evening, Chancellor Hitler delivers his first radio address. The ministers stand behind him in a unified show of support.

Hitler begins by recalling the difficult days of the Weimar Republic, when poverty and hunger weakened so many.

Dissension and hatred broke out among us. Millions of the best German men and women from all walks of life watched in profound distress as the unity of the nation disintegrated and dissolved in a tangle of egotistical political opinions, economic interests, and ideological differences.

Hitler identifies Communists as the cause of chaos and violence in the streets and declares that Germany will remain in shambles if left-wing renegades take control of the government. He praises President Hindenburg's valor as a field marshal in the Great War of 1914–1918 and asks the men and women of Germany to grant them four years to rebuild the country.

Within four years, the German peasant must be saved from impoverishment. Within four years unemployment must be finally overcome.... Now German people, give us four years, and then pass judgment on us!

Hitler steps away from the microphone. The dark-suited ministers congratulate him.

6.

Now Hitler sets into motion a plan. The two Nazi ministers he has appointed will help him execute it.

Minister of the Interior Wilhelm Frick will draft legislation that will enable Hitler to assume totalitarian control over the economy and all other aspects of the political and cultural landscape.

Minister Without Portfolio Hermann Göring will go on to receive more illustrious titles (minister of the interior for Prussia, minister of aviation), and a more eccentric one (Reich master of the hunt and of the forests). Most consequential, he will create the Gestapo, short for Geheime Staatspolizei (Secret State Police), which will quickly become one of the most devastatingly efficient tools of cruelty and persecution in Germany.

Meanwhile, Chancellor Hitler will invalidate the Weimar Constitution, destroy Germany's parliamentary democracy, and engineer its complete and total transformation into a dictatorship.

All this, in just six months.

A Whisper, a Nod

1933

1.

In 1933 the Germans who are opposed to the principles that constitute the black, beating heart of the Third Reich are dispersed among the membership rolls of trade unions and rivalrous left-wing political parties. It's no secret that scrappy factions of Communists and Social Democrats have agitated against Nazis since the early 1920s, although they will soon be driven underground. The resistance, such as it is, is far from a united coalition.

Mildred calls the group that comes to the apartment a discussion circle. In time, she and Arvid will shorten the name and refer to it simply as the Circle. Some members are Mildred's students. Some are friends. Some are friends of friends. They are factory workers and writers, lawyers and professors. They are Jewish, Catholic, Protestant, atheist.

And so the Circle begins—as a whisper behind closed doors, a nod on the sidewalk.

They meet in cafés. They stroll through the Tiergarten. They come to the apartment and distribute themselves on the sofa and the chairs and, when there are no seats left, across the wood-planked floor. Their discussions last hours, carrying them deep into the night.

What is happening? they ask. *What can we do?*

2.

How do we recruit young Germans?

The Circle discusses this question frequently. Mildred says she has the answer: We go where young Germans go. Schools are bursting with teenagers and young adults who could be persuaded to fight Nazis.

Some in the Circle are skeptical. A good number of those teenagers and young adults are Nazis.

"Nazis or snobs," scoffs one of them, a young woman from Frankfurt. Aloof and at times acidic, with a high, patrician forehead, she could be mistaken for a snob herself, though she's a passionate champion of the working class. (Years later, the woman—her name is Greta Lorke—will write about that day, recalling the conversation they had, the "searching look" on Mildred's face.)

"I can't stand snobs," Greta says. "They might as well be Nazis."

"Take a look at them," Mildred tells her, "an actual look."

Greta hears the implication loud and clear. Mildred is accusing her of myopia, if not outright blindness.

A week later, Greta shows up at the BAG. Grudgingly, she looks. What she sees are not snobs or Nazis but people in ragged clothes with thin limbs, wan faces.

"Ashamedly, I told Mildred she was right, completely correct," Greta wrote in her memoir.

The next time Mildred meets a group of BAG students in the Tiergarten, Greta goes too. The Tiergarten accommodates their discussion well. Its stark beauty in winter is bracing. Bare branches are dark against the sky. A network of paths, some dirt, some paved, some cobblestone, are covered with a dusting of snow. But the beauty has been violated. There are swastikas painted on lampposts, etched into tree trunks and the slats of wooden benches.

They walk from monument to monument, statue to statue, and discuss what Greta calls "crumbling heroes." She's following Mildred's lead, taking a circuitous path as she talks to the students, asking them innocuous questions that give way to more pointed ones, guiding the conversation nimbly toward the threat of fascism. Recruitment disguised as a history lesson.

3.

Of all the people in the Circle, Greta has known Mildred the longest. They met at the University of Wisconsin.

Greta came to learn about Mildred gradually after spotting her from afar. At first she knew her only by sight: a serious student getting a master's degree who dressed modestly, favoring long skirts and long sleeves, and kept her hair off her face. Buttoned up, but not always. On Friday nights, Mildred would carry on with a group of student revolutionaries, a fizzy, feisty mix of suffragettes, socialists, Marxists, and Leninists. Presiding over this group — they called themselves the Friday Niters — was Professor John Commons, who had a reputation for delivering electrifying lectures about the corruptions of capitalism.

Back then, Greta didn't know what she believed. She joined the Friday Niters hoping she'd find out.

Greta spoke English haltingly, with a strong German accent. She knew only one other student from Germany, Arvid Harnack. They were sitting on the grass with paper plates in their laps heaped with potato salad and hot dogs. An American-style picnic, entirely foreign to her. Seated around them in animated clusters were other Friday Niters — all, or nearly all, American. Greta was stung with self-consciousness. She didn't like Arvid speaking to her in German, not when she was trying to blend in.

But Arvid kept gabbing. And bragging. He had a law degree and was now working on a PhD. He spoke about his eminent uncle Adolf von Harnack and about his dissertation under Professor Commons, who was shaping his views about American labor unions. Greta didn't need such a lengthy catalog of Arvid's accomplishments; not now when all she was trying to do was eat a hot dog.

One winter night she saw Arvid skating across a frozen lake. This time, he was with a young woman. In another moment, they were gliding to the bank, where Greta was. Greta found Arvid's girlfriend "exceptionally pretty." Her blond hair lay on her shoulders loose and long. Her skin was pale, her nose and chin rosy from the cold. Her cheekbones were finely chiseled. But her eyes, Greta thought, were "the prettiest thing—large and blue under dark eyelashes." The girlfriend introduced herself as Mildred Harnack.

Greta wasn't used to seeing her this way, her hair freed from its bun. And she wasn't Arvid's girlfriend, she was *his wife*.

A bonfire burned nearby, at the top of a snow-covered hill. A group of students gathered around it, roasting mutton on sticks. Mildred and Arvid hiked up the hill to join them. Greta followed. The group underwent a subtle shift. Everyone seemed to gravitate toward the couple, to vie for Mildred's and Arvid's attention. Especially Mildred's. Someone brought her a blanket, another offered a stick, another speared a chunk of raw meat for her.

"No one seemed to expect that she, like us, would roast the meat herself," Greta wrote.

Did they dote on Mildred because she was pretty? No; there were plenty of pretty girls at the bonfire. Greta, ever practical, wasted little time on pointless musings. She didn't vie for Mildred's attention that night. She didn't bring her blankets or sticks. She didn't fawn over Mildred, much less like her.

Greta put it bluntly: "It was not friendship at first sight."

She was equally put off by Mildred's literary bent, which struck Greta as irritatingly sentimental. Sometimes, out of the blue, Mildred quoted Homer or Shakespeare, in a voice so soft it seemed as if she were speaking to herself. No matter. Loud or soft, poetry-reciting meant one thing.

"To me," Greta wrote, "it was deadly."

A WEEK OR TWO later, Greta was caught off guard when Mildred invited her over for dinner. Against her better judgment, Greta accepted the invitation.

"I had to force myself," Greta wrote.

The dinner defied expectation. So did the hostess who served it. Mildred, so graceful on ice skates, was, to Greta's mind, a walking disaster,

awkward in all practical things of life. She couldn't iron a blouse without it ending up more wrinkled than before, or it had singe marks. She invited guests to dinner in order to try out a new, wonderful recipe, but forgot the most important seasonings. The rice pot boiled over, the cake didn't rise, the vegetables weren't cooked. Her shoestrings broke on every hike. She had delicate, slender, and expressive hands, but they were two left hands, which never mastered the pitfalls of objects.

Greta was also baffled by the questions Mildred asked her during dinner: "Have you read about the struggles of the American worker?" "Do you want to see the Ford and Chevrolet plants?" "Do you know about the organizational structures capitalism has created?"

Mildred, tremulous whisperer of Shakespeare and Homer, wanted to talk politics, not poetry.

4.

A hike. An ordinary hike. This was what Greta was expecting. When they weren't canoeing on the lakes, her classmates at UW were heading off to the hills. One fine spring day Greta joined them. The snow had melted, and everywhere you looked, wildflowers pushed up through thawing dirt. Greta followed her classmates, Mildred among them, as they charged up a hill.

This was no ordinary hike, it turned out. It had a name: "Follow Your Nose Through Thick and Thin."

There were rules. Head in a straight line. If there is a fence in your path, climb it. If there is a lake, swim to the other side. If there is a house, knock on the front door and inform whoever answers that you must enter the house and leave through the back door. No matter what obstacle you encounter, keep going, *through thick and thin*.

Greta, fond of rules, was giddy.

The rules weren't constraining; they allowed her, paradoxically, to let loose. Follow Your Nose Through Thick and Thin was a crazy romp through the countryside. Sometimes when Greta knocked on someone's door, she was invited in for pancakes or cinnamon toast or "one of the wonderful ice creams which were produced on larger farms." After their romp, she and her American friends lay "in the shade of nut trees" and "let the wonderful spicy larva-like blossoms fall down on us." They told one another stories. Funny stories, sad stories, stories about hometowns, parents, childhoods. Lying there in the litter of blossoms was Mildred.

"Slowly a picture developed from Mildred's stories," Greta reflected.

Mildred wasn't a pampered American ice-skating princess. She had grown up poor. This surprised Greta, who had grown up poor too. Her father was a metalworker, her mother a seamstress.

5.

At some point in 1933, Arvid runs into Greta on a sidewalk in Berlin. The last time they saw each other was in Wisconsin. Since then, she has moved back to Germany and settled in Frankfurt.

What is she doing in Berlin? Arvid wants to know. What a coincidence that he bumped into her! Later, she will wonder whether it was really a coincidence.

Greta doesn't know how long she will be in Berlin. In Frankfurt, she was enrolled in a PhD program and worked as the assistant to a prominent sociology professor at Goethe University. The professor was fired. He was a Jew. All Jewish professors have been fired from Goethe University.

Arvid tells her that he and Mildred are assembling some kind of group, a loose network of like-minded people. A "circle of acquaintances" is how he puts it. He wants to know whether she has any connections to factory workers. He wants to establish contact with poor, working-class Berliners but is finding this difficult. Greta can see why. Arvid Harnack, descendant of the great scholar Adolf von Harnack, eminent theologian and former adviser to Kaiser Wilhelm II, is not someone poor people would listen to. They would listen to *her,* though. Her working-class roots could be an asset. To what end isn't immediately clear.

Greta agrees to go to a meeting.

6.

Greta is now a core member of the Circle. The location of their meetings varies. It's safer that way. Sometimes they meet in "a small rowhouse, the type that was built after the first World War," Greta remembered. "We sat on all the chairs brought from all over the entire house and talked about the measures the Nazis had taken so far."

Sometimes the Circle meets "on the path to a boathouse in Pichelsdorf." Here, walking along the Havel River, they're far from prying eyes and ears. They have what they seek most: privacy and a place to strategize.

The People's Radio

1933–1934

1.

Now that Hitler has seized power, he needs to hold on to it. It's not enough for the Nazi Party to be the largest party in the Reichstag. The vast majority of Germans must support him. To win them over, the government must control all media. It is to this end that Hitler creates the Reich Ministry for Public Enlightenment and Propaganda and puts Joseph Goebbels in charge of it.

Once, Goebbels aspired to be a writer. In 1921, at the age of twenty-four, Goebbels received a PhD (he wrote his dissertation on an obscure nineteenth-century playwright), and he struggled for several years to build a respectable career. He wrote a novel that no publisher would publish, two plays that no producer would produce, and when he turned his attention to journalism, no newspaper would hire him. When he encountered his idol Hitler, his luck began to change. In 1926, Goebbels delivered a speech about propaganda at a Nazi Party rally in Weimar. Hitler was so impressed that he named the twenty-nine-year-old failed writer the leader of the Berlin branch of the Nazi Party. In the seven years since, Goebbels has proven himself to be one of Hitler's most devoted acolytes. His new position in Hitler's cabinet strengthens his resolve to support the man he has described in his diary as a "genius."

2.

Goebbels wastes no time in setting up seven departments in the Reich Chamber of Culture to oversee Germany's newspapers, film, radio, music, visual arts, theater, and literature.

Germany's celebrated free press is no more. Hundreds of newspapers are banned, and Jewish-owned publishing houses are forced out of business. Nazis seize control of Ullstein, the largest publishing company in Germany, forcing the Jewish family members who own it to resign from the board of directors and sell their stock. An "editor's law" prohibits Jewish writers and editors from working. The Reich Chamber of Culture, under Goebbels's ruthless eye, dictates what can and cannot be published.

Germany's theater and film industries are purged of all Jewish writers, actors, producers, and directors.

Germany's museums are purged of art that is not *Germanic*. Paintings by Cézanne, Picasso, van Gogh, Gauguin, and Matisse are no longer worthy of exhibition, as Hitler considers them too modern, too decadent, too *degenerate*. The man who was twice rejected by art school will go on to cocurate an exhibition of "Great German Art," held in a building he helped design, a feat of architecture that Hitler brags is "unparalleled and inimitable."

Along with the purging of Jews comes the elimination of people in the arts who belong to opposing political parties. Painters, writers, musicians, architects, producers, directors—anyone who is a Communist or a Social Democrat or suspected of being one is forbidden to work in these professions.

And while all media is put in the service of spreading Hitler's ideology, it is radio that will become the Nazi government's most powerful instrument of propaganda.

3.

What if every German, young or old, rich or poor, city- or country-dweller, could hear Hitler's voice, even if the person lived miles from his megaphone? So mused Goebbels, who understood that newsreels screened in theaters reached only people who watched films and that the printed word reached only people who read newspapers, and even then, reading the Führer's speech was a step removed from actually hearing it. Goebbels seized on the notion that he could use radio to coax ideas into people's heads, repeating again and again core messages of Hitler's ideology. For the first time in history, Germans living in the most remote regions of the country could be reached, even the destitute and uneducated, even the apolitical. All it required was getting radios into their hands.

Goebbels gleefully ordered manufacturers to produce a radio that everyone could afford. The first model cost thirty-five Reichsmark—what a factory worker or manual laborer earned in a week—and was payable in installments. Goebbels gave the cheap radio a name—"the People's Radio"—and a model number that corresponded to the date Hitler became chancellor.

Six million units sold within a year.

The People's Radio was designed with a limited range to ensure that only German stations could be heard. Turning the dial to a station broadcasting from London was an exercise in frustration, the whistling static a reminder that the Nazi government didn't want its citizens to hear news from other countries.

Now that Germans were cut off from the rest of the world, Nazi propaganda would be all the more successful.

4.

"It would not have been possible for us to take power
or to use it in the ways we have without the radio."
—Joseph Goebbels, August 18, 1933

5.

Mildred doesn't own a People's Radio and never will. The radio she listens to is a Blaupunkt, a gift from Arvid's brother, Falk Harnack. The Blaupunkt is encased in wood that is polished to a sheen. It is a thing of beauty. It features both longwave and shortwave reception and a dial that moves a thin horizontal line across an array of even thinner horizontal lines representing radio frequencies. Turn the dial, and you can hear the magnificent thunder of a Beethoven symphony or the more delicate strains of a Bach violin sonata, but this isn't why Mildred likes the Blaupunkt. Its shortwave reception enables it to pick up foreign news broadcasts. Radio programs produced in other countries are quickly becoming the only reliable sources of news. Falk knows how important news is to Mildred. He turns twenty in March. Mildred calls him *mein kleiner Bruder.* My little brother.

The Blaupunkt is manufactured in a town near Berlin. The first model was produced in 1923, the year Hitler—then a thirty-four-year-old misfit—convinced a group of twenty young men to start a revolution in Munich, firing a pistol in a beer hall. The failed coup came to be known as the Beer Hall Putsch, and it landed Hitler in prison. He wrote the first volume of his manifesto *Mein Kampf* there, formulating his plans for another, more massive, revolution.

Hitler's latest revolution will fail too—this is what Mildred believes right now. She's not alone. Arvid believes this, as do many of their friends who consider themselves politically astute. They're convinced that Germans will revolt against this lunatic politician. It's just a matter of time.

The Reichstag Fire

1933

1.

"Now it will be easy," Goebbels scribbles in his diary. "And this time, naturally, there is no lack of money."

On February 20—two and a half weeks after Hitler is appointed chancellor—twenty-four of Germany's leading industrialists sit around a long, rectangular table. Gustav Krupp, a tycoon who runs Friedrich Krupp, a weapons manufacturer, is here. So are Georg von Schnitzler, a board member of I. G. Farben, the world's largest chemical conglomerate; Albert Vögler, head of United Steel Works, a massive mining corporation; August Rosterg, general director of Wintershall, Germany's largest producer of crude oil; Hugo Stinnes Jr., board member of a major German coal syndicate; and Ludwig von Winterfeld, board member of Siemens and Halske, the largest electrical-engineering equipment manufacturer in Europe.

Hitler sits at the head of the table. "Private enterprise cannot be maintained in the age of democracy," he begins. "It is conceivable only if the people have a sound idea of authority." Hitler pledges to eliminate left-wing opponents and destroy trade unions. He promises to initiate the process of rearmament and restore the military to its former glory.

The twenty-four businessmen listen. Perhaps, now and then, they nod.

Hitler mentions the upcoming Reichstag election. The Nazi Party must gain thirty-three more seats, he insists. "This is not impossible if we exert all our strength."

When Hitler is done speaking, the host of the meeting, a shrewd economist named Hjalmar Schacht, asks the businessmen to reach into their wallets and support the Nazi cause.

The businessmen fork over three million Reichsmark.

2.

Hitler wants to become the supreme sole ruler of Germany, but he doesn't have the power to do this. The Weimar Constitution stands in his way.

How does a dictator overthrow a democracy? Bullets and blood, usually. Violent revolution, military coup.

Hitler does it differently.

3.

Some call it luck. Some call it something else. Less than a month after Hitler is appointed chancellor, an arsonist lights a match in the Reichstag.

The arsonist isn't German. He's an immigrant from Holland, a twenty-four-year-old out-of-work bricklayer, later described by the chief of the Prussian secret police, Rudolf Diels, as "naked from the waist upwards, smeared with dirt and sweating...with a wild triumphant gleam in the burning eyes of his pale, haggard young face." Diels, who has a flair for the dramatic, observed the filthy young man charging "through the big corridors with his burning shirt, which he brandished in his right hand like a torch." Diels took care to note that the arsonist's pockets bulged with Communist pamphlets.

Fire brigades arrive, sirens blaring. Berliners rush out their doors, coats over their pajamas, to watch the firemen aim their hoses at the enormous steel-and-glass dome that crowns the Reichstag, built when Germany was ruled by a monarchy. The dome collapses, as does much of the building.

Hitler is there. So are President Hindenburg, Vice-Chancellor Papen, Goebbels, and Göring.

Göring steps forward. He is in every way an outsize man, with a swelling belly and an appetite for extravagance in food, drink, and dress. He is known for the hunting parties he throws at his lavish country estate, where he greets his guests, as one later recalled, wearing "high leather boots, a leather jerkin, white shirtsleeves, a huntsman's broadbrimmed hat on his head and a six-foot hunting spear in his hand." What Göring wears tonight is equally exhibitionist, a uniform gleaming with medals that boast of his twenty-two victories as a fighter pilot in the Great War of 1914–1918.

"This is a Communist crime against the new government!" he cries.

The words that he hollers into the smoke-filled air are noted by Vice-Chancellor Papen, who observes that Göring is in a tizzy, sweating copiously. The immigrant bricklayer is *clearly* part of a Communist plot, declares Göring, and tonight marks "the beginning of a Communist revolution."

"There will be no mercy now," Hitler shouts. "Every Communist official will be shot where he is found! The Communist deputies must be hanged this very night! Everybody in league with the Communists must be arrested! There will no longer be any leniency for the Social Democrats either!"

The fire is still smoldering when Göring corners the chief of the Prussian secret police and orders him to arrest the opposition. Thirty-three-year-old Rudolf Diels will do such a splendid job that he gets a promotion. Göring will name him chief of the Gestapo.

At approximately midnight, a mass arrest begins.

Storm Troopers break into homes, drag men out of their beds, and deposit them in barracks and holding cells. More than four thousand Communists and Social Democrats are imprisoned, among them members of the Reichstag.

The next morning, Hitler uses the fire as a pretext to declare a national emergency, pressuring President Hindenburg to sign a decree that suspends indefinitely all seven sections of the Weimar Constitution guaranteeing basic civil liberties to Germans.

The decree abolishes freedom of speech and freedom of the press. No longer can Germans attend rallies and march in demonstrations against the Nazi government, as the decree abolishes the right to assembly. Letters and telephone calls can now be monitored by the Nazi government, as the decree abolishes the right to privacy. Storm Troopers, the Gestapo, and anyone else with a badge can raid any home without a search warrant.

The order is called the "Decree of the Reich President for the Protection of the People and State," and it grants the Nazi government the right to silence all opposition.

4.

DECREE OF THE REICH PRESIDENT FOR THE PROTECTION OF THE PEOPLE AND STATE

Pursuant to Article 48, Section 2, of the Reich Constitution, the following is decreed as a defensive measure against Communist acts of violence endangering the state:

1. Suspension of Basic Rights

Articles 114, 115, 117, 118, 123, 124, and 153 of the Constitution of the German Reich are suspended until further notice. Thus, restrictions to personal liberty, to the right of free expression of opinion, including freedom of the press, to the right of assembly and the right of association; and violations of the privacy of postal, telegraphic, and telephonic communications, and warrants for house-searches, orders for confiscations as well as restrictions on property, are also permissible beyond the legal limits otherwise prescribed...

2. Reich Government as Executive State Authority

If in a state the measures necessary for the restoration of public security and order are not taken, the Reich Government may temporarily take over the powers of the highest state authority...

3. Imposition of the Death Penalty

The crimes which under the Criminal Code are punishable with penitentiary for life are to be punished with death: i.e., in Sections 81 (high treason), 229 (poisoning), 306 (arson), 311 (explosion), 312 (flooding), 315, Paragraph 2 (damage to railway facilities), 324 (public endangerment through poison)...

Signed:

The Reich President: Paul von Hindenburg

The Reich Chancellor: Adolf Hitler

The Reich Minister of the Interior: Wilhelm Frick

The Reich Minister of Justice: Franz Gürtner

Berlin

February 28, 1933

5.

March 5, 1933. As crews clear away the charred rubble of what remains of the Reichstag building, an election is held.

Six days ago, Hitler gutted the Weimar Constitution. He did it legally, right under everyone's nose, without bullets or blood. Germans have lost nearly all their rights—all but one. They still have the right to vote. Germany is still a democracy, not a dictatorship. Representatives in the Reichstag are still elected, and the body still functions as Germany's parliament, with the power to approve budgets and legislation.

In the days leading up to the election, Goebbels undertakes a massive publicity campaign. "Radio and press are at our disposal," he writes in his diary. "We shall stage a masterpiece of propaganda."

The radio broadcasts Hitler's promises far and wide. All morning and afternoon, trucks outfitted with loudspeakers circle streets and country lanes, bringing Hitler's voice to bustling city squares and quiet neighborhoods. An inflammatory report released by the government announces the discovery of documents proving that Communists have been plotting "terrorist acts" against Germany, planning to burn down not only the Reichstag but also "government buildings, museums, mansions."

At the polling sites, swastikas are on full display — on armbands, posters, flags, banners. Storm Troopers, the SS, and a paramilitary veterans' army called the Stahlhelm — Steel Helmets — are monitoring the polls. Anyone who wants to cast a vote must walk past rows of armed Nazis.

In the face of all this fearmongering and intimidation, Germans show up at the polls in droves. The voter turnout is 89 percent.

6.

It's not the victory Hitler had hoped for.

The Nazi Party gets 44 percent of the vote. Fifty-six percent of German voters cast their ballots for another party.

A majority is required to pass any new law in the Reichstag, which puts Hitler in a pickle. Any law that supports the Nazi agenda will most likely be rejected.

7.

Thirteen days later, Hitler asks the Reichstag to pass a new law.

He makes his request while standing on the grand stage of the Kroll Opera House, where the Reichstag convenes now that the other building is a charred wreck. Five hundred twenty-five representatives are present. They sit in red velvet chairs. Above them, crystal chandeliers hang from gilded chains. Cherubs carved into woodwork gaze down at the aisles, clogged with Storm Troopers standing at attention with "scarred bully faces," notes the American journalist William Shirer, seated in back. The setting is strange enough, but it's the law itself that is most unusual. It will put the members of the Reichstag out of work.

Not permanently, Hitler assures them. Just for four years. Essentially, he's asking the Reichstag to take a very long holiday.

The Reichstag members, seated in their red velvet chairs, consider his request, which necessitates a change to the Weimar Constitution. Any constitutional change requires two-thirds of the Reichstag to support it.

One representative stands. He is Otto Wels, leader of the Social Democrats. Many of his friends and colleagues were arrested after the Reichstag fire. He speaks, according to Shirer, "quietly and with great dignity."

We German Social Democrats pledge ourselves solemnly in this historic hour to the principles of humanity and justice, of freedom.

Wels refuses to support Hitler's law. He urges his colleagues to do the same. No law, Wels tells Hitler, "can give you the power to destroy ideas which are eternal and indestructible." Wels sits down.

The Reichstag members cast their votes: 441 in favor, 84 against. This gives the Nazis far more than a two-thirds majority. In a spectacle of cowardice and political opportunism, the politicians support Hitler and pass a new law.

Hitler calls it the "Law to Remove the Distress of People and Reich." It will come to be known as the "Enabling Act." In five short paragraphs, it guts what remains of the Weimar Constitution and transforms Germany into a dictatorship.

And it's all done legally. Not by armed revolution, not by a bloody coup. But in an opera house, among cherubs.

An Act of Sabotage

1933–1934

1.

Mildred is pregnant.

For the past two years she has been doing abdominal exercises to prepare her body for pregnancy. The book she bought depicts exactly how she should position her arms and lift her torso to do a proper sit-up. The book hasn't prepared her for what she should do now.

2.

The role of women is to populate Germany with good Germans. This is what Minister of Public Enlightenment and Propaganda Joseph Goebbels announces in a speech he delivers in a crowded hall in Berlin. He has given his speech a humdrum title—"German Women"—but he delivers it with verve.

Women during the Weimar era were granted too many rights, Goebbels tells the crowd. Women shouldn't hold public office or compete with men in the workplace. "The feminization of men always leads to the masculinization of women," he says, and the net result is profound despair for both sexes.

"A fundamental change is necessary!" Goebbels bellows into the microphone:

The first, best, and most suitable place for the woman is in the family, and her most glorious duty is to give children to her people and nation, children who can continue the line of generations and who guarantee the immortality of the nation!

It's essentially impossible to find a condom in Berlin or anywhere else in Germany. Contraception was readily available in major cities by the end of the Weimar Republic. Vending machines dispensed condoms in men's public restrooms. Clinics provided free condoms. Now they're illegal.

3.

Hitler tells the Nazi Women's League that a woman's world is "her husband, her family, her children, and her home." He criticizes the concept of "women's emancipation," insisting that it "is merely an invention of the Jewish intellect."

After the thunderous applause dies down, he continues:

We do not think it proper for woman to invade the world of man, to enter his territory; instead, we think it natural for these worlds to remain separate.... And that is why woman has always been man's helper and, as such, his most loyal friend, and it is also why man has always been his wife's protector and, as such, her best friend!

4.

Across Germany, women lose their jobs.

Over nineteen thousand women in leadership positions at the ministries and in regional and local government offices are immediately fired. Women lawyers are dismissed from firms. Women physicians are ousted from clinics. Restaurant owners are threatened by police if they don't sack their waitresses and replace them with men.

Women who aren't fired are encouraged to give up their jobs to make room for unemployed men. Goebbels mounts a vigorous propaganda campaign against so-called double-earners—families in which a husband and wife both hold jobs.

5.

Young women are discouraged from going to college. A new quota restricts the number of women who can enroll in a German university to 10 percent. There were over eighteen thousand female university students in Germany before Hitler took power, a number that soon plummets to 5,447.

The curriculum in German high schools is revamped. Girls are required to take classes in cooking, cleaning, and mending. The single goal of a young woman's education is to prepare for motherhood.

Hitler establishes his mother's birthday, August 12, as the new Mother's Day and declares it a national holiday.

6.

Mildred takes a train to Grunewald to visit Arvid's cousin Agnes von Zahn-Harnack, whom she adores. Agnes is an ardent women's rights activist who until recently was president of the powerful Bund Deutscher Frauenvereine (BDF)—the Federation of German Women's Associations—which has over five hundred thousand members. Agnes is outraged that women across Germany are losing their jobs, jobs that have subsequently "fallen into men's hands."

In 1908 Agnes von Zahn-Harnack had the distinction of being the very first woman to enroll at the University of Berlin. During the Weimar Republic she cofounded the Deutscher Akademikerinnenbund — German Association of Women Academics—and gave birth to a daughter, Margarete, who is fifteen now and is fond of telling Mildred and anyone else who pays a visit that she wants to be a doctor when she grows up.

These days, it seems like a pipe dream.

7.

"No more Paris models," Hitler tells German fashion editor Hela Strehl. From now on, German magazines must depict German women who are untainted by the French or any other foreign influence. Hitler wants the models to dress in a distinctly *German* way.

"German men want real German women again," asserts a 1933 Nazi handbook. The farmer's wife is celebrated as the feminine ideal: healthy and strong, unsullied by perfume or paint. Suntanned skin is fetishized, along with the traditional German folk costume—*Tracht*—worn by the peasants of yore in the Alpine regions of Bavaria and Austria.

German women are urged to throw out their lipstick, hair dye, and high heels.

Hitler establishes the Deutsches Modeamt—German Fashion Institute—and assigns Goebbels's wife, Magda, to serve as honorary president. Blond-haired, blue-eyed Magda Goebbels seems perfect for the job, a model of Aryan beauty and fertility who recently gave birth to a daughter, Helga. (Between 1934 and 1940 Magda will have five more children: Hildegard, Helmut, Holdine, Hedwig, and Heidrun.) Hitler may be flattered by her fidelity to the letter *H,* but he is also disappointed by her performance as honorary president. Magda is worrisomely uncooperative in her new role, flouncing into the Deutsches Modeamt headquarters in haute couture (she wears Ferragamo heels), voicing her own opinions while chain-smoking slender cigarettes from a gold-tipped holder. After she tells a journalist that "the German woman of the future should be stylish, beautiful, and intelligent," Magda Goebbels is booted from Deutsches Modeamt.

Deutsches Modeamt is renamed Deutsches Mode-Institut. Propaganda Minister Goebbels will make arrangements for fashion editor Hela Strehl—who happens to be one of his many mistresses—to be hired by Deutsches Mode-Institut.

8.

German women are urged to have as many children as possible. A bronze medallion etched with the words *Ehrenzeichen der Deutschen Mutter*—the Cross of Honor of the German Mother—is awarded to a woman on the birth of her fourth child. For her sixth child, the medallion is silver; for her eighth, gold.

Kindersegen—women blessed with children—are praised as national heroines. You see them everywhere, on posters, in magazines: images of young blond smiling women cradling numerous cherubic babies.

The Law for the Encouragement of Marriage is passed. If two people get married, they can receive a state loan of 1,000 Reichsmark—equivalent to one-fifth of a worker's annual income—as long as the wife promises to "immediately leave" her job. If she gives birth to one baby, the couple receives a credit of 250 Reichsmark; if she has a second baby, 500 Reichsmark; if she has a third, 750 Reichsmark. The entire loan is forgiven the day her fourth baby is born.

Income-tax deductions are awarded to married couples with children. Parents of four children can deduct 60 percent from their taxable gross income. Parents of six children pay no income tax at all.

Newspapers carry stories about German gynecologists facing criminal charges. Gynecologists may receive the death penalty if they are found guilty of terminating an unwanted pregnancy, but only if the woman is Aryan, "racially pure."

There is no penalty for terminating the pregnancy of a woman who is "racially inferior."

9.

Mildred slips away for a few days to London, where she has made an appointment. Abortions are considered an act of sabotage against Germany's future, but she can't have a baby. Not now.

She tells no one about the doctor's appointment—no one except her mother. Georgina Fish mails the London doctor a check for fifty-six dollars. How she scraped together the money is a mystery.

Mildred types a letter to her mother.

I am grateful for sending what you did to England. It's all right. Words about it are unnecessary. Please don't write anything more about it.

Mildred's Recruits

1933–1934

> chologie und Geschichte in Berlin.
> 32. *Johanna Schulze*, Buchhalterin, studiert nicht.
> 33. *Käthe Stombierek*, Bücherrevisorin, studiert nicht.
> 34. *Richard Theus*, Fernmeldemonteur, jetzt ohne Beruf, studiert Elektrotechnik in Berlin.
> 35. *Paul Thomas*, Schmied, z. Zt. arbeitslos, studiert Mathematik in Berlin.
> 36 *Marthuise Tollert* Kontoristin studiert Medizin in

1.

In 1933, the Circle is not large. There are about a dozen members. Soon, the number of people who show up to meetings will grow.

2.

Mildred recruits Wilhelm Utech into the Circle.

He's unemployed and has been taking classes at the BAG since 1932. At first, he hides his involvement from his wife. He worries she'll be angry—or worse, turn him in. When he heads off to a meeting, he tells her he's going to an "English tutoring session."

One day Wilhelm Utech is arrested and thrown into a concentration camp. His crime is distributing leaflets that criticize Hitler's regime. He is interrogated and beaten. For a year he languishes there. When he is finally released, he heads home and tells his wife everything. Martha Utech doesn't turn him in. She joins the Circle.

3.

Mildred recruits Paul Thomas into the Circle.

Paul Thomas fought in the First World War when he was a teenager and lost his right arm. Part of his face is puckered with scar tissue. He's a friend of one of her former students at the University of Berlin. After she taught her last class there, she invited him to take her class at the BAG.

On the class register Paul Thomas is number 35. He's *arbeitslos*—unemployed—like so many of his friends in Berlin.

4.

Mildred recruits Bodo Schlösinger into the Circle.

Bodo is a fair-haired tailor with a talent for languages. He shuffles into Mildred's class at the BAG after a long day squinting at stitches.

Bodo won't squint at stitches forever. Soon, his degree from the BAG will open the door to a much better job. Bodo's fluency in Russian and English will be a tremendous asset to the Circle, though he doesn't yet know how. The woman Bodo will marry, a secretary named Rose who works at a factory in Chemnitz, will also join the Circle.

5.

They can't meet at Mildred and Arvid's apartment anymore. The walls and ceilings are too thin, and the possibility that a neighbor may overhear them is too great. A young man wearing round wire-framed eyeglasses offers to host meetings at his apartment. His name is Karl Behrens. He's one of the most devoted members of the Circle.

Karl has the aristocratic bearing and long, lean face of a greyhound, though he has no pedigree to speak of. He didn't go to school with rich men or grow up near them. He doesn't even have a high-school diploma.

At seventeen he joined the Hitler Youth. The full name—Hitlerjugend, Bund der deutschen Arbeiterjugend (Hitler Youth,

League of German Worker Youth)—emphasizes the poor, working-class origins of many of its recruits. Karl marched in rallies wearing a uniform that resembled the one Storm Troopers wear: brown shirt, black shorts, and a swastika armband. A white horizontal stripe across the swastika distinguishes a Hitler Youth's armband from a Storm Trooper's.

At eighteen, he became a Storm Trooper.

At twenty-two, he did something radical. He quit the Storm Troopers and decided to return to school.

He walked into his first class at the BAG at the end of an exhausting day working at a factory that manufactured gas lamps. Mildred awakened the revolutionary in him. Now, he smuggles into the factory leaflets that denounce Hitler and leaves them in piles near the machinery, slips them into mailboxes and under doors.

6.

Mildred starts to look outside the BAG for recruits. It is a delicate, dangerous undertaking.

It begins, frequently, with a book. Mildred lends one to anyone she has her eye on. This allows her to suggest they meet again, when she'll ask her prospective recruit a mild question or two about the book, laying the foundation for a discussion that will soon turn political.

Sometimes it begins with a conversation that might be about anything at all and that takes place in public or private, in a crowded restaurant or in a neighbor's apartment. Mildred knows Gestapo informers could be anywhere—sitting next to her on the U-Bahn, loitering at the corner newsstand, sniffing roses at the florist's, drinking tea in her neighbor's kitchen. The risks are many. If she reveals too quickly that she's in the resistance, she could be arrested. If she keeps her political opinions concealed too long, she could lose a valuable recruit.

She develops a sly technique. Others in the Circle use it too.

Pretend you're a Nazi. Don't beat around the bush. Tell the shopkeeper or the factory worker or the friend of a friend that you admire something Hitler did or are otherwise sympathetic to Nazi policies and see how the person responds. "The object was to lead the other person to reveal his political attitude," her recruit Wilhelm Utech remembered. "This 'testing' was to be carried out very carefully, so that we did not reveal ourselves prematurely and thus endanger our work."

The sly technique could cause colossal misunderstandings, of course. On a trip to London, Mildred tries to recruit the writer Rebecca West, who scoffs when Mildred gravely tells her that Hitler adores her books. "I threw her out of the front door," West recalled in a letter.

Tumbling Like Dominoes

1933

1.

On April 1, 1933, there is a national boycott of all Jewish businesses. Storm Troopers and SS men stand outside the stores' entrances, forbidding anyone to go in.

On April 7, 1933, the Law for the Restoration of the Professional Civil Service excludes Jews and the "politically unreliable" from becoming professors, teachers, or judges. The Law on the Admission to the Legal Profession forbids Jews to become lawyers.

On April 25, 1933, the Law Against Overcrowding in Schools and Universities limits the number of Jewish students allowed to receive public education. No more than 5 percent of the students in a school or university may be Jewish.

2.

On July 14, 1933, the Law for the Prevention of Genetically Diseased Offspring legalizes forced sterilization of people deemed mentally ill or physically disabled. An estimated four hundred thousand Germans are sterilized. Most are between the ages of twenty and forty. The compulsory surgeries are evenly divided between men and women. Men receive vasectomies; women undergo tubal ligation—their fallopian tubes surgically cut, tied, or crushed.

3.

It is now a crime to criticize the Nazi government. The Malicious Practices Act prohibits Germans from expressing their disapproval about anything Hitler says or does. Even a joke could bring the Gestapo to your door.

Newspapers and magazines that once lampooned the Nazi Party go silent. The editors at *Simplicissimus* escape imprisonment by pledging in the April 1, 1933, issue to adopt a "loyal attitude" toward Hitler. In the April 16 issue, the editors announce that their articles will no longer be "critical and negative."

The *Münchener Post* publishes articles with urgent headlines like GERMANY UNDER THE HITLER REGIME: POLITICAL MURDER AND TERROR and BRUTAL TERROR IN THE STREETS OF MUNICH and OUTLAWS AND MURDERERS IN POWER until Storm Troopers raid the editorial office and throw everyone in prison. One of the journalists, Fritz Gerlich, is transported to the concentration camp at Dachau, where he is murdered by the SS.

4.

The words *arrested* and *imprisoned* are no longer used.

Protective custody — *Schutzhaft* — is the term that the Nazi government prefers.

If you are a German under protective custody, you have no legal remedies at your disposal. No lawyers can intervene, because you are not technically under arrest. If you are dragged out of your bed, bludgeoned, denied legal counsel, thrown into a cell, and left to languish there, bleeding, for an indefinite period, it is for your own protection and for the protection of peace and order in Germany.

5.

Persuading Germans to fight back is getting increasingly difficult. The systematic prohibition of all forms of opposition — leaflets, posters, rallies, meetings, marches — is wildly effective. Many throw up their hands and say there is *nichts dagegen zu machen*—nothing to do about it.

6.

"The majority tumbled like dominoes," as Emmi Bonhoeffer put it in an interview many years later.

Mildred loves visiting Emmi and all the other Bonhoeffers. Emmi is married to Dietrich Bonhoeffer's brother Klaus. Their home is in a wealthy neighborhood in Berlin, on Bendlerstrasse, steps from the Tiergarten. Dinners are occasions for a loud, cheerful volley of opinions on politics and philosophy, music and art. The Bonhoeffers are openly contemptuous of Hitler.

In April, Dietrich Bonhoeffer wrote an essay criticizing church leaders who refused to defend Jews. A few weeks later, he committed treason when he contacted Rabbi Stephen Wise in New York and urged the Jewish leader to inform President Roosevelt about Hitler's treatment of Jews. Dietrich won't be silenced.

Neither will Dietrich's grandmother, who defied the April 1 boycott to buy a quarter pound of butter. When a Storm Trooper guarding the entrance of the store warned her not to buy butter from a Jew, the ninety-one-year-old woman rapped her cane against his jackboots and strode in, declaring, "I shall buy my butter where I always buy it."

Mildred is beginning to feel less comfortable in her own home. It's not far from Emmi's, just three miles or so, but it might as well be a world away. Loud, cheerful dinners aren't possible at Hasenheide 61. The walls and ceilings and floors aren't thick enough to prevent an eavesdropper from hearing what they say. She and Arvid share the fourth floor with another couple, separated by a single sliding door. Can they be trusted?

Mildred's fears aren't unfounded. Stories about neighbors betraying neighbors have already begun to circulate.

7.

In the spring of 1933, a group of prisoners arrive at a holding facility ten miles north of Munich. The facility is a former munitions factory. There are twenty barracks on the grounds, many of which can hold two hundred people. Some barracks are larger, accommodating two hundred fifty. The barracks are made of brick and are in disrepair, the bricks broken, the mortar crumbling. Soon, the barracks will be spruced up. The prisoners will do all the work. One hundred state police—Landespolizei—guard the facility. A barrier of barbed wire has been stretched around the area—three strands, spaced evenly apart—preventing escape.

These details are announced to a group of journalists who have been invited to a press conference. It's Monday, the beginning of what will be a busy week for the journalists and perhaps even busier for the mild-mannered man who stands before them. He has a bookish demeanor, wears black-rimmed glasses. He's in charge of the holding facility, which he calls a *camp*.

The camp is located near a picturesque town called Dachau. This is the very first camp established under Hitler's regime, he explains to the journalists. It will serve as a model for other camps.

The journalists ask questions and scribble in their notebooks as they listen to this reasonable man, who introduces himself as Heinrich Himmler, the head of the SS.

Himmler is thirty-two. He studied agronomy in college and worked briefly on a farm raising chickens. Now he directs his talent for classifying flora and fauna to the SS officers who apply to work at this concentration camp. Requirements are strict. Pure German blood is a must.

Right now, Dachau holds approximately one hundred twenty Communists, Social Democrats, and other left-wing opponents of the Nazi Party who were arrested after the Reichstag fire. At first, they were sent to courthouse jails. But leaving them there put too much economic strain on the apparatus of the criminal justice system, Himmler explains, and it would be inappropriate to let them go free.

This, then, is the rationale for Dachau. It's called a *concentration camp* because all the individuals who threaten the security of Germany are concentrated here.

A journalist at the press conference submits an article to his newspaper, *Dachauer Volksblatt.* On April 6, 1933, the article appears under the headline THE FORMER GUNPOWDER FACTORY IN DACHAU A CONCENTRATION CAMP FOR POLITICAL PRISONERS. The journalist describes Dachau as a work camp and reassures the reader that "protective custody of individuals would not be continued any longer than necessary." After the prisoners rebuild the crumbling brick buildings, he writes,

> they will be led out in small groups of about fifty men into the countryside, where extensive land cultivation projects wait to be implemented. Perhaps later some of the camp inmates will be offered the possibility of settling here.

No one brought to Dachau will want to settle here, of course. Over the next twelve years, more than two hundred thousand people will be imprisoned in Dachau. An estimated forty thousand will die here.

8.

Dachau is the first concentration camp in Nazi Germany and serves as a model for other large camps that will soon be built. In the spring and summer of 1933, hundreds of smaller, makeshift camps spring up in cities and towns across Germany. These early camps function as jails for people under "protective custody" outside the jurisdiction of municipal courts, and they are by no means identical. Hotels, restaurants, and hostels are converted into camps. Even pubs and old castles hold prisoners. They are run by Storm Troopers and SS officers and function, in the words of one Communist, as "Nazi torture dens." In Berlin alone, there are 170 makeshift camps in 1933, mainly in working-class neighborhoods like Kreuzberg and Wedding.

In 1936, another major concentration camp is built: Sachsenhausen. In 1937, another: Buchenwald. Two more are established in

1938—Mauthausen and Flossenbürg—followed by Ravensbrück, a concentration camp exclusively for women, in 1939.

During the Second World War, the number of camps explode to twenty-seven main camps and over eleven hundred satellite camps across Germany and Nazi-occupied countries, including Austria, Poland, Czechoslovakia, France, Belgium, the Netherlands, Lithuania, Latvia, and Estonia. In 1940, Auschwitz opens. In 1942, the mass deportation of Jews to the camp begins. A lethal gas, Zyklon B, is used to murder them. Auschwitz and other camps engineered for mass murder play a central role in what Nazis called the Final Solution—the extermination of European Jews known as the Holocaust.

9.

The day Dachau opens, March 22, 1933, anti-Semitism is rampant. Among the Communists and Social Democrats imprisoned at Dachau, Jews are singled out and bludgeoned by Nazi guards. Over a six-week stretch in April and May, eight of twelve prisoners who are murdered are Jewish.

When an attorney from the Munich state prosecutor's office shows up at Dachau to investigate the murders, Himmler holds a press conference. He wears his black SS uniform. The image he projects is less the militaristic head of a sadistic corps of officers than a mild-mannered intellectual. Behind his round, black-rimmed glasses, his eyes blink thoughtfully, evoking the abstracted air of the agronomist he once aspired to be.

The murders were not premeditated, he tells the journalists. The prisoners had been "auf der Flucht erschossen"—shot while trying to escape—a phrase that will soon become a shopworn Nazi euphemism for murder.

10.

In 1933, Jews are not rounded up and imprisoned in significant numbers—not yet. In the early days of the Nazi regime, Hitler targets political opponents first.

There are twenty thousand political prisoners by March 1933.

By the end of the year, over two hundred thousand Communists, Social Democrats, and trade unionists have been put in "protective custody" at concentration camps. The Circle discusses and debates — often heatedly — the central question: Stay or go? Stay and risk arrest, imprisonment, death? Go and abandon Germany to the Nazis, who are hell-bent on destroying it?

Mildred sees swastikas on cigarette packages, coffee cans, cake pans. Every day, Nazi propaganda disseminates misinformation and false promises. Every day, Hitler wins more German hearts and minds.

And it's all happening so fast.

Torched

1933

1.

May 10, 1933 — three and a half months after Hitler becomes chancellor.

First, they make a bed of sand. On this bed they lay logs, criss-crossing them, stacking them with care. A haphazard jumble won't do; the spaces between logs ensure that oxygen will circulate. The logs form a pyre twelve feet square and five feet high.

At eleven p.m. they light torches. Their ranks grow as they march through the streets of Berlin, ending at the square across from the university. The torches illuminate their faces. Their cheeks are smooth or pockmarked by acne. Their foreheads are unfurrowed by wrinkles. They are teenagers. They heap book after book onto the logs and hold their torches to them. The pages catch.

A gleeful Goebbels steps up to a podium adorned with swastikas. He addresses the students, hollering into a loudspeaker.

The age of extreme Jewish intellectualism has now ended... these flames not only illuminate the final end of an old era; they also light up the new!

The scene is one "which had not been witnessed in the Western world since the late Middle Ages," writes the American journalist William Shirer. He watches the fire crackle horrifically, the pages of twenty-five thousand books turning to ashes.

*   *   *

Books by American writers like Ernest Hemingway, Upton Sinclair, Sinclair Lewis, Theodore Dreiser, Jack London, John Dos Passos, and Helen Keller.

Books by British writers like Joseph Conrad, Aldous Huxley, D. H. Lawrence, and H. G. Wells.

French writers like André Gide and Victor Hugo.

Irish writers like James Joyce.

Russian writers like Isaac Babel, Fyodor Dostoyevsky, Maxim Gorky, Vladimir Nabokov, and Leo Tolstoy.

And a whole slew of German writers: Vicki Baum, Walter Benjamin, Ernst Bloch, Bertolt Brecht, Max Brod, Otto Dix, Alfred Döblin, Albert Einstein, Friedrich Engels, Lion Feuchtwanger, Marieluise Fleisser, Leonhard Frank, Sigmund Freud, Iwan Goll, George Grosz, Jaroslav Hašek, Werner Hegemann, Heinrich Heine, Magnus Hirschfeld, Ödön von Horváth, Heinrich Eduard Jacob, Franz Kafka, Georg Kaiser, Erich Kästner, Alfred Kerr, Egon Kisch, Siegfried Kracauer, Karl Kraus, Theodor Lessing, Alexander Lernet-Holenia, Karl Liebknecht, Georg Lukács, Rosa Luxemburg, Heinrich Mann, Klaus Mann, Thomas Mann, Ludwig Marcuse, Karl Marx, Robert Musil, Carl von Ossietzky, Erwin Piscator, Alfred Polgar, Gertrud von Puttkamer, Erich Maria Remarque, Ludwig Renn, Joachim Ringelnatz, Joseph Roth, Nelly Sachs, Felix Salten, Anna Seghers, Arthur Schnitzler, Carl Sternheim, Bertha von Suttner, Ernst Toller, Kurt Tucholsky, Jakob Wassermann, Frank Wedekind, Grete Weiskopf, Franz Werfel, Arnold Zweig, Stefan Zweig.

2.

The Nazi fraternity that burns all these books mobilizes members in thirty-four universities to stage identical book burnings that

night. Press releases announce that the burnings are meant to be a
Säuberung—a cleansing—symbolically purifying German language
and literature of "un-German" elements for the benefit of the *Volk*.
Volk means "people," but the Nazi fraternity follows Hitler's lead in
using it in an exclusionary way; only people belonging to the Aryan
race are considered *Volk*.

Teenagers race through neighborhood streets putting up posters
with pots of paste, spreading the word. Each poster lists twelve
decrees, including

> MAINTAINING PURITY OF LANGUAGE AND
> LITERATURE IS UP TO YOU! YOUR *VOLK* HAS
> ENTRUSTED YOU WITH THE FAITHFUL
> PRESERVATION OF LANGUAGE.

And

> OUR MOST DANGEROUS ADVERSARY IS THE
> JEW AND ANYONE WHO DOES HIS BIDDING.

And

> THE JEW CAN THINK ONLY IN JEWISH TERMS.
> WHEN HE WRITES IN GERMAN, HE TELLS
> LIES. ANY GERMAN WHO WRITES IN
> GERMAN BUT WHOSE THINKING IS
> UN-GERMAN IS A TRAITOR!

3.

Teenagers in the underground resistance race through the streets
and campuses, pasting up posters of their own that also list twelve
decrees, including

> ALL ANTI-SEMITIC STUDENTS ARE ASSHOLES!

And

> ASSHOLES DO NOT BELONG AT THE
> UNIVERSITY, THEY BELONG IN
> THE SHITHOUSE.

And

> EVERY DECENT HUMAN BEING IS ASHAMED
> TO SAY THAT THIS IS THE GERMAN WAY.

Dietrich Does Battle with the Aryan Clause

1933–1934

1.

At an international ecumenical conference held in Sofia, Bulgaria, Dietrich Bonhoeffer pushes for a resolution to condemn the German Lutheran Church's support of the *Arierparagraph* — Aryan clause — which first appeared in Nazi legislation in April and is rapidly being used to exclude Jews from all professions, unions, businesses, associations, and organizations in Germany. Dietrich's proposed resolution begins:

> We especially deplore the fact that the Reich measures against the Jews in Germany have had such an effect on public opinion that in some circles the Jewish race is considered a race of inferior status.

Clergymen from the United States, France, Great Britain, and other countries discuss Dietrich's resolution.

The resolution passes. But when Dietrich returns to Germany, he faces powerful opposition.

2.

Dietrich writes a manifesto that urges the German Lutheran Church to reject the Aryan clause. He finds a printer who turns the manifesto into leaflets. Dietrich and a few like-minded pastors distribute the leaflets to clergy, nail the leaflets to trees.

The leaflets do nothing.

The German Lutheran Church stands by its support of the Aryan clause. Eighteen pastors of Jewish descent are ejected from their positions.

3.

The Vatican signs a treaty with the Nazi government. It begins:

> His Holiness Pope Pius XI and the president of the German Reich, moved by the common desire to consolidate and promote the friendly relations existing between the Holy See and the German Reich and wishing to regulate lastingly, in a manner satisfying to both parties, the relations between the Catholic Church and the state for the entire territory of the German Reich, have decided to conclude a solemn agreement.

And ends with a secret appendix that elucidates the role of priests and other members of the clergy in the event that the Nazi government imposes a military draft.

The treaty—officially known as a concordat—grants Catholics various rights in Nazi Germany, including the freedom to worship. In return, Catholic bishops must take the following oath of allegiance:

> I swear and promise before God and on the Holy Gospel, as befits a bishop, loyalty to the German Reich.

Vice-Chancellor Papen represents the German government at the signing ceremony on July 20, 1933. Cardinal Eugenio Pacelli—who will become Pope Pius XII in 1939—acts as Pope Pius XI's representative. With the stroke of a pen, the Vatican grants moral legitimacy to Hitler.

4.

Now that Hitler has the Catholics, he pursues the Protestants.

He consolidates the various splinters into a single *Reichskirche*—Reich church—and recommends the appointment of a somewhat obscure, fiercely anti-Semitic pastor as bishop. On September 27, 1933, by a unanimous vote at a meeting of the National Synod, the church leadership approves Bishop Ludwig Müller, a man who wears a cross on his breast and a swastika in his heart.

5.

Dietrich Bonhoeffer is inside the Castle Church in Wittenberg, listening to Bishop Müller blabber on about the glories of Hitler. In 1517, a thirty-three-year-old German friar named Martin Luther nailed his ninety-five theses to the door of this church, an act that catalyzed the Reformation. Luther is entombed beneath the pulpit where Bishop Müller stands now, lifting his arms to the heavens, his voice filling the church, solemn and reverberant:

> The Lord has called us into the breach as His warriors! We look upon the German movement for liberation and its leader, our Chancellor, as a gift of God!

Dietrich sits there, silent and appalled.

6.

A month later, Dietrich turns down an offer for a parish post in Berlin.

He sits down to compose a letter to his mentor, a Swiss Protestant theologian named Karl Barth.

"I feel that in some way I don't understand, I find myself in radical opposition to all my friends," he writes, admitting that he has become "increasingly isolated with my views of things." He concludes, "All this has frightened me and shaken my confidence."

In October 1933, Dietrich decides to leave Germany. He accepts a job as a pastor in London.

Arvid Burns His
Own Book

1933–1934

1.

Here is Mildred, walking home after teaching a class, her head
stuffed with questions. It's late. She's tired. Predicting what will
happen next is as alarming as it is inconceivable. A number of her
BAG students are Jewish. If they try to flee Germany, they will need
to have all the right documents with all the right stamps. Mildred
will do her best to help them. She has contacts at the U.S. embassy.

She climbs the four flights of stairs to her apartment, unlocks the
front door. Maybe Arvid is home, maybe he isn't.

2.

ARPLAN is no more. For several years, Arvid was secretary of the
group. In meetings held in Berlin and Moscow, ARPLAN members—among them German scholars, writers, politicians, and
playwrights—discussed heatedly why capitalism during the Weimar era left so many hungry and homeless. American capitalism
seemed equally flawed; the United States was now in the depths of
the Great Depression. Many ARPLAN members concluded that
Germany and other democracies should look to the Soviet Union
for answers. ARPLAN's president, Friedrich Lenz, promoted the
idea that Germany should model its economy on the Soviet planned
economy. Lenz was Arvid's doctoral dissertation adviser.

Last week, the Gestapo raided Lenz's apartment, and the Justus Liebig University fired him.

Arvid can't apply for a position at the Justus Liebig University or the University of Berlin or indeed any university in Germany. His area of expertise — U.S. labor movements and Soviet political theory — is too controversial. He could be branded as "politically unreliable," just as Lenz was.

3.

Arvid burns his own book, hastily stuffing his manuscript, page by page, into the coal stove. Rowohlt Verlag was just days away from publishing his thick tome on the Soviet economy. Now it would mark him as a Communist. He shovels the ashes into a pail and bolts out the door.

The Landwehr canal shimmers in the sun. Arvid dumps the ashes into it, then heads straight to the publisher; there, he smashes the printing plates to pieces. He will take no chances. A single page seized by the Gestapo could put him in Dachau.

All that work. All those years.

4.

Before leaving for Rowohlt Verlag with his pail of ashes, Arvid had intended to burn another book. But the pages took too long to catch. Maybe the coals weren't hot enough. He needed to get to Rowohlt Verlag before the office closed. Mildred promised she'd burn it, and Arvid raced out the door.

The book is Arvid's dissertation, "The Pre-Marxist Labor Movement in the United States." The title alone could summon the Gestapo. The manuscript hasn't been typeset yet — there are no plates to be smashed. It's just a stack of pages on a shelf by his desk.

Mildred stuffs Arvid's dissertation into a bag and hurries off to the American Church in Berlin. The pastor's wife accepts the bag and promises to keep Arvid's dissertation safe.

Where will she hide it? In the basement of the church? Up in the rafters? She won't say. She is a devout young woman with lips that clamp shut like a vise. No secrets escape—it's better for everyone that way.

Her name is Martha Turner. She and her husband, Ewart, moved to Berlin in 1930. Next year, they will flee Germany and settle in Dracut, a small town in Massachusetts just north of Boston. She will take Arvid's manuscript with her and hide it in the attic of their clapboard house. In an interview years later, Martha Turner will recall that Mildred and Arvid were "very careful" and "very afraid."

5.

Every Sunday, two Nazis in uniform march through the doors of the American Church and sit in a pew. They're impossible to ignore. What are they doing here? Germany has transformed into a police state so quickly, it seems possible that it will all change again tomorrow and return to the way it was before. The pews fill with people dressed in their Sunday best, pleats pressed, shoes polished to a sheen. Perhaps they catch the eyes of friends and acquaintances, perhaps they smile at each other and nod as they always do, but now the wordless greeting is charged with the knowledge that they are being watched.

The Boy

III

American in Berlin

1938–1939

Pupil Donald Heath	Aug - Oct	Dec.	Feb.
Days present			2 5
Days absent			
Punctuality			S
School Spirit			S
Cooperation			S
Self Discipline			S
Study Habits			S
Improvement in Appreciation, and Knowledge of:			
Nature			S
Science			S
Health			S
Biology			
Improvement in:			
English			U S
German			N S
French			
Latin			
Journalism			
Improvement in Knowledge of:			
History			S
Geography			S
Social Science			
Mathematics Arithmetic			S
Spelling			S
Grammar			
Writing			S
Drawing			S
Art History			S
Music			S
Poetry			S
Reading			
Mythology			S
Phonics			S
Callisthenics			

1.

The boy's name is Don, short for Donald. His full name is Donald Read Heath Jr. His father is Donald Read Heath Sr.

In letters, Donald Heath Sr. calls the boy Young Don.

so thorough.
Young Don is getting along pretty well.
He also is developing intellectually. he read
The Three Musketeers" during the summer

So does the boy's mother, Louise.

Young Don has begun music lessons — twice a

Growing up, Don feels runty, forever straining an arm and craning his neck to reach and see something too far, too high. His sister, Sue, seven years older, calls him her baby brother, dooming him to diapers when he's a kid in pants. The freckles dotting his nose make things worse. His hero is John Wayne, that brave and rugged cowboy, immense in stature and renown. But Don's freckles don't declare him as brave or rugged or immense. They make him, in the eyes of most people he meets, adorable.

Which gives him a distinct advantage, he will come to realize. He can carry a blue knapsack through Berlin without arousing suspicion. An adorable boy is on his way to school, someone might think.

Picture him: freckle-faced and sly, leaving Mildred's apartment with the knapsack. He retraces his steps to the Nollendorfplatz U-Bahn station, where he sees a pair of SS officers, *Totenkopf*—skulls—grinning on their collars. He knows Germans call the SS Schutzstaffel. Behind closed doors, his father has other names for them.

He ducks his head and slips nimbly past them. Races down the stairs. Speed-walks to the far end of the platform. And waits. Any minute now, the train will come. Nollendorfplatz, he thinks. Next stop will be Viktoria-Luise-Platz, then Bayerischer Platz, then Stadtpark. His father made him memorize the route. His father is at the U.S. embassy now, consumed with preparations for a clandestine trip to Washington he'll take in a couple of weeks. The embassy is housed in the cavernous and stately Blücher Palace, years ago scorched by fire and recently laboriously restored. Its limestone walls are the color of butterscotch and stretch in one direction to the Brandenburg Gate, where automobiles and bicycles stream between its fluted columns. Behind Blücher Palace there's a skating rink—in spring, when the snow melts, it will transform into a sloshy tennis court—and a walled villa that is home to Minister of Public Enlightenment and Propaganda Joseph Goebbels. Once, Don accompanied his father to an embassy tea, an event attended by high-ranking Nazi officials, including Goebbels. To Don's eleven-year-old eyes, he looked like a puny man with a limp. Goebbels chuckled and patted Don's head, complimenting him on his German. *You don't sound like an American boy!* he boomed.

Sometime later, at the opera, Don spots Hitler fewer than ten feet away, on the balcony. Four balconies grace the Staatsoper Unter den Linden—the State Opera House—which features Corinthian columns and opulent crimson velvet and gilded statues (or, as his mother, Louise, writes in a letter, "red plush to the nth degree with naked figures hanging out at sides in prominent places—lots of gold roses, etc.") and which, like all German cultural institutions, is under Nazi control. The Heaths have season tickets and come here once a month, on a Sunday night. Louise Heath loves opera. Donald Heath doesn't, but his job requires him to maintain social contact with high-ranking Nazis, who do.

Look, Don whispers. *The balcony.*

Louise, seated on his left, nods, putting a forefinger to her lips. Donald, seated on his right, whispers, *Close your eyes.*

Don does as he is told.

Now concentrate. Hard. Even harder.

It's a game they play, father and son. A kind of sorcery. If they concentrate hard enough, they can make Hitler stop breathing.

2.

Don was born in Switzerland on New Year's Day 1928 in a hospital one and a half kilometers from the U.S. embassy in Bern. After Switzerland, he lived in Port-au-Prince, Haiti. After Haiti, Topeka, Kansas. After Topeka, Silver Spring, Maryland. And now Germany.

He arrives by steamer ship just after his tenth birthday. He worries he won't learn to speak German quickly enough, but within a week he can pronounce *Mutter* and *Vater* and *Schwester* like a native Berliner. His sister, Sue, now seventeen, has trouble with the language—she's hard of hearing, a consequence of scarlet fever in her infancy—so she's put in the care of their grandparents in Topeka, who enroll her in a girls' school in Colorado. Sue's letters to Berlin are sweet, giddy accounts of the friends she makes and the horses she rides. Don wishes he could ride a horse. He misses his friends too. He had a whole battalion of them in Silver Spring.

Sunday morning Don goes to the American Church in Berlin, near Nollendorfplatz. Before the service, the vestibule is jam-packed with well-heeled parents and children, most of them American or British. His own parents stand among them, shaking hands, introducing themselves. *Topeka,* he hears Louise Heath say after a woman extends a white-gloved hand and asks in a fluty voice where they are from.

When the woman asks what his name is, Don is too humiliated to answer. All the well-heeled children are staring at him, some of them slack-jawed, some sniggering, taking in the sight of his corduroy knickers, his scuffed-up knee boots, his mackinaw. Nearest him stands a girl in a pearl-colored coat with a matching muff for her hands and puffs for her ears. She thinks his mackinaw is very, very funny. In Silver Spring, you can horse around with your friends all winter and no one blinks an eye at your mackinaw, even when you wear it to church. Here at the American Church in Berlin, children are different.

Later, Don's father sits him down and reminds him that the sons and daughters of diplomats are, more often than not, rich. Some are *obscenely rich,* the scions of oil magnates and railroad barons and newspaper moguls. Back in the States, the Great Depression is going on, but you wouldn't know it by the way the diplomats here carry on. Wealth does things to people, his father says, *makes them cockeyed.*

MONDAY MORNING IS DON'S first day at school. Mulling over the previous day's humiliation, he fears the worst. The American School is west of the Tiergarten, on Platanenallee, a street lined with gaunt plane trees. Walking through the wrought-iron gate, Don recognizes a few boys from the American Church, but most of the students aren't the wealthy offspring of diplomats; they are ordinary kids from nearby neighborhoods.

By the end of the week he has made a few friends: two boys and a girl. The boys speak German, the girl speaks Polish; their parents have enrolled them in the American School to learn English. Soon, the girl and one of the boys will be required by German law to wear yellow fabric stars sewn onto their clothing.

Thirty percent of students at the American School are Jewish. The school also employs Jewish teachers and is housed in a building owned by a Jewish woman. It was founded a decade earlier by an American couple, Gregor and Edna Ziemer. Now the Ziemers are under constant Gestapo scrutiny. German schools are required by law to base their curriculum on a manual with the ponderous title *Erziehung und Unterricht in der Höheren Schule: Amtliche Ausgabe des Reichs und Preuszischen Ministeriums für Wissenschaft, Erziehung, und Volksbildung* (Education and Instruction in the Higher Schools: Official Publication of the Reich and Prussian Ministry of Knowledge, Education, and National Culture) that features such dictates as

the student should be made to feel the superiority of the Nordic Germanic race

and

Boys of fourteen should study songs of medieval foot soldiers, modern soldier songs, marching songs.... Boys of sixteen are to learn military folk songs and an opera by Wagner.

But Gregor and Edna Ziemer ignore the government mandate. The school remains open, an achievement that has everything to do with the Ziemers' ties to American diplomats in Berlin.

Every morning that winter, Don buttons his mackinaw and trudges down Berlin's snow-choked streets to the school's iron gate.

In February, he doesn't miss a day of school. He improves his knowledge of history, geography, and arithmetic as well as drawing, music, and poetry. His command of the English language is, in Edna Ziemer's estimation, "Very satisfactory." His command of German is not. Still, he's cooperative and demonstrates a degree of self-discipline that she finds "Satisfactory."

3.

Living in Berlin is different from living in Silver Spring, Don quickly discovers. The Ziemers' ten-year-old daughter, Patsy, composes a list of all the things that are forbidden—*verboten*—in Germany:

Verboten in Germany
To start a fire in your yard
To pick up wood in the forest
To listen to Russia over the radio
To bring any Communistic papers into Germany
To ask the dentist to put gold in your teeth
To say the least little thing against the Nazis
To eat more than one egg, or try to buy more than your amount
    of butter
To leave Germany without permission
To go to churches where preachers were who were not Nazis
To take money out
To throw away any tin cans, or toothpaste tubes, or tin foil, or
    paper
To throw away any old food
To fly foreign flags
To have big meetings with Jews
To have any foreign money in the house
To have a Jewish servant
To have your door open after eight o'clock at night
To play piano, or make any noise between two and four, or after
    ten at night
To read books written by writers who were not Nazis

To walk on the grass in the parks

Patsy also makes a list of the uniforms she sees in Germany:

<u>Uniforms in Germany</u>

The regular army uniform, gray-green, with hundreds of different numbers and braids, and tassels, and epaulets, and buttons, and caps

The S.A. (*Sturmabteilung*) with hundreds of different numbers and stripes...round caps with big visors, black boots, and Swastika armbands...brown shirts

The S.S. (*Schutzstaffel*) all in black, but sometimes with white belts and white gloves, and many different kinds of numbers on their arms

The regular police in blue, sometimes with caps, sometimes with helmets

The tank drivers, all in black, baggy trousers, and berets on their heads

The forest soldiers, all in green

The Hitler Youth, wearing shirts like the S.A., but wearing the numbers of their troops on their arms

The BDM girls, with blue skirts, and white waists, and also with many different numbers and stripes

Goering's soldiers, with different uniforms almost every month

Ribbentrop's men, with bright blue uniforms.

DON SOON BECOMES AWARE of a feeling he can't name, halfway between an ache and an itch and impossible to ignore. He senses agitation in the air, whisperings of war. Sitting in one place at school is hard enough, but by springtime he can barely keep a pencil in his grip. Hitler orders German troops to cross the Austrian border, declaring an *Anschluss*—political union—with the country, and sets his sights on his next conquest: Czechoslovakia.

Don gets an earful whenever his father comes home from the embassy and switches on the radio, a satchel-size device that pops and squeals as he turns the dial past the intervals of thick static to the BBC broadcast. Donald Heath keeps the volume low and instructs Don not to tell any of his German friends what he hears on the BBC.

4.

In the summer of 1938, a Berlin court issues an order for the American School to close. Nazi officials object that the school makes no distinction between Jewish and non-Jewish pupils. Officials at the U.S. embassy intervene, and with some reluctance German authorities permit the school to open again in September. The American School will close its doors permanently the following year when war breaks out and the Ziemers will flee to Minnesota, but of course ten-year-old Don doesn't know this when he walks down Platanenallee on the morning of his first day as a fifth-grader. Several yards from the school's wrought-iron gate, something hard smacks his head.

A rock.

Don spots a blond-haired boy standing under a plane tree. Black shoes, black socks, black shorts, brown shirt. The shirt is emblazoned with a swastika. He's a student at the German school that's directly across the street, chock-full of boys wearing Hitler Youth uniforms.

The boy throws a second rock at Don. A third.

Don lunges for a stone and throws it. Gregor Ziemer appears and drags him behind the wrought-iron gate. *Don't fight back,* Ziemer warns him sharply, *or they'll close us down again.*

AFTER SCHOOL, LISTLESS AND antsy, Don takes to shooting his air rifle from the roof of his house, loading it with hunks of raw potato he filches from the kitchen when Mamzelle the cook isn't looking. One day Mamzelle catches him and marches him to his mother. Louise Heath sighs at the sight of the air rifle, swipes it from his grip, and instructs him to go blow off some steam with his friends. Don fills a pocket with pfennigs and goes to the park. He runs around pelting squirrels. When he's done, he scrounges in the dirt for the coins. Squirrel hunting is something Don does alone. He has no friends to play with in Schöneberg Park. His friend Mole lives in another neighborhood. Mole is in a gang called Trenck's Panduren. Don sees them together sometimes, a rowdy pack of German boys who live in a neighborhood so different from his own that it might as well be another country. Don lives on Innsbrücker Strasse, a street lined with elegant buildings and houses. Don wishes he had a gang too.

Don's air rifle was a present from someone at the embassy—maybe his father's secretary, Miss Ulrich, maybe someone else. All the boys in Trenck's Panduren have them. Don's was made by a German company called Diana, known for manufacturing barrels that can easily accommodate whatever ammunition a boy stuffs in. Sometimes Don shoots real pellets instead of potato hunks. Sometimes he pretends he is shooting at Goebbels. Sometimes he pretends he's shooting at Hitler.

Don't Dawdle

1939

1.

Don stands on the U-Bahn platform jiggling his leg, watching the train approach. Two distant lights in a dark tunnel growing larger.

On the train he finds a seat, slides the knapsack off his shoulders, and sets it on his lap. He wants to tell his friend Mole about Mildred, about the job he's doing for his father, about what's in his knapsack. Mole is off somewhere roaming the streets wearing some old man's pants cinched at the waist so they won't fall down. If Don could get off the U-Bahn and find Mole, he would, but he can't.

Don't dawdle after seeing Mildred, his father told him. *And don't horse around with Mole. Go straight home.*

Home is Innsbrücker Strasse 44, a six-story apartment building that overlooks a duck pond in Schöneberg Park. The Heaths occupy the top two floors, which contain an assortment of rooms.

There's a music room with a piano.

There's a living room with a bookcase, a Chippendale table, and several upholstered chairs.

There's a dining room bright with mirrored walls.

The bedrooms are on the sixth floor. In the summer, tomato plants ripen on a wraparound terrace—the sunporch, Don's mother calls it. It's the only place in the home where a confidential conversation can be held, since the interior of the apartment is bugged and the phones are tapped. At first this was just a suspicion Louise Heath harbored, but now she's convinced of it. Every few months, a clutch of Germans claiming to be from the electric company arrive at the apartment unannounced. Louise protests that she did not call the electric company, and the men insist that their visit is warranted. For repairs, they say.

The owner of the building is Hela Strehl, one of Goebbels's many mistresses. She is the former fashion editor who is now director of the Deutsches Mode-Institut, which Hitler masterminded to promote the image of the ideal woman, one who will bear numerous children to populate Germany with a master race. Such a woman, according to Hitler's specifications, has Aryan features, eschews makeup, exercises frequently, and wears a dirndl.

Hela doesn't wear a dirndl, nor does she eschew makeup. Her hypocrisy isn't lost on the tenants in the building. She has a way of lifting her pencil-thin eyebrows and forcing a lipsticked smile when she passes them in the hallway that suggests she trusts no one. The feeling is mutual, of course.

2.

The train hurtles forward, station to station.

Viktoria-Luise-Platz.

Bayerischer Platz.

Stadtpark.

The doors gasp open. Don leaps out. The knapsack heavy on his back, he speed-walks up the stairs and out of the U-Bahn station. He runs all the way to Innsbrücker Strasse, spots his apartment building. No one is outside.

He flings open the door, hits the stairs, races up the first flight, second, third—and runs smack into Hela Strehl, who says what she always says when she sees people in the hallway.

Heil Hitler!

Don lowers his head and says nothing. This is a mistake.

Every building has its Gestapo informant. At Innsbrücker Strasse 44, the informant is most certainly Goebbels's mistress. It was Mildred who told Don this, insisting that he must be very, very careful around Hela Strehl. Yes, he is an American and the adorable son of a diplomat at the U.S. embassy, but diplomatic immunity does not necessarily apply in a dictatorship.

Hela continues on her way. Don waits for her to stop, turn around, scold him, threaten to report him. She doesn't.

Relief.

He dashes up the stairs to the fifth floor, the knapsack banging against his back, bursts through the front door, and makes a beeline for his bedroom. Slams the door. Throws off the knapsack. It's crammed with books.

Inside one book is a piece of paper. Mildred folded it twice, like a letter.

Mildred
IV

The Proper Care of Cactus Plants

1933–1935

1.

Hitler brags—absurdly—that the Third Reich will last "a thousand years."

Mildred and Arvid and everyone else in the Circle still believe it will collapse within a year, two years, three years tops. Germans just need to keep the pressure on and *resist*.

2.

In Berlin's working-class neighborhoods, clandestine clusters of anti-Nazi agitators produce leaflets that report local news and call for revolution. One leaflet describes a skirmish with the police following a food shortage at a market; another details oppressive working conditions at a telephone factory. Satirical poems and cartoons intermingle with screeds against Hitler. Some leaflets are typed and reproduced one sheet at a time using a pan of gelatin, a roller, and violet-colored aniline ink. Some are handwritten; producing a dozen copies or more is a painstakingly long process.

3.

The banned newspaper *Rote Fahne*—Red Flag—manages to put out three hundred thousand copies in March 1933, a print run that continues two or three times a month for roughly a year. In the spring of 1934, the Gestapo raids the production facilities, confiscates the newspapers, and hauls all the journalists and printers to a concentration camp.

A few months later, printers in Düsseldorf, Cologne, and Solingen-Ohligs resume production. The printer in Solingen-Ohligs, a man named Georg, sends five thousand copies to Berlin in crates several times a month until early 1935, when the Gestapo tracks him down.

4.

The now-illegal German Communist Party — Kommunistische Partei Deutschlandsor, or KPD — goes underground and produces leaflets that agitate for the overthrow of Hitler's regime. After the Gestapo shuts down a slew of basement printing operations run by KPD cells in Germany, production is moved to secret facilities in France, Czechoslovakia, the Netherlands, and Switzerland. Between 1933 and 1935, the KPD produces over a million leaflets a year.

The Social Democratic Party transforms into the Social Democratic Party in Exile (SOPADE) and establishes an outpost in Prague (in 1938, SOPADE will move to Paris; in 1940, to London). The bulletins its members produce on mint-green paper compile the reports of scouts in Berlin, Hamburg, and other cities. These "green reports," as they come to be known, describe conditions in Nazi Germany, including the rampant anti-Semitism Jews experience on a daily basis.

The couriers who smuggle the leaflets and reports into Germany face a harrowing journey. Some drive cars; some take trains. A group called the Transportkolonne Otto loads bundles of banned newspapers produced in Switzerland onto boats that stealthily maneuver up the Rhine River.

The Gestapo employs spies to hunt down couriers. Arrests and murders are discouragingly frequent. In 1934, the Gestapo seizes 1,238,202 leaflets; in 1935, 1,670,300.

5.

The voices of opposition try to fool the Gestapo.

Covers of underground pamphlets display deceptive titles like *Cookery Book with 70 Approved Recipes* and *The Proper Care of Cactus Plants*.

Skiing in the Black Forest is a compendium of speeches delivered by left-wing politicians. *Home Heating by Electricity* features an excerpt from a book published in Paris in August 1933 called *The Brown Book of the Hitler Terror and the Burning of the Reichstag*, which proposes a controversial theory: Nazis were the ones who torched the Reichstag.

Fair Bright Transparent

1933–1934

> landscape. She used to write unsigned postcards to me from all parts of
> the country. In a ~~beautiful small clear~~ delicate ~~blue~~ hand, ~~as simple and pure as her~~
> personality, she wrote exquisite poetic lines as singingly lovely as her
> voice. She and Arvid were both nature lovers of the sort one finds only

> He wore, of course, the Nazi uniform.
> Mildred could have made friends very easily but she ~~chose to do it~~ slowly
> as caution was absolutly essential to her work. She was slow to speak
> or express opinions; she listened quietly, weighing and evaluating the
> words, thoughts and ~~implications~~ motivations in conversation. She was

> Therefore when she did speak she commanded attention; her words were thought
> ful, sometimes ambiguous when it was necessary to feel people out, per-
> suasive and charged with an unobtrusive logic. It was fascinating to watch
> her subtle, ~~probing~~ approach to people whose sympathy she wanted to enlist
> im the underground.

1.

And, then, Mildred makes a friend.

Years later, this friend will jot down her impressions of Mildred,
remembering that her skin was "fair bright transparent" and her
dress "simple."

Mildred sends her postcards from all parts of the country. She doesn't write much, just a poetic line or two. She doesn't sign the postcards because she likes surprising her new friend with an anonymous note, and she's beginning to accustom herself to concealment.

2.

Mildred prefers to make friends slowly. Her new friend sees this firsthand, watching her with other people. Mildred is cautious. Her friend won't understand why until they've known each other awhile. Sometimes Mildred speaks to people in a way that's deliberately "ambiguous," choosing her words carefully, waiting to learn what they think, how they feel. She doesn't interrogate people so much as coax information from them.

"It was fascinating," her friend writes, "to watch her subtle approach to people whose sympathy she wanted to enlist in the underground."

3.

Her friend's name is Martha Dodd. She arrived in Berlin on July 13, 1933, with her parents and older brother.

Martha is twenty-four. She went to college at the University of Chicago, where her father was a professor of American history, and she worked briefly as an assistant overseeing the book reviews at the *Chicago Tribune*. Her dream is to be a writer—and not just any writer but a great, famous American writer.

Martha is already good friends with several great, famous American writers: the poet Carl Sandburg, the playwright and novelist Thornton Wilder. This startles Mildred. Mildred lectures about famous American writers, but she doesn't know them personally. She leads an unglamorous life.

That's what Martha loves about her. Mildred "is very poor and real and fine," she writes in a letter to Thornton Wilder.

The friendship between Mildred and Martha blossoms on the streets of Berlin in the bright, pollen-dusted light of late summer.

Side by side, they stroll along the Unter den Linden, inhaling the bracing, citrusy scent of linden trees; they duck into cafés and sip cold drinks in the fan-blown air; they meet at the American Women's Club, where Mildred gives lunchtime lectures about contemporary American novelists. Wives and daughters of diplomats are among the women who fill the club's plush, walnut-paneled rooms to hear her, and they all want to meet Mildred's new friend, the daughter of Ambassador William Dodd. Dodd is a demi-step away from Franklin D. Roosevelt himself, who appointed him to be ambassador in Berlin after winning the presidency last November in a landslide.

4.

Mildred meets William Dodd soon enough. He's not adjusting easily to being an ambassador. His colleagues at the U.S. embassy consort with Washington's elite, obscenely wealthy men who seem more interested in hobnobbing at cocktail parties than in putting in an honest day's work.

Ambassador Dodd is the son of farmers. Mildred doesn't need him to explain. She knows farmers and recognizes in the ambassador a down-to-earth, Midwestern modesty. She can practically sniff it, the way you know whether milk is fresh or sour.

He shows Mildred the handwritten manuscript of the book he's working on, an enormous opus he has titled "The Rise and Fall of the Old South." Will she type it for him? He can pay her a small sum.

Mildred says she will. Arvid still can't find a job, so her teaching salary is their only source of income right now. After rent, coffee, canned sausages, and a few vegetables, they've got nearly nothing left, just a few coins for a neighbor who provides a loaf of bread once a week, tying it to the doorknob in a kerchief. The dress Mildred likes to lecture in is old—in her words, "worn to spiderwebs." The sight of it doesn't bother her students at the BAG—their clothing is even more threadbare—but it raises the plucked eyebrows of the well-dressed members of the American Women's Club.

"Please excuse me for mentioning it," she writes to her mother, "but I'm wondering whether anyone in the family has any clothes which she doesn't want."

A package arrives a month or so later. The shabby, shapeless dresses her mother scrounged up are wrong, all wrong. Mildred might as well wear an old curtain.

5.

Martha tells Mildred that she has a connection to a newspaper in Berlin, one Goebbels hasn't touched yet.

So it's decided: they will team up and write a book column.

Martha dashes off a letter to Thornton Wilder. The newspaper is called *Berlin Topics*. "It is lousy," Martha tells him petulantly.

> *But we might be able to build up a little colony . . . I mean following.*
> *Get people together who like books and authors.*

Martha doesn't want her real name in the column's byline. She concocts a pseudonym: Mr. Wesley Repor. Mildred decides to publish under her own name. Other aspects of her life require concealment, not this.

What books should they write about? Mildred admires the Hogarth Press, a small publishing company Virginia Woolf and her husband, Leonard, run out of their dining room in London. In 1932, they published a scathing critique of German anti-Semitism called *A Letter to Adolf Hitler,* by Louis Golding. The Hogarth Press also released a novel about coal miners, *Saturday Night at the Greyhound*, by John Hampson — perhaps not as bold as *A Letter to Adolf Hitler,* but the novel might raise the hackles of Nazi censors, who see in every working-class character a traitorous nod to Communism.

Martha is ecstatic. As always, the daughter of Ambassador Dodd thrills to the idea of doing something subversive.

6.

High society suits Martha.

She lives with her parents and brother in a palatial mansion on Tiergartenstrasse with a ballroom and servants' quarters, nothing like their ho-hum house in Chicago. Nearly every day an embossed card arrives inviting her to a tea, a lunch, a dinner, a dance. Martha hardly speaks a word of German or Russian or French, but she introduces herself to foreign attachés and diplomats anyway, getting by on spunk alone. She's got a sweet smile that creases easily into sassy, alluring almond-shaped eyes, and chin-length hair that she transforms with rollers into adorable curls. She is petite, but her presence is commanding. A spitfire at parties, she loves to argue almost as much as she loves to dance.

When excited, she talks a blue streak. Her exuberance is infectious, and Mildred slips swiftly into absorbing conversations. They talk about books. They talk about Berlin. Martha reveals that she's not just friends with Carl Sandburg—they had a torrid love affair. Usually shy about her private life, Mildred finds herself opening up in the presence of her new friend. Martha is six years younger—not much of an age difference, though as their friendship develops, Mildred will notice it more.

Mildred isn't looking for a recruit, not this time. She yearns for a confidante. She spends so much time alone.

7.

Mildred sits at her desk, picks up a pen.

"Mother," she writes. "This afternoon I have been with Martha."

It was nearly night when Mildred left Martha's mansion and walked back to her apartment, taking a winding path through the Tiergarten. Her heart still thrummed with the conversation they'd had. For hours they'd talked about men. How can she describe it all in a way her mother would understand?

She sets the nib of her pen on the sheet of paper before her. A red candle flickers. A vase holds three winter roses. Through the arched window she can glimpse the night sky, black as the ink that spills from her pen.

She writes about Arvid, about the wonder of loving a man who looks at the world the way she does, a man "who also longs to put his fingers feelingly into life." She writes until she exhausts her powers of expression.

Time for bed.

The bedroom is cold. She slips under a thin blanket. Soon, Arvid will slip in beside her. Outside, it's snowing.

Two Kinds of Parties

1933–1935

1.

November 12, 1933. A Sunday afternoon. The *Berlin Topics* book column hits newsstands today, and Mildred is throwing a party at her apartment to celebrate. Daylight streams through the arched window, and festive candles burn on every surface that isn't covered with books. She boils water for tea. She sets out a tray of bread, cheese, and liverwurst.

Martha would have preferred champagne to tea and caviar to liverwurst, but there is nothing to be done now. As she makes the rounds, greeting friends and accepting their compliments, she takes in the decor. Mildred's book-strewn home has a certain charm. She spots a vase of pussy willows, slender brown stalks poking out every which way. A curiosity. Mildred has placed a candle behind the vase. The flame makes the shadows of pussy willows dance on the wall.

Is it "sense or nonsense"? Martha can't decide.

2.

A few weeks ago Martha threw a party of her own. There were cocktails and canapés and, best of all, a spectacular guest, a *criminal:* Ernst von Salomon, a German novelist who received a five-year prison sentence for his role in the 1922 assassination of Germany's foreign minister, Walther Rathenau. The party was packed to the gills with American diplomats and their wives—exactly the type of people Martha loves to scandalize.

Later, she wrote to Thornton Wilder, "I produced to the astonishment (there was a little hushed gasping and whispering behind hands from the oh so proper gathering) of the diplomatic right set Ernst von Salomon! accomplice in the Rathenau murder.... He is much worthwhile."

3.

Martha somehow can't help herself; she has fallen in love with a Nazi.

Rudolf Diels, the handsome head of the Gestapo, has taken to stalking her, creeping under her bedroom window. Swooning, Martha scribbles in a letter to Thornton—

> *The snow is soft and deep lying here—a copper smoke mist over Berlin by day and the brilliance of the falling moon by night. The gravel squeaks under my window at night—the sinister faced, lovely lipped and gaunt Diels . . . must be watching me.*

But she doesn't dare breathe a word about the affair to Mildred. She knows that Mildred is in some kind of resistance group and is exceedingly cautious and might very well end their friendship if she suspected Martha was romantically involved with Diels.

The scars etched into Rudolf Diels's cheeks and mouth are from fencing, something young men in Germany do during college to prove their courage. They're known as bragging scars— *Renommierschmisse.* In her memoir, Martha will recall that "he had the most sinister, scar-torn face I had ever seen." He was "tall and slender." His hair was "luxuriant." His eyes were "black, cruel, and penetrating." He didn't walk—he "crept on cat's feet."

Bugged

1933–1935

1.

Rudolf Diels confides in Martha, telling her all about the Nazis he knows, about their "intrigues and inter-party struggles and hatreds."

He seems to enjoy terrifying her.

The American embassy is bugged, he tells her. *So is your home. The telephones are tapped, the servants are spies, nothing is secret.*

2.

Martha's father begins to take certain precautions. The Tiergarten, beloved by Berliners as the verdant heart of the city, is a popular place for horseback riders, dog-walkers, bird-watchers, dress-paraders, baby-carriage-pushers, and promenading lovers. It's also a destination for Ambassador Dodd and his colleagues at the U.S. embassy when they need to have a private conversation.

Martha knows this. But the idea that her own home is bugged is something she isn't prepared to absorb.

The living-room chandelier takes on a sinister aspect. Are there microphones concealed somewhere among the crystals? And what about the kitchen? Could there be some sort of recording device inside the oven? In the bedroom? In the stuffing of the mattress? Is there *any* privacy? In the anxious, febrile dramatizations that play out in Martha's mind, nothing seems preposterous.

Martha muffles all the telephones with pillows, but this isn't enough. When her father comes home, she convinces Ambassador

Dodd to put cardboard boxes lined with cotton batting over the telephones.

She hears about a mysterious new mechanical device that can record someone's conversation in one room if it is "placed against the wall of an adjoining room." Maybe there are dozens of these devices in the mansion. Maybe they have all been placed there, Martha speculates, "with the collusion of our servants, whom we never trusted."

Martha finds herself in "a nervous state that almost bordered on hysterical."

3.

Mildred seems entirely unfazed.

Now and then, she visits the mansion to drop off a large envelope. Inside are pages she has typed for Martha's father—a chapter or two of "The Rise and Fall of the Old South." Standing in the entryway, she makes only the blandest conversation.

Sometimes, though, Mildred puts a finger to her lips and motions for Martha to follow her up the stairs to the bathroom, where she whispers almost inaudibly into her ear. Bathrooms, says Mildred, are difficult to wire. She also likes loud restaurants, open meadows.

Martha's head spins. Somehow, Mildred accepts the shocking possibility that their homes are bugged the same way she has accepted the news that books were burned in pyres across Germany—as a fact that must be dealt with.

4.

It's odd, how Mildred disappears. Abruptly, she'll go off on a trip to somewhere in Germany or farther away, to Switzerland or England or Russia. Then she sends a postcard. Nearly always, Mildred leaves it unsigned.

One day a letter arrives. Martha recognizes the handwriting.

Do you like beer in old steins on a big scrubbed wooden table with wurst or frankfurters and flowers from the garden and candlelight

shed from old hammered brass holders? Do you like tea under fruit
trees in the garden? Do you like sheep with triangular heads so
sharp-boned, and horses and cows?

Mildred is inviting her to a weekend trip. It will be just the two
of them—they'll have a whole house to themselves. The house
belongs to a friend. At the bottom of the letter, Mildred adds:
"Nobody need be told about the trip."

Esthonia, and Other Imaginary Women

1934–1935

1.

The invitations Emmi Bonhoeffer sends out are embossed, on stationery the color of cream. In an elegant script it is noted that Mildred will deliver three lectures on three Saturdays in spring. The lectures will be held at Bendlerstrasse 36, the home of Mildred's relatives Emmi and Klaus Bonhoeffer, and "will be followed by informal discussion." It is also noted that the lectures are "under the patronage of the American Embassy."

At five o'clock on Saturday, April 21, 1934, Mildred stands before a lively group of critics, journalists, and professors and introduces herself. Among them are Jews and leftists. Some have lost their jobs. Some will lose them soon. The focus of her lectures, Mildred explains, is the American South. Two weeks ago, she discussed the Mississippi-born author William Faulkner. The week after next, she will talk about the young novelist Thomas Wolfe, from North Carolina. Tonight, she will lecture about an author from South Carolina named Julia Peterkin, the first Southerner to win the Pulitzer Prize. Most likely, no one in the room has heard of Julia Peterkin, much less read her 1928 novel *Scarlet Sister Mary,* about a young black woman living in the segregated South. Mildred wants the people in this room to understand how Jim Crow laws affect every aspect of daily life. Schools and churches, buses and drinking fountains, restrooms and restaurants—everywhere you look in the South, you see

"Colored" signs, "Whites Only" signs, a constant reminder of the racial segregation that is enforced by acts of violence committed by ordinary American citizens, uniformed police, and the white-hooded vigilantes of the Ku Klux Klan.

The parallel with Germany is obvious. Signs are cropping up in Berlin and across the country: "Jews Are Not Wanted Here," "Jews Prohibited," "Jews Forbidden in This Town."

2.

Afterward, Mildred writes to her mother and tells her about the lecture. Before putting the invitation in an envelope, she scrawls an elliptical note in black ink:

> *Since then the group has held together in an interesting way.*

3.

In what *interesting way,* exactly?

Mildred's writing is becoming increasingly vague. She makes veiled references to political gatherings. She uses coded language she hopes the recipient will be able to decipher. Words must be understood in context, since she knows Nazi censors are reading her mail.

One strategy she uses is to say the opposite of what she means. She's horrified to see Hitler Youth marching in a May Day parade, but in a letter to her mother, Mildred writes:

> *How beautiful it was. Thousands, thousands, and thousands of people marched in order singing and playing through the majestic streets. . . . Well, it is a very beautiful, serious thing — serious as death — and I hope it will never be perverted again! Think this over, for I want you to understand me.*

4.

Before she moved to Germany, Mildred took a small sum from her savings and invested it. When she wants to know how the investment is doing, she writes to her mother and asks:

> *How is Esthonia? Is her health all right or have the hard times hit her too? We are thinking about her and hoping we shall hear about her in January. Dear old cat. She used to have kittens pretty regularly. How about this year?*

Esthonia isn't a woman or a cat; it's a treasury bond. And *kittens* doesn't mean baby cats; it means interest.

Mildred isn't the only one who uses codes to communicate. The whole Harnack clan does, including the Bonhoeffers, the Delbrücks, and the Dohnányis.

They're careful about answering the front door. A certain number of knocks tell those inside who you are. Telephone conversations conceal thickets of meaning underneath benign observations about meals and weather. If you say, *Now I have to go to prayer,* it means you're planning to listen to an illegal foreign broadcast on your Blaupunkt radio. If you say, *She is in the hospital,* it means she has been arrested. If you say, *He has gone on a trip,* it means he has been thrown into a concentration camp.

And what then? If someone in the family is arrested and thrown into a concentration camp, how do you communicate with the prisoner? The question is discussed with great care. Families are occasionally allowed to bring a book or two to a prisoner, so books, they decide, can be used to deliver news and instructions. By placing a tiny dot under a letter, you can spell out a word over many pages, and a whole sentence over many more.

There are other ways to conceal messages too. Some prisons allow families to bring clothing and food. Letters can be sewn into the hems of pants and dresses. Tiny bits of paper can be mixed into a jar of dried beans. They practice writing in minuscule script.

Arvid Gets a Job

1934–1935

1.

Mildred is officially the breadwinner now. Every morning, she wakes up with this knowledge, feeling the weight of it. The money she earns from teaching at the BAG is barely enough to cover the bills. She cuts corners where she can. She drinks cheap ersatz coffee made from corn and skips meals when the cupboard is bare. Arvid is despondent. He doesn't know what to do about his career. The manuscript that's hidden in the American Church may be published one day, or it may not. Either way, academia is closed to him for the foreseeable future. He grows increasingly agitated. Mildred writes a story about the arguments they have and stashes it in a drawer. She doesn't intend to publish it—not now, anyway.

Arvid paces around the apartment and snaps at Mildred, losing his temper at the slightest provocation. "How often do I have to tell you to take your books out of the bathroom?" he cries. "Or do I have to do it myself?"

To keep the apartment tidy, they have worked out a system: She's in charge of one room, he's in charge of the other. He lights the coals in the porcelain stove, and she keeps the kitchen clean. But the sink fills with dishes. Crumbs litter the countertop. She forgets to return the big platter she has borrowed from the landlady. "You don't do a thing," Arvid moans. Mildred neglects to cook dinner sometimes. She's careless with her belongings. She leaves her books in piles everywhere, while Arvid lines up his books neatly, making a fetish of it.

Worst of all, the man who was once so generous with his love, so eager to share everything, has taken to calling the living room *his* room.

"It's mine too," she insists. "Yours is mine and mine's yours."

"It's only mine and I don't want to see anyone else in it," Arvid snaps.

Aghast, Mildred grabs the platter, puts on her coat and cap, and marches out the door.

Arvid follows her into the hallway. He's sorry now. He doesn't want her to go out by herself. They can return the platter together.

"No," Mildred says. "I want to be alone."

2.

Thousands of women are in prison now, their numbers steadily increasing. Many found liberation a decade ago, during the years of the Weimar Republic, taking jobs as secretaries, journalists, factory workers, lawyers, physicians, professors. Now they are arrested for their affiliation with left-wing parties. If they are mothers, their children are sent to Nazi-run foster homes. Many of these women will never see their children again.

A German woman is sent to a women's prison near Hanover called Moringen. Her husband was once an esteemed politician in the Reichstag. Because he represented the Communist Party, he was rounded up with all the other Communists, tortured in Dachau, and left to die. When she was arrested, her children were ripped from her arms. Now she writes to her sister in America, pleading for assistance.

> *Unfortunately we are in a bad way. Theodor, my dear husband, died suddenly in Dachau four months ago. Our three children have been put in the state welfare home in Munich. I am in the women's camp at Moringen. I no longer have a penny to my name.*

But the letter is rejected by Nazi censors. She's forced to rewrite it, scrub it clean:

Unfortunately things are not going exactly as we might wish. Theodor, my dear husband, died four months ago. Our three children live in Munich, 27 Brenner Strasse, I live in Moringen, near Hanover, 32 Breite Strasse. I would be grateful to you if you could send me a small sum of money.

3.

From Arvid's family there is both bad and good news.

The bad news: Arvid's cousin Ernst von Harnack has been arrested.

Until recently, he was mayor of the town of Merseburg. Ernst has upheld the Harnack tradition of challenging dogma, drawing around him a swirl of controversy by arguing vociferously against the Nazi Party; it's the reason he was ousted from his job. Now he's under suspicion as an enemy of the state after voicing his support for several Social Democrats and union leaders who have been incarcerated and tortured in concentration camps. The family is horrified. No one knows if Ernst will be sent to a concentration camp and tortured too.

And the good news: Arvid's cousin Klaus Bonhoeffer has finally found a job for Arvid. It's not in academia, but Arvid doesn't care. Klaus works as a lawyer for Lufthansa Airlines and has made arrangements for Arvid to be hired as a law clerk, a job that will give Arvid a much-needed paycheck, but money isn't the only draw. Lufthansa schedules routine flights into numerous countries throughout Europe. Arvid hasn't worked out a clear strategy yet, but he sees an opportunity to establish connections with other countries that will aid the resistance.

4.

Arvid works long hours at the office, devoting himself to his new job.

Most nights Mildred comes home to an empty apartment and eats dinner alone. She fills the lonely hours with work. There are always lectures to prepare, and she's hopelessly behind on her dissertation, a nagging concern; she really should be *done* by now.

Now and then, women and men arrive with banned books stashed in purses or wedged under waistbands. By discussing books that challenge the tenets of the Nazi regime, they can prepare for its defeat—which Mildred and Arvid and everyone else in the Circle still believe is imminent.

After they leave, the apartment is quiet again.

She reads a book, writes a letter. She lies on the floor, does some sit-ups. Boils water for tea. The longer Arvid stays at the office, the more she worries he has been arrested.

Then, at last: the soft metal scratching of a key in the lock.

Relief. He's home.

Thieves, Forgers, Liars, Traitors

1934–1935

1.

Mildred is leading more meetings now, and the Circle is expanding. Over the next four years, it will link with another resistance circle, and another, and another—Tat Kreis, Gegner Kreis, and Rittmeister Kreis—in an interlocking chain.

2.

"Many in the group which formed over the years were young, joyous people, full of energy and enthusiasm," recalled one of them, a Jewish writer named Günther Weisenborn whose books were banned in 1933.

Leaflets are the first weapon in their arsenal.

Finding enough paper to print the leaflets is difficult. So is obtaining typewriter ribbons, carbon paper, envelopes, stamps. As controls in the Nazi police state tighten, they resort to stealing supplies.

"Of course we took precautions, wore gloves, used different typewriters, and carefully destroyed carbon papers," remembered Weisenborn.

They leave leaflets in piles in phone booths, public restrooms, parks, train stations. They mail them to perfect strangers, finding addresses by flipping through the Berlin phone book. They can't go to a post office with a pile of envelopes without inviting suspicion, so they divide the large piles into smaller ones and take turns dropping them into mailboxes all around Berlin.

The leaflets urge Germans to *resist, resist, resist.*

Relentless Nazi brutality invigorates their conviction that they must fight back steadily, diligently, without hesitation. They set up safe houses and help Jews escape Germany. They forge ration cards, identity cards, exit papers. In this way, Germans in the resistance become thieves and forgers.

Traitors too. To fight your own country is an act of treason.

And what if your friends or family don't share your political views? What if your husband or wife is afraid of the Nazi government or, worse, admires it? To join the Circle means you have to invent excuses for abrupt absences, disappear into the night without an explanation. You have to accustom yourself to half-truths and deceptions, to lying again and again, even to those you love. You become wary, distrustful. You watch your acquaintances for signs that they are Gestapo informants. Stories about children reporting their parents begin to circulate. The Circle's members turn into anxious people, paranoid people.

But Mildred doesn't consider herself particularly anxious. She doesn't think of herself as a traitor either. Her task is simple: to persuade as many Germans as possible to join the resistance.

Rudolf Ditzen, aka Hans Fallada

1934

1.

With the money he makes from his bestselling novel, the German writer Rudolf Ditzen buys a farmhouse in a remote village nestled in the hills of Mecklenburg. Mildred has never been to this village, nor does she know him personally, but she knows his editor, who offers to make an introduction.

Mildred is curious about Rudolf. His novel touched a nerve when it was published in 1932, and she understands why. It's about an office clerk and a shop assistant who struggle through chronic job insecurity and financial pressures brought on by the birth of their son. They're the spitting images of her students at the BAG, caught in a downward spiral of poverty and shame. Germans flocked to buy his novel—it's called *Little Man, What Now?*—with whatever coins they could scrounge. By March 1933, it had sold forty-two thousand copies in Germany. He published it under a pseudonym: Hans Fallada.

Despite his recent success, Rudolf isn't doing well. He worries about his career constantly. Last year he was faced with a decision: Should he join the Reichsverband Deutscher Schriftsteller, the Union of German Authors? Writers who didn't would never see their books published in Germany. So he joined. He saw no other way.

Since then he has written two books. One is a 580-page novel called *Once We Had a Child* that he completed in three months, a frenetic pace that left him breathless with exhaustion. Abscesses on his gums sent him into surgery three times, and both his children got whooping cough. But it's the other novel that has caused him the most misery. *Once a Jailbird* is about a man who goes to prison. The book is a raw critique of the criminal justice system in Germany. He knows it will be considered controversial, not least because it features a homosexual relationship and a sympathetic depiction of an unmarried mother. To placate the Nazis, he decides to write a foreword that expresses gratitude for the changes society has undergone since Hitler became chancellor. The "ridiculous, grotesque, and pitiful" characters and circumstances depicted in the book are, he assures the reader, "a thing of the past."

His editor hates the foreword. It's "too ingratiating," he insists. *Take it out.* Ernst Rowohlt is an industry titan in Germany, president of Rowohlt Verlag, a publishing house that continues to print books by Jewish authors and keep Jewish editors on staff. He is not easily deterred.

But Rudolf refuses. He has a wife and a son and a little baby. He has reached a point in his career where he can't afford to take chances. The foreword must stay. He won't change a word. Last spring he was arrested after a stranger accused him of plotting to assassinate Hitler. Storm Troopers searched his farmhouse for three hours. They found no evidence of anything but threw him in prison anyway. He languished there for ten days. The experience rattled him, and he never wants to repeat it.

Leave Germany, Rowohlt advises him. *Sell your farmhouse.*

But Rudolf says he can't. Can't and won't. The farmhouse is his pride and joy. He will, in his words, "swallow the bitter pill."

The bitter pill is making him ill, or so it seems to Rowohlt, who knows many authors who have remained in Germany and many authors who have fled. Authors in the first category say they're waiting for Hitler's regime to collapse, and in the meantime they'll keep a low profile, retreat into the comfort of family, avoid ruffling Nazi feathers. Authors in the second category believe authors in the first category are bootlicking fools.

Thomas Mann, who will go on to win the Nobel Prize in Literature, belongs in the second category. Mann reads *Once a Jailbird* in Switzerland, where he has exiled himself and continues to publish novels on his own terms, without groveling or bootlicking. The foreword disgusts him. On March 14, 1934, Mann scribbles furiously in his diary:

> In order to be published in Germany a book has to disown and deny its humane philosophy in an introduction.

2.

Mildred visits Rudolf Ditzen on May 27, 1934. Ernst Rowohlt can't accompany her, but his twenty-six-year-old son, Heinrich Ledig-Rowohlt, can.

Mildred invites Martha Dodd to join them.

Their friendship suffered a setback after Mildred discovered that Martha was dating the chief of the Gestapo. Since then, Martha seems to have come to her senses. Her obsession with the sinisterly handsome Rudolf Diels was, she admits, a childish mistake. Mildred accepts this dramatic turnaround with coolheaded approval.

Martha's new lover, a Russian named Boris Vinogradov, gallantly offered to drive. Mildred, Martha, and Heinrich pile into the back seat of a convertible Ford Cabriolet and Boris steers them north, leaving behind the traffic-choked boulevards of Berlin. Carwitz is their destination, a quaint village in Mecklenburg, a region dotted with pristine blue lakes. The trip takes three hours. After they drive an hour or so, the country roads narrow. Acacia trees spring up on either side, fragrant with blossoms that cluster and hang like grapes. Chestnut trees carry their blossoms like candles, cones of white thrusting up through the leaves. The conversation drifts to Rudolf and his regrettable foreword, but a violent change in weather drowns it out. They hear cracks of thunder, see flashes of lightning. It's a spring storm. The rain falls warm and heavy, and a strong wind shakes the trees.

Boris speeds on, undaunted. He refuses to put up the convertible's top, to the delight of his passengers. They lift their faces to the pelting rain, laughing. By the time they reach Carwitz, they are thoroughly drenched.

THE RAIN STOPS. THE sun brightens. A dog appears, barking.

Rudolf Ditzen emerges from the farmhouse and walks down a slanting pathway to greet them, followed by his four-year-old son and his wife, Suse, who cradles a baby in her arms. Country life seems to suit them; all radiate contentment.

He proposes a tour. In the sunshine, their wet clothes can dry off. He leads them around the farmhouse. There's a magnificent vegetable garden. Beyond it, a blue lake sparkles. Mildred says she wants to walk to the lake. Not alone—she wants Rudolf to come with her. He accepts her invitation, leaving the others to make their way back to the farmhouse.

Side by side, Mildred and Rudolf stroll on. She tells him about Lake Michigan. When she was a child, she'd kick off her shoes and run barefoot in the sand. She'd swim in the sun for hours, until her skin was burned.

"It must be difficult for you to live in a foreign country," Rudolf observes.

Mildred admits it is.

He lights a cigarette, takes a drag. A cloud of smoke rises. "I could never write in another language," he says, "or live anywhere else but Germany."

"Perhaps it's less important *where* you live," she says, "than *how* you live."

In the country, surrounded by cows, a man can write in peace. This is what Rudolf tells Mildred, who holds him with a level gaze.

"Can you really write whatever you want?"

"Depends on your point of view," he says. He tells her about the difficulties writers face in Germany, the demands.

I don't need you to explain, she could respond, *you're not telling me anything I don't know.* But she keeps silent. She will let him say what he needs to say. And so he goes on and on about how the government can ban this word or that word but language itself can't be banned, language is something alive, something that belongs to the people of Germany. She lets him prattle on about the people. The *Volk*.

"So, yes," he concludes, "I believe you can still write in Germany if you observe the necessary regulations and give in a little. Not in the important things, of course."

"What is important and what is unimportant?" Mildred asks.

Another drag. A rising cloud of smoke.

IN THE WANING AFTERNOON light, Rudolf's wife lays out a simple country supper. The conversation rambles pleasantly.

Martha's Russian lover remains silent. Now and then, Boris Vinogradov beams a smile at Martha, who beams one back. Their communication seems to consist entirely of smiles and hand signals.

After supper Mildred and Martha go out for a walk, the dog trailing after them. The men stay behind to play chess—Boris watching, Rudolf and Heinrich facing off. Heinrich disapproves of the foreword to *Once a Jailbird* and tells Rudolf so. Rudolf grows furious.

NO ONE SPEAKS MUCH on the drive back to Berlin. Boris maneuvers the convertible Ford Cabriolet away from the farmhouse and along the winding country roads. His passengers are lost in their own thoughts. When Mildred breaks the silence, she speaks of the tortured, cowardly author who held their attention for the better part of the day. At one point, she asked Rudolf why he'd given up. His face turned scarlet. Then he went quiet.

Mildred won't recruit him into the Circle. No one knows this had been her ulterior motive—not Heinrich, not Martha, not Martha's new Russian lover.

Boris Vinogradov grips the steering wheel, speeding past lone cottages and empty fields. His headlights send beams of yellow into the blackness.

The Night of the Long Knives

1934

1.

Days before the killing spree begins, three men meet in a well-lighted office.

They are Hitler's most loyal lackeys. The youngest is just thirty years old. Last month he was named the new chief of the Gestapo. Seated beside him is the thirty-three-year-old leader of the SS and architect of the concentration-camp system. The third man doesn't sit; he paces back and forth. The well-lighted office belongs to him. At forty-one, he is their superior in age and rank, presiding over both the Ministry of the Interior for Prussia and the Ministry of Aviation. Last year, he masterminded the creation of the Gestapo and served as its first chief.

The three men are Reinhard Heydrich, Heinrich Himmler, and Hermann Göring. Each will see his career flourish spectacularly in the coming years, collecting appointments and cabinet positions as avidly as boys collect marbles.

It's been nearly a year and a half since Hitler became chancellor, and some Germans are growing weary. There are grumblings that the new laws are too stringent. A vocal segment of wealthy, right-wing conservatives are demanding a stop to the arbitrary arrests and street violence. The economy is showing signs of significant improvement—by June 1934, unemployment has fallen by more than 50 percent—but Nazi thuggery threatens to undermine stability. The pulse of fear can be felt throughout Germany. Whispers of a second revolution are in the air. In some towns, worries about another crippling recession are driving people into panicked buying and hoarding.

Hitler's three loyal lackeys know there are several ways to address these problems.

First, they could spread the word that Germans are much better off now than they were a year and a half ago. But they are already doing this.

Second, they could arrest the opposition. Anyone who questions Hitler's policies counts as the opposition; right-wing conservatives and fellow Nazis are no exception. But arresting them is not the same as silencing them.

Which brings them to a third option: shoot the opposition.

2.

One man is missing from the well-lighted office. His name is Ernst Röhm. He has been Hitler's political ally and close friend for fourteen years. When Hitler was an upstart politician giving speeches in beer halls, Röhm was there, protecting him, recruiting followers. Everyone else has to address Hitler as Mein Führer. But Röhm calls him Adolf. Sometimes, Röhm is even cheekier. Sometimes, he calls him Adi.

Hitler and Röhm—Adi and Ernst—are joined at the hip. Everyone knows it. And many—including the three men in the well-lit office—resent it.

Röhm is the leader of the Storm Troopers. He has three million men under his command, seven and a half million if you count recruits from the Steel Helmets, a veterans' organization. The sheer numbers are staggering. Röhm's force is the size of a full-fledged army. Compare this with the SS, which has a measly fifty thousand men.

As head of the SS, Himmler feels outmanned. So does Heydrich; the Gestapo will never approach Röhm's numbers. Göring, too, chafes at Röhm's popularity.

Even Hitler is growing uneasy. What would happen if Röhm

decided to turn against him, spearhead a revolution? The very idea sends Hitler into paranoid fits.

Ernst has to go.

3.

On June 30, 1934, Ernst Röhm is arrested and thrown in jail.

The next morning, two SS officers enter his cell. Suicide, they explain, is within his rights. They give him a gun.

Röhm accepts the weapon—a loaded Browning—but refuses to kill himself. So they shoot him dead.

4.

The killing spree goes on for three days. It will come to be known as the Röhm Purge. It will also acquire another name: the Night of the Long Knives.

The SS murder a slew of politicians, including a number of men who work for Vice-Chancellor Papen. The vice-chancellor's press secretary, Herbert von Bose, is shot. The vice-chancellor's speech-writer is shot. The vice-chancellor's friend is shot. The vice-chancellor himself narrowly escapes murder; instead, Papen is placed under house arrest.

In Berlin, one hundred fifty Storm Troopers are lined up against a wall and shot.

In Munich, a man is playing cello in the study of his apartment while his wife prepares dinner and their three children, ages nine, eight, and two, play a game. The doorbell rings. Four SS officers march in and arrest him. Later, they shoot him and deliver his casket to his wife with an apology. The man wasn't who they thought he was. They'd confused Willi Schmid, a music critic, with Willi Schmidt, a Storm Trooper.

Over a thousand people are arrested.

Hitler orders the Ministry of Justice to retroactively legalize what has happened, promising to deliver a speech that will explain everything.

5.

THE REICH GOVERNMENT HAS ENACTED THE FOLLOWING LAW RELATING TO NATIONAL EMERGENCY DEFENSE MEASURES

The measures taken on 30 June and 1 and 2 July 1934 to suppress attempts at treason and high treason are legal emergency measures in defense of the state.

The Reich Chancellor: Adolf Hitler

The Reich Minister of the Interior: Wilhelm Frick

The Reich Minister of Justice: Franz Gürtner

Berlin

July 3, 1934

6.

Hitler's speech is broadcast on the radio. He raves about a gang of traitors who had been conspiring to overthrow the government with the help of another, unnamed country. He alludes darkly to his friend Röhm, claiming he was plotting to assassinate him.

Let it be known that no one can threaten Germany's existence—which depends on its internal law and order—and escape unpunished! And let it be known that if you raise your hand to strike this country, you will face certain death!

7.

Hitler's threat is clear and unambiguous, blunt as a hammer. *Certain death.*

Time to move, Mildred and Arvid decide.

They find a small place tucked away in a secluded part of Wannsee, a suburb of Berlin. It isn't far from their former apartment, just fifteen miles or so, but it might as well be another world with its dense, mossy woods and two lakes, a small one and a large one. They used to swim in the small one on Sundays. They'd sit on their towels and eat sandwiches in the sunshine, letting it bake the water off their skin. They'd return to Berlin feeling rested and ready to face another week of work.

Now is a different time. A bloody massacre has occurred in broad daylight. Countless people have been shot in the back, in the face, in the chest, their bodies dumped into ditches or stuffed into caskets and delivered to their wives. In some cases, wives were murdered too.

Gangsters. Germany is being governed by gangsters.

8.

Mildred needs to think, to figure out the wisest course of action.

Every morning before breakfast, she and Arvid take a walk and talk about what they should do. In the afternoon, she writes. Writing is deeply satisfying these days and helps get her mind off gangsters, at least for a little while.

The book column with Martha Dodd is over. After three months and a half dozen columns, Martha has lost interest, alluding vaguely to other demands on her time. Probably for the best. Martha wasn't much of a collaborator; Mildred wrote most of the articles herself. She gave up the pretense of having a coauthor in the last and final column—it was about Hervey Allen's epically long novel *Anthony Adverse*—and signed it with her own initials.

9.

Mildred writes a note to Martha. In the rush to leave Berlin, she hadn't said goodbye.

She mentions that she's reading a book about a man who is lonely and worried about the destructive forces in his country and goes insane.

Mildred isn't going insane, but the strain of living in Germany is beginning to take its toll.

> Dear Martha, We have moved to Wannsee, Tristanstrasse 27, HO 5671. And in the confusion I have not written to you. Here the stars are nearer than in the H...

This is not one of Mildred's anonymous postcards. This time, she signs her name.

> ...good sun for you, I... Love from Mildred

10.

Nine a.m., August 2, 1934. President Paul von Hindenburg is dead. After a prolonged illness, the eighty-six-year-old leader has taken his final breath.

Three hours later, the government issues a statement.

The role of president has been abolished. The role of vice-chancellor is a thing of the past. Adolf Hitler is now the supreme, sole leader of Germany.

Mildred hears the news on the radio. Arvid is with her, pacing the room.

The Boy

V

A *Molekül* and Other Small Things

1939

1.

The first time, Don didn't notice whether Mildred's apartment was quiet or loud, dark or light, warm or cold. Now he knows: quiet, light, cold.

He hears a ticking sound. His gaze lands on the porcelain stove in the corner of the room. Coal burns inside it. Some charred lumps are in a heap behind a little door with holes. A thick pipe stretches to the ceiling, carrying the smoke outside, into the cold gray air. Colder outside than inside, but not much.

He takes off his knapsack and coat, soggy with snow.

Mildred drapes his coat over a wooden chair near the stove. *Put your knapsack over there,* she says, pointing to the sofa. It's upholstered, with wooden armrests. Her favorite place to read, he'll learn over the next year and a half. He'll also learn that oranges are her favorite fruit and that she loves flowers more than almost anything. He sits next to her.

Now take out your book, she says.

Don does as he's told, unzipping his knapsack.

She points to a paragraph. Her finger looks different from his mother's. His mother's nails are red and shiny. Mildred's are plain.

The words on the page are a slippery path, periods and commas like pebbles. He stumbles. He forges ahead, stumbles again. He doesn't know what book this is or why she wants him to read it out loud. He'd rather read *Anthony Adverse*. He found it on a table at the American Women's Club, where his mother likes to eat lunch. *Anthony Adverse* is a thick book, 1,224 pages—more if you count the table of contents, which divides the book into nine parts. The first part is "In Which the Seed Falls in the Enchanted Forest." The second is "In Which the Roots of the Tree Are Exposed." The third is "In Which the Roots of the Tree Are Torn Loose." And on and on to the ninth: "In Which the Tree Is Cut Down." The book Mildred wants him to read is about poor people from Oklahoma. The title— *The Grapes of Wrath*—makes him think of fruit, not people.

He's done reading the paragraph. He says he's tired. He looks down at his feet. Jiggles his leg. Mildred takes a sip of tea.

Well, she says at last. *This can be a short lesson, then.*

She rises from the sofa and instructs him to put his book back in his knapsack. Before he zips the zipper, she slips in a note. When he goes home, he will give it to his mother. Later, when his father comes home from the embassy, Louise will pass the note on to him.

Don't forget your coat.

Don remembers that she put his coat on the chair beside the stove. She helps him put it on. The coat is warm now.

2.

After the lesson, Don goes to find Mole on Hauptstrasse.

Mole is short for *molecule*, or *Molekül* in German. Meaning a small thing, a speck. Several years ago, when Mole was playing with older, taller boys on Hauptstrasse, they called him this, and the nickname stuck.

Mole's real name is Günther Möllmann. His family is poor. His clothes are secondhand, too big. Mole's older brother is in the army. He was drafted. He'd always wanted to join, so he would have volunteered even if he hadn't been. Mole explained this to Don when they met.

Mole is Don's age. He's too young to join his older brother in the army, but if he is drafted one day, he'll go. He'll have no choice. *But I won't shoot you,* he tells Don.

I won't shoot you either, Don tells his friend.

Their fathers fought on opposite sides in the Great War. Don and Mole wonder if their fathers would be friends now. The idea is so unfathomable that they laugh, picturing it.

3.

One day, Don takes a photograph of Mole in the park.

He aims the camera the way his father has taught him, making sure Mole is smack in the center. The sun is low, and the shadow Don casts is long and wide, blackening Mole's leg from the knee down.

4.

There are four other boys in Mole's gang. One is named Achim, another is Peter, and another is Siggy. Achim's full name is Joachim

Steinberg. Peter's is Peter Muenzberg. Siggy is short for Siegfried. And then there's Pladik. They're all poor and they all live on Hauptstrasse. At first Achim, Peter, Siggy, and Pladik didn't want an American boy in their gang, but they changed their minds the day they saw Don on his Flexible Flyer.

It was freezing that day, snow freshly fallen. Don was in the park sliding down a steep snowy hill. Mole's gang took in the sight of him, a lone American boy riding a wooden sled with red runners. The sled had a magnificent design painted on it, an eagle with outstretched wings holding a red banner in its beak. On the banner were the words FLEXIBLE FLYER in triumphant capital letters.

When Don reached the bottom of the hill, they rushed over. They all wanted to ride it too. Mole stepped forward and told them they couldn't. Not unless Don joined their gang.

This made Don love Mole even more.

The gang used to be called Trenck's Panduren but they changed the name after Don joined. Now they call it the Kansas Jack Gang.

The Kansas Jack Gang

1939

1.

Don isn't from Kansas, of course. He was born in Switzerland, but this is a technicality he didn't explain to Mole. Kansas is what Don considers his home, since this is where his mother and his father were born and raised.

Mole loves Kansas. So do Achim, Peter, Siggy, and Pladik. They've all read about Kansas in books by the German author Karl May, who writes about the American West, about cowboys and Indians and an Apache chief named Winnetou.

2.

Slip your hand into his pocket and you'll find a few pfennigs, a packet of Dr. Oetker's pudding powder, maybe a marble or two.

The pfennigs are for nuts. A man standing on the street corner across from Mildred's apartment sells them from a cart. The pudding powder is another treat, best consumed by ripping off the top of the packet and sticking your tongue inside. The marbles can be traded for pfennigs, or pudding powder, or coils of scrap tin, or nearly anything else that German boys scrabbling around Berlin have stuffed in their pockets.

The routes Don takes to Mildred's apartment are as various as the currency he collects. "The wolf was certain of intercepting Red Riding Hood because she always took the same route to Grandma's hut," his father reminded him. Sometimes he walks down

Bülowstrasse to the American Church, where he climbs the stairs to the steeple for a bird's-eye view. Sometimes he walks as far as the canal. Sometimes he takes a detour through the Berlin Zoo. There, he gazes at the elephant seals through fingerprint-smeared aquarium glass, careful to check in the reflection whether someone is following him.

3.

You have a good memory, Mildred tells Don when he rattles off the names of all the characters in Karl May's books and the animals he saw at the Berlin Zoo. She asks him which route he took to her apartment. He recites the names of the streets and U-Bahn station stops. When their lesson is done, she slips a note into his knapsack.

A good memory is essential in espionage, though Don won't know what *espionage* means for many years.

Mildred
VI

Fragment

Questionnaire
Plötzensee Prison, Berlin
February 16, 1943

Do you have especially strong passions?   No
(Drinking, smoking, sexual excess?)

A New Strategy

1935

1.

In February 1935, Mildred and Arvid return to Berlin, moving into an apartment at Woyrschstrasse 46. They have formulated a new plan. It's a radical shift in strategy.

The Circle is too small, and too weak. Fighting fascism with books and leaflets isn't enough. Paper is a poor weapon against the supreme, sole leader of Germany. A stronger weapon is needed, one that will penetrate the very core of the Nazi government and destroy it from within.

2.

Every morning, the neighbors can see Arvid walking down four flights of stairs and out the front door, gripping a briefcase.

As for what's in the briefcase, the neighbors may only guess. Arvid has gotten a job at the Ministry of Economics. The documents he handles are strictly confidential. He is responsible for writing reports that his boss, Hjalmar Schacht, brings to meetings with Hitler. Arvid hopes to build his own reputation as a brilliant analyst of economic conditions. His impersonation of a dutiful servant of the Third Reich and his discretion in word and deed have already won him the admiration of his colleagues at the Ministry of Economics, who greet him every morning as he enters the building with raised, stiff arms: *Heil!*

Heil! Arvid responds, raising his own.

3.

Arvid is now in direct daily contact with high-ranking Nazis, learning their secrets, reading their documents.

He conceals raw fear behind a bland expression. He seems, in the words of his nephew Wolfgang, "almost bored." Behind round spectacles, Arvid's eyes are soft and unfocused, making him appear professorial, lost in abstraction. The teenage bully who shoved a stick in his eye so many years ago unknowingly did him a service. Arvid's blind eye is a kind of camouflage.

The Nazis around him are even blinder. It will be five years before one of them suspects that Arvid Harnack is in the resistance.

4.

Mildred worries about Arvid.

Any Nazi bureaucrat who takes the merest glance at Arvid's past and present affiliations could demand his arrest. His former involvement with ARPLAN would be reason enough.

Arvid assures Mildred that bureaucrats miss important details as often as they discover them, and an impressive lineage opens doors in a fascist dictatorship as well as it does in a capitalist democracy. Over the years, a succession of doors has opened for Arvid in social and professional settings whenever he mentions that he's the nephew of the great Adolf von Harnack. Sometimes he doesn't even need to mention this; his name alone is recognized.

Born in 1851, Adolf von Harnack was a prolific theologian who helped draft a section of the Weimar Constitution after the First World War. He scandalized the fusty, dusty factions of the church with his provocative teachings. Nothing was taboo, he insisted; every word in the Bible should be subject to scrutiny. Uncle Adolf (as Arvid called him) lived in Grunewald, a suburb of Berlin dense with birch trees and prosperous families, in a three-story house on Kunz-Buntschuhstrasse that was large enough to accommodate a wife and seven children. Hans Delbrück, a historian and member of the Reichstag, lived on the same street with his wife and seven children. Around the corner, in a big yellow house on Wangenheim-Strasse, lived a professor of psychiatry named Karl Bonhoeffer with his wife and eight children.

The Harnacks, the Delbrücks, and the Bonhoeffers all intermarried. Toddlers, children, and teenagers spilled out of their houses. When Arvid turned twelve, he got to know them well. The train ride from his home in Jena to Grunewald took the better part of the morning, but the gaggle of cousins who greeted him when he arrived made it worthwhile. He befriended the cousins closest to him in age. Klaus Bonhoeffer was also twelve, Justus Delbrück was a year younger, Emmi Delbrück was four years younger, and both Max Delbrück and Dietrich Bonhoeffer were five years younger. (The Bonhoeffer boys went to school with a boy named Hans von Dohnányi, who would also marry into the family.)

Adolf von Harnack's fame in Germany has only grown since his death in 1930, when he was mourned in a grand memorial service attended by a minister of state, a minister of interior, a minister of culture, and a throng of Harnacks, Delbrücks, Dohnányis, and Bonhoeffers. Dietrich Bonhoeffer, then just twenty-four, delivered a poignant eulogy. Mildred sat up front next to Arvid, holding his hand. Toward the end, Dietrich praised Adolf von Harnack as a man

> who formed his free judgment afresh time and time again, and went on to express it clearly despite the fear-ridden restraint of the majority.

The memorial was held at the Harnack House, erected the previous year with funds provided by the state of Prussia to serve as a meeting place for esteemed scientists, artists, ambassadors, and public intellectuals. A guest book over the years boasted the names of several Nobel Prize winners: the Indian poet Rabindranath Tagore; the German physicists Albert Einstein, Max Planck, and Werner Heisenberg. Here, in a stately hall named after Goethe, Einstein presented his theory of relativity for the very first time.

How much has changed since then—and how *rapidly*.

On February 4, 1935, high-ranking Nazis, including Goebbels and

Hitler himself, gathered at the Harnack House to attend the opening of the German national film archive—the Reichsfilmarchiv—the first of its kind, a Nazi triumph.

Arvid was horrified.

Still, all this will help him execute his new strategy: to position himself directly under the Führer's nose.

Bye-Bye, Treaty of Versailles

1935

1.

On March 16, 1935, Hitler announces a new law: all German males between the ages of eighteen and forty-five will be required to serve in the military. The law is a blatant violation of the Treaty of Versailles, drawn up after the First World War by its victors — the United States, the United Kingdom, France, and Italy — which prohibits Germany from building tanks, military aircraft, and submarines and limits the size of the German army to one hundred thousand volunteers. Compulsory military service is forbidden, but Hitler hopes that the world will overlook what he's done, especially when he steps up to a microphone and assures everyone he wants *peace*.

On March 17, he says,

Germans don't want war. We want to be peaceful and happy.

On May 1, he says,

Germans want nothing else than peace with the rest of the world.

On May 21, he says,

Germany needs peace and desires peace.

On August 11, he says,

We wish for peace.

On August 28, he says,

We have declared a hundred times that we wish for peace.

Hitler is well aware that the Great War of 1914 to 1918 is a sore spot for the Germans who huddle by their People's Radios to hear him. He knows that the mere mention of the Treaty of Versailles could make them collectively wince.

Signed in the summer of 1919, the Treaty of Versailles required Germany to claim full responsibility for starting the war. Germany's emperor, Wilhelm II—who delivered the order to fire the first shot—abdicated and fled to the Netherlands, where he ensconced himself in yet another splendid castle. The castle had a fleet of dutiful servants, a charming view of the countryside, and a sibilant name, Huis Doorn. While Wilhelm II guzzled wine from gold goblets beneath a massive chandelier, ordinary Germans had to suffer the consequences of the treaty, which aimed to weaken their country so it would never again pose a threat to the world. Most enfeebling was the provision that required Germany to pay a colossal sum. (It took Germany more than ninety years—until October 2010—to pay off the debt.)

The first payment was due in 1921. Germany's new democratic government struggled to come up with the sum and attempted to solve the problem by simply printing more money. Two thousand printing presses produced a seemingly ceaseless supply of banknotes. Inflation skyrocketed. The economy was so volatile that prices would often soar in a single afternoon; a cup of coffee that cost 5,000 marks at 1:00 p.m. would cost 14,000 marks a few hours later. As the value of German currency plummeted, purchasing anything became an absurdity. A wheelbarrow of money couldn't buy a single newspaper. The German journalist Bella Fromm wrote in her diary:

When you go shopping, you have to carry your banknotes in suitcases. In order to mail a letter inside Germany, I had to pay several million marks for a stamp.

People with pensions or bank accounts lost nearly all their money. Rampant theft, homelessness, and starvation followed. Suicides escalated, reaching record levels. Newspapers published lists of the dead; magazines published articles on despair. "There is not much to add," begins one article.

It pounds daily on the nerves: the insanity of numbers, the uncertain future, today, and tomorrow become doubtful once more overnight. An epidemic of fear, naked need: lines of shoppers, long since an unaccustomed sight, once more form in front of shops, first in front of one, then in front of all. No disease is as contagious as this one....Rice, 80,000 marks a pound yesterday, costs 160,000 marks today, and tomorrow perhaps twice as much; the day after, the man behind the counter will shrug his shoulders, "No more rice." Well then, noodles! "No more noodles."

By the winter of 1923, forty-two billion marks was worth one American cent. The collapse was complete.

The German artist Käthe Kollwitz roamed the garbage-strewn streets of Berlin, pasting posters on walls and billboards. Her posters were cries of anguish. Above an openmouthed figure, scrawled in large black letters, were the words *Nie Wieder Krieg!*—"Never Again War!" It was a sentiment shared by many.

2.

Kollwitz's art has been removed from Germany's galleries. She is among the artists whose work is considered offensive, subversive, *degenerate*. Her posters have been torn down, the streets of Berlin have been scrubbed clean, but the memory of the horrific economic collapse lingers. The middle class, the working class, and wealthy, property-owning aristocrats all experienced devastation; no one was exempt.

Or *nearly* no one. The great German industrialists not only survived hyperinflation, they profited from it. During the 1920s, the tycoons at the helms of the massive chemical conglomerate I. G. Farben and the weapons manufacturer Friedrich Krupp knew hyperinflation made manufacturing German goods cheap and easy to export to other countries. While most of the population in Germany suffered grievously, these tycoons amassed even larger fortunes. They were also among the industrialists who wrote big checks to support the Nazi Party immediately after Hitler took power in 1933—and who stand to profit handsomely from rearmament now.

Tommy

1935

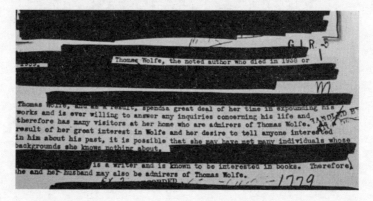

1.

In the gin-soaked pages of Thomas Wolfe's diary, she is always Mrs. Harnack, never Mildred. The first time they meet and over the next few years, she keeps herself at an affectionate distance, halfway between a wink and a warm handshake. She prefers to be an enigma rather than risk exposing herself.

St. Pauli Bar is on Rankestrasse, a ten-minute walk from Mildred's apartment. Wolfe knows nothing about her, just that she's an American who wants to interview him.

Wolfe's a day late. He was scheduled to arrive in Berlin on May 6, but he had some sort of trouble getting here. It doesn't matter. She's face-to-face with him now at St. Pauli Bar, his long legs sprawled out from a chair much too small for him. It's impossible to be inconspicuous when you're with Thomas Wolfe. He's a giant of a man, six foot seven. He stoops his shoulders when he lumbers into a room; still, he towers over everyone in it. He has a huge, shaggy mass of hair, which makes him seem even taller, and dark, unusually penetrating eyes.

Mildred asks about his hometown. This seems a good place to start. She has never been to Asheville or anywhere in North Carolina. The farthest south she has been is Chevy Chase, Maryland, where her sister Harriette lives, but she doesn't mention this.

"I haven't dared to go home to the South since I wrote my first book," Wolfe says, and he goes off like a shot from there. He loves talking almost as much as he loves writing. Maybe more. He writes as fast as he can, as if possessed by a demon. Always in a fevered rush to put his thoughts down, he fills page after page, scribbling for days and weeks at a time, until his hand hurts and his eyes sting, and the stack of pages beside him inches upward, growing mountainous.

"I wrote and wrote and wrote," Wolfe tells Mildred. "Every time I'd get a hundred thousand pages piled up, I'd take them to my friend Max Perkins of Scribner. And every time he'd say, 'That's good, that's the real stuff. But it's only the knee joint.' Or, 'It's only an arm.'" In Wolfe's mind, his book was a statue and he couldn't arrange all the pieces properly. That's what he needed Perkins for, he tells Mildred, to put it all together.

Look Homeward, Angel is Wolfe's first novel. Published in 1929, it was hailed as a masterpiece in the United States. In Germany, too, the book was wildly successful. It's all crammed in there, all of America: the teachers and preachers and traveling salesmen; the trains, the big cities and small towns; the wide plains and starry skies; the wish for more, more, more. Every page spills over with wild effusions of words. *Look Homeward, Angel* is as huge and over-blown as Thomas Wolfe himself, and German readers can't get enough of him.

The feeling is mutual; Thomas Wolfe can't get enough of Germany. Everywhere he goes, people seem charmed by him—the cab-drivers, the trolley men, the salesgirls, the waiters. Even the writers—the ones who haven't fled the country—treat him with warmhearted respect. He loves Berlin's streets and parks. He goes crazy for the trolleys, the gingerbread houses, the flowers spilling from window boxes. He plans to stay here until he runs out of money or overstays his welcome, and neither seems a possibility anytime soon. Nearly every day he will be spotted lumbering down a side-walk somewhere, loose-limbed and gesticulating wildly, deep in conversation with a companion. He will become a regular fixture at the Romanisches Café. His mighty height and childlike exuberance awaken in the Germans he meets a kind of awe. As his German edi-tor, Heinrich Ledig-Rowohlt, puts it, Wolfe is "the embodiment of the free world that we in Hitler's prison were longing for."

THE INTERVIEW AT ST. Pauli Bar is going well.

Wolfe orders another drink from the bartender, then another. Toward the end of the interview, he grows pensive and tells Mildred he was hurt in his youth. "So many Americans are," he adds.

Mildred nods. She's nearly the same age as Thomas Wolfe—thirty-two to his thirty-four—and he isn't the only one who had a difficult childhood. Her mother ran a boardinghouse, just as Wolfe's mother did. Her father, like his, was a raving drunk. But Mildred doesn't tell him any of this.

Wolfe drains his glass with gusto. It's time for him to shuffle off. Tomorrow Martha Dodd is throwing a big party at her mansion and he's the guest of honor. Will he see Mildred there? She assures him he will.

Wolfe pushes away from the table, rises to his full height, and lumbers amiably out. The interview has lasted an hour or so. Mil-dred has learned a great deal about him and he's learned nearly nothing about her, which is how she wants it.

Mildred's notebook is a riot of scribblings. She slides it into her leather satchel. Now she just needs to get home and make sense of it all. She walks out of the bar. It's a warm spring night. Rankestrasse is bright and busy, streaming with headlights. This time tomorrow she will be at the party, surrounded by a lively jumble of journalists, editors, and novelists. Standing beside her with a winning smile, the gleeful center of attention, will be a very drunk Thomas Wolfe. Or, as Martha Dodd has taken to calling him, Tommy.

2.

Martha hasn't even met him yet and already she's given him a nickname. Tommy this, Tommy that; he's all she has talked about in the weeks of planning the party, which she calls a tea. It will be held from five p.m. to eight p.m., but she envisions a much more raucous event than the word *tea* implies. Alcohol will be served liberally, and the celebration will surely continue after eight, if not in the stately hall of the U.S. embassy, then at the Taverne, where she's chummy with the owner and can persuade him to stay open until the wee hours of the morning. Martha dashes off a handwritten note to her guest of honor on embossed U.S. embassy stationery.

> *It is such an event when a writer comes to town that we become quite hysterical over it. Like a pack of maddened savage dogs all of literary Berlin is on your scent. I should mention that I'm also a writer. My brother, Bill, and my father are historians, not diplomats in the common sense. I would be delighted to do anything for you, including taking you dancing, drinking, sunning, and motoring. My father will arrange anything you require as a tourist. I am tremendously anxious to see you, mainly of course because I admire your work so immensely.*

Boris Vinogradov still hasn't returned to Berlin. For a few months, her Russian lover was in Moscow, but now he's somewhere in Romania. Boris teases her—no, tortures her—with hints about marriage, but he hasn't proposed, nor has he given her anything along the lines of a definitive plan. How long will he be in Romania? When will he return to Berlin? Boris doesn't know. It seems his hands are tied by forces beyond his control. The ink she spills in her letters expresses her deep, abiding love and inextinguishable passion for him. Soon they will be reunited, and in the meantime she will dream of no one else.

But Wolfe's impending arrival banishes Boris from her dreams.

3.

Sometime before the party, Martha asks Mildred to take charge of the guest list. The guests must all be prominent and literary, Martha tells her, the type of people Tommy would want to meet. Tommy's New York editor, Maxwell Perkins of Scribner's, can't come, but no matter. Donald Klopfer, publisher of Random House, happens to be visiting Berlin and should be added to the list, as should Tommy's German publisher, Ernst Rowohlt of Rowohlt Verlag. Surely the biggest publisher in America and the biggest publisher in Germany will draw all sorts of poets, writers, and journalists, like a flame draws ragged moths. It will be, Martha hopes, Berlin's biggest literary event of the year.

4.

May 8, 1935. At five p.m., the guests begin to fill the banquet hall on the ground floor of the Dodd mansion. Donald Klopfer arrives, a sleek, commanding presence. Journalists from the *New York Times,* the *Herald Tribune,* the *Chicago Daily News,* the *Christian Science Monitor,* and the Hearst press arrive, wives at their sides. Sigrid Schultz of the *Chicago Tribune* strides in, petite and indomitable. The bespectacled Louis Lochner, bureau chief of the Associated Press in Berlin, shuffles in. The Americans have arrived.

As for the Germans, young, chestnut-haired Margret Boveri from the *Berliner Tageblatt* is here. The irrepressible Bella Fromm is here too. She's writing a gossip column in the English-language *Continental Post* now that the *Vossische Zeitung* no longer employs Jews.

Ernst Rowohlt, with his big, booming voice, moves conspicuously through the room with his more taciturn son, Heinrich Ledig-Rowohlt, who quietly notes the small smattering of German authors in attendance. It's impossible to ignore the obvious. The absence of others "showed very clearly to what an extent the tree of our literature was already stripped of its leaves," Heinrich wrote several years later. "All the great names of German letters had emigrated."

Martha Dodd flutters around the banquet hall in a festive dress, greeting them all. At the center of the room is a German poet. He has a "strong, suffering face," she observes. Several months ago, the poet's wife was arrested and thrown into a concentration camp. Martha can't help but notice that the guests are all "standing around drinking heavily and devouring plates of food." Many of them, she realizes, are "poor and actually ill-fed." Some are Jewish; they look "uncomfortable and self-conscious."

Mildred is here, eyeing the guests as she mills around the banquet hall. She aims to interact "with as many guests as possible" in order to "increase the sources of information."

Thomas Wolfe bursts into the room and quickly becomes the center of attention. He may be drunker than anyone else here. He wants to play a parlor game: Who Goes Nazi? The object of this game, he says, is to find the Nazis in the room.

Wolfe shambles around, narrowing his eyes at the guests, taking their measure. "I don't trust him!" he cries suddenly, jabbing his finger at one man.

Some of the guests are amused. Some hide their discomfort behind laughter. Some are aghast.

5.

Mildred swiftly writes two articles about Thomas Wolfe, one for the *Continental Post* and one for *Berliner Tageblatt*. She wants Martha to read them.

But Martha may be too distracted now that she and Tommy are officially an item. The two of them have been spotted well past midnight drinking cocktails at the Romanisches Café. They have also been seen staggering out of the Taverne in the light of dawn.

Thomas Wolfe describes Martha as "a little middle western flirt—with little shining stick out teeth, and a little 'sure that would be swell' sort of voice." She is, he writes, "a butterfly hovering around my penis."

6.

Mildred invites Wolfe to join her for a walk in the Tiergarten. If they were alone, it might be possible to have a more lengthy, serious talk. He's having tremendous fun in Germany and doesn't seem to understand how grave the situation is.

She wants to tell him to open his eyes. But his mind is fixated on *parties parties parties, girls girls girls.*

7.

Thomas Wolfe's Diary

Perkins cable—don't let Rowohlt in yet—sold continental rights in America, etc...taxi hotel—Ledig...goulash, wine, etc.—good—a dreamy summer's afternoon—the lovely dreamy shimmer of the trees in the Kurfürstendamm—the lovely girls—in spring summery dresses...strawberry ripe ripe ripe...left Ledig 5:30—[_____] called—asked her to hotel [2 times]—noticed disquieting penil symptoms—but all right—so to Martha Dodd's in taxi at 8:00 o'clock—said good bye to [_____]—sent her home—so to dine with Dodds—later alone with Martha talking, fighting, crying—so to Romanisches Café with Martha at 2 a.m.—few people there—so 2 drinks on terrace (weinbrand u.s.w. cognac etc.) watching light pale the western skies...so at closing of café to Taverne—there after closing hours by invitation—so there hearing American music until 4:30 or 5—so home to embassy

by cab—so looted icebox in great kitchen—so to library—ate
sandwiches...So up at 1—bathed, dressed—lunch with
Dodds—so with Martha talking all afternoon—3 or 4 drinks
(whiskies)...so called Martha saying I was busy talking to
people most important—so shaved—looked at penis...
dressed in grey, rough Tweed—so out on streets...the sweet
trees of the Kurfürstendamm—the cars—the busses—the
people flowing past—and the Germans and night—now
night.

8.

To be an American in Berlin is to turn a blind eye to atrocity.

Wolfe isn't the only one. Most American expats Mildred meets
in Berlin are largely untouched by what's going on around them.
Over a sumptuous dinner at the Hotel Adlon, they can have an
absorbing discussion about an article they read in a newspaper published in New York or Paris or London or Zurich that arrived in
Berlin a day or two after publication. They can sigh about this
inconvenience and change the subject to a broadcast they heard on
the BBC—a live show at the London Palladium featuring none
other than Duke Ellington and his jazz orchestra. The Germans sitting at a nearby table and the Polish waiter pouring water into their
goblets have no such luxury; listening to Ellington—*Negermusik*—
would bring the Gestapo to their door.

9.

On the evening of May 21, 1935, Hitler delivers a speech in the
Reichstag. It's a full house. The entire diplomatic corps is in attendance. Ambassadors from France, England, Italy, Japan, and Poland
sit in the front row. Ambassador Dodd sits in the third row. The
American journalist William Shirer watches it all from the section
of seats allotted to the press, noting the "six hundred or so sausage-
necked, shaved-headed, brown-clad yes-men, who rise and shout
almost every time Hitler pauses for breath."

The presence of Storm Troopers is no surprise; what stuns Shirer is the subject of Hitler's speech: peace.

"Germany wants peace!" Hitler hollers. "No one of us means to threaten anybody!"

The journalists seated around Shirer can't believe their ears either. Hitler vows that he won't invade Poland—

We recognize Poland as the home of a great and nationally conscious people!

and swears he will reduce his military arsenal—

Germany declares herself ready to agree to any limitation whatsoever of the caliber of artillery, battleships, cruisers and torpedo boats!

and outlines a thirteen-point proposal for maintaining peace.

Hitler has hollered about peace before, but not like this. His speech stands apart for its specificity and length. His thirteen-point proposal convinces not only Germans that he's telling the truth but also people in other countries, including those he will invade.

A credulous journalist for the *Times of London,* recognized as one of Britain's most influential newspapers, writes that Hitler's speech "turns out to be reasonable, straightforward, and comprehensive.... It is to be hoped that the speech will be taken everywhere as a sincere and well-considered utterance meaning precisely what it says."

Thomas Wolfe listens to Hitler's speech on a radio at Martha's house. He has spent the afternoon with her—a boozy lunch at Schlichter's, followed by cocktails at the Hotel Adlon. At five the next morning, he scrawls several pages in his journal. He will recall "the solid magnificence of the house—even in porter's quarters— and the green trees of yards outside fading into last light." He will remember "talking and quarreling" with Martha and the drinks they had afterward. But he won't remember a word of Hitler's speech.

Monkey Business

1935

1.

In the stately halls of the U.S. embassy in Berlin, tales of Martha Dodd's escapades have been making the rounds. Several embassy men have alerted top officials at the State Department in DC about Martha. First Secretary Raymond Geist described her indiscretions in vivid detail to Wilbur Carr, chief of consular services. In a letter marked "personal and confidential," Consul General George Messersmith told Western European Division chief Jay Pierrepont Moffat about Martha's relationship with the Harvard-educated German businessman Ernst Hanfstaengl, expressing his suspicion that it was "undesirable." Martha's flirtation with the tall, muscular military officer Fritz Wiedemann has raised diplomats' eyebrows, and there is speculation that she has carried on with Ernst Udet, a stunt pilot celebrated for his corkscrew spins.

Of course, Martha's dalliance with Gestapo chief Rudolf Diels has not escaped notice, nor has her affair with the Russian diplomat Boris Vinogradov. She seems to pick up men and set them down again without much examination. (First a Nazi! Then a Communist!)

And now she's been canoodling with a famous American novelist. How long will her fling with Thomas Wolfe last?

2.

The truth is, Martha hasn't forgotten about Boris Vinogradov.

Although she doesn't speak Russian and barely speaks German and his English is awful, it doesn't matter. They have found other ways to communicate. Boris is tall and broad-shouldered, with thick hair she can run her hands through. When words are absolutely necessary, they volley between his rudimentary English and a kind of pidgin German. Boris has what you'd call a diplomat's grasp of the language, the range of his vocabulary confined to questions a man might ask at a dinner party or a dance. They met, according to one account, at Sigrid Schultz's party, and he wooed her at a dance several weeks later.

"I am in the Soviet embassy," said Boris. *"Haben Sie Angst?"* Are you afraid?

The rakish twinkle in his eye told her she shouldn't be...or perhaps she should. Dizzy and with a thudding heart, she slipped her hand into his. He was a dud on the dance floor, but when he moved his lips to her ear and whispered, "I would like to see you again," she felt a delicious shiver shoot straight down to her toes.

They went to Paris. Then, on a whim, she flew to Russia to tour her lover's homeland, a trip that caused "a near diplomatic scandal." Photographers were waiting for her on the tarmac. She arrived wearing a polka-dot blouse, a swingy skirt, and a hat that she tilted, like Marlene Dietrich's. Flashbulbs flashed, and Martha smiled winningly, posing by the door of a small Junkers plane.

First stop, Leningrad. Then Moscow. Then a boat cruise down the Volga River with stops in delightfully alliterative cities: Samara, Saratov, and Stalingrad. She was enchanted by what she saw. The factories were marvels. Once, the poor had toiled away for hours on end, oppressed by wealthy aristocrats; now they worked in perfect harmony.

They work seven hours a day, have an hour for lunch and recreation, and two weeks' to a month's paid vacation every year, and enjoy every sixth day as a holiday. Former palaces and mansions, and their parks, are turned into homes of culture and rest, playgrounds, medical centers, children's schools or vacation places. All of this is done for workers by other workers who are the head of the state, as a beginning toward giving them the privileges and opportunities they deserve as the creators of the nation's wealth.

Dazzled, Martha didn't realize that the guide who led her on this tour—"a pretty rosy-faced girl"—had been instructed to present a carefully crafted vision of Russia, a Potemkin village at every stop.

In Leningrad, Martha had lunch with an American diplomat and heard something shocking. He claimed that between 1932 and 1933, Stalin had engineered the murder of millions of Ukrainians. The diplomat was William Bullitt, U.S. ambassador to the Soviet Union. He was "attractive," she decided, "with intense light eyes," though he was "bald-headed" and had a "glistening face." There was nothing about a Ukrainian genocide in the newspapers. Ambassador Bullitt, she decided, was "a man to be suspicious of and one not to be trusted."

In Martha's wide, sky-blue eyes, Russia was a peaceful nation. "What pleased me most," she wrote, "was the absolute lack of military display. I saw a few Red Army soldiers, and even one small parade, but they were all so simple, so inconspicuously dressed, so modest and even careless in appearance, I could hardly believe they were part of the formidable Soviet Red Army."

All Russians—men and women, children and babies, even the elderly—seemed irrepressibly happy. She couldn't help but observe that "there seemed to be a sort of ebullient vitality and love of life everywhere."

Stalin wasn't murderous, Martha decided. The murderous one was Hitler.

3.

After Martha's trip to Russia, her relationship with Boris grew more serious. On one heart-stirring occasion, he invited her to lunch at the Soviet embassy and slurred a toast: "To Martha, my wife!"

She and Boris have already been through so much together.

After all, Boris was with her on what might have been the most frightful night she has ever experienced. They'd spent the whole afternoon together, sunbathing on a secluded lake near Wannsee. Driving back to Berlin, Boris—who was especially fond of speeding—noticed with dismay that the traffic was unusually heavy. Entire boulevards were blocked off. Sidewalks that usually streamed with people on Saturday nights were empty. As he steered his convertible toward the Tiergarten, military vehicles came into view— trucks brimming with soldiers, tanks with machine guns jutting from their mounts. Swarms of green-uniformed police and black-uniformed SS officers spilled onto the streets. But no Storm Troopers. Brown uniforms were conspicuously absent.

The Night of the Long Knives made an indelible impression on Martha, cementing her view that Hitler had to be stopped. The fact that all those Storm Troopers were slaughtered was shocking enough; it was even more incomprehensible that Hitler had ordered the murder of high-ranking men in his own regime, including Ernst Röhm, supposedly his closest friend. "Hitler surely couldn't shoot all people who opposed him," she'd thought then.

Well, she's wiser now. Whatever trials lie ahead, Martha can face them with pluck and courage with Boris by her side.

Except he isn't by her side. He hasn't been for months.

4.

The letters Boris send her drip with sentiment and exclamation marks.

> *Martha! I want to see you, I need to tell you that I also have not forgotten my little adorable lovely Martha!*

> *I love you, Martha!*

It's true they've had some spats. In a moment of adoration, Boris sent Martha three little ceramic monkeys. In a moment of fury, Martha sent the monkeys back. The monkeys were like their children, caught between squabbling spouses. One little monkey covered its eyes, another covered its ears, another covered its mouth—see no evil, hear no evil, speak no evil. Did Boris understand the meaning of the monkeys?

He returned them, with a note.

> *Your three monkeys have grown (they have become big) and want to be with you. . . . I have to tell you very frankly: three monkeys have longed for you.*

So now Martha has the monkeys again, and she and Boris are back to the way they used to be, squabbling spouses with their children caught between them, except that they're not spouses. Will her Russian lover ever propose?

5.

Thomas Wolfe was a welcome distraction from the monkey business, but now he's gone too. He'd intended to take a trip to Russia; her rhapsodic accounts about her new favorite country had evidently piqued his curiosity. But then, for whatever reason, he abruptly abandoned the plan—and abandoned her. After a sloppy farewell, Tommy left Berlin, heading off to Copenhagen. Her broken heart could have been easily mended by Boris.

But Boris has vanished.

The Soviet embassy booted him from Berlin practically overnight. The story he tells her is vague. He is needed in Moscow, that is all.

Rindersteak Nazi

1935

1.

In the late spring of 1935, Mildred and Arvid invite Greta Lorke to join them for dinner in their new apartment. Greta arrives with her new boyfriend, a brooding man with heavy brows. His name is Adam Kuckhoff. He is the former editor of a political magazine called *Die Tat* (the Action) and has written several plays and a novel. He's working on a second novel now. Its subject is provocative: Germany has started a vicious, bloody war, and the protagonist must decide whether he will be a patriot or a rebel. Most likely, the book will be banned.

Adam Kuckhoff has his own resistance circle in Berlin: Tat Kreis. It's a small group of about seven men, a few of whom Adam met when he edited *Die Tat*. An intersection of the Circle with Adam's group could be advantageous.

Mildred "set the table festively with the old family silver," Greta recalls in her memoir. She doesn't elaborate, but by now we know Mildred well enough to fill in the blanks: candles flickering, a simple jar filled with flowers, and a meal that's most likely bland or burned or both.

Arvid has been at the Ministry of Economics long enough to form conclusions about the documents that pass from the hands of his Nazi colleagues to his desk, but he waits until they finish eating before he gives any indication that he intends to broach the topic.

First, he checks the apartment for wires. Then he climbs up to the neighbor's attic, which Greta sees is "full of old junk and hard to get through." Once he's convinced that "not one sound from the conversation we were having" could be heard by the neighbors, he begins speaking—though quietly, in an urgent whisper. With all his precautions, he's still worried about eavesdroppers.

Hitler's "peace" speech was a sham, a dog-and-pony show, the work of an inveterate liar. The documents Arvid has seen tell the truth, proving beyond a shadow of a doubt that peace plays no role in Germany's future. Hitler, he says, is "preparing for war."

2.

Hjalmar Schacht is a shrewd operator, impossible to pin down. Does he support Hitler's plans for war? Arvid contemplates the question as he goes about his day at the Ministry of Economics, prodding it as a tongue does a loose tooth.

Arvid may not know that his boss secretly collected three million Reichsmark from Germany's leading industrialists immediately after Hitler took power, but he is undoubtedly aware of the man's accolades. Hjalmar Schacht became president of the Reichsbank in 1923 and was credited with rescuing Germany from hyperinflation, which brought him international acclaim as the nation's "financial wizard." Schacht resigned in 1930. Roughly a month after the February 20, 1933, meeting with industrialists, Hitler reappointed Schacht as president of the Reichsbank. Schacht's allegiances are difficult to pin down. He admires the British economist John Maynard Keynes and praises aspects of President Roosevelt's New Deal policies. He has even encouraged Hitler to introduce a public works program similar to Roosevelt's. Schacht is, in a word, inscrutable. Sometimes he seems to be a staunch supporter of Hitler; sometimes his praise of the Führer comes off as insincere.

Schacht has put Arvid in charge of American-German trade relations. In this role, Arvid is required to strengthen his social ties with diplomats at the U.S. embassy. It is a perfect camouflage. He can position himself shoulder to shoulder with men he hopes will become valuable allies in bringing Hitler down.

Arvid sits across from Schacht in closed-door meetings. He

shuffles papers, lights a pipe. Smoke curls into the air. It's a kind of scrim. Through it, Arvid studies Schacht's face, alert to every twitch.

3.

Schacht is a member of the Deutscher Klub, an elite club that's crawling with Nazis. Arvid wonders whether he should join too. Other members include wealthy industrialists and high-ranking officers in the German military. SS chief Heinrich Himmler sits on the board. If Arvid joins their club, it will burnish the illusion that he is a fiercely loyal Nazi. Even better, it will widen his access to military intelligence. How thoroughly should he take on the identity of a person he despises? Uttering "Heil Hitler" dozens of times a day pains him enough.

There's a term for what Arvid is: a *Rindersteak*—beefsteak— Nazi. Nazi brown on the outside, lefty red on the inside. In such a guise, Arvid can justify becoming a member of the Deutscher Klub. But he won't join the Nazi Party. It's a line he will not—*cannot*— cross.

4.

After three months at the Ministry of Economics, Arvid is well on his way to perfecting his masquerade. He plays the part of a Nazi convincingly. He can deliver a stiff-armed salute and sign all his letters *Heil Hitler* without flinching. He regularly attends meetings of the Deutscher Klub, where he befriends military officers and industrialists who stand to profit tremendously if Hitler starts a war.

Today is July 15, 1935. Perhaps, as Arvid walks through the cavernous building to his office this morning, hearing the marble hallways echo with his footsteps, he thinks it's an ordinary day.

Perhaps it is.

But not for Artur Artusov, whose office is roughly one thousand miles northeast of Berlin. Artusov is the director of a department at the NKVD, Stalin's secret police and foreign intelligence agency, headquartered in Moscow. A steely-eyed man with the build and smashed nose of a boxer, Artusov has known about Arvid for quite a while now and has been waiting for the right moment to strike. The moment has arrived.

Artusov calls a meeting and instructs his colleagues to "expedite preparations for Harnack's recruitment."

An Old Pal from ARPLAN

1935

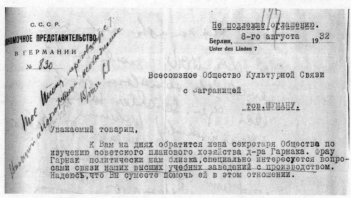

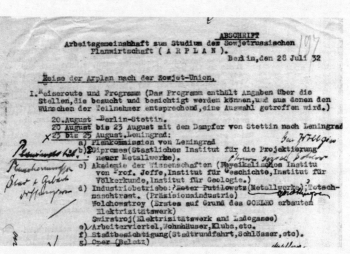

1.

Two months later, on August 8, 1935, a Russian named Alexander Hirschfeld approaches Arvid. Does he have a moment to talk?

The moment lasts three hours.

2.

Alexander Hirschfeld is an amiable, well-educated man who introduced himself to Arvid sometime in late 1931. Arvid was setting up ARPLAN then, and Hirschfeld volunteered to help. He drew up a list of prominent people who could be recruited into ARPLAN and invited Arvid to events at the Soviet embassy, where he introduced him to a slew of Russian diplomats and officials. Hirschfeld had a scholar's intellect—he would later write a doctoral dissertation on the Treaty of Versailles—and quickly earned Arvid's admiration. Arvid did not for a moment suspect that Hirschfeld had a hidden agenda.

In the summer of 1932, Arvid traveled to Moscow with ARPLAN's president, Friedrich Lenz, and a handpicked delegation of twenty-four German scholars, scientists, writers, and politicians. It was an ideologically diverse group representing both the left and right wings who sat in a large conference room and discussed the dire state of Germany's economy. The Soviet planned economy was a revolutionary model that appeared to be successful—could Germany adopt certain aspects of it? Hirschfeld orchestrated the three-week conference, sending Arvid and the others on tightly supervised tours of housing developments, farms, and power stations. They finished off with a jaunt to a seaside resort in Odessa.

Admiration gave way to trust. Arvid began to confide in Hirschfeld.

Hirschfeld helped set up another organization based in Berlin, called Bund Geistiger Berufe, or BGB. Outwardly, the BGB presented itself as a club for academics, scientists, and other working professionals that promoted goodwill between Germans and Russians and was unaffiliated with any particular political party, although many of its members were sympathetic to the left wing. In Hirschfeld's words, the BGB sought to "unite radical intellectuals along professional lines...under the banner of struggle." Arvid promptly joined the BGB.

Trust gave way to friendship. All the while, Arvid remained unaware that Hirschfeld was taking careful notes.

The BGB wasn't apolitical. It was, in fact, a cover organization established by the Communist Party with a secret purpose: to spread "ideological influence in those circles of the intelligentsia that, for various reasons, were hesitant to join a mass movement." Hirschfeld kept close tabs on the group and sent to Moscow membership lists, summaries of meetings, and profiles of members. Arvid, he wrote, is "very close to us" and "should be invited to the Soviet Union *at any cost.*"

In befriending Arvid, Hirschfeld was laying seed that he hoped to harvest later. That day has come.

Spies often work under diplomatic cover, and Alexander Hirschfeld is no exception. He holds a legitimate position as first secretary at the Soviet embassy in Berlin. He is also an authorized representative of a Soviet "friendship society" called the All-Union Society for Cultural Ties Abroad, otherwise known as VOKS. In both roles, he can cultivate relationships with Germans like Arvid, who may be of interest to Soviet intelligence, while slyly concealing that he is a military intelligence agent in the Red Army.

In the chummy jargon of Soviet espionage, the Red Army and the NKVD are *sosedi*—neighbors. Because the Red Army and the NKVD have overlapping jurisdictions—military intelligence and foreign intelligence—the agencies can be as rivalrous as siblings vying for parental favor. In this case, they have cooperated. Arvid is a valuable asset, and squabbling will get them nowhere.

3.

The two men find a place where they can talk freely. Hirschfeld warns Arvid that his work in the Circle is putting him at risk. It's far too dangerous to agitate so openly against Hitler. By cooperating with Soviet intelligence, Arvid can fight Hitler more effectively.

Hirschfeld makes a persuasive case. Still, Arvid isn't convinced. He's a German anti-fascist, not a spy for Moscow. He will not mindlessly obey orders.

Hirschfeld explains — patiently — that there are rules Arvid must follow. They are for his own protection. Arvid will be required to disassociate himself from left-wing groups, for example. Ties that carry even a taint of Communist ideology must be cut ruthlessly.

Arvid isn't sure he can agree to this. He would have to distance himself from so many old friends and acquaintances, as well as new friends like Adam Kuckhoff. Even if, theoretically, he cut these ties, he wouldn't know how to deliver intelligence to Russia without getting caught. He doesn't know the proper procedure. He has absolutely no training in espionage.

We will train you, Alexander Hirschfeld tells him. After the meeting, Hirschfeld writes a detailed memo that he sends to Moscow Center, headquarters for Soviet intelligence. Unquestionably, Hirschfeld is a good spy. Arvid regards him as an old pal from the glory days of ARPLAN, someone he can trust, which is precisely why Moscow Center sent him to do the wooing.

4.

Arvid is assigned a control officer named Naum Belkin. Fluent in Arabic, German, French, and Spanish, Belkin is a seasoned, cosmopolitan spy who has worked undercover in Yemen, Iran, Saudi Arabia, Uruguay, and Spain and who projects the supercilious air of an aristocrat. When posing for a photograph, he lifts his chin and holds his narrow nose high.

Belkin explains the rules of secrecy — *konspiratsia* — that Arvid must follow. Arvid insists he doesn't want to be treated as a spy. He will whisper secrets into Moscow's ear as a representative of the anti-fascist underground, nothing more. He will not accept money. He will not sign an oath of loyalty to Soviet intelligence.

Many men find Arvid admirably uncompromising. Belkin probably isn't one of them. An oath of loyalty is integral to the relationship between spy and spymaster. Without one, the risks to Moscow Center are pronounced. Still, whatever objections Belkin may have don't deter him from sending an enciphered memo to Moscow Center under the code name Kadi to confirm he has successfully recruited his target: Arvid Harnack, senior official in the Ministry of Economics.

Moscow Center opens a case file and gives Arvid his own code name: Balt.

Spies Among Us

1935–1936

1.

It has been two years since Martha Dodd set foot in Berlin, arriving just six months after Hitler was appointed chancellor. A magnificent train had roared into a magnificent station, palatial in its dimensions, with a soaring, barrel-vaulted roof, a marvel of steel. Pronouncing the name of the station, Lehrter Bahnhof, meant abandoning the flat, nasal vowels she'd grown accustomed to in Chicago. She would do her level best. She had a new role to play. The moment she stepped off the train, she underwent a regal transformation. No longer was she the daughter of Professor Dodd, a fusty, dusty scholar on the faculty of the University of Chicago, but of *Ambassador* Dodd. In the world of diplomacy, her father was at the very top of the hierarchy. A crowd surged onto the platform to greet her—her very own retinue of diplomats and newspapermen and photographers. Flashbulbs flashed, "a steady stream of blinding light," and she posed for them with orchids in her arms. In their eyes, she was a princess. The little hat she wore might as well have been a tiara.

Two years. For Martha, it has been a kaleidoscopic whirlwind of parties, extravagant dinners, and elegant teas with some of the most powerful and influential political figures in Germany, including Hjalmar Schacht, Hermann Göring, Joseph Goebbels, and—on one occasion—Hitler himself. As a fly on the sumptuous walls of the mansion she calls home—one room is covered in emerald damask, another in ruby tapestry, another in pink satin—Martha has a commanding view of the political stage. She catches snatches of confidential conversations between her father and his State Department colleagues who come over for dinner. In a letter to Thornton Wilder soon after her arrival, she writes, "I am told state secrets." A year later, she has even more to brag about.

> I have heard Schacht say not more than two weeks ago things that would make a roaring front cover headline and would probably bring the system crashing about his head (it will of course anyway)....I know some of the dirtiest tricks that are being played on the international chessboard mostly being played by the English who are swine from start to finish....My head is swollen with the snobbery I feel about being as success-ful as I am at balancing myself not less gracefully than the other 400,000 angels on the pin point of European security.

The drama of it all is fizzy, delicious; she bathes in it, guzzles it like champagne. Lately, though, Martha has been feeling low. Boris is still stuck in Moscow, and she's still madly in love with him. In his letters, he drops hints that he wants to marry her.

Martha has no idea that her Russian lover is already married, with a wife and child in Moscow. She also has no idea that Boris is a spy.

2.

On June 5, 1935—two weeks after Hitler's "peace" speech—Boris Vinogradov (code name Alex) sends an enciphered cable to the NKVD.

> The situation with the American woman (Martha Dodd) at present is as follows: She is currently in B., and I have received a letter from her in which she writes that she still loves me and dreams of marrying me.

3.

Six months later, while attending a lavish reception at the Soviet embassy, Martha bumps into a dark-haired man with a strong Russian accent. He strikes up a conversation with her, introducing himself as Dmitri Bukhartsev. He says he's a journalist who works for the newspaper *Izvestia*.

The job with *Izvestia* is his cover. He's actually a spy, code name Emir.

Dmitri has a weak chin and a strong gaze. His career as a journalist is impressive. He has worked at *Komsomolskaya Pravda* and as bureau chief of the Russian news agency TASS. Martha finds Dmitri so agreeable that she sees him again and again. She tells him all about the "swinish behavior" displayed by Ambassador Bullitt, a man she believes is unfit to be U.S. ambassador to the Soviet Union. She tells him all about her father, too, confiding details about a letter Ambassador Dodd wrote to the State Department in Washington, DC. She lets it be known that, as the daughter of a diplomat, she's privy to numerous secrets of this sort. Dmitri knows this, of course. It is precisely why the NKVD has targeted her.

4.

It doesn't take much persuasion to convince Martha to become a spy. Dmitri explains that he will be her control officer. Martha doesn't know what a control officer is, but she is an eager student and will learn everything she needs to learn. She tells him she is "intensively" reading a book written by Stalin. It's an English translation of the Russian, and her teacher is deeply knowledgeable. Dmitri notes the teacher's name—"Harnack." Dmitri cables a top-secret memo to Moscow Center:

> Martha says that the main interest in her life is secret assistance to the cause of the revolution. She agrees to use her position to work in this direction, provided that the possibility of blowing her cover or discrediting her father is eliminated.

Beheadings Are Back

1935–1936

1.

It's monstrous but true: beheadings are back.

Hitler's regime has revived this gruesome punishment, which was effectively banned during the Weimar Republic. By 1935, the death penalty is mandated for forty-seven crimes and recommended for 2,539 others. The definition of a *crime* has expanded to include "attacks on the national community," and the definition of *attacks* has expanded to include just about anything anyone does to oppose Hitler.

Beheadings are carried out at a prison in Berlin called Plötzensee. The executioner there is Karl Gröpler, a sixty-five-year-old man who makes a modest living as the owner of a laundry. Gröpler's contract with the Reich Ministry of Justice states that he is responsible for bringing his own chopping block, bench, and ax to the beheadings, all of which he carries out with theatrical precision in the prison courtyard. Usually in attendance are several court officials, a representative from the state attorney's office, a member of the clergy, a physician, an official from Plötzensee, and a cluster of witnesses, who all watch Gröpler stride into a bright spotlight wearing a black top hat, a black tailcoat, and spotless white gloves. Three young men—Gröpler's assistants—lead the prisoner to the bench and position the chopping block under the prisoner's head. The state prosecutor reads aloud the death sentence and a court official gives the directive: "Executioner, do your duty." Gröpler raises his ax and brings it down.

In 1935, seventy-nine men and nine women are beheaded by Gröpler.

Beheadings at Plötzensee aren't a secret. Lurid details are splashed across the pages of German newspapers and make headlines in the United States.

The beheadings of two young women charged with treason scandalized readers of the *Washington Post,* which published an article on February 24, 1935, under the tabloid-worthy headline HERR HITLER HAD AXES TO GRIND. The *New York Times,* the *Chicago Daily Tribune,* and *Time* magazine also covered the story. American readers were treated to descriptions of Gröpler's macabre costume, his white-gloved grip on the ax. A prison guard who watched the beheadings provided all the details about the two women: how they walked calmly to the chopping block, one at a time, dressed in blue prison garments, their wrists shackled behind their backs; how they didn't have to be dragged to the scaffold as men often do. "What impressed us most," the guard said, "was that neither of them murmured a single word."

In Germany, the names of these young women—Baroness Benita von Falkenhayn and Renate von Natzmer—are known to anyone who reads *Völkischer Beobachter,* the Nazi Party newspaper controlled by Goebbels, which ran a sensationalistic front-page article about their alleged crime. The women were caught whispering military secrets to a handsome Polish diplomat, according to the article, secrets that concerned a new type of German airplane being manufactured in a Berlin factory. Hitler himself rejected their appeals for clemency. Treason, he warned, would not be tolerated.

2.

At the BAG, Mildred continues to serenade her students with American protest songs. "John Brown's Body" is especially resonant now. John Brown was executed the same way some German men in the resistance will be executed: by slow strangulation, on gallows constructed with sadistic care. Not now, but in due time, after the Gestapo catches up with them. Their crime? Same as John Brown's: treason.

Many German women in the resistance will be executed in a manner that is equally barbarous: by guillotine. Why aren't these women hanged? From the Nazi point of view, the supple necks of the weaker sex must be treated differently, and a blade kills more quickly than a rope. It is the Nazis' special perversity to make such a distinction, to view head-chopping as more humane than hanging.

They are gruesome, these stories, and they seem to circle around Mildred. Stories about treason, death by hanging—decapitation too.

3.

A headless man. Mildred had shuddered, hearing the story. Arvid's cousin Ernst von Harnack told it to her a few years ago when she stopped by for a visit.

It didn't help that Ernst and Anne von Harnack lived in a stone castle with a dungeon built during the Middle Ages. A labyrinthian hallway echoed ominously when Ernst led her to the room where she would sleep. From the window, she could see the Saale River etching its way through the hills of Merseburg, a town that was so quiet at night that she could hear the scampering of mice.

Centuries ago, Ernst told her, a page who had worked in the castle somehow found himself in trouble. Did he displease a monarch? Probably so. Did the punishment fit the crime? Probably not. Whatever his crime, the blade came down, slicing off his head. Now a headless ghost haunts the rooms of the castle. *Especially,* Ernst said, *your room.*

Mildred had lived in Germany long enough to develop a feel for what passed as German wit. She knew Ernst was teasing. Still, long after she'd said good night, she lay awake in the low-ceilinged bedroom as a headless apparition slipped through cold stone walls and hovered above her bed. Ernst had put the image into her head; now she couldn't get rid of it.

In the raw light of morning, Mildred wrote a letter to her mother and confessed that she never wanted to sleep in Ernst and Anne's castle again.

4.

One spring evening after a class at the BAG, Mildred walks with her student Emil along Tauentzienstrasse, a wide boulevard near the Tiergarten. They're heading to the S-Bahn station by the Berlin Zoo. Emil has written anti-Nazi leaflets under the alias Emko for a Communist resistance group and suffered the blows of batons under Gestapo interrogation. Emil suspects he may be under Gestapo surveillance. Still, he won't stop fighting Hitler. Emil wants to help the Circle. He knows two bookshop owners with secret stashes of banned books.

Mildred and Emil are so deep in conversation, Emil writes later, that they don't notice the commotion ahead. People are thronging the entrance of a movie theater. SS officers shove them aside, shouting at them to move. The grand doors open and a man emerges. The crowd erupts, cheering as if the man were a matinee idol.

It's Hitler. The sinister smudge of his mustache. His eyes startlingly blue.

A middle-aged woman swoons, crying out, "What an historic moment!"

Mildred and Emil walk on in silence. They reach the S-Bahn station. They nod goodbye. *We still have so much work to do.* This is what Emil thinks. He knows Mildred is thinking it too. Words are unnecessary.

5.

The Nazis close down the BAG. Mildred has lost a primary source for recruitment.

A number of her students ask if they can stay in contact with her. Sometimes they pile into a café. Sometimes they fill Mildred's apartment. She makes tea for them all, boiling the water on her white porcelain stove. They sit in the living room and talk for hours, Mildred jumping up from the sofa every now and then to put the kettle on again or read aloud a passage from an American novel banned by Goebbels's censors. She wants them all to see "the new developments in Germany with fresh eyes."

Widerstand

1935–1937

1.

Resistance takes two forms: passive and active.

Passive acts of resistance are called *Resistenz*. Refusing to fly Germany's new flag—a giant swastika—is one example. Refusing to say "Heil Hitler" is another. Buy a train ticket, walk into a shop—every transaction is freighted with the expectation that you will initiate or conclude it with these words. Some take the risk, pay the price: arrest, a stint behind bars or worse. Some find a substitute expression. Saying *Grüss Gott*—God bless you—is a useful way to dodge *Heil Hitler.*

Active acts of resistance are called *Widerstand*. Help a Jewish friend escape Germany, and you are performing an act of *Widerstand*. Write a leaflet that criticizes Hitler's regime, slip one into someone's mailbox or coat pocket, smuggle some into a train station, and you are engaging in *Widerstand*. These crimes are punishable by a year or two in a concentration camp.

Arvid's espionage is another example of *Widerstand*.

2.

Mildred has been leading meetings of the Circle for about a year now. Arvid's got little time to spare these days, but even if he could manage to squeeze in a meeting, the rules of *konspiratsia* have him in a bind. He is forbidden to associate with Communists and Social Democrats, and the Circle is chock-full of them.

If Mildred is busy, her devoted BAG recruit Karl Behrens steps in. Karl's round wire-framed spectacles and intelligent gaze resemble Arvid's, but in other respects he's very different. His life has been harder. He boasts no family pedigree that eases his way into the clubs and inner circles of the elite.

Karl has left his job at the gas-lamp factory. Now he works as a locksmith at AEG, a company that produces electric motors, steam turbines, transformers, cables, switches, and fuses. Karl doesn't know that AEG contributed sixty thousand Reichsmark to the Nazi Party at the meeting Hitler held a month after he was appointed chancellor. What he knows is that business appears to be going well. He smuggles in copies of an underground anti-Nazi newspaper called *Der Gegen-Angriff* (Counterattack). Its name is a direct response to the Nazi newspaper *Der Angriff* (Attack).

After a meeting, Mildred turns on her Blaupunkt, careful to keep the volume low. She presses an ear to the speaker. Through the pops and squeals, she can hear a BBC program. President Roosevelt is giving a speech. Mildred scribbles furiously. She translates what she's written into German, types the words onto sheets of paper that are then transformed into leaflets. The Circle smuggles them into Berlin's factories, leaving them in small piles for workers to discover.

3.

On September 15, 1935, the Law for the Protection of German Blood and German Honor is passed. Sex between Jews and non-Jews is now illegal. It is also illegal for Jews to marry non-Jews. A woman with "German blood" under the age of forty-five cannot work in a Jewish house, as she might tempt a Jewish man to have sex with her, which could result in a mixed-blood baby, a *Mischling*. Jews in violation of this law face penalties that include hard labor, imprisonment, and a fine.

On the same day, the Reich Citizenship Law is passed. It explicitly excludes Jews from citizenship in Germany.

These two laws will come to be known as the Nuremberg Laws. Now Germany has established an explicit legal framework for the marginalization of Jews, the segregation of Jews, the confinement of Jews, and, ultimately, the extermination of Jews.

4.

Mildred will help Jews escape. She reaches this decision easily, knowing that she can exploit her ties to the U.S. embassy through her relationships with former Consul General Messersmith and Ambassador Dodd and, with deft and subtle maneuvering, obtain the visas Jews require to cross the German border.

A Jewish editor named Max Tau asks if she can do anything for him. Mildred orchestrates Tau's escape to Norway.

A Jewish student at the BAG lingers after class. Samson Knoll wants to escape to the United States. Also, he has a relative who knows someone who wants to flee Germany. Mildred discreetly makes the necessary arrangements.

5.

Over a fourteen-month period in 1935 and 1936, 2,197 people in underground resistance groups in Berlin are arrested. Over twelve thousand people across Germany are arrested in 1936 for distributing anti-Nazi leaflets.

Two of Mildred's BAG recruits are arrested.

Karl Behrens is accused of distributing copies of *Der Gegen-Angriff*. In prison, Behrens is beaten, interrogated, beaten some more, then released. The Gestapo officer who interrogated him, a stickler for proper protocol, uncovered no evidence. Behrens confessed to nothing.

Wilhelm Utech is caught red-handed. The Gestapo confiscates his leaflets and hauls him to a concentration camp, where he languishes for a year.

6.

The others don't stop. They smuggle leaflets into phone booths and U-Bahn stations, stuff them into people's coat pockets, fold them into envelopes. Someone writes addresses, someone else slaps on stamps. The addresses belong to journalists, politicians, professors, members of the Catholic Church.

"We kept strict discipline and secrecy," recalled Günther Weisenborn, a member of Gegner Kreis, an underground group that will soon intersect with the Circle. "We were divided into a series of subgroups which distributed leaflets in many factories." The factories in Berlin are crammed with die-hard Communists and Nazis. Extreme left and extreme right work shoulder to shoulder. Tattletales are everywhere. If Weisenborn slips a leaflet into the wrong hands, the Gestapo will hear about it.

"Our work was both exciting and nerve-racking," Weisenborn admitted.

They disguise their meetings as cocktail receptions, potluck dinners, birthday parties. "To any outsider our meetings would have seemed like convivial gatherings," recalled a doctor named Elfriede Paul. "Some people came later, some left earlier. In any case, we deliberated until late at night whenever a special question had to be addressed or a particular action planned."

Elfriede Paul agrees to host meetings at her clinic after she sees her final patient of the day. Others host meetings in basements, attics, living rooms.

7.

In 1936, the Gestapo collects 1,643,200 leaflets denouncing the Nazi regime. The number is noted meticulously in their records, a testament to an underground resistance Hitler wants to quash. The Gestapo obtains the leaflets in various ways: by seizing them from the hands of opponents, by raiding homes and discovering them in drawers or behind walls or under floorboards, or by more devious methods.

An ordinary citizen who finds a leaflet in her mailbox can report the offense to the local police station. The Gestapo relies on citizens like this to assist in policing neighborhoods and rooting out the resistance. As the number of snitches and gossips and snoops and denouncers increases, the Gestapo develops a classification system, distinguishing between an *Informationsperson* (information person), a *Wahrmann* (truth man), a *Gewährsmann* (informer), a *Gegnermann* (opponent man), a *Zuverlässigerperson* (reliable person), and an *Auskunftmann* (information man). At the top of the hierarchy are elite informers called *Vertrauensmänner* (men of confidence), designated as "VM" in Gestapo reports. VM are paid Gestapo spies who write their reports in code and deposit them in designated postboxes. Often, they masquerade as Hitler's enemies. In the language of espionage, they are moles. The most skillful VM penetrate a resistance group's inner core and befriend its members, earning their trust, learning their secrets, reporting it all to the Gestapo.

8.

During the first three months of 1936, Hitler keeps telling the world that he wants *peace*.

On January 10, he says,

There is not a single German who desires war.

On January 30, he says,

Just as we have always preached peace in the domestic life of our people, so we wish also to be a peace-loving force among other people. We cannot repeat that too often.

On March 16, he says,

My aim is peace.

9.

On March 7, 1936, Hitler orders 3,300 soldiers to march into the Rhineland, a region in Germany that borders France. The maneuver is another blatant violation of the Treaty of Versailles, which designates the region as a demilitarized zone. Germany is not allowed to erect fortifications or train any troops here. Strictly speaking, if a single soldier shouldering a loaded Mauser rifle plants a single boot onto the Rhineland, it is a breach of the treaty.

No bullets are fired that day. The maneuver is a kind of performance, a powerful piece of theater. Hitler has alerted the world that Germany won't be crippled by a punishing treaty any longer. He's gambling that he'll get away with it.

He does.

10.

That summer, the Spanish Civil War erupts.

Hitler sends German soldiers and munitions to Franco, who is leading a fascist military coup against Spain's newly elected democratic government. Göring is delighted about the deal, seeing it as a prime opportunity to test out his brand-new air force, the Luftwaffe. Germans won't learn about any of this by reading a censored newspaper or listening to their People's Radios, so Gegner Kreis produces a slew of leaflets.

A Jewish artist named Elisabeth Schumacher designs them. She spends countless hours devising ingenious ways to produce leaflets of varying sizes, minimizing words and photographs so they can fit on paper as small as a postage stamp. "Night after night," Elfriede Paul recalled, "she photographed images from the Spanish Civil War, minimizing texts, even poems." The leaflets include details about the number of troops, tanks, submarines, and aircraft that Franco receives from Hitler. These details are snatched from top-secret documents by an officer in the Reich Ministry of Aviation who, like Arvid, is posing as a Nazi and stealing secrets. He is Harro Schulze-Boysen, the twenty-six-year-old leader of Gegner Kreis.

11.

Harro Schulze-Boysen visits Mildred and Arvid's apartment. In the book-crammed living room of Woyrschstrasse 46, the three of them have a lively discussion about the resistance. Harro is tall and blond and lean. He has already spent time in a concentration camp. Scars on his chiseled chin and cheekbones bear evidence of torture. One of his ears is mutilated, more than half of it hacked off. His crime was "preparations for high treason." He published an anti-Nazi underground newspaper called *Gegner* (Opponent) until SS officers raided the office and smashed the printing press. They dragged Harro and another *Gegner* writer to a concentration camp on the outskirts of Berlin, where they were stripped naked and flogged with lead-weighted whips. After Harro was released, the pain in his kidneys was so severe that he had to be hospitalized. His friend's injuries were even worse. He died.

Unquestionably, Harro Schulze-Boysen is a fierce and charismatic anti-fascist, but he makes Mildred and Arvid uneasy. His light blue eyes seem too bright, shining with the recklessness of a man with a vendetta. An alliance with Harro, they decide, would be "too dangerous."

Ernst and Ernst

1935–1937

1.

"I have put my revenge in cold storage," Harro Schulze-Boysen told Ernst von Salomon shortly after he was released from the concentration camp. Harro ran into him on a crowded sidewalk in Berlin. Harro's face was so disfigured that Ernst didn't recognize his friend at first. "His features were very different," Ernst reflected years later in a memoir. "He had lost half an ear and his face was covered with inflamed wounds that had scarcely healed."

2.

Ernst von Salomon has spent time behind bars, though for entirely different reasons than Schulze-Boysen. He drove the getaway car for the men who assassinated Foreign Minister Walther Rathenau in 1922, attempted a murder in 1927, and tried to bomb the Reichstag in 1929. Since then, he has written four novels. His publisher is Ernst Rowohlt, the publishing titan who founded Rowohlt Verlag and who stands at the center of a web of social and professional connections that link Ernst von Salomon to Mildred. Among these links are Thomas Wolfe and Hans Fallada (aka Rudolf Ditzen), both published by Rowohlt, and Martha Dodd, who has invited Ernst Rowohlt and Ernst von Salomon to countless parties, hoping to curry favor with men in publishing who can help her when she writes a book of her own.

3.

"Martha Dodd invited me to her receptions and parties," Ernst von Salomon wrote in his memoir, "where dignified servants in white gloves passed mildly opalescent and mildly intoxicating cocktails together with little slices of white bread covered with pale, chopped vegetables and herbs." Her guests were

> smart young men with perfect manners and an imperfect knowledge of languages: some wore the elegant black uniform of the Foreign Ministry, which so discouragingly resembled that of the SS; a great number of the guests were real SS men.

It was a fantastically odd assemblage. Nowhere but Berlin would you find Hitler's ministry men and SS thugs intermingling with American, French, and Russian diplomats. Usually, Ernst von Salomon stood alone, watching them "smiling attractively or laughing gaily at Martha Dodd's witty sallies." He "decided gloomily" that Martha's suitors were "easier on the eye" than he.

Ernst von Salomon bears a striking resemblance to Alfred Hitchcock, wattles and all, and smokes a nearly identical calabash pipe. Still, the four novels he has published coupled with his reputation as a murderer ensure that his mailbox overflows with invitations that are "printed on the most expensive paper—skillfully lithographed invitations to social gatherings presided over by highly placed personages, by powerful patrons of the arts, by revolutionary organizations in full bloom, by greatly respected establishments both national and foreign." He much prefers the "clear vodka, caviar, and trout in aspic" served at Russian embassy soirees to the "thin-blooded cocktails" and tasteless canapés he chokes down at American embassy events. "I only very rarely got drunk," Ernst von Salomon recalled, "unlike Rowohlt."

4.

Ernst Rowohlt is under siege. Not since he founded Rowohlt Verlag, in 1908, has he been in such danger of going out of business. The list of writers his publishing house can no longer publish is punishingly long, and continues to lengthen. Any author who comes within sniffing distance of a left-wing political party is added to the list, as is anyone who is a Jew or who seems sympathetic to Jews. Ernst Rowohlt is proud that his list of American authors includes the mighty Hemingway, but even Hemingway has been deemed *verboten* by the Nazis, who have decided that his novel *A Farewell to Arms* is too critical of war, the work of a dangerous pacifist. Rowohlt scrambles to negotiate contracts with writers who have fled Germany and are now living in exile in other countries—Switzerland, France, and America are common destinations—and racks his brain for sly ways to evade Nazi censors, who are ruthless and frequently inept.

Two frowning men appear at the doorway. They aren't wearing uniforms, but they are clearly Gestapo.

Ernst Rowohlt, a big man with a booming voice, invites them into his office and, with the graciousness he shows his most trusted friends, offers them cigars. They refuse.

"What good news do you bring me?" Ernst Rowohlt booms.

One of the officers replies in a clipped monotone that they have come to seize all copies of *Babbitt*. The title of the novel, spit from the lips of this German, sounds like *Bahbiett*.

Ernst Rowohlt opens a bottle of schnapps, pours himself a glass— he doesn't offer any to the Gestapo—and leans back luxuriantly in his chair. "A publishing house isn't a place where books are written, typed, printed, bound, packed, and sold," he says, "but rather what you might call the administrative headquarters which controls all these disparate activities, or the roof which covers a host of specialized forms of production." He takes a sip of schnapps and continues, dreamily: "So if you wish to seize *Bahbiett* you must go to the place where it is to be found, namely to the printers or to the bookshops, but not to me. Apart from that, *Bahbiett* is not published by me but by the Transmare-Verlag, which was wound up some years ago. Furthermore *Bahbiett* is not the book you are after. It is by Sinclair Lewis. The author you have in mind is Upton Sinclair, who is likewise not published by me. Nor has he been published in Germany these many years."

A look of confusion spreads over the Gestapo officers' faces. One of them says, "In that case we must use the telephone."

After they are gone, Ernst Rowohlt emerges from his office, grinning widely. The editors who have been eavesdropping on the conversation gaze at their boss in astonishment, knowing full well that Rowohlt told the Gestapo two monstrous lies. Upton Sinclair isn't the author of *Babbitt;* Sinclair Lewis is. And Rowohlt *did* publish novels by Sinclair Lewis, who in 1930 had the honor of being the first American ever to win the Nobel Prize in Literature. Rowohlt is exceedingly proud that he had the foresight to acquire the rights to all of Sinclair Lewis's novels, and he has put his son, Heinrich Ledig-Rowohlt, in charge of them.

5.

It has been over a year since Mildred, Heinrich Ledig-Rowohlt, Martha Dodd, and Boris Vinogradov piled into a convertible Ford Cabriolet and sped off to the country to visit Rudolf Ditzen, aka Hans Fallada. After the trip, Mildred wondered whether her talks with Rudolf would have a positive influence on him. It seemed so, at first. He stopped pandering to Nazi censors and in a letter declared with fresh resolve, "I have nothing to hide and I am not going to keep my eyes shut."

But his resolve quickly wore off. Every time Rudolf Ditzen sat down to write, he felt constrained by self-consciousness. He couldn't stop thinking about the audience for his work. Nazi censors invaded his imagination, hovering insidiously over his typewriter, condemning and scrutinizing each half-formed thought. Words stuttered out of him limp and lifeless. The stress of writing wore him down completely.

On April 29, 1935, Ditzen announces, "I can't write anymore," and suffers a full-blown nervous breakdown. His wife, Suse, packs his suitcase and sends him off to the Charité hospital in Berlin, where he is now receiving treatment for hallucinations. The psychiatrist presiding over Ditzen's treatment is Karl Bonhoeffer, father of Arvid's cousins Dietrich and Klaus.

6.

One evening in 1936, Ernst von Salomon stands in the hallway of Mildred and Arvid's apartment. Ernst isn't alone. His girlfriend, Ille, stands beside him, as does Harro Schulze-Boysen. Harro is the reason they're here. He received an invitation to a small party Mildred and Arvid are hosting tonight, and he asked Ernst and Ille to join him. Behind the door are the muted sounds of revelry.

More than a year has passed since Harro was last here. Hitler's military aid to Franco on the battlefields of the Spanish Civil War has increased; so have Harro's efforts to sabotage the Führer, but he doesn't breathe a word about Gegner Kreis or the leaflets they produce to friends like Ernst von Salomon, whose allegiances are tricky to pin down. Harro knows Ernst hates Nazis, though he's not a Communist or a Social Democrat. He's sympathetic to conservative points of view and used to write for a right-wing newspaper.

Ernst and Ille live in the same neighborhood as Harro, who drives an old though stylish automobile and spends Sundays in his sailboat, maneuvering it over the windswept lakes of Wannsee. Harro has piercing blue eyes, wheat-colored hair, and a winning smile. He wears his scars well. He is as handsome as he is cagey. Ernst senses that Harro is up to something at the Reich Ministry of Aviation and presses him.

"I stick flags into maps," Harro tells him wryly. "All sorts of prettily colored little flags into very ugly old maps."

The front door swings open. Mildred introduces herself and invites them in.

Ernst has bumped into her several times already at social gatherings, including events at the Russian and the American embassies. He knows Mildred and Arvid have "an assured place in diplomatic circles."

He takes in the surroundings with the eye of a novelist. He notes the furniture in the apartment, the size of the room where the guests are mingling. He observes the mantelpiece, how Mildred and Arvid lean against it while carrying on a conversation. There are about a dozen people here, a motley crew of diplomats, writers, businessmen, and bureaucrats from Hitler's ministries.

After an hour or so, Ernst and Ille say their goodbyes and head to the front door.

Ille can barely contain herself. Usually, she waits until she's on the street before she starts gossiping. But the moment the door closes, she blurts, "It looks all wrong to me. I feel there's something very, very wrong."

Ille describes the way Mildred and Arvid were "quite casually discussing things . . . things, well, any one of the things they discussed could cost them their heads."

Ernst says nothing. They descend four flights of stairs. "Promise me this!" Ille cries. "Promise we'll never go there again!"

It's dark out. They walk along Woyrschstrasse, heading home.

"They stand there, well-dressed, decent-looking people, and they talk about 'cross-channels of communication'—do you know what that means?" Ille pauses, aghast. "They describe Hitler and Himmler," she goes on, "as utter fools."

Ille overheard one of the party guests talking about a "source" in Zurich. She watched him hand a "yellow envelope" to another man, who glanced at her and said, with a wink, "Strictly confidential."

Was that a joke? Or were there secrets in the yellow envelope? When she cautiously introduced herself to these men, she learned that one was "a ministerial Councillor" and the other was "an adjutant." They promptly introduced her to their friend who was "in the SS" and to another man who was "a diplomat."

Ille gasps, remembering, and glares at Ernst. "Tell me, can you understand it all?"

"Yes, yes, that's the way it is," Ernst says.

"And Harro, good old Harro," Ille cries. "I heard him saying to another man—they were discussing somebody: 'He's another dull fellow we'll have to shoot.' Harro! Our old Harro talking about shooting people. . . . But I won't hear any more about shooting people! I won't! I don't want to have people shooting people here and people shooting people there, and who shoots who? I won't have it!"

"I won't either," Ernst says. He wants to go home now. He doesn't want to stand here in the street talking about shooting.

"Do you know what they're up to, those people? They're starting a revolution."

Ernst and Ille have reached Friedrichstrasse. He urges her to keep walking, but she won't budge. She shouts in the dark, "I've had enough of revolutions!"

7.

Ernst von Salomon decides to sever his relationship with Harro Schulze-Boysen. He promises Ille he will never go sailing on the Wannsee or canoeing around the Spreewald or even speak to their friend from the Reich Air Ministry ever again.

But first, he wants to say goodbye.

Ernst and Harro trade a few witticisms. Then Ernst grows serious. He tells Harro that his activities in the resistance are dangerous. And more — they're treasonous. He is committing "a crime."

Harro's winning smile fades. His eyes harden.

"Inactivity," Harro says, is "the greatest crime of all."

8.

In 1937 there are only six men in Harro Schulze-Boysen's resistance group. If Gegner Kreis and the Circle worked together, they could expand their reach, but Mildred and Arvid remain reluctant. For the time being, the groups will fight fascism separately.

Still, a chain is beginning to form.

In 1937 Greta Lorke gets pregnant and marries her boyfriend, Adam Kuckhoff, forging a link in the chain connecting his resistance group, Tat Kreis, with the Circle.

Gegner Kreis will form a third link in the chain three years from now, when the world is on fire.

Identity Crisis

1936–1937

1.

Mildred and Arvid pack their belongings at Woyrschstrasse 46. They're moving again. The street is the same. The apartment building is just a few blocks north, a stone's throw away from the old one. Mildred writes her new address on an envelope — Woyrschstrasse 16 — and mails a letter to her mother.

The proximity of their new apartment to Gestapo headquarters is unnerving. Only one mile away. Mildred frequently sees Gestapo officers driving in her neighborhood. Sometimes the men are in uniform; sometimes they're not. They're easy to spot in their glossy black Mercedes sedans crawling around the streets like wicked beetles.

2.

Among Berliners it's well known that the Gestapo keeps a card file on every agitator or suspected agitator who could threaten Hitler's regime. Mildred wonders whether her own name is on a card. It's possible, certainly possible.

Any day now, she might hear Gestapo fists pounding on her front door. Or she could open her mailbox and find a letter in it instructing her to report to Prinz-Albrecht-Strasse 8 for questioning. The letter would put her in an impossible bind. If she didn't report to Gestapo headquarters, she could be arrested. If she did report to Gestapo headquarters, she could also be arrested.

Every neighborhood has a Nazi "block warden." Mildred spots him in his brown uniform ornamented with gold banding and red epaulettes strolling up and down the sidewalk. If he sees her slipping a leaflet into a phone booth or overhears her criticizing Hitler, he will report her. Block wardens are the eyes and ears of the Gestapo. There are over two hundred thousand block wardens right now, a number that will soon grow to two million. In Berlin's factories, foremen take over the role of the block wardens. A worker at the weapons manufacturer Friedrich Krupp remembered, "You couldn't say anything, the foreman was always standing behind you."

Her friends are disappearing. Are they in hiding, waiting to see how wide a net the Gestapo will cast? Or have they been arrested? If they're languishing in prison cells somewhere, Mildred would have no way of knowing. If someone in the Circle doesn't show up for a meeting, she can reasonably assume the worst.

3.

Himmler, the sadistic former chicken farmer who has distinguished himself by leading the SS and masterminding the construction of concentration camps, presides over the rapid expansion of the Nazi police state. The SD (Sicherheitsdienst des Reichsführers-SS, or Security Service) is a division of the SS that will grow to become a vast intelligence agency. The Gestapo and the criminal police (Kriminalpolizei, or Kripo) will be integrated under the name SiPo (Sicherheitspolizei). Eventually, the SD and SiPo will merge into one centralized agency called the RSHA (Reichssicherheits-hauptamt, or Reich Security Main Office), a massive, metastasizing bureaucracy divided into seven main offices and at least a hundred departments and subdepartments that collectively aim to defeat all enemies of Germany, both inside and outside its borders.

Göring has a rash of new responsibilities. His collection of official titles is already considerable, including minister of the interior for Prussia, minister of aviation, commissar for raw materials and for-eign currency, commander in chief of the Luftwaffe, and Reich master of the hunt and of the forests. On October 18, 1936, Hitler puts him in charge of the Four-Year Plan, an ambitious scheme to boost employment, stimulate coal production, amass rubber, metal, and fuel, and make Germany's economy entirely self-sufficient within four years. Göring promptly holds a secret meeting. He invites men from Hitler's ministries and a bunch of tycoons who run Germany's largest companies, including I. G. Farben.

> The battle we are now approaching demands a colossal measure of production capacity.... We are already on the threshold of mobilization and we are already at war. All that is lacking is the actual shooting.

The primary objective of the Four-Year Plan is to prepare Germany for war. In a confidential memo, Hitler writes,

> Just as we are now producing 700,000 or 800,000 tons of petroleum, we could be producing 3 million tons. Just as we are today manufacturing a few thousand tons of rubber, we could already be producing 70,000 or 80,000 tons per year. Just as we have stepped up the production of iron ore from 2½ million tons to 7 million tons, so we could be processing 20 or 25 million tons of German iron ore, and if necessary even 30 million....

> I thus set the following task:
> The German army must be operational within four years.
> The German economy must be fit for war within four years.

4.

After much agonizing, Arvid joins the Nazi Party, becoming member number 4153569. His cover is, at last, complete.

Dozens of men at the Deutscher Klub consider Arvid their friend. Some are rabidly fascist, some are naive opportunists, some are in the underground resistance. Some become his sources.

The NKVD is suitably impressed. The German who adamantly refused to be considered a spy is proving himself to be as shrewd and effective as a seasoned paid agent. The reports in Arvid's file reveal that he consistently supplies Moscow Center with high-grade intelligence, including

valuable documentary materials on the German currency and
economy
secret summary tables of all Germany's investments abroad
the German foreign debt
secret lists of goods liable to importation into Germany.

5.

Meanwhile, Mildred convincingly plays the part of a Nazi wife, carrying on her own masquerade.

To keep her job at the BAG she was required to join a Nazi teachers' union, a mandate imposed by the Nazi regime in 1933. Now she strengthens her Aryan credentials by joining the Daughters of the American Revolution—which requires her to submit proof of bloodline lineage—and assuming a leadership position in the Berlin-based chapter of the organization. At social events with Arvid's colleagues, she proves herself capable of slipping seamlessly into the persona of the sort of wife they would approve of, pretending she's an American woman who is as loyal to the Nazi cause as her German husband is.

By all indications, the Nazis are fooled. Even Moscow is aware of how effectively she plays her role. In a memo that will turn up in an NKVD file she is described as

bold, tall, blue eyes... typically German-looking... an intensely Nordic type.

Mildred appears to be the perfect complement to Arvid, who is

also blond, blue eyed (wears glasses)... very Nordic looking.

As a couple, Mildred and Arvid both have "good contacts with Nazi women and men."

6.

She is Mildred Harnack. Sometimes she's Mildred Fish-Harnack. Sometimes she's Mildred Harnack-Fish.

She is a woman.

She is a wife.

She is an American.

Sometimes she's an American leader of a German resistance group. Sometimes she's the American wife of a German in the resistance. Sometimes she's the American wife of a Nazi.

Once, Mildred was recognizable to herself. Now, she isn't.

It happens slowly, bit by bit. She wouldn't have been able to pinpoint the exact moment when she looked in the mirror and saw another woman gazing back. She is the same, more or less—same hair, skin, nose, chin—but do her eyes give her away? Do they shine a bit too brightly, betraying flashes of fear? Not consistently, but at odd moments, when she thinks she's unobserved?

It's in this state of mind, perhaps, that Mildred boards a steamer ship and goes home.

VII

Homecoming

1937

1.

The Mili they see is not the Mili they remember. She's twitchy. Jumpy. Walking around Milwaukee, she doesn't look like someone who once lived here. She looks like a stranger. Before talking to anyone, she glances over her shoulder and then from side to side. In Berlin, it's called *der deutsche Blick*—the German look—but no one knows this. All they know is that Mili is acting oddly.

It has been more than seven years since they last saw her. She can't stay long. She's on what she calls a lecture tour, which means she'll head off soon. She mentions some cities: Chicago, Philadelphia, New York. The very word *lecture* is off-putting to the Fish family. *Lecture.* Like she's telling people what to do. *Lecture.* Like she's all hoity-toity.

Marbeau Fish—everyone calls him Bob—takes her around the dairy farm where he rents a patch of land. Bob remembers the day she got married here. Everyone in the family was happy for Mili then, even as they allowed that she might be making a mistake marrying Arvid. Now, Bob Fish considers the possibility that they'd been right. His sister's strange behavior is getting stranger. She seems uncomfortable at home. She used to crack jokes. Now she doesn't even crack a smile.

Why Mili waited so long to visit, nobody knows. But they may have guessed why she's here now: she misses her mother. Mildred is thirty-four and childless. This strikes the Fish family as the biggest tragedy of all. Mildred has always been headstrong, but that shouldn't stop her from getting pregnant. Look at Harriette. Look at Marion. Mildred's older sisters are plenty headstrong, and they have six children between them. And look at Georgina, who reared them all, a woman who is so headstrong she refuses all medicine, even if she's suffering.

Mildred spends several days at Bob's home in Evansville, "much of the time in private conversation." On the last night, to his considerable alarm, she murmurs in a voice barely above a whisper that "she knew she had been followed out of Germany & was, in fact, under surveillance." Right now. At this very moment, outside the house. Bob Fish glances out the window, sees nothing out of the ordinary, and considers the possibility that his sister is crazy.

2.

Francis Birch is puzzled when Mildred doesn't show up at the train station. She'd called him to let him know the date she would arrive in Cambridge, Massachusetts, and asked whether he and his wife would mind if she stayed the night. Of course not, he told her.

Francis carried a torch for Mildred at Western High. During their senior year they'd spent countless hours together. They were both in Miss Merrill's journalism class; they both wrote for the school newspaper, the *Western Breeze;* and they both signed up to be editors of the yearbook. Sometimes they shared the same table at the cafeteria, where he watched her negotiate the puzzle of which polished fork was the correct one for salad. She was different from the well-to-do girls he knew, girls with impeccable table manners. Mildred's articles for the *Western Breeze* tackled numerous topics. Her conversations, too, ranged far and wide. Francis found her admirably "introspective" and "concerned with things." Francis had an abiding interest in science; he would go on to get a doctorate in physics at Harvard, writing his dissertation on the thermodynamics of mercury.

At the station, the train arrives, then leaves, disgorging huge puffs of steam. Francis walks up and down the platform, looking for Mildred. She'd mailed him a recent photograph so he would know what she looked like. She hadn't changed much at all: the same wheat-colored hair, the same gray-blue eyes, her gaze an alloy of gentleness and steely resolve.

He goes back home and waits late into the night for the telephone to ring, certain that she will call and blurt out an apology, explaining a mix-up with the train schedule. But she doesn't call. Not that night, not the next, not ever. "It was very strange, very unlike her," Francis reflected later.

3.

In New York, Mildred stays with a friend from college. More than a decade ago, she and Clara Leiser sat in the same classroom at the University of Wisconsin, scribbling notes during lectures given by Professor William Ellery Leonard.

Now Clara lives in a narrow, four-story row house in the West Village. Clara is writing a biography about Leonard, a book she began twelve years ago. She's as meticulous as she is scatterbrained, filling drawers and shoeboxes with every letter, poem, essay, and scrap of paper Leonard sends her. Clara has been preparing for Mildred's visit for weeks. In a letter to Leonard, she writes:

> *Did I tell you that Mildred Fish wrote that she was coming over in January and asked whether she could stay with me because she couldn't take any money with her and didn't know where she would sleep?*

The moment Mildred arrives at 16 St. Luke's Place, Clara senses something is off. Mildred's jitteriness is pronounced, but it's more than her nerves that rattle Clara. Mildred seems hardened somehow. Every day Mildred makes "a fetish," as Clara puts it, "of morning & evening exercises." The girl she knew in college is gone. She wonders what Leonard would make of "the 1937 Mildred Fish" and admits,

> *I envy her will power, almost I envy a certain ruthlessness she's developed in pursuing her own interests & plans, no matter how rude part of the process may be.*

A few days after arriving, Mildred delivers a lecture at New York University and uses Clara's telephone to call Thomas Wolfe. Clara knows that Mildred published an article about him in the *Berliner Tageblatt* and another in the *Continental Post*. She knows that Mildred introduced Wolfe to Martha Dodd, the daughter of the U.S. ambassador in Berlin, and that the three of them went to parties and gallivanted with writers and editors. She knows that Mildred is now acquainted with Wolfe's editor, the venerable Maxwell Perkins at Scribner's, who also edits Hemingway and Fitzgerald, and she knows that Mildred plans to visit Perkins's office while she's in New York.

Clara doesn't like hearing about any of it, not one bit. She has her own literary ambitions.

Mildred stays at Clara Leiser's home for fourteen long days. Clara fills the pages of letters to William Ellery Leonard with gossipy put-downs. Mildred, she complains, is condescending, utterly convinced that "anybody she approaches concerning a 'lecture' will be delighted & greatly benefited by the mere meeting of her."

Despite her misgivings, Clara throws a big New York party for Mildred, inviting about fifty people from UW, many of whom cross state lines to attend.

4.

Mildred has changed. They all try to put their fingers on how, exactly. She speaks German fluently and has made herself into some kind of scholar; this much they know. In spite of these accomplishments, Mildred doesn't seem happy. Not even a little. The easygoing, radiant Mildred has been replaced by someone brittler. Stonier. The light in her is gone, snuffed out. Mady Emmerling thinks Mildred seems "extremely frightened, cautious and reserved as if she felt there was someone looking over her shoulder all the time." Dorothy Meyer tries to engage Mildred in a friendly conversation. She has heard through the grapevine that Mildred visited Russia. She asks Mildred about the trip.

"We don't talk about that," Mildred responds.

Later, after Mildred kisses her goodbye, Dorothy turns to her husband and says, "I have the feeling I've just been kissed by a Nazi."

Dorothy isn't alone in that belief. Others form the same conclusion.

5.

Harriette invites Mildred to stay a few days in Maryland. She and Fred still live on Brookville Road in Chevy Chase, where Mildred spent her senior year of high school.

Mildred arrives at the front door clutching a suitcase. The bedroom where she'll sleep is the one she stayed in back then, with brown wallpaper and a picture window. Through it, she can see a patch of lawn and the elm tree that was once a slim seedling, so much broader and taller now. She sets down her suitcase and joins the family at the dinner table. Harriette's daughters are all grown up. Marion is twenty-two, and Janey—she prefers Jane now—is almost twenty-one.

Marion notices a change in Aunt Mili. She's "kind of strained, sort of roughened," she recalled years later. She used to talk in a way that made sense. Now she's "slightly off." Harriette is studying her too. The odd rigidity, the severity in her facial expressions—it all adds up: *Nazi.* Harriette hasn't the slightest idea how to handle the situation, and her husband isn't much help. Fred keeps telling Mili, in the stern voice he reserves for disciplining their children, *Don't go back to Germany. Stay with us.*

She tells him she can't. *Why?* he wants to know.

Mili says something mysterious then. "I hold Arvid's head in my hands."

6.

The day Mildred is to depart, Harriette is happy to see her go. Almost happy, anyway. Mildred has caused too much friction in the family, and worse—Jane is thoroughly captivated by her. The entire visit, Harriette has bristled, watching her almost-twenty-one-year-old daughter hang on Mildred's every word.

Georgina's Tremors, Big and Small

1937–1938

1.

America no longer holds the comforts of home. During her visit, Mildred notices that friends and even family treat her differently. It is the same wherever she goes—New York, Pennsylvania, Maryland, even Wisconsin. She seems odd to everyone. Her years abroad have changed her. No one understands why she left Wisconsin in the first place and why she won't return. Americans can't grasp—how could they?—what is happening in Germany now.

We read the papers, Harriette insists. *We know what's going on.*

The papers tell you nothing, Mildred informs her older sister. She leaves it at that. She can't say more.

2.

Jane lingers in the doorway, watching Mildred pack her suitcase. She wants to know everything about Berlin, *everything.* Mildred is tired—the trip has taken a toll—but her niece's passionate curiosity awakens something in her. Perhaps she's reminded of an earlier version of herself.

3.

Before Mildred returns to Germany, she pays a visit to her mother. The details of the visit are lost to history.

What is known is this: Georgina Fish is holed up in a small room in a town called Wauwatosa, a stone's throw from Milwaukee.

And this: she is dying.

4.

Now Mildred is back in Berlin. Wherever she goes, she senses the mute gaze of strangers. She does her best to blend in; still, she is conspicuous. Her command of German is excellent, but her accent always gives her away.

Why do you remain in Germany?

Countless times Mildred has been asked this question. Countless times the person asking it—a shopkeeper, a stranger on the street— is unconvinced when she answers, *Because my life is here.*

Arvid is here, the Circle is here, but the recognition that Germany isn't the country she once loved can't be avoided. The cruelty, the barbarity, the outright sadism, are horrifying. Still, she holds on to the hope that fascism can be fought. All those Nazis goosestepping their way through the halls of government can be defeated, the reins of power ripped from their hands. Germany, if given the chance, could become a prototype for countries around the world to follow, a model of fairness, decency, and equality. This is Mildred's adamant belief.

5.

In college, Mildred awakened to the idea that the political left provided an answer to the problem of poverty. What began at UW as a spirited debate with the Friday Niters soon hardened into a heartfelt conviction that the rich in America were too rich, the poor too poor. "If capitalism keeps on the path it is going," she wrote, "the coming years will bring the enormous wealth of a very few and the misery and want of the common people."

Capitalism was broken; Black Tuesday and the Great Depression that followed convinced her of that all the more. America was doomed, and Germany was no better off. Mildred despaired over the masses of unemployed people she saw in Berlin, the ragged beggars, the impoverished children. "Ninety-six percent of the German people possess no property and live from hand to mouth," she wrote in February 1931. Six months later: "In Berlin one never forgets the wan faces." In them, she kept seeing Georgina. Sometimes she "walked through the streets at night and saw a woman whose face showed the signs of a struggle such as yours," she confessed to her mother. "I could have knelt and kissed her dress."

Russia, it seemed, offered hope. Lenin's writings on the need for equality between the sexes brought Mildred to her feet. When students visited the apartment, she'd dash to her bookshelves for his dog-eared books and read passages aloud. Lenin railed against the "old, bourgeois humiliation of women." How much more enlightened these proclamations were than the Nazi view, which held that women should limit the scope of their activities and concern themselves with only three things: *Kinder, Küche, Kirche*—children, kitchen, church.

Five months before Hitler came to power, Mildred visited Moscow. "It's good for a woman to go traveling alone," she wrote. She was twenty-nine years old, deeply inspired by what she perceived as Lenin's vision for women in the future:

> *Women are allowed to work in whatever fields they wish . . . They are paid the same as the men for the same work. When they are pregnant their work is made lighter for them, but not taken away from them. They receive two months' vacation with pay and all necessary care before confinement and two months after confinement. They are not forced to bear children, but are encouraged to use birth control measures and are allowed to use abortion to a certain extent.*

She knew her mother knew nothing about Lenin, so she took it upon herself to educate Georgina. She explained that Lenin was a leftist revolutionary who had led a revolt against the monarchy in 1917, ending centuries of imperial rule. No longer was land the sole property of wealthy aristocrats. Land was returned to the peasants, and Lenin was hailed by many as a hero. Mildred hoped her mother—who was living on a shoestring and always would, who had suffered a life of toil and still did, and who undoubtedly felt unvalued throughout it all—would view Lenin as a hero too.

Georgina didn't. Mildred's letters frightened her.

Georgina was in her late sixties then. She was still making a meager living typing letters for men, just as she'd done when Mildred was a girl. Every day sapped the dwindling reservoir of her strength. In previous letters, she admitted she hadn't been feeling well lately; her energy wasn't what it used to be. She mustered a sufficient amount now to compose a fresh letter, aiming to put into words her alarm. She worried that Mildred had been swept away by a tide of some sort or had wandered off on a wayward path. She especially didn't understand why Mildred was writing so much about *Reds*.

Mildred tried again. "I am so sorry you have been troubled," she wrote.

> *I cannot explain all in one letter—or even in many—though I shall do what I can to help you to see that I am on a good path. I can say that the best forces of love, strength, perseverance, conscientiousness, and thoughtfulness which existed and slumbered in me are now quietly and purposefully awakening and moving in response to something which study, thought, and experience have proved and are daily proving to me is worthwhile.*

Study, thought, and experience had convinced Mildred that Germany suffered from the same moral ailment as America. Men in power thought "only of the individual and the soul of the well-to-do" and ignored the poor. So: fascism must be fought—capitalism too.

When Mildred made comparisons between America and Russia, the gulf of misunderstanding deepened.

"You are quite right in saying that America could not follow the same path as Russia," Mildred wrote.

Every country has its own requirements. The point is only that the principles would have to be the same in both cases: namely the equal good of all.

The more Mildred broke down into simplistic terms what she meant, the more off her rocker she sounded to Georgina. Georgina was known to the Fish family as a woman of few words, but whenever she got a letter from Mildred, everyone got an earful.

6.

For a while, it's Georgina's son who hears most of it. Georgina moves into Bob's modest shack by the dairy farm when her health begins to deteriorate. She moves to her daughter Marion's house in Wauwatosa when the tremors in her hands and feet get more pronounced. Her voice acquires a tremor too. The truth is, she doesn't make much sense. Whatever ailment she suffers from, she refuses all treatment. A devout and stoic Christian Scientist, Georgina Fish will take nothing but a glass of clear, cold water.

7.

On February 22, 1938, Georgina Fish takes her last breath.

No matter how many times Mildred remembers that her mother is gone, her grief is no less potent than when she first heard the news. The immensity of it is incalculable.

Mildred travels to Paris alone. Somewhere north of the Seine, she gets lost. She approaches a woman who looks roughly her age and asks for directions in the few words of French she knows.

The woman responds in German. "Surely you are Frau Harnack?"

Mona Wollheim. They were classmates at the Justus Liebig University in Giessen. But Mildred doesn't seem to remember, or understand. Mona is so unsettled by her odd behavior that she holds on to the memory for many years.

Jane in Love

1937–1938

1.

Two months, Harriette tells Jane. That is all. Then you get on the ship and come back to America. Harriette has lined up a job for Jane in September, just to be sure.

2.

On June 17, 1937, Jane Esch, age twenty-one, boards the SS *St. Louis,* bound for Hamburg. In a letter to her parents, she writes the date as a German would: day, then month, then year: *17 Juni 1937.* Already she is switching the order of things, trying out a new way. She has enclosed today's menu with her letter ("See that menu—I mean *Speisekarte?*"). Already she's showing off her German.

3.

Jane writes the next letter on the train. She's captivated by the German countryside. "The cows look just like ours," she writes.

> *The soil is very rich and black.... Everything seems laid out in miniature, all so carefully cultivated and precisely planned. Neat little farmhouses of brick, decorated much more than ours, and brick barns. Trees lining all the dirt roads, very exact, like a countryside set up with toys, for children.*

The train arrives in Berlin and disgorges its passengers. Except for an occasional tromp to Washington, DC, where her father commutes to work, Jane has never set foot outside Chevy Chase. Her hair is cut short, right at the chin. She has curled the ends up with an iron, so they flip skyward.

4.

In her letters, Jane does her best to put into words a culture shock of immense proportions.

26 June 1937

For the last couple of days I've been walking about Berlin getting acquainted. It's a very interesting city, and lots of fun getting to know it. The women here are plumper and frowzier. Their shoes and stockings are awful looking. There are lots of blondes, many more than we see in Washington.

9 July 1937

A nice thing about the cafés here is that you can sit at a table outdoors as long as you like, and write or read or chat. They seem to expect everyone to do it. . . . Everywhere you go here, instead of serving lemonade or punch they serve Bowle, pronounced bohle.

9 Aug 1937

It's been terribly hot here the last few days. They say it comes from America, like women smoking on the streets & wearing shorts and raising whoopee at midnight in beer parlors. What an idea most of them have of Americans, anyway! Irresponsible children with too much money and an awful accent, who make too much noise and wear too much makeup. . . . Please when I get home don't give me any boiled potatoes—please!

A single bite of Mildred's waterlogged potatoes prompts Jane's cheerful declaration that she'll take care of meals from now on. Jane just as cheerfully does all the shopping. "I'm getting expert at making bargains in German," she writes. "Today I was very proud of myself because I got two pork chops for sixty instead of seventy pfennigs (2½ pfennigs equal a cent). Then I cook dinner for Mildred and me and do the dishes."

Arvid works so late at the ministry that he misses most of these meals.

Mildred has grown accustomed to eating alone, opening a can of something and heating it up, but now she can enjoy the sweet, spirited companionship of her twenty-one-year-old niece. Jane makes everything easier.

5.

In every letter Jane writes to her parents are rhapsodic accounts of her time with Mildred and Arvid—the symphonies, the operas, the fascinating discussions, the Sunday strolls with friends and relatives through the countryside.

"A couple of nights ago we went to see some friends of Arvid's called the Delbrücks," Jane writes. "The whole family was there— an old mother, about seven grown children with husbands & wives, etc. I couldn't get them all straight."

One of the seven catches her eye. His name is Max. He isn't just Arvid's friend; he is his cousin. Max sits next to Jane and explains the family tree. She feigns comprehension. She's too spellbound to pay attention. Max Delbrück is thirty-one and gorgeous. He has a PhD in physics and has just been awarded a Rockefeller Fellowship. He tells Jane that in Copenhagen he studied under the great Danish physicist Niels Bohr. This September, Max will move to California, where he will conduct important research at Caltech.

Jane's heart skips when Max asks, *May I take you to a concert?*

The concert is held in a cavernous church constructed an impossibly long time ago, before Martin Luther was born. A plangent organ swells in Brahms's "Ein Deutsches Requiem," and Jane's heart swells along with it. Max Delbrück sits beside her on a pew. When violins merge with the organ and reach a crescendo, Max Delbrück's lips tremble. She considers the possibility that she is in love.

6.

August 22 is the date on Jane's return ticket. Until then, she will cram in as much as she can. Max wants to take her dancing. Another admirer wants to show her Frederick the Great's palace. Mildred wants to show her every river and lake and canal in Berlin.

On August 12, Mildred takes her to the Thuringian countryside. Jane admires the "tawny fields of harvesting grain striped and squared with patches of green.... And on the skyline, blue smoky mountains."

On August 13, Mildred takes her to Weimar. Jane swoons at the houses where Goethe, Schiller, and Liszt once lived. It seems impossible that she's permitted to sit down at Liszt's piano and play it, her fingers touching the same ivory keys the great composer's fingers caressed. In a letter to her parents, she writes,

> *A week from tomorrow I'll be on the ship. If I don't write again it's because I'm so busy seeing everything at the last minute. There surely is a lot to see!*

7.

But she isn't on the ship. She decides to stay. A week later, she goes on a Sunday stroll and falls in love.

The man who walks beside her on a leaf-shaded trail is thirty-five, the same age as Mildred. They're heading toward a lake in Wannsee, where Mildred and Arvid used to rent an apartment. He is some kind of economist, like Arvid, and speaks English with a kind of deference, like Arvid—haltingly, gently, pronouncing the *W* in *Wannsee* like it's a soft *V*: *Vahn-say*.

The way he looks at her makes her forget all about Max Delbrück. He is tall and broad-shouldered and his eyes are as blue as the cloudless sky.

His name is Otto. She has never met a man named Otto. She says his name over and over again—*Ot-to, Ot-to, Ot-to*—enchanted by the way it makes her lips purse together, like a kiss.

8.

The letter Jane composes to her parents is several pages long. She outlines her plans. She will learn German and teach English. She will enroll in classes at the University of Berlin and study the history of music. After six months, she will take a steamer ship back to America.

9.

On September 3, she goes swimming with Otto. The lake is luminous, and there are swans. German swans seem different from American swans, though she can't quite say how. The differences between German and American young women are much easier to grasp.

Jane wants to be more like a German young woman.

When you want to go swimming you sort of wriggle out of what underclothes you have, and slip on your suit unconcernedly, all underneath your dress. It doesn't matter whether other people are around or not.

After swimming, Jane dries herself off with a towel and lies next to Otto. She doesn't dare mention him in the letter.

10.

"I have been going out with a friend of Arvid's from the Economics Ministry lately," she writes two months later.

He's an economist, and has written several books, and is teaching a course at the University of Berlin on statistics this semester, and next semester on the economic conditions in Europe. Besides that he's good-looking.

Otto recently took her to a ball at the Hotel Esplanade, a magnificent building with baroque flourishes.

The rooms are hung with crystal chandeliers that are big gobs of sparkle. The walls look like a wedding cake.

Weddings are very much on Jane's mind. Nine days later, she sends her parents another letter:

The picture I am enclosing is of Otto Donner, the man about whom I wrote in my last letter. He and I love each other very much, and are engaged to be married.

My Little Girl

1937–1938

Saturday, Nov. 27, 1937

My Little Girl,

I wish I could avoid hurting you. My first reaction, upon reading your letter last night, was to wait a
week before replying, but after one of the most wretched nights
of my life, this morning it seems to me that this is one of the

It is not that I have any objection to Otto personally - I know
that any man you might choose is bound to be worthy. But marriage involves so very much more than one single man!

I know you and that you are impulsive and have powerful emotions. And I know that, married or single, you are going
to be in love a good many times in your lifetime. I wonder if

<del>RESTRICTED</del>

OFFICE OF U. S. CHIEF OF COUNSEL FOR WAR CRIMES
APO 696-A
EVIDENCE DIVISION
INTERROGATION BRANCH

Restricted Classification
Removed Per
Executive Order 10501

INTERROGATION SUMMARY NO. 1754

Interrogation of : Otto DONNER, Chief of the Research Office for
War Economy

Shortly before the outbreak of the war informant got a
position with the Ministry of Economics, where HARMACK, a friend
of subject, was working. In the house of HARMACK, subject met
his future wife, an American. In 1938 DONNER went to the States

1.

Harriette is furious. Mildred is euphoric.

2.

Harriette writes a letter to Jane. "My Little Girl," she begins.

> *After one of the most wretched nights of my life, this morning it seems to me . . . I should speak plainly. I know you and that you are impulsive and have powerful emotions. And I know that, married or single, you are going to be in love a good many times in your lifetime . . .*

> *Either you must choose to remain childless as Mildred has done, thus sacrificing the greatest satisfaction life holds, or you must be resigned to squandering your love on sons who will be victims of the inevitable European wars to come.*

> *I wrote Mildred explicitly asking that she defer urging you to come to Berlin until you had time to find yourself. After all, there are plenty of fine American men with qualifications as high as any European has . . .*

> *So, my very warm-hearted and hot-blooded child, if in all your life you ever listen to what I have to say, please listen now. Please come home before you marry.*

3.

Jane does not go home. She is twenty-one and in love. She will marry Otto on a spring evening in 1938.

4.

Jane shares the good news in a letter to Max Delbrück.

Max is in California studying the chromosomes of the fruit fly. His fascination with physics is giving way to a fascination with biology. He will escape Hitler entirely and spend the rest of his career in the United States, conducting research that will earn him a Nobel Prize.

Max's brother Justus Delbrück takes a different path. He remains in Germany.

In 1938 Justus Delbrück is practicing law and hatching various plans to overthrow the Nazi government. One plan will take precedence over the others. Justus Delbrück will join Ernst von Harnack, Dietrich Bonhoeffer, Klaus Bonhoeffer, and Hans von Dohnányi in a 1944 conspiracy to assassinate Hitler.

Jane will meet them all—Justus, Ernst, Dietrich, Klaus, and Hans—but she won't know they are in the resistance. She remains blissfully unaware that there is such a thing as a resistance. Not once does she suspect that Sunday strolls serve a clandestine purpose: Mildred and Arvid use them as a cover to obtain or deliver messages and top-secret intelligence smuggled out from Hitler's ministries.

One Sunday, Mildred, Arvid, Jane, and Otto head off to Wannsee with rucksacks. They walk around the periphery of a small lake—Jane practices pronouncing its name, Kleiner Wannsee—until they find a spot where they can spread out a picnic blanket. Jane gazes at the wedding band on her hand. She's still not used to seeing it there.

They eat sandwiches in the sunshine.

Otto's father is a blacksmith. His working-class roots impress Mildred and Arvid. Not once does Jane suspect that Otto Donner is one of their sources.

A Circle Within the Circle

1937–1938

1.

Wolfgang Havemann hasn't forgotten the night he watched the torch-light parade with Uncle Arvid. Since then, he has joined the Circle. At law school, he keeps a low profile, sitting beside students who are ardent Nazis. He makes small talk with them, laughs at their jokes. No one guesses that he is in the underground resistance. Not the students, not the professors, not even his own Nazi boot–licking father.

As the Circle grows, they develop strict rules to avoid arrest.

"Everyone knew that arrest might mean death," Wolfgang remembered.

> We often didn't know the true names of each other. We used aliases so that even if you were arrested, you could only tell them you were "with Kurt." Then they couldn't find him.

Arvid wonders whether Wolfgang would be suitable for spy work. Mildred wonders too.

Wolfgang agrees to hide the typewriter Mildred uses for leaflets in his apartment, but he's not sure about espionage. In time, Wolfgang will make up his mind, and Moscow Center will assign him a code name: Italian.

So it is that a circle of spies within the Circle begins to emerge.

2.

Two of Mildred's BAG recruits sign on to be spies.

Karl Behrens has gotten a promotion at the AEG factory. As a newly minted mechanical engineer, Karl is now ideally positioned to smuggle out blueprints that AEG is using to produce electric motors and steam turbines for Hitler's war machine. Moscow Center gives him the code name Beamer.

Wilhelm Utech endures a string of interrogations at the concentration camp he has been hauled to. Distributing leaflets is a crime that suggests he's in a resistance group, but the SS guards assigned to beat the truth out of him fail. After he is released, he finds Mildred and assures her that he revealed nothing about the Circle. The brutality he experienced while incarcerated has convinced him that they should use whatever weapons are required to fight Hitler. Moscow Center gives him the code name Worker.

3.

By now, Arvid has cultivated friendships with a number of sources at the Deutscher Klub, including a man called Titzien (code name

Albanian), a tycoon with contacts in the German military, and Hans Rupp (code name Turk), a senior accountant at I. G. Farben. Arvid has also tapped Baron von Wohlzogen-Neuhaus (code name Greek), an acquaintance from his ARPLAN days who has just been given a post as a senior official in the Oberkommando der Wehrmacht— High Command of the German Armed Forces—which oversees the army, navy, and air force. Collectively, these Deutscher Klub sources furnish Arvid with a wealth of information about Hitler's preparations for war as outlined in his Four-Year Plan.

Naum Belkin, Arvid's control officer, was posted to Spain in 1936, so spymaster Boris Gordon now supervises Arvid directly.

4.

Boris Gordon has his eye on Mildred too.

Mildred has been elected president of the American Women's Club, an establishment jam-packed with the wealthy wives of diplomats. As an invited guest at formal teas and parties hosted by various foreign embassies in Berlin, she frequently rubs shoulders with ambassadors and other high-ranking officials. Mildred's contacts at the U.S. embassy, in particular, make her highly desirable. So, too, do her contacts within the highest ranks of Hitler's government: dutiful, gullible Nazis who remain unaware of her true feelings toward them. Moscow Center has kept a file on Mildred since the ARPLAN days, when she took four trips to the Soviet Union. Twice she traveled to Moscow alone. She carried a folded piece of paper in her satchel with a list of addresses and navigated her way to the friends who awaited her arrival. One was a leader of the Comintern who cooperated with the GRU and planned to "use her" for "work in Finland." Whether Mildred carried out this work is unknown; most of her file remains classified.

Gordon gives Mildred a code name: Japonka. Moscow Center slips a photograph into her file.

It remains unknown whether Mildred ever met Gordon or knew he had assigned her a code name. According to all available accounts,

Mildred doesn't involve herself with the NKVD right now. She keeps her focus on the Circle.

5.

The Circle is optimistic. Hitler may want to start a war, but he can be stopped before the first shot is fired. The cooperation of other countries is essential.

A Child, Almost

1937–1938

1.

While Arvid whispers military secrets into Moscow's ear, Mildred gets a job as a literary scout for the Berlin-based publishing company Rütten and Loening. The job is her cover, a sly way for her to travel to other countries and meet with contacts without raising Gestapo eyebrows.

She travels to Norway, Denmark, Switzerland, France, England.

Sometimes she travels alone, sometimes with Arvid. Sometimes she tracks down Arvid after she arrives.

Then she sits in a room. She is the sole American. The other chairs are filled by Europeans who think of themselves as anti-fascists or comrades or revolutionaries participating in what they regard as an international struggle against fascism. Hitler isn't the only threat. Fascism is on the march throughout Europe right now. Mussolini is tyrannizing Italy, and Franco is massacring civilians in the Spanish Civil War. Democracies seem to be toppling everywhere; iron-fisted dictators rule the day.

In Paris, Mildred sits with Arvid and a clutch of Communists. By associating with them, Arvid is brazenly defying the rules of *konspiratsia*. He doesn't care; he will take this risk. The way he sees it, he's a leader in the German resistance, not a spy for the NKVD.

Arvid is evolving right before Mildred's eyes. The cautious graduate student she married is metamorphosing into a bolder man. He even buys a motorcycle.

2.

Arvid's cousins continue to deepen their involvement in the resistance.

Dietrich Bonhoeffer is gaining recognition in other countries as a German pastor who is fiercely opposed to Hitler, and he has received an invitation from Mahatma Gandhi to meet with him in India. In Germany, Dietrich has organized a group of two thousand pastors called the Bekennende Kirche—Confessing Church—that is agitating against the Nazification of Protestant churches. The Gestapo arrests more than eight hundred of these pastors.

Klaus Bonhoeffer has been promoted to director of the legal department at Lufthansa and is helping Arvid, Mildred, and at least a dozen others in the resistance to expand their contacts across Germany's borders. Lufthansa schedules routine flights into numerous countries throughout Europe, enabling frequent courier runs under the cover of a commercial airline.

3.

Hans von Dohnányi—who is married to Dietrich and Klaus Bonhoeffer's sister, Christine—has been meticulously collecting evidence of Nazi crimes since 1934, indexing them in a ledger, a "chronicle of shame," which he hides in a safe thirty miles south of Berlin. His job at the Ministry of Justice allows him access to thousands of pages of evidence, including the classified records of prisons and concentration camps. He will have all the documentation he needs to prosecute Hitler, Himmler, Göring, and other high-ranking Nazis if a coup brings them to their knees.

For most of 1937, there isn't a shred of evidence that anyone in Hitler's inner circle is seriously contemplating a coup.

But when a captain in Hans von Dohnányi's network of confidential sources tells him about a belligerent tirade that Hitler delivered to military top brass on November 5, 1937, Dohnányi senses a shift. War is imminent, the source tells him, corroborating what Arvid has been hearing from his own sources.

But Hans learns something more: two generals strongly objected to Hitler's desire to start a war in Europe. In February 1938, the two generals are ousted from their posts. One is defamed as a homosexual, and the other is accused of marrying a prostitute. Hitler then declares himself the supreme commander of the armed forces and announces a massive reorganization of Germany's military leadership. Fourteen generals are forced to retire. In their place, Hitler installs generals who swear allegiance to their new supreme commander.

So it is that in 1938, a plot to assassinate Hitler is born.

It involves Hans Oster, deputy head of the Abwehr (German military intelligence); Admiral Wilhelm Canaris, chief of the Abwehr; Colonel-General Ludwig Beck, chief of the army general staff; and a small cluster of military officers, politicians, and diplomats. Their plan is deceptively simple: a group of armed Germans will storm the Reich Chancellery and shoot Hitler. It will come to be known as the Oster conspiracy.

In August and September 1938, several conspirators meet with Foreign Secretary Lord Halifax and other British statesmen and tell them about their plan to extinguish the Nazi regime. They intend to assassinate Hitler when he invades Czechoslovakia, which they predict will happen any day now. Already, Hitler has positioned troops along the Czech border and is threatening to attack unless the Sudetenland region of Czechoslovakia is surrendered to Germany. The conspirators urge the British government to oppose Hitler's land grab.

But Prime Minister Neville Chamberlain attempts to negotiate with Hitler instead, hoping to avoid armed conflict. In a September 27 BBC radio broadcast, Chamberlain describes Hitler's warmongering in Czechoslovakia as "a quarrel in a faraway country between people of whom we know nothing."

On the morning of September 28, 1938, the German conspirators assemble at army headquarters and distribute arms and ammunition, preparing to storm the Reich Chancellery. But the coup is abruptly called off. On September 29, in a surprising turn of events, Neville Chamberlain, Prime Minister Édouard Daladier of France, and Italy's fascist dictator Benito Mussolini meet in Munich to sign a document that gives Hitler what he wants: the Sudetenland.

The news is a blow to Hans Oster, Wilhelm Canaris, Ludwig Beck, and others in the Oster conspiracy, who understand that they will have little support for their coup now. The Munich agreement is widely hailed as a triumph of diplomacy. Upon his return from Munich, Chamberlain announces to the cheering crowd that assembles at Heston airport in West London that the agreement he signed with Hitler promises "peace for our time."

The Oster conspiracy is unsuccessful, but it lays the groundwork for conspiracies to come.

4.

The resistance begins to form new alliances, the connections between them as fragile and intricate as spiderwebs.

In the winter of 1938, Arvid's cousins Ernst von Harnack and Klaus Bonhoeffer join a small group of Germans to discuss how they can crush Hitler. The men convene in a stone-walled room at Ernst's medieval castle in Merseburg. A "Unity Front," they decide, could erase the divisions separating right- and left-wing opposition to Hitler. Thanks to Hans von Dohnányi, Ernst and Klaus know that there are conservative military officers at the heart of the Third Reich who oppose Hitler.

This meeting marks the beginning of a resistance effort that will culminate when Ernst von Harnack, Klaus Bonhoeffer, Dietrich Bonhoeffer, Justus Delbrück, and Hans von Dohnányi join forces with Oster, Canaris, Beck, and other high-ranking military officers. Code-named Walküre (Valkyrie), the plot will become the most historically well-known attempt to assassinate Hitler.

5.

As the Spanish Civil War rages on, Hitler's military aid to Franco's army increases. What he receives in return is not money but minerals—specifically, iron, copper, and sulfur—materials that enable Hitler to build up his own military. If Franco wins his war, Hitler knows Germany will gain another military advantage: U-boat bases on the Atlantic coast.

An anti-fascist German radio station in Madrid called Deutsche Freiheitssender broadcasts daily reports on the war, appealing to Germans to oppose Hitler's support for Franco. Germans in the underground resistance can tune in on their Blaupunkts to hear instructions on how to sabotage German armaments factories, preventing the shipment of weapons to Spain.

Mildred is moved to take greater risks. At one meeting of the Circle, Mildred tells members to look for ways to support the anti-fascists in Spain and sabotage German military aid. If they obtain enough explosives, they can blow up key communications centers.

6.

And then, quite suddenly, Mildred discovers that she's pregnant.

7.

Two friends invite her to a town called Gremsmühlen for a two-week holiday. Franziska and Rudolf Heberle have known Mildred for over a decade. When Mildred arrives, they notice that she has almost nothing in her suitcase and only one white blouse. They also notice that Mildred seems ill, or sad, or both.

Gremsmühlen is one of those picturesque German towns that entranced her when she was a newlywed. It's situated near a lake. Perhaps she goes swimming; perhaps not. She misses Arvid, who is in Washington, DC, on official business for the Ministry of Economics. Every American official Arvid meets in the State Department believes he's a devout Nazi. The man he pretends to be is a horrible, horrible lie.

Lies spill out of Mildred too.

She tells Franziska she isn't ill, nor is she sad. She keeps up the pretense that all is well for most of the trip. Finally, in the kitchen, Mildred confides that she had a miscarriage.

"Her sorrow astonished me," Franziska recalled later in a letter, "because I believed that she intentionally had no children because of her political work."

8.

"A. has been away," Mildred writes in a letter to her brother, Bob, "so it has been a bit lonely."

The stream of letters Mildred used to send home slows to a trickle. She has no one to confide in anymore, not really.

Stalin and the Dwarf

1937–1938

1.

Martha Dodd can't stop thinking about Boris. He's not in Moscow anymore—he's in Warsaw. "Darling," she writes.

> *You cannot imagine, darling, how often you have been with me, how I have constantly thought about you, worried about you.*

She hatches a plan. She could fly out to Warsaw. She could stay at a "small hotel" and they could have a secret rendezvous—she wouldn't tell a soul.

> *Maybe we could leave Warsaw for a day or two and drive into the countryside. I would come by myself, of course, and my parents completely agree that I do as I wish—after all, I'm 28 years old, and I'm very independent!*

Martha writes another letter, this time addressing it to "the Soviet Government."

> *I, Martha Dodd, U.S. citizen, have known Boris Vinogradov for three years in Berlin and other places, and we have agreed to ask official permission to marry.*

2.

Martha flies to Warsaw. Boris obligingly whispers sweet nothings into her ear, keeping up the ruse that he will marry her soon, soon, very soon. Months ago, Boris cabled a confidential memo to Moscow Center:

I don't quite understand why you have taken such an approving stance regarding our wedding? I asked you to tell her that this is completely impossible and in any case will not work out.

But it did no good. His plea was ignored.

Boris has no intention of marrying Martha, of course. He has been married twice already, the first time to a woman named Tatiana, the second to Vassa, his current wife.

3.

Martha is ordered by Moscow Center to cut off contact with anyone who is a Communist or a Communist sympathizer, the same instructions Arvid, Karl, and Wilhelm received when they were recruited. In a signed statement dated March 14, 1937, Martha promises to deliver top-secret information about the United States:

At present I have access mainly to the personal confidential correspondence of my father and the State Department, as well as the President of the U.S. The source of information on military and naval matters, as well as aviation, is solely personal contact with the personnel of our embassy.

She points out that her father "has great influence" over President Roosevelt and Secretary of State Cordell Hull and reveals that he won't be ambassador for much longer as "he personally wants to quit." She would be more than willing to push for whichever man Moscow Center hopes to see as the next U.S. ambassador in Berlin and asks, "Do you have anybody in mind?"

Martha's willingness to spy on her own father and guide his decisions impresses the NKVD leadership so thoroughly that Stalin himself is alerted about her recruitment in a memo marked "TOP SECRET For your eyes only." The memo is composed by Nikolay Ivanovich Yezhov, head of the NKVD and commissar of State Security, known to his colleagues by his nickname, the Dwarf. "Comrade Stalin," he wrote.

Martha Dodd, daughter of the American Ambassador in Berlin . . . described in her statement her social status, her father's status, and prospects of her further work for us. Forwarding a copy of the letter, I ask instructions about Martha Dodd's use.

4.

The Dwarf is short and walks with a limp, characteristics he uncannily shares with his German enemy Goebbels. The Dwarf is by no means an idle man. Several years ago, Stalin assigned him to the Purge Commission, which periodically ejects Russians from the Communist Party. A bloodless purge has given way to a bloody one. At present, the Dwarf is engaged in a murderous housecleaning. The very day the Dwarf asks Stalin how best to employ Martha Dodd as an NKVD spy, scores of Soviet military officers are rounded up and sent to gulags, prison camps in Siberia. What began as Stalin's vengeance against political enemies (real or — as is more frequently the case — imagined) is spilling over into the civilian population. They are dragged into forests and shot. Over forty thousand residents of Leningrad are murdered in 1937 — a number that reaches sixty thousand in 1938. More than half a century later, their bones will be exhumed from a mass grave, nearly all bearing a single bullet hole in the back of the skull.

The Great Purge averages one thousand murders a day between 1936 and 1938. Because executions are carried out at night and mass graves are hidden, most of the population remains blissfully ignorant of Stalin's killing spree.

In 1937, Stalin regards the Dwarf as a fiercely loyal comrade, a distinction not easily won, though easily lost. Few are better acquainted with Stalin's fickle, vengeful heart than the Dwarf, who demonstrated his devotion to the Communist dictator by spraying mercury on the curtains of his own office and blaming it on Genrikh Yagoda, then director of the NKVD. Yagoda was arrested, charged with treason, and dragged before a panel of judges at the last of three so-called Moscow Show Trials in March 1938, when the mercury-tainted curtains were presented as conclusive evidence that Yagoda was a German spy plotting to poison the Dwarf and perhaps Stalin too. After the judges pronounced a guilty verdict, Yagoda was shot in the head. The Dwarf was all too happy to take Yagoda's place as the new director of the NKVD.

5.

Moscow Center instructs Boris Vinogradov to leave Warsaw and report to the Soviet embassy in Berlin. During a drinking binge with the American journalist H. R. Knickerbocker—Knick, Boris calls him—he confides that he must return to Moscow. In the euphemism employed by the Dwarf, Boris has been "recalled." In Moscow, he will be questioned, but Boris tells Knick he's not worried. He's a loyal Communist, he fought in the Red Army; his interrogators would never conclude that he's an enemy of Russia. The two men converse in Russian; Knick is nearly fluent. Knick puts it to Boris straight: "If you have reason to believe that you have been falsely denounced, will you go back or will you choose exile in the West?"

Exile, in Boris's mind, is not an option. Nor is refusing to return to Moscow, where the Dwarf is waiting for him.

6.

Martha meets with her control officer, who instructs her to sneak into her father's office, read his reports to President Roosevelt, and write "a brief summary" of the contents. Her Soviet handlers are particularly interested in "information about Germany, Japan, and Poland."

Martha receives "200 American dollars, 10 rubles, and gifts bought for 500 rubles," and a firm directive to cut off all telephone contact with Boris Vinogradov. She may write letters to her Russian lover, but the letters cannot be sent using the regular postal service. A courier is suggested as an alternative. A memo in her file indicates that all the love letters she writes from now on will be intercepted by the NKVD, and an unnamed Russian agent will compose Boris's replies.

7.

Boris returns to Moscow and checks into room 925 at the Moskva Hotel, which faces the Kremlin. He is arrested, tortured, and deposited in a prison cell. On August 28, 1938, he is sentenced to death by a Soviet military court, dragged to a secret NKVD mass-execution site, and shot.

Boris's Last Letter

1937–1938

1.

Mildred and Martha meet in a crowded restaurant in Berlin. They find a table in a corner.

Mildred is guarded. Lowering her voice, she tells Martha that the Circle has widened.

Years later, Martha will write about their conversation. Mildred is "rarely demonstrative," but later that night, when they are walking in the Tiergarten after their dinner, Mildred kisses Martha on the cheek—"quickly"—and walks away.

2.

Ambassador Dodd resigns. His four and a half years in Berlin have worn him down. Since 1934, Dodd has been telling the State Department that Hitler poses a threat to Germany and the world, and he is outraged that his warnings have had little to no effect on American foreign policy. Dodd knows he is unpopular among his State Department colleagues and suspects that for many months Undersecretary of State Sumner Welles has been working behind the scenes to eject him as ambassador.

On December 29, 1937, William Dodd concludes what he describes as his "sad years in Berlin" and boards the SS *Washington*.

A reporter from the *New York Times* is waiting on the dock when the SS *Washington* pulls into New York Harbor. The reporter notes that Dodd is "greeted by his daughter, Martha, who returned from Germany a few weeks ago."

3.

Martha moves into an apartment in New York located on a tree-lined block near Gramercy Park.

On January 8, 1938, a spy named Iskhak Akhmerov (code name Jung) receives a directive from Moscow:

> We are informing you that our source...Miss Martha Dodd, daughter of the former Amer. Ambassador to Germany Dodd is currently in your city.
>
> You must make contact with her upon receiving a special cable regarding this. Her address: Irving Place, New York City. You need to come to her home early in the morning between 8 and 9 o'clock and say: *I want to give you regards from Bob Norman.*

Martha is assigned a new control officer, code name Igor.

A Harvard-educated millionaire quickly attracts her attention. After a brief courtship, they marry. A spy cables the news to Moscow Center:

> She lives in a rich apartment on 57th Street, has two servants, a driver, and a personal secretary.

One day Martha receives an envelope in her mailbox. It's from Boris.

> *I love you, I'm full of you, I dream of you and us.*

Martha reads the sentence over and over again, deeply moved.

"It was a sad, sad letter," she will write many years later, "and a very loyal one (I still have it) and was his farewell I guess to me and to life. They say he was shot after this."

Martha will never suspect that the letter was written by a spy pretending to be Boris after Boris was shot.

4.

Martha's new husband attempts to buy his way into a post as an ambassador, offering fifty thousand dollars to the Democratic Party. He hopes to be installed at the U.S. embassy in Moscow. An NKVD spy stationed in New York sends a cable to Moscow Center:

> She is very keen on her plan to go to Moscow as the wife of the american ambassador.

> His offer is rejected.

5.

Martha continues to spy for Moscow Center.

In years to come, she will grow accustomed to thinking of herself as a member of the German resistance, equating spying on her own father with aiding the resistance. After the war, in a passage that is as self-dramatizing as it is untrue, she will write, "We, all of us... were in the German underground from 1933 to 1943. I am the only one left."

Seeking Allies

1938–1939

1.

Stalin issues orders for more mass murders.

The Dwarf presides over thousands of executions, then thousands more. Soon, the Dwarf himself comes under suspicion, and he is arrested in the spring of 1939. Later, he is shot in the head.

2.

The Russian embassy in Berlin is eerily empty. Among Arvid's contacts there, five out of nine have been executed.

Arvid's NKVD control officer, Boris Gordon, is executed.

Stalin's conviction that Trotskyite enemies and foreign spies are out to get him utterly paralyzes his intelligence operations. At precisely the time in history when Stalin needs accurate, high-level intelligence about Hitler, he murders all the spies who could provide it.

The Dwarf is replaced by an NKVD officer with far less experience. Baby-faced neophytes try to wear the well-worn shoes of the recently killed. This is the norm, according to one disgruntled Soviet agent:

New people came to fill the offices—young, happy, confident in the rightness of their being there. They received high titles and positions. The authorities did not skimp on buying souls and loyalty. A young man with two pips on his uniform could be promoted in a few days to wearing rhomboids, the equivalent of the old general's rank, and move into an office that still retained the smoke of the favorite tobacco of the previous tenants.

For the next two years, Arvid will hear nothing, not a peep, from the Russians.

3.

Now what?

Over the past three years, Arvid has given the Soviets classified information about Germany's foreign trade agreements and investments indicating that Hitler has been steering Germany toward full economic independence. Hitler has also been rapidly expanding his military, aiming to triple the size of the army, and building a fleet of bombers, laying the groundwork for war.

Who can Arvid give information to now?

Mildred has cultivated contacts at the U.S. embassy, but nothing substantial has come of her conversations with Messersmith or Ambassador Dodd, and now they're both gone. A Yale-educated diplomat named Hugh Wilson is the new ambassador in Berlin, and he is nothing like Dodd, who always made his hatred of Hitler plain. Ambassador Wilson believes that the American press is "Jewish controlled" and praises Hitler as "the man who has pulled his people from moral and economic despair."

There has been some high-stakes turnover at the Ministry of Economics too. Arvid's boss, Hjalmar Schacht—who was embroiled in a very public power struggle with Göring over the Four-Year Plan—left in a huff in protest over Germany's military buildup, which Schacht, never one to mince words, regards as foolish and wasteful.

Schacht's replacement is Walther Funk, a nasty Nazi who has no objection to a military buildup and is presently consumed with an elaborate scheme to confiscate Jewish property.

Arvid's loathing for Walther Funk knows no bounds.

4.

The political situation in Germany was complicated in previous years. Now, in August 1939, it makes no sense. In a maneuver that stunned not only Arvid and Mildred and the Circle but everyone else on the planet, the Soviet Union and Germany join forces.

In a room packed with photographers, a stout, mustachioed man and a slim, clean-shaven man sign a nonaggression agreement. They are Stalin's and Hitler's foreign affairs ministers, Molotov and Ribbentrop, who smile for the cameras, no hatchets in sight. Under the Molotov-Ribbentrop Pact, Stalin and Hitler are no longer bitter enemies. Communism and Fascism shake hands.

5.

A few days before Christmas, Hitler sends Stalin a note:

Best wishes for your personal well-being as well as for the prosperous future of the peoples of the friendly Soviet Union.

Stalin sends a thank-you to Hitler—

Please accept my appreciation for the congratulations and for the kind wishes for the peoples of the Soviet Union.

—and a note to Hitler's foreign minister, Ribbentrop:

The friendship of the peoples of Germany and the Soviet Union, cemented by blood, has every reason to be lasting and firm.

6.

Now what? Now what?

The Boy
VIII

Morgenthau's Man

1937–1939

9.45		2.00	
10.00		2.15	
10.15	*Donald Heath*	2.30	
10.30	*Banking Liquidation*	2.45	
10.45	*Feis*	3.00	*Jo...*
11.00	*Mexico*	3.15	

1.

Donald Heath hadn't planned to get his son involved. Not initially.

Over the previous fifteen years, he'd shuffled from one middling consular assignment to another, hoping to break into the diplomatic

274 ALL THE FREQUENT TROUBLES OF OUR DAYS

ranks of the foreign service. That he'd managed to break into consular work at all was an achievement. Heath was the first in his family to go to college. He got through two and a half years at Washburn University in Topeka before talking his way into a job as a journalist for United Press.

What he lacked in stature—in his socks, he barely reached five foot five—he made up for in charisma. He was a hit at parties. He remembered everyone's name in a crowded room. He had an inexhaustible supply of oddball stories and welcomed punch lines with a loud laugh. If there was a piano nearby, he'd play it, and if his fingers hit the wrong keys—by his own admission, he was no Irving Berlin—he'd laugh louder. As a reporter, he had a nose for sniffing out a good story and a knack for coaxing information from tight-lipped sources.

Still, Donald Heath had bigger ambitions. When the First World War broke out he fought in the infantry in France and resolved to change his life if he was fortunate enough to survive. Whether due to fortune or fate—he couldn't decide which—he did. Newly discharged, he dropped gallantly to one knee and promised a girl from Topeka that he'd be an ambassador one day. *Get up off the ground,* Louise Bell declared. They married. Within a month, they were living in Romania, where Heath had talked his way into a job with the U.S. State Department as vice-consul.

Over the next decade he paid his dues in the consular service, accepting transfers to Poland, Switzerland, and Haiti, earning the respect and admiration of his colleagues but never managing to ascend above the rank of consul. To be an ambassador was to occupy a rarefied realm dominated by Ivy Leaguers with family fortunes and powerful social connections all but closed to a former journalist from Topeka. Heath knew the State Department discouraged men without wealth from applying for diplomatic positions, but he took the required written examination anyway and passed it easily. At Heath's oral examination, a panel of foreign service officers evaluated his fitness for such a posting, using criteria such as "style, grace, poise, and above all, birth." Heath was undaunted. He'd been around diplomats long enough to know how to behave like a member of

Mildred.
Milwaukee,
Wisconsin, 1916

Arvid. Jena,
Germany, 1917

Mildred and
her mother,
Georgina Fish, a
self-taught
stenographer

During adolescence,
Mildred was inspired
by the women's suffrage
movement in Wisconsin,
the first state to ratify the
Nineteenth Amendment to
grant women
the right to vote.

In 1925, Mildred received a BA in humanities from the University of Wisconsin, which offered free tuition to Wisconsin residents.

Mildred and Arvid met when they were graduate students. Both advocated for left-wing social and economic reform. After marrying in Wisconsin in 1926, they hitchhiked to Colorado and joined a picket line of coal miners on strike.

Mildred was awarded a master's degree from the University of Wisconsin in 1926. In 1929, she moved to Germany to pursue a PhD.

Mildred and Arvid planned to teach at universities in Germany and the United States once they received their doctorate degrees.

Mildred with Arvid's family in Jena, Germany. (*Left to right*) Wulf Auerbach, Clara Harnack, Falk Harnack, Angela Harnack, Inge Auerbach, Mildred Harnack, Johannes Auerbach, Arvid Harnack, Claus Auerbach. Inge's husband, Johannes, was a Jew; Wulf and Claus were considered Mischlinge—mixed blood—by the Nazi regime.

In 1932, Mildred and Arvid began holding clandestine meetings in their Berlin apartment to discuss strategies of resistance against the Nazi Party. Mildred recruited German anti-fascists into the group, which she nicknamed the Circle.

At the U.S. embassy in Berlin, Kansas-born Donald Heath sent top-secret cables to the State Department in 1938 and 1939, about Hitler's preparations for war. Among his intelligence contacts were Mildred and Arvid.

After Germany invaded Poland, Louise and Donald Heath aided the resistance, using their son, Don, as a courier.

Don Heath, Jr., 1939

The Resistance in Berlin: Gestapo Mug Shots

Karl Behrens

Cato Bontjes van Beek

Erika von Brockdorff

Hans Coppi

Hilde Coppi

Arvid Harnack

Mildred Harnack

Wolfgang Havemann

Adam Kuckhoff

The Resistance in Berlin: Gestapo Mug Shots

Greta Kuckhoff

Elfriede Paul

Rose Schlösinger

Oda Schottmüller

Harro Schulze-Boysen

Libertas Schulze-Boysen

Elisabeth Schumacher

Kurt Schumacher

Günther Weisenborn

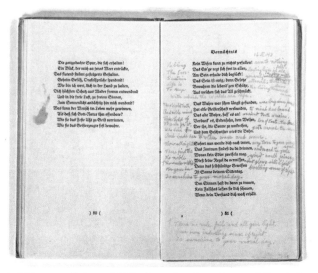

At Plötzensee Prison, Mildred translated a volume of Goethe's poetry. The book was smuggled out by Harald Poelchau, a prison chaplain who was secretly in the resistance.

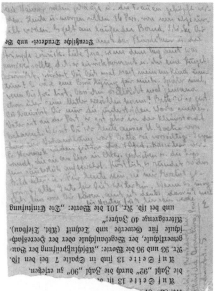

A note smuggled out of Charlottenburg Prison, written by a young woman in the resistance who was executed three months after Mildred.

their club. If style, grace, and poise could trump birth, he'd be an ambassador soon enough.

He left the oral examination exhilarated. But the promotion he'd hoped for didn't come. He remained a consul.

So Heath changed tactics. He quit consular work and landed a job at the Division of Latin American Affairs in Washington, DC. There, he rubbed shoulders with President Franklin D. Roosevelt's right-hand man, Sumner Welles. Welles presided over a massive reorganization of the State Department in 1937, and he was sufficiently impressed by Heath to recommend him for a new position—one in the foreign service.

Finally, the break Heath had been waiting for.

Heath was forty-three. Welles was forty-five. Both men had toiled since their twenties to advance their careers, but Welles was leagues ahead, just twenty-eight when he became chief of the Division of Latin American Affairs, where Heath was currently a middle-aged *assistant* chief. Welles had the pedigree Heath did not. He had been born into an exceptionally wealthy family in New York, like President Roosevelt, and educated at Groton and Harvard, also like President Roosevelt. He served as ambassador of Cuba—a fawning *New York Times* profile had described him as "the most talked-of diplomat in the service of the United States Government"—and as assistant secretary of state before President Roosevelt appointed him to his current position, undersecretary of state. At six foot three, Welles towered over Heath in the most literal sense too. Welles got his suits tailored in London and carried an ivory-tipped cane wherever he went, though nothing was wrong with his legs. Heath regarded him with a potent mixture of annoyance, envy, and immense gratitude.

A colleague of mine needs someone like you, Welles told him. *Someone different.*

Heath didn't need Welles to spell out what he meant by *different.* He asked where the job was. Welles, known for his crisp and concise manner, said, *Germany. It's somewhat dangerous.*

Heath reminded Roosevelt's undersecretary of state that he'd fought in the trenches in France. Whatever the job was, he was the man for it.

★   ★   ★

DONALD HEATH'S NEW ASSIGNMENT was officially announced on November 6, 1937, and published in the December 1937 issue of *American Foreign Service Journal:*

> Donald R. Heath of Topeka, Kansas, who has been serving in the Department of State, assigned to Berlin, Germany.

The issue landed in Heath's mailbox before he'd hashed out all the details with Welles's colleague, a man who was considered one of President Roosevelt's closest confidants.

2.

At 10:15 a.m. on December 14, 1937, Donald Heath entered a wood-paneled corner office at 1500 Pennsylvania Avenue for his first on-the-books meeting with Secretary of the Treasury Henry Morgenthau Jr. It was a Tuesday. Morgenthau's mornings were typically jammed with meetings, but today his desk calendar showed a considerably lighter load. He had a full half hour for Heath.

The two men discussed Heath's new position. The job description was not, in the strictest sense, straightforward. Heath was taking on not just one job, but two.

As first secretary at the American embassy in Berlin, Heath would work under the auspices of the State Department. Easy enough. Heath had held consular positions since 1920 and was well acquainted with the responsibilities of a first secretary. Here's where it got tricky: someone already had the job. The eminently capable Raymond Geist, a Harvard man, had been first secretary for nearly a decade. Morgenthau didn't intend to advocate for Geist's dismissal. He wanted Geist to keep doing what he was doing while Heath took on some of it. *Some,* but not too much, as Heath would need to devote most of his time to his second job, which was the real, off-the-books reason Heath was being dispatched to Berlin. The second job wasn't within the ranks of the State Department. It didn't even have a name.

Across the Atlantic, the man who had been appointed Germany's chancellor on January 30, 1933, had been steadily and determinedly mounting a lunatic campaign to extinguish the Jewish population and rule a broad swath of Western and Eastern Europe, if not the world. Other major powers had systems in place to acquire and analyze intelligence about threats, both internal and external, to their national security. The Brits had MI5 and MI6. The Soviets had the NKVD and the GRU. The Germans had the Abwehr.

What did the United States have? A mishmash.

The State Department, the FBI, the army, the navy, and the Treasury Department operated as separate, isolated agencies that competed against one another for presidential favor. Each agency had its own way of obtaining intelligence, and there was little to no sharing among them. It would be three and a half years before President Roosevelt authorized the creation of the first centralized intelligence agency of the United States, christening it the Office of the Coordinator of Strategic Information. Roosevelt appointed the charismatic William "Wild Bill" Donovan to run it, granting him military authority. Fierce objections followed from the upper ranks of the military and law enforcement, who joined forces against the new agency, hoping "to strangle this unwanted newcomer at birth." In a feeble effort to appease them, Roosevelt excised the word *Strategic* from the agency's name, and on July 11, 1941, the agency was rechristened the Office of the Coordinator of Information. Eleven months later, fraught with internal tensions and political bickering— FBI director J. Edgar Hoover called the COI "Roosevelt's folly"— the agency was scrapped and the Office of Strategic Services was born. Two agencies followed—the Strategic Services Unit in 1945 and the Central Intelligence Group in 1946—before the Central Intelligence Agency came into being in 1947.

In 1937, Assistant Secretary of State George Messersmith was well aware of the pronounced U.S. intelligence void in Germany. "We may be headed into stormy seas," he wrote in a ten-page letter to a colleague, stressing the need for comprehensive information about the German government, specifically economic intelligence. "We need to have the very best Department and the very best Foreign Service that we can have."

Meanwhile, the secretary of the treasury was formulating an audacious plan of his own. Morgenthau had long ago concluded that the reports the diplomats and attachés in Berlin dispatched to Washington were nearly useless to him. He didn't want summaries of newspaper articles or street gossip. He wanted numbers. He wanted facts. He wanted feet-on-the-ground intelligence, and he was gobsmacked that he couldn't get it.

He wanted to find out whether Hitler was preparing for war and how he planned to finance it. He wanted to know whether Germany would repay its debts to American creditors or default on them. He wanted a breakdown of Germany's money-market position, its foreign-exchange position, its gold reserves. He wanted a man who could cozy up to high-ranking Nazis and coax secrets from them, a man he didn't have to share with scores of State Department colleagues, a man who was his and his alone. The treasury secretary wanted his own personal spy.

So it was that Donald Heath became an intelligence agent in Berlin at an unusual moment in the history of American espionage. On the brink of a second world war, the United States was the only global power without a centralized intelligence agency. The gathering of foreign intelligence, what there was of it, was relegated to the diplomats and attachés. From January 1938 to November 1941, Donald Heath occupied a no-man's-land, a territory staked out somewhere in the nexus between the Treasury Department, the State Department, and the soon-to-be-formed Office of the Coordinator of Information.

The title Morgenthau devised for Heath was treasury attaché. Informally, Heath's colleagues called him "Morgenthau's Man." Neither title appeared in the *American Foreign Service Journal*.

3.

On January 15, 1938, his first day on the job, Donald Heath composed a list of men. He kept the list in the top drawer of his desk. Every so often he'd add a name to the list or cross one out.

At the top of his list: Hjalmar Schacht.

Hjalmar Schacht is president of the Reichsbank, Germany's central bank. Until recently, Schacht was also head of the Reich Ministry of Economics. Praised in international newspapers as a wizard of international finance, Schacht was credited with rescuing Germany from hyperinflation, and in the mid-1930s he became Hitler's darling. Since then, the most powerful economist in Germany has grown disillusioned with the Führer and resigned from the Reich Ministry of Economics on December 8, 1937.

Schacht cannot be trusted. This was the opinion held by the State Department, including Secretary of State Cordell Hull, Undersecretary of State Sumner Welles, and President Roosevelt himself. Ambassador William Dodd had held a different view—rumor had it that he actually *liked* Schacht—but Dodd was gone, having resigned from his post before Heath walked through the embassy doors.

Heath knew he was on his own. He was given an office with a large walnut desk. He was given a terrifically competent secretary, Miss Ulrich. And he was given virtually no instructions on what to do or how to do it aside from Morgenthau's directive to write reports and send them to him in DC. Walking to work on the morning of his first day, Heath passed a long, seemingly endless line of people, one that stretched from the Tiergarten all the way to the embassy's entrance and on through the doors to the consular section.

Men and women, young and old, rich and poor, were desperate to escape and pleading for visas that many would never receive. Restrictive immigration quotas limited the number of Germans who could legally seek refuge in the United States, and the rules favored the rich. Telephones rang incessantly. The sound of typewriters clattering resembled nothing so much as gunfire. The spectacle was unnerving, unlike anything Heath had experienced as a consul.

The embassy section was quieter. Up a broad, elegant staircase, there was a balcony where diplomats smoked and joked and watched Nazis goose-step across Pariser Platz.

What Donald Heath was up to exactly was not entirely clear to the people he worked with, from the secretaries on up to

Ambassador Hugh Wilson, who sent a carefully worded letter of protest labeled *personal and confidential* to Assistant Secretary of State Messersmith. A few weeks later, he sent a second letter to Messersmith, reminding him that "nobody discussed with me the work Heath was to do."

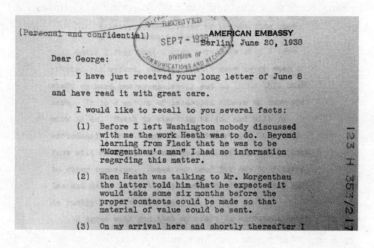

(Personal and confidential)   RECEIVED   **AMERICAN EMBASSY**

SEP 7 - 1938   Berlin, June 20, 1938

DIVISION OF COMMUNICATIONS AND RECORDS

Dear George:

     I have just received your long letter of June 8 and have read it with great care.

     I would like to recall to you several facts:

(1)   Before I left Washington nobody discussed with me the work Heath was to do. Beyond learning from Flack that he was to be "Morgenthau's man" I had no information regarding this matter.

(2)   When Heath was talking to Mr. Morgenthau the latter told him that he expected it would take some six months before the proper contacts could be made so that material of value could be sent.

(3)   On my arrival here and shortly thereafter I

4.

Meanwhile, Heath has made contact with Hjalmar Schacht.

Heath and Schacht meet for lunch at the Hotel Adlon, stroll through the Tiergarten after work, and on at least one occasion, Schacht shows up at Heath's home. By June, Heath has coaxed from the president of the Reichsbank enough information to write his first report for Morgenthau.

Every week or so, a detailed report with the subject line "From Heath to Treasury" reaches Washington by cable. If Heath's report is highly confidential, Miss Ulrich will slip it into a diplomatic pouch to be delivered by courier, typically by steamer ship and now and then by airplane. The most confidential information is never entrusted to cables or couriers; Heath is required to communicate it in person, which means frequent travel between Berlin and Washington, DC.

Sometimes Heath's trip is clandestine and goes unremarked upon. Sometimes it is reported in the *American Foreign Service Journal,* its purpose described vaguely as "principally on business connected with the Treasury Department."

Donald R. Heath

William F. Scotten

Donald R. Heath, First Secretary at Berlin, arrived in New York City on February 18 on the S.S. *Aquitania* and subsequently divided his time between New York and Washington, principally on business connected with the Treasury Department. He sailed for his post on March 15 on the S.S. *President Harding.*

Joy Ride

1938

1.

The daughter of mild-mannered Midwestern farmers, Louise Heath often skirts confrontation, pressing her lips together to keep words she might regret later from spilling out. But after six months in Berlin, she's less inclined to remain silent. When Donald comes home from the embassy, exhausted, and asks how her day was, she tells him, *Fine, fine,* mindful of Mamzelle the cook, who bustles around them, dishing up dinner, clearing plates, always within earshot. Once Mamzelle is gone, Louise hustles her husband out to the sunporch and treats him to a lengthy account of the day's intrigues and betrayals. She can't help it—the words burst out of her. Earlier, she caught Mamzelle looking through a drawer in the music room. Mamzelle claimed she was looking for a spoon.

The flower lady who has a shop on the first floor thinks Mamzelle is a Gestapo spy. In the same breath, the flower lady discloses that she's required to give the Gestapo a list of the names and addresses of the people Louise sends flowers to.

It is in this atmosphere of paranoia that Louise discovers that the Gestapo is following her. She'll leave the apartment to run an errand, driving a car the embassy has provided, and in the rearview mirror she'll see a black vehicle trailing close behind.

2.

One morning Louise decides to attend a lunch lecture at the American Women's Club. She brings Young Don with her. *It will be educational,* she tells him.

They're in the embassy car. Louise glances in the rearview mirror. Following them is a Volkswagen crammed with Gestapo trainees, some of whom look as young as sixteen. Louise floors the accelerator. The Volkswagen stays close behind. She has a full tank of gas and guesses that the teenage trainees don't. She merges with traffic onto the Autobahn, the Gestapo on her tail.

Don, squirming in the passenger seat, steals anxious glances at the Volkswagen in the rearview mirror.

Louise drives on, lips pressed together, eyes fixed on the road ahead as if daring it to defeat her. Her lipstick is blood red. Her nose is freshly powdered. Her hair is swept up in a bun. At some point, she pulls off the Autobahn and drives along country roads until, at last, the Gestapo trainees run out of gas.

Ha! she exclaims, and makes a sharp U-turn.

Awestruck, Don watches his mother lean out the window and wave at the teenage Nazis, screeching past their stalled Volkswagen.

Goodbye, boys!

3.

Most days, Louise is careful to keep her composure. She sails through the rooms at Innsbrücker Strasse 44 with a light step, managing the household and a full social calendar with ease. The pages of her datebook are crowded with embassy lunches and teas, dinners and cocktail parties, and the many other obligations demanded of her as Mrs. Donald Heath.

Mamzelle the cook is devoted to her—or at least claims to be.

So is Aladar Weigal, the Hungarian driver assigned to transport Donald to the embassy. Aladar doubles as a butler when Louise hosts a social event at home. He has already told her that he's required to report to the Gestapo once a month and tell them all he has seen and heard at Innsbrücker Strasse 44.

Aladar swears he will never say anything incriminating.

The flower lady on the first floor assures Louise that Aladar can be trusted.

4.

The moment Louise steps into Hela Strehl's apartment, she feels anxious.

Don can see it in his mother's eyes, the way they dart around the room from the piano to the lamp to Hela herself.

Will you take a photograph of us? she asks Goebbels's mistress. Her impulse is documentation, not celebration. Hela says she will. Many photographs show Louise smiling warmly, but this isn't one of them.

Later, she slips the photograph into an envelope and mails it to her mother in Topeka. She wants to give her mother a glimpse of her life in Berlin. She wants to show her how big Young Don is getting.

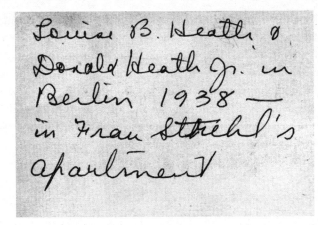

Louise B. Heath &
Donald Heath Jr. in
Berlin 1938 —
in Frau Strehl's
apartment

5.

Louise sets out to attend another lunch at the American Women's Club, and this time, the Gestapo mercifully leaves her alone. She drives to Bellevuestrasse 5, just south of the Tiergarten, and parks her car at the curb.

Walking in, she notices a woman moving through the sumptuously furnished rooms with the ease of someone who knows its contours intimately, pausing to say a word to this or that acquaintance, drawing from each a respectful nod, a smile, an embrace. The woman is president of the American Women's Club. She is blond though not at all glamorous. She wears no makeup or jewelry. Her dress is plain. Her hair is pulled back in a serviceable bun.

Louise has spotted Mildred Harnack in crowded rooms twice before, once at the American Church and once at a party hosted by a diplomat. Mildred seems to know nearly all the Americans living in Berlin—the journalists, the diplomats and their wives—or is at least on nodding terms with them. Although Louise hasn't yet introduced herself to Mildred, she's heard plenty about the president of the American Women's Club from its members, who gather to hear Mildred deliver lunchtime lectures about Thomas Wolfe, Theodore Dreiser, Willa Cather, and other American writers whose books Louise has never cracked open.

Donald is eager to meet Mildred's husband, a German named Arvid Harnack who works at the Reich Ministry of Economics, until recently under Hjalmar Schacht, one of Donald's best sources. Donald wants to turn Arvid into a source too, but so far he has eluded him, not returning a single phone call.

Now Louise approaches Mildred and introduces herself. Louise Heath is schooled in the art of diplomacy and knows full well that the best way to reach an unreachable man is through his wife.

Lunch Before Kristallnacht

1938

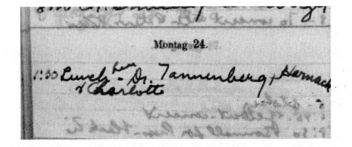

1.

At one o'clock on October 24, 1938, Mildred and Arvid Harnack eat lunch with the Heaths. Other guests include Charlotte Gilbert, the wife of Consul Prentiss Gilbert, and Wilhelm Tannenberg, first secretary at the German embassy in Washington, DC. The lunch is held on the fifth floor, in the Heaths' apartment in a small dining room painted cinnamon red. One wall is mirrored, making the dark room seem larger. A chandelier suspended from the ceiling casts chinks of light onto a table set for six.

The conversation during the meal is, we may assume, bland, congenial chitchat. But it marks the beginning of a courtship of sorts between the Heaths and the Harnacks. They sense that their sympathies are aligned and proceed to test the theory that they can be useful to each other during a series of casual social encounters. Donald and Arvid will begin meeting regularly in the chandelier-lit dining room of the Hotel Adlon on Pariser Platz, directly across from the U.S. embassy. Louise will begin meeting Mildred at the American Women's Club or in the pews of the American Church.

2.

Two and a half weeks after the lunch, Associated Press journalist Louis Lochner files a story that begins

> The greatest wave of anti-Jewish violence since Adolf Hitler came to power in 1933 swept Nazi Germany today.

Lochner's story is among the first to reach the English-speaking world about an orgy of brutality that erupts across Germany, Austria, and regions of the Sudetenland in Czechoslovakia during the evening and early-morning hours of November 9–10, 1938. In major cities, suburban towns, and rural villages, mobs of Nazis go on a rampage, setting fire to synagogues, barging into Jewish homes and stores, smashing everything in sight. The broken glass on the streets and sidewalks will later lend a name to the horrific episode: Kristallnacht—the Night of Broken Glass.

Journalist Sigrid Schultz writes a story that appears in the *Chicago Tribune* with the headline HOMES BURNED; STORES LOOTED; TERROR REIGNS: MOBS RUN WILD IN GERMAN STREETS. She reports,

> In Berlin an American walking down the Kurfürstendamm, one of the city's principal thoroughfares, saw a mob haul a Jew out of a store, knock him down, and trample on him until his shrieks stopped.

And

> Young men in leather jackets approached windows of Jewish stores...with crowbars.

And

In the poorest Jewish streets near Alexanderplatz, kitchen cabinets and other furniture of Jewish inhabitants were heaved out of windows, chinaware was spilt all over the street. The furniture was piled together and bonfires were lit.

A Jewish man in a town at the foot of the Black Forest is startled when ten Gestapo officers burst through the front door of his home, followed by an SS officer and a police officer.

"The policeman threw my wife to the ground," Simon Ackermann later recalled, "while the SS man flailed away at me like a madman. The policeman wanted to throw my three-year-old daughter out the window but I held her tight." Simon was dragged out the door and forced into a procession of other Jews through the neighborhood. "The whole town was on the streets. Many screamed like drunkards, yelling out 'Beat the Jews to death.'"

Across Germany, 267 synagogues and 7,500 Jewish-owned stores are destroyed. Ninety-one Jews are murdered. Innumerable Jewish women are raped. An estimated twenty thousand to thirty thousand Jewish men are arrested and sent to Dachau, Buchenwald, and Sachsenhausen.

Thanks to Berlin-based foreign correspondents like Lochner and Schultz, the horrors of Kristallnacht become known to the rest of the world. It is the first time the Nazi regime openly carries out a mass arrest of Jews specifically because they are Jews.

3.

Goebbels holds a press conference to castigate Lochner, Schultz, and other foreign correspondents for writing what he insists are false stories. No stores were looted. No Jews were killed. The violence was a "spontaneous demonstration" by ordinary citizens who were outraged after reading a newspaper article about a seventeen-year-old Polish Jew who had shot someone at the German embassy in Paris several days earlier. The teenager, Goebbels explains, had been "systematically trained" to commit this crime by a "Jewish organization."

Of course, the teenager hadn't been trained by an organization, nor was Kristallnacht "spontaneous." It was masterminded by Goebbels and Reinhard Heydrich, chief of the Gestapo, who saw in the teenager's crime a convenient pretext to instigate violence. Among the Nazi documents seized after the war was a confidential message that Heydrich sent to all police stations at 1:20 a.m. on November 10 outlining the procedures officers should follow for the planned event. The message ended with a detailed statement directing officers to arrest and send to concentration camps as many healthy male Jews as they could.

4.

Kristallnacht marks the end of one thing and the beginning of something else. What it is the beginning of, no one at the U.S. embassy in Berlin can fathom. Consuls and diplomats pass each other in the halls, tongue-tied and shaken to the core. Ambassador Hugh Wilson is "recalled for consultations to Washington," as the official line goes, which everyone at the embassy knows is a euphemism for *got the hell out.*

He never returns.

Scrambling to fill the void, the State Department gives Consul Prentiss Gilbert a hasty promotion to chargé d'affaires, a notch below ambassador. Gilbert dies of heart failure five months later.

It's a time of tremendous chaos within the embassy and outside its doors. The line of people desperate to escape Germany is seemingly interminable and will stay that way through the next year. "Refugees were to be found in every nook and cranny of [the building], many of them begging to be allowed to spend the night," remembered one of Heath's colleagues at the U.S. embassy in Berlin, Consul William Russell.

There was no European country which would admit a German or a Polish Jewish refugee unless he could first show that he was registered with the American Consulate for an immigration visa. There were times when the crowds got too much for us—especially the time they pushed through two heavy glass and brass doors.

In the midst of the chaos, Donald Heath keeps writing his reports. His list of sources grows after Kristallnacht, and Arvid Harnack is among them.

Getting to Be Pretty Good

1938–1939

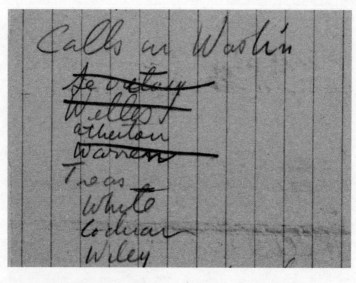

1.

On December 13, 1938 — exactly one year after Donald Heath met with Henry Morgenthau to discuss his new position — Morgenthau convenes a meeting in his office. It's 9:30 a.m. In the room are ten men and one woman (Miss Chauncey, a secretary). The meeting is recorded and will later be meticulously transcribed.

About ten minutes in, Harry White, who has recently been named director of the Division of Monetary Research at the Treasury, says

```
White:      I don't know whether you have noticed, but Heath,
            the man who went over for the State Department to
            Germany - his cables are getting to be pretty
            good.  There was a long time when we got nothing,   |
            but they are beginning now.
```

Morgenthau agrees, and says he wants to talk to Heath face-to-face.

On February 4, 1939, Secretary of State Cordell Hull sends a telegram to Donald Heath directing him to come to Washington, DC. Heath boards the SS *Aquitania* and arrives on February 17.

In DC, Heath gives Morgenthau a typed summary of the intelligence he has obtained from his key sources Hjalmar Schacht and Arvid Harnack about Hitler's armament program.

"Heath has all the stuff," Morgenthau tells his Treasury Department colleagues.

2.

Back in Berlin, Donald Heath writes a letter to Morgenthau and describes a recent weekend walk with Arvid, who advocates for "an unmistakable firm stand" against Hitler.

3.

Arvid knows all about the massive profits I. G. Farben is making thanks to his confidential source Turk, who sees all the balance sheets. The chemical conglomerate is currently producing vast quantities of synthetic fuels, oils, rubber, and plastic as Hitler prepares for war. During a weekend walk, Arvid tells Donald Heath about Germany's reserves of strategic raw materials, including petroleum.

Appeasement won't restrain Hitler. Arvid emphasizes this point again and again in his conversations with Heath.

On April 24, 1939, Heath sends a cable to Morgenthau:

> The Embassy has received reliable information that the German Embassy in London has been informed by Chamberlain that Great Britain is prepared to release to the Reich most of the Czech gold reserve which was on deposit in London.... This news is surprising to Reich officials who look on it with somewhat amused disdain. They interpret it as an indication that Chamberlain is still inclined to gestures of "appeasement" and a belief that financial enticements can be used to buy off the Reich.

4.

The U.S. embassy is in a state of chaos. After Chargé d'Affaires Prentiss Gilbert's death, the State Department scrambles to find a diplomat to take his place. In May 1939, the post is awarded to Alexander Kirk, the Yale- and Harvard-educated heir of a laundry-detergent fortune.

Chargé d'Affaires Kirk arrives in Berlin splendidly attired. After introducing himself to Donald Heath and other key personnel at the embassy, he devotes himself to the task of looking for a mansion that meets his standards.

5.

And now it is summer. Arvid takes a trip to DC. He is traveling under the auspices of the Ministry of Economics to discuss a German-American trade agreement but takes advantage of the opportunity to meet with several of Donald Heath's colleagues in the Treasury Department.

Hitler, he warns them, must be stopped.

Arvid mentions his source at I. G. Farben who knows all about the company's hidden assets in America. The moment Hitler starts this war—not *if* he does, but *when*—these assets must be seized by the U.S. government. Arvid is especially adamant on this point.

But it's no use. Arvid returns to Germany with the conviction that the men in the Treasury Department didn't take him seriously.

6.

This is a pattern that repeats again and again. As early as 1937, emissaries from the German resistance attempted to make contact with the U.S. and British governments and warn them about the threat Hitler poses to the rest of the world. But statesmen in the West remain profoundly skeptical that a German resistance actually exists.

An illustrative memo written by an official at the British Foreign Office asks: "Are the stories which reach us of dissident groups in Germany genuine?"

7.

The archives tell us a great deal. Historians have relied on them in the decades that followed the Second World War to piece together the story of the German resistance, or part of it, anyway.

Much is missing from them.

The voluminous archives at the National Archives, the Library of Congress, and the Franklin D. Roosevelt Presidential Library don't tell us that in the summer of 1939, Donald Heath informed Chargé d'Affaires Kirk that he had received intelligence indicating that "Nazi military aggression would shortly occur," or that Kirk gave him a "pitying" look and said, "My dear Don, even somebody as stupid as myself...knows there's not going to be any war."

The archives tell us that Donald Heath reported to Secretary of Treasury Morgenthau, Secretary of State Hull, and Undersecretary of State Welles accounts of confidential conversations he had with Reichsbank president Hjalmar Schacht, but don't indicate that Schacht asked Heath not to send these accounts "by cable because the Nazis had 'broken' the American codes" or that Heath sent them by cable anyway—

```
recounted I had an unusual dual assignment.  On the one hand I had
been directed to keep in touch with Schacht who was head of the
Reichsbank and to report under my own name any important information
received from him by Diplomatic Pouch to the State Department.  Schacht
had asked that my conversations with him not be reported by cable
because the Nazis had'broken"the American Codes.  On this occasion
```

—because he "thought the information too urgent to send by Diplomatic Pouch." The archives don't inform us that State Department officials rejected Arvid Harnack's offer to deliver confidential information about Hitler's preparations for war, or that they believed he was lying when he insisted that he was in the resistance.

So many stories remain untold.

8.

Immediately after Arvid returns from DC, he and Mildred visit Donald and Louise Heath and stay up very late, talking about what could possibly be done. They visit the Heaths again on August 26, 1939, and open a bottle of wine, deciding for the remainder of the night to forget Hitler. In a moment of tipsy hilarity, Donald pounces on the piano and Mildred thrusts her arms out theatrically, the way she'd once done in high-school plays, performing a waltz step that takes her into a twirl. There she is, twirling and whirling and bursting into song—yes, Mildred starts to sing, and she is "so funny singing," Louise Heath would later write in her diary.

The Heaths' seventeen-year-old daughter, Sue, is there too, transfixed by the sight of Mildred, who, whirling even faster now, lifts her voice into "operatic registers" as Sue's parents hiccup with laughter.

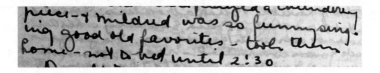

gone to bed, but I was allowed to stay up.   In two months I would be

18 and back at college in the States.

My father played some Schubert on the piano, and Mildred, restless,

got up and whirled around in a waltz step. When my father finished the
to sing something in German
piece she began whirling faster , her arms flinging out, her

voice going up into an operatic register. Father grinned and began to

accompany her accompaniment on the piano. I could see his shoulders

shoulders heaving with laughter, but I couldn't understand all the

German words, being delivered by Mildred . Even my mother

had become helpless with laughter. Only Arvid

Upstairs in his bedroom, her brother, Don, is asleep, too young
to understand any of it.

A Fateful Decision

1939

1.

Don spends most of the summer of 1939 in a German town near the Polish border with a family called the Zitzewitzes, who own a castle there. A boy Don nicknames Boobie takes him sparrow shooting, and nearly every day he goes swimming in a lake.

A rubber tube keeps him afloat. There are loons that keep their distance, white smudges on the water, while he kicks and splashes, snug in the middle of the tube. He likes watching them swim in a line, slow and serene, a faraway parade. Likes chasing them too. Once, riding in a motorboat, the Zitzewitzes and Don chase four loons around the lake. The flurry of white feathers makes him giddy. The Zitzewitzes feed him lobsters. Ice cream too—Don can polish off four helpings in a single sitting. One day Don swims in the cold, majestic Baltic Sea—the Ostsee, the Zitzewitzes call it—and surprises himself: he can swim on his own, without the tube.

Dear Ma and Pa.
I went to the ost see, gosh it was cold, I swam with a rubber tube and surprised myself by swimming without one. The bees are eating out of the honey bowl.

The castle the Zitzewitzes call home is cold and massive. There are endless passageways inside and endless rows of vegetables on the estate surrounding it, but what impresses Don most are the bees.

Don likes to wake up before dawn and run outside to see a farmer dressed in rumpled work clothes tend the bees. Don helps him scrape the comb, sending ribbons of runny honey into a pot the farmer holds with grubby hands. The lantern in the dirt gives off a soft yellow sputter.

2.

The Zitzewitzes tell Don it's time to return to Berlin. The morning of his departure he dashes out to see the bees and hears a magnificent boom. Then another, and another.

Thunder.

Two weeks later the booming won't stop. This time it isn't thunder. The Second World War has begun.

3.

While bombs rain on Poland, Donald Heath works sixteen hours a day at the U.S. embassy in Berlin. Only a skeleton staff remains. The State Department has issued instructions for all but the most critical personnel to leave Germany. Clerks and secretaries throw their belongings into steamer trunks. The wives and children of diplomats are dispatched to Norway, where they wait until arrangements can be made for their safe transport back to the States.

4.

The city streets are eerily empty. The train station is just the opposite: sheer pandemonium. This is Louise Heath's first impression as she hustles Young Don through the grand, arched entry of the Anhalter Bahnhof, which is thronged with panicked people. There is a stench of unwashed bodies, a potent brew of sweat and fear that Louise finds nearly unbearable. She bribes the conductor to let them get on the train going to the port town of Warnemünde.

In Warnemünde she buys two ferry tickets to Copenhagen.

In Copenhagen, Louise and Don board a train to Oslo.

In Oslo, they look for a hotel. The first two are full. The third, Hotel Bristol, has a vacancy ("got one single room at Bristol," she scribbles in her diary). After a fitful sleep and a cold breakfast, Louise takes Don sightseeing. Among the distractions are a fleet of Viking ships and a twelfth-century church "with faint painting on the walls." The day ends with a visit to a museum that housed the *Fram,* a vessel that voyaged to the South Pole. Don is delighted by the *Fram,* but is otherwise listless and cross.

5.

They spend all of September in Oslo.

Young Don makes friends with some of the children at the Hotel Bristol, and Louise socializes with their mothers. She will always remember this strange, anxious time. The cold, Nordic mornings, the glossy fish on plates of ice, the sense of holding her breath. She follows news of the war in whatever newspapers she can get her hands on. On lucky days, the *London Times.* On other days, she makes do with the *Deutsche Allgemeine Zeitung,* puzzling out the words with a dog-eared German-English dictionary. She scribbles notes in her diary:

> On September 5: "horrible bombings in Warsaw."
> On September 14: "rumors of Russian mobilization."
> On September 24: "Warsaw finally taken."
> On September 29: "Warsaw really taken now."

In October the *London Times* is even harder to find. Louise pages through German newspapers, dictionary in hand, appalled. There is "nothing but repetition of great success in the war . . . German papers full of most disgusting accusations—every day call Churchill more names."

On November 4, Louise gets a telegram from Donald:

COME BACK TO BERLIN.

Finally, Donald has a plan. She has been waiting for this telegram all month.

"Mad rush all day," Louise writes in her diary. "Great silence on train — no one spoke.... Rumors of heavy bloodshed in Czechoslovakia."

6.

In Berlin, Louise and Donald Heath discuss what to do with Young Don. The American School is closed for good now — the Ziemers have fled — and the diplomats at the U.S. embassy have sent their children off to boarding schools in Switzerland or back to the States. Donald says he has a plan for Young Don. It's so far-fetched Louise can't quite wrap her mind around it.

On November 15, Louise goes to the American Women's Club to hear Mildred give a lecture. Mildred speaks about "the idea of hope in Emerson, Walt Whitman."

Hope. Perhaps Louise feels, for a slim moment, reassured.

7.

November 19:

> *At nite we went over the question of Don... seems as tho I <u>cannot</u> let him go.*

November 20:

> *Couldn't keep from weeping when I tucked him in and heard his prayers. We talked late into the nite, Donald and I, wavering on the wisest choice.*

November 21:

> *Early at the same question. Donald left without deciding... said we'd go over whole question at noon & at noon we decided we'd wait at least one more day.*

8.

On November 22, 1939, Donald and Louise come to a decision. Young Don will remain in Berlin. Louise listens to her husband's rationale for using their son as a courier for Mildred. Later, she writes in her diary, "I feel really as tho it is a mistake."

Air Raid

1940

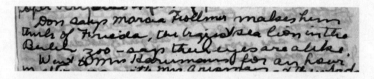

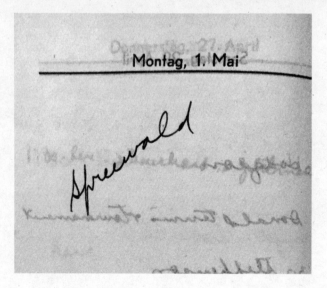

1.

Sometimes Don takes the S-Bahn to Zoologischer Garten. The biggest elephant seal in the Berlin Zoo is named Frieda. Don likes watching her swim. Frieda has long whiskers and sad eyes.

Sometimes he takes the U-Bahn to Nollendorfplatz.

Sometimes he takes it to Stadtpark.

No matter which route he takes to Mildred's apartment, he passes the charred remains of a burned-down synagogue. The memory of Kristallnacht is impossible to erase.

2.

Don misses his friends at the American School. In a photograph taken of his class last year, he stood with his arm slung around the shoulder of another boy, who is Jewish. That boy is gone now.

3.

The paper Mildred slips into Don's knapsack looks like a letter.

Dear Louise, it begins. *How are you doing today? I hope all is well with you and Donald.* It goes on in this dull way for several sentences. *The weather has been so cold, hasn't it? We ran out of coal last night.*

At the end of the letter, an invitation, equally bland.

Arvid and I would love for you and Donald to join us for a walk in the Spreewald, it might say. *We can pack a picnic lunch.*

4.

The Spreewald is a heavily wooded region sixty miles southeast of Berlin, far enough that they feel reasonably sure they aren't being followed. They meet on a Sunday, giving their rendezvous the appearance of a leisurely outing.

Mildred and Arvid travel there by train. Louise and Donald go by car, Young Don in the back seat. Don waits for the moment his father brings the car to a stop, then leaps out.

He's the lookout and has dressed the part. Black short pants, tan knee socks, tan shirt, and a black cap—the uniform of the Deutsches Jungvolk in der Hitlerjugend, a division of Hitler Youth for boys between ten and fourteen. The uniform is Young Don's own idea. Mole stole it for him.

Don runs deep into the forest. On a tree-lined path, Mildred and Arvid are waiting. Don finds them, turns around and runs to his parents, then leads them back to Mildred and Arvid.

As the four of them stroll through the Spreewald, Arvid gives Donald confidential information from the Ministry of Economics that he can't risk putting in writing. Don runs ahead, keeping an eye out for people on the path. If he spots anyone, he'll start singing the Nazi anthem "Horst Wessel Lied"—a warning to his father and Arvid to stop talking.

They continue to meet, often on Sundays, sometimes there, sometimes at the boat lift (*Schiffshebewerk*) in Lüneberg, where they walk alongside the enormous hydraulic hoists that lift ships out of the sea.

Sometimes, a man named Otto Donner joins them. Otto works with Arvid at the Ministry of Economics.

Don runs up ahead, dressed in his Deutsches Jungvolk uniform. He is always the lookout, a job he knows is important, but sometimes he wishes he could listen to their conversation instead. He hears Otto yelling and Arvid yelling back. He even hears his father yelling—all three, arguing fiercely. Don wonders what they're arguing about.

A moment later, he spots two Germans in uniform striding up the path. Heart thumping, he bursts into song:

Die Fahne hoch! Die Reihen fest geschlossen!
SA marschiert mit ruhig festem Schritt!

5.

The war will start soon, Don overhears Mildred say. She is in the living room with his parents, and Arvid is with her. It's late at night. This is the only time of day Mildred and Arvid visit—after Mamzelle the cook has left.

6.

Be careful, Berliners say. Nazi informants are everywhere. Watching. Listening. With neighbors, watch what you say. And with friends? You never know. Alliances shift. Your friend could become your enemy. Your enemy could become your friend.

Germany and Russia have become friends. This is what Don learns from his father, who explains that the two countries promised that they won't take military action against each other for ten years. His father is flabbergasted. Germany and Russia were bitter enemies in the First World War. *Now they've buried the hatchet?* his father exclaims.

7.

Sometimes Don goes to Mildred's apartment late in the afternoon, and when he leaves it's nearly night. The sidewalk is slippery with ice, and his shadow on it is long, the color of coal. The smell of coal stings his nostrils. Smoke spews from chimneys, drifts in cloud clusters above apartment buildings. Sometimes Don sees no smoke, which means there's no coal. Inside, people huddle in ice-cold rooms, shivering in moth-eaten overcoats. Hitler planned for this war. The men in his ministries calculated how much bread and potatoes Germans would need, but they didn't plan for this cold.

Trucks don't deliver coal anymore. There aren't enough trucks, and there isn't enough gas to fuel them. If you want coal, you have to go to the railway. Coal is piled high in mounds. Women trudge there dragging suitcases, pushing empty baby carriages. Children pull empty toy wagons. They pile as much as they can into their suitcases and baby carriages and toy wagons and trudge back home.

Sometimes there's no coal at the railway. No coal means no hot water. As a consequence, Don doesn't take baths as often as he used to. This is a relief. Don has never liked baths. His father has begun to take his baths at work.

"At the Embassy two large tin bathtubs are installed upstairs," Donald Heath's colleague William Russell writes in a memoir,

> one for women and one for men. Women employees of the Embassy must telephone one of the stenographers a day ahead if they want an appointment for the bathtub. They have twenty minutes to take their bath and get out. We men have not been put on bath schedules, it being practically impossible to tell a man what newspaper he shall read or what hour he shall take his bath.

While Donald Heath and William Russell enjoy privileges their female colleagues do not, they must accustom themselves to other deprivations. Stores no longer sell shaving cream, razors, or cigars. Toilet paper is no longer white—it's brown, and is called "unity paper." Louise Heath shares her husband's disdain for it; she doesn't know how a whole family can survive on "one roll of toilet paper (more like sandpaper) for our family every 10 days." Soap has a new name too, "unity soap." Families are allowed a single bar a month, which "was supposed to suffice for face washing, dish washing, bathing and all laundering." Groceries are also strictly rationed. One-pot Sundays are instituted. German women are instructed to fill a pot with old vegetables and meat scraps for the Sunday meal and calculate how much money they save. When a Nazi Party worker bangs on their doors, they must deposit this money in a can.

Meanwhile, some stores in Berlin display pyramids of canned goods that are not for sale, intended to present the illusion "that there were unlimited supplies in the Reich."

8.

As food shortages worsen, Berliners tell bad jokes:

What's the difference between India and Germany?

In India one man starves for everybody. In Germany everybody starves for one man.

9.

The sound of wooden shoes fills the street. *Clappity-clap, clappity-clap.* No one in Berlin has rubber-soled shoes anymore. Rubber is needed for the war.

10.

In April 1940, Hitler invades Denmark and Norway.

In May, Hitler invades Belgium, Holland, and Luxembourg.

In June, Hitler invades France.

Boys enact bloody battles. You see them on the streets of Berlin, invisible rifles in their arms. Some drive make-believe tanks, simulating engines, sputtering their lips, *bbbbbbbbbbbbrrrrrrrrrrr,* releasing fine sprays of spit.

Six weeks later, France surrenders.

11.

A single shrill note, piercing the air.

The first time Don hears it, he's not frightened. He imagines a fire truck racing through the streets of Berlin. Wherever the fire is, the firemen are ready for it. They stop traffic. Neighbors huddle on the sidewalk, grateful that a truckful of tall men in helmets and coveralls are coming to the rescue. Children trapped in smoke-filled rooms will be rescued, and right in the nick of time a mewling kitten will emerge from the blaze, fur singed but otherwise intact, cupped in a fireman's meaty palm.

But there is no fire.

The single shrill note is a warning. The Allies might drop bombs on Berlin. It's important to be prepared, says his mother, who calls it an *air alarm*. His father calls it an *air raid*. Don secretly hopes that he'll hear it again.

12.

The second time he hears it, he's still not scared.

The single shrill note sends everyone scrambling to the air raid shelter in the basement, all the people in Innsbrücker Strasse 44. They are frenzied, their eyes wide with panic, though they try to remain calm.

Mamzelle hates the air alarm. So does his mother. Don crouches next to them in the shelter, feeling a wild, exuberant thumping in his chest.

13.

Hitler has conquered most of Western Europe. The Luftwaffe is now the largest air force in Europe. Britain braces for bombs.

The Blitz — short for Blitzkrieg, or lightning war — begins in September 1940. For fifty-seven consecutive nights, the Luftwaffe bombs London, lighting up the city's famed dismal gray skies. A bushy-eyebrowed North Carolinian named Edward Murrow arrives in the smoke-choked city. CBS Radio has hired him to broadcast daily reports to Americans.

"This is London," Murrow begins, emphasis on the *this*. He lifts his microphone above his head so listeners can hear what war sounds like. An explosion rips the air. He places his microphone on the ground. The sound of footsteps: Londoners retreating to bomb shelters. He climbs to a rooftop. "For reasons of national as well as personal security," he says, "I am unable to tell you the exact location from which I am speaking." Murrow broadcasts to Americans' imaginations as much as their ears.

Off to my left, far away in the distance, I can see just that faint red angry snap of anti-aircraft bursts against the steel blue sky.... Now you'll hear two bursts a little nearer in a moment. There they are. That hard, stony sound.

Murrow's radio reports on the Blitz draw ordinary Americans into the Second World War, bringing it right into their homes. Still, President Roosevelt doesn't want the United States to get pulled into what he considers to be Europe's war. For more than a year, Britain will fight Germany alone.

14.

Black headlines scream from Berlin's newspaper kiosks. ARE THE ROOSEVELTS JEWS? one asks.

15.

A British bomb detonates near the Heaths' apartment. Louise Heath marks the date in her diary: September 11, 1940.

On September 12, a bomb goes off near the U.S. embassy, approximately one hundred fifty yards from the Brandenburg Gate, estimates William Shirer, who will write about it in *Berlin Diary*. A splinter from the bomb

crashed through the double window of the office of Donald Heath, our First Secretary. It cut a neat hole in the two windows, continued directly over Don's desk, and penetrated four inches into the wall on the far side of the room.

The same day, a Jewish professor forced to live in a communal *Judenhaus*—Jews' house—scrawls in his diary:

> For three weeks now the Berliners have been sitting in their cellars night after night; yesterday they were hit very hard.

16.

A single shrill note, piercing the air.

Now when Don hears it, the thumping in his chest isn't excitement. It's fear.

Louise Heath's Diary

1940

1.

The cover of Louise Heath's diary is tough black leather. She writes in it nearly every day. Sometimes, when she isn't home, Don flips through the pages, idly wondering what would happen if she burst into the room and caught him reading it. The threat of punishment makes his stomach turn with a queasy mixture of excitement and shame.

Louise Heath's handwriting is compact and neat, the letters slanting uniformly forward, evoking a woman who is inclined toward brisk optimism, a wife and mother who confronts life's challenges by looking sensibly on the bright side. Gazing at it, Don is reassured. All is right in the world. If he turned the page and her handwriting was loopy and erratic, slanting every which way, he might feel unnerved, as if his mother had suddenly acquired a strange foreign accent or replaced her sensible, low-heeled leather pumps with clown shoes.

Louise Heath also keeps a datebook. If she has to take the car to the mechanic or get her hair shampooed or go to a cocktail party at the Russian embassy and make small talk with Hermann Göring and Joachim von Ribbentrop, she writes it down.

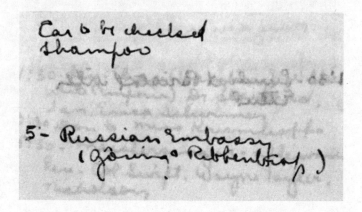

Don sometimes sees his own name. The first two days of 1940, his name appears twice.

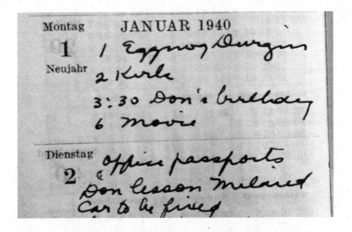

2.

On January 1, after eggnog and before Don blows out twelve candles on his birthday cake, Louise and Donald Heath have a late lunch
with Chargé d'Affaires Alexander Kirk. A chargé d'affaires is one
rank below ambassador. This is problematic from the perspective of
American diplomacy. Diplomatic doors that open to an ambassador
remain closed to a chargé d'affaires. Kirk can't have lunch with
high-ranking German officials or otherwise meet with them. The
U.S. embassy occupies a kind of "twilight zone between diplomatic
normality and non-recognition."

Young Don doesn't understand the difference between an ambassador and a chargé d'affaires or why doors that were once open and
are now closed would pose a problem for the American government
during a world war. What he knows is that his father doesn't like
Kirk, and Kirk doesn't like his father, though you wouldn't see it if
you watched the two of them together, smiling and nodding and
clapping each other on the back. His mother doesn't like Kirk either,
but it's harder for her to hide what she feels. When Louise Heath is
in Kirk's presence, distaste sours her face as though she just bit down
on a lemon seed.

Kirk refuses to live in just any old mansion. Months go by before he finds one that passes muster. Louise slips a photograph of it into an envelope and sends it to her family in Topeka.

"Mr. Kirk's residence here," she writes with frank sarcasm, "has only forty rooms."

Mamzelle and Mildred and Mole

1940

1.

Mamzelle's pastries are shaped like stars and crescent moons that leave golden, greasy crumbs in Don's hands. She was born in France and likes to be called Mademoiselle. Don can't twist his tongue around it so he calls her Mamzelle.

Mamzelle is paid by the U.S. embassy to cook for the Heath family. She obtains provisions set aside for diplomats at the embassy, which has made an arrangement with Danish dairies for "a weekly shipment of Canadian bacon, cheese, eggs, and butter."

You're very lucky to be American, she tells Don. *German boys don't eat real butter.*

Every night after Mamzelle finishes washing the dinner dishes, she calls, *Bonsoir! Bonsoir!* on her way out the door.

2.

One day Mamzelle shows Don a German newspaper with gruesome pictures of Poland. The Polish people committed horrible atrocities in a town called Bromberg, she tells him, chopping off the legs and arms of German farmers, cutting the tongues out of their mouths. Mamzelle insists that these atrocities are the fault of two British men, Prime Minister Winston Churchill and Foreign Secretary Anthony Eden.

Mamzelle likes spoiling Don, stuffing his pockets with her pastries, feeding him ice cream. She lets him lift the bowl to his mouth and lick the melted ice cream pooling at the bottom, something his mother would never allow. Mamzelle asks him, *Who are your mother's friends? Who are your father's friends?* When Don has a lesson with Mildred, Mamzelle gives him two pastries. *One is for your teacher,* she says.

3.

Tell me how you got here.

Don recites the names of streets, the U–Bahn station stops.

You have a good memory, Mildred says.

She keeps telling him this. Don can't believe his ears. His teacher back in Silver Spring had branded him distractible and a slow learner.

Did anyone try to talk to you? Mildred asks.

Don shakes his head. He drapes his coat over the back of the chair. *Here,* he says, withdrawing a small cloth bag from his knapsack. Inside are two star-shaped pastries. He reaches into his knapsack once more and withdraws a brown paper bag. Inside is an orange. *From my mother,* he tells her. Oranges are even harder to obtain than butter. Mildred brings the orange to her nose and takes a long, grateful sniff.

The next day, Mamzelle peppers him with questions. *Where does your teacher live? What does she tell you?*

Lifting a bowl of ice cream to his mouth, Don pretends he doesn't remember. Sweet ice cream melts on his tongue.

4.

One day Mildred shows Don a map. She's going to a park in Potsdam and wonders whether Don can come.

Don takes the S–Bahn to Potsdam. Mildred meets him at the station. She hugs him. She looks tired. Together, they walk to the park.

She tells him she's meeting a lady from Leipzig. She wants Don to trail behind. If he sees anyone following them, he must whistle the danger song. If he doesn't see anyone following them, he must whistle the safe song.

The danger song, as always, is "Horst Wessel Lied." The safe song is "The Hunter and His Dog."

Don has worn his Deutsches Jungvolk uniform for the occasion. His beloved air rifle is slung over his back, and he has a pocketful of pellets. When his mother saw him leave the house, she frowned and said, *You don't have to wear all that.*

He feels his pulse quicken now, watching Mildred approach a woman, a satchel in her hand. They greet each other like old friends.

Don follows them at a distance. There is the smell of earth and rain. It's spring. Squirrels scramble up trees and across the path, and on any other day he would shoot pellets at them. But Don is looking for Gestapo. Sometimes they wear uniforms, sometimes they don't.

Don whistles the safe song.

A moment later, Mildred and the lady from Leipzig exchange satchels.

5.

October 31, 1940. Germany loses the Battle of Britain.

Don is ecstatic. He races up the stairs to the roof of his house, loads his air rifle with hunks of raw potato, and shoots at the sky, where a crow flying past metamorphoses into a Messerschmitt Bf 109. When he runs out of potato, he loads it with lead slugs and shoots at a stack of tin cans, then tosses the rifle aside and spreads his arms, transforming into a Spitfire with a courageous RAF pilot in the cockpit.

The next time he sees Mole, he shoots him.

Mole cries out and reels around, his face registering shock.

Don drops his air rifle. Then picks it up again. He doesn't know what to do.

A slug isn't a bullet. Mole will be all right. Still, the expression on his face is horrible to see. Spit leaks out the corner of Mole's mouth, and his eyes fill with tears.

Mildred

IX

Fragment

Questionnaire
Plötzensee Prison, Berlin
February 16, 1943

Last place of residence?   Berlin, Woyrschstrasse 16

Where did you last work for longer   University of Berlin
than a week?

How many times have you previously Never
been convicted?

How many children do you have?   None

Foreign Excellent Trench Coats

1940

1.

In 1940 the cozy handshake between Stalin and Hitler is tightening. They follow up their nonaggression pact with a trade agreement, making them partners in both war and business. Stalin sends Hitler wheat, cotton, rubber, iron, nickel, tin, platinum, cobalt, and crude oil. In exchange for these strategic raw materials, Hitler sends Stalin artillery and warplanes, including Germany's brand-new Junkers Ju 88 combat aircraft and Messerschmitt Bf 109 and Bf 110 fighter planes, as well as an assortment of turbines, generators, diesel engines, and explosives.

Hitler prizes the Russian oil above all else. Oil is the lifeblood of the German military machine. Stalin sends him 606,600 tons of it in 1940. Russian oil fuels the German panzer divisions that roll across France and up to the shores of the English Channel in the spring. Russian oil fuels the German warplanes that rain bombs on Britain through the summer, fall, and winter.

2.

Meanwhile, Hitler is hatching a plan to double-cross Stalin and invade the Soviet Union.

First he needs to conquer Britain. Then he can focus his attention on the vast expanse of the east and claim the Soviet Union—or a chunk of it—as his own. It is an audacious scheme, not least because Hitler has been sending Stalin all those Messerschmitts and Junkers knowing full well that when he attacks the Soviet Union, Russian troops will use them to kill Germans.

3.

Stalin, of course, is hatching a scheme of his own.

He has already murdered millions of his own people in the Soviet Famine of 1932–33 and the Great Purge of 1936–38. Many of his best spies are among those whose bodies are buried in mass graves in Moscow and its outskirts. Stalin promised Hitler that he wouldn't spy on Germany, a condition of the cozy handshake, but Stalin has no intention of keeping his promise.

He promptly issues orders to activate a sprawling spy network in the countries surrounding Germany, with city capitals serving as bases of operation. Agents, technicians, liaisons, couriers, cipher clerks, and radio operators are swiftly dispatched to Brussels, Amsterdam, Copenhagen, Geneva, and Paris.

In Brussels, a pair of Moscow-trained agents set up an import-export company to serve as a cover for their espionage. They name their company Foreign Excellent Trench Coats.

By 1940 Foreign Excellent Trench Coats has been up and running for over a year. It is fully outfitted with a radio transmitter to send and receive encrypted messages as well as a codebook and cipher pads for decrypting the messages. A fireplace in the office serves a dual purpose: to warm the agents during winter months and to incinerate messages.

4.

A secret symphony plays over the airwaves as operators at Foreign Excellent Trench Coats and in Soviet cells scattered across countries surrounding Germany tap out messages to Moscow Center.

In 1940, the Germans don't hear the symphony. They don't even know it exists.

Corsican Drops a Bombshell

1940

1.

On the morning of September 17, 1940, Arvid hears a knock on the front door. He isn't expecting anyone. Mildred has traveled alone to Czechoslovakia and won't be home for several days.

Arvid doesn't like strangers at his door. Warily, he opens it.

The stranger gives Arvid his name: Alexander Erdberg. A faint Russian accent colors his vowels. Arvid studies him. He is dark-haired and square-jawed. He says that he knows Arvid's old friend from ARPLAN Alexander Hirschfeld. Arvid hasn't heard Hirschfeld's name uttered by anyone in more than two years—not since Stalin's bloody purges cleaned out the Soviet embassy in Berlin. Hirschfeld is alive, one of the lucky few who escaped execution. This, at any rate, is what Alexander Erdberg claims, insisting, *We need your help.* In March, the strangers knocking on the door were Gestapo. One of Arvid's colleagues at the Ministry of Economics— he doesn't know who—had tipped them off. Heart pounding, Arvid watched the officers raid the apartment, spilling the contents of every drawer onto the floor, ransacking the closets, looking for leaflets, stolen documents, anything that would merit his arrest. The Gestapo left empty-handed. Since then, he has walked a knife's edge.

Alexander Erdberg proposes that they meet again, leaving Arvid to wonder whether he is who he says he is. He could be Gestapo.

2.

Alexander Erdberg is an alias. His real name is Alexander Mikhailovich Korotkov. At nineteen, Korotkov worked as an elevator operator at a building in Moscow's Lubyanka Square, headquarters of the Soviet secret police, known then as the OGPU. Korotkov caught the eye of OGPU top brass, who admired his athleticism on the tennis courts of the OGPU's lavish sports club. He was promoted to clerk and quickly ascended the ranks of Soviet intelligence.

Now, at thirty-one, Korotkov works for the NKVD under diplomatic cover as third secretary at the Soviet embassy. He goes there immediately after seeing Arvid and sends an enciphered message to Moscow Center confirming that he has restored contact with Balt.

3.

Six days later, Arvid hears another knock on his door.

This time, Korotkov drives him to the Soviet embassy, where they can talk without worrying about the Gestapo. In the time between their first encounter and this one, Arvid has decided to trust Korotkov. He reiterates his terms. He won't be ordered around, and he won't accept money.

Korotkov listens with the sympathetic patience of a seasoned spy. He asks Arvid how his resistance group is structured. How many members? How are they recruited? Arvid tells him that Mildred is crucially involved in "carefully selecting and drawing in new recruits" and describes the circles within circles that compose the Circle, which has grown to sixty members.

After the meeting, Korotkov sends Moscow Center an enciphered message:

At present, within the larger circle, centers have been formed, each of which is dedicated to the education and training of a small group . . . while not all of the members of the circle know one another, something of a chain exists.

4.

Moscow Center is displeased. One of the key principles of *konspiratsia* is compartmentalization. Too many people in the Circle know each other. The Gestapo could easily unravel the entire network by arresting a few members and torturing out of them the names of others.

Still, Pavel Fitin, the thirty-two-year-old director of NKVD foreign intelligence, wants to replenish an agency that has suffered a bloody purge. Fitin is woefully inexperienced. The agents who have managed to evade execution are jittery and demoralized. Already, Fitin has sent two hundred hastily trained agents to other countries, hoping to resuscitate his depleted networks. A group of sixty Germans who are willing to risk their lives and commit treason can be useful to him, provided that Arvid is both trustworthy and willing to trust. Korotkov assures his superiors that Arvid is "an honest person, a truly moral person, who says what he means." Moscow Center authorizes the arrangement, advising Korotkov to conduct "a very careful treatment of Harnack so that a wall of distrust did not arise."

Korotkov assigns Arvid a new code name. Balt is no more. Now he is Corsican.

5.

Three days later, on September 26, 1940, Arvid sends Korotkov his first intelligence report. It's a bombshell.

Korotkov immediately sends an enciphered message to Moscow Center, alerting his superiors that an officer in the High Command of the Wehrmacht

has told Corsican that by the beginning of next year Germany will be ready for war with the Soviet Union.

Libs and Mildred Among the Cups and Spoons

1940

TOP SECRET

M.1.

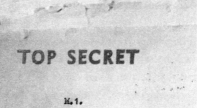

SCHULZE-BOYSEN, Libertas.

nee HAAS-HEYE.

4221geu/3

ESPIONAGE: Deeply implicated in her husband's intelligence work from 1936 onwards, and his deputy during the war years.

PERSONAL PARTICULARS:

Nationality: German

Description: Extremely attractive, wealthy.

Occupation: Writer, art and film critic.

Relatives: Daughter of a Swedish countess, nee EULENBERG, related to Count DOUGLAS. Parents owned estate at Giebenburg, at which GOERING was a frequent visitor.

ADDRESSES: 2, Weitzstrasse, Berlin-Charlottenburg.

119, Altenburger Allee, Berlin-Charlottenburg.

1.

Harro Schulze-Boysen's wife is twenty-seven. She has dark blond hair cut at the chin and a snub nose. Her name is Libertas; Harro calls her Libs.

Libs likes to show off her wealth, or so it seems to Greta Kuckhoff. The first time they meet, she produces a photograph of a massive castle in Liebenberg that belongs to her grandfather. Greta gives the photograph back to her, unimpressed. She is peeved by Harro's wife—who enjoyed a pampered childhood in that castle, followed by finishing school in Switzerland—and by Harro, too, who strikes her as an annoyingly adolescent hedonist. Greta has a nickname for him: "Schu-Boy."

Greta is a mother now; her son, Ule, is three. "It was so rare to have a child in our circle," she wrote, noting that "Libertas didn't have one" and "Mildred wholeheartedly wished for one."

Despite her irritation, Greta helps to arrange a meeting between Mildred and Libertas in Hohnstein, a small town one hundred fifty miles south of Berlin. A cottage with a narrow kitchen "protected from all eyes and ears" will serve as the perfect place for a rendezvous. She gives Mildred a key to a side entrance door.

Later, when Greta is alone with Ule, she wraps her arms around him. "I needed to hold my child tightly," she remembered. "I could see very clearly: From now on death was near us."

2.

Mildred meets Libertas in the narrow kitchen. She wants to get a good sense of her before their husbands meet again. She knows Harro's wife is an aristocrat, the granddaughter of a prince.

There is so much Mildred doesn't know.

Libertas's family castle in Liebenberg is near Göring's country estate—just twenty miles away. Göring keeps lion cubs as pets and has a vast collection of plundered art at the estate, which is situated between two lakes in a beautiful forest and has a name—Carinhall—a tribute to his Swedish wife, Carin, who died young. His second wife, an actress named Emmy, lives there now. The architect who designed Carinhall in 1934 went on to design the stadium that hosted the 1936 Summer Olympics in Berlin. Göring didn't pay a dime for his country estate; the Nazi government footed the bill in full.

Libertas's proximity to the architect of the Gestapo may be chilling, but it has paid social dividends. When Libertas was twenty-two, Göring invited her to an extravagant hunting party at Carinhall, where she watched princes and foreign dignitaries join the self-appointed hunting master of the Reich in chasing after stags with rifles. Libertas had been a member of the Nazi Party then.

She had a change of heart when she fell in love with Harro.

Now, Libertas considers herself as committed to the resistance as he is. Göring isn't a hindrance; in fact, the supreme commander of the Luftwaffe has helped smooth Harro's way toward professional advancement. Göring was one of the guests at Libertas and Harro's wedding, held in the chapel of her family castle. Harro's swift promotion followed. Göring is entirely unaware that Harro despises him. Indeed, Göring's fondness for Libertas's husband is so widely known among Luftwaffe lieutenants that Harro can walk out the door with top-secret blueprints and bombing-target maps without anyone raising an eyebrow.

Mildred still isn't sure about Harro. She's not sure about his wife either. That afternoon in the kitchen, among the cups and spoons, Mildred listens carefully to Libertas, taking the measure of her political convictions.

AGIS and Other Agitations

1940–1942

1.

After Mildred meets with Libertas, Arvid meets with Harro.

Harro's resistance group, Gegner Kreis, has grown since Mildred and Arvid sat down with Harro in their living room five years ago. There are now approximately twenty members.

Arvid's opinion of Harro hasn't changed much. He still believes Harro is too "fervent." But circumstances are dire now. The world is so much worse.

2.

The Circle expands.

In 1940, Harro Schulze-Boysen's Gegner Kreis forms a third link in the chain along with Adam Kuckhoff's Tat Kreis.

3.

In 1941 Gegner Kreis intersects with Rittmeister Kreis, a small resistance group with a neurologist named John Rittmeister at its center. He is director of a clinic in Berlin and describes himself as a "humanist." He agrees to help Harro with a new leaflet campaign.

The leaflets are signed *AGIS*. It's John Rittmeister's idea, a reference to Agis IV, the idealistic king of Sparta who aimed to abolish inequity and redistribute land held by the wealthy. The leaflets are a call to action, urging Germans to oppose Hitler's regime. Emblazoned across the top of one leaflet are the words "Call for Resistance."

Over the next two years, members of the Circle, Gegner Kreis, Tat Kreis, and Rittmeister Kreis collaborate to produce a slew of leaflets with titles like

What Is a Majority?
Why the War Is Lost
Freedom and Violence
Revealing Certificate of the North-German Industry About the
    Circumstances Leading to the War
Call to the Workers of the Mind and the Fist Not to Fight Against
    Russia
Call for All Professions and Organizations to Oppose the
    Government
Organize the Revolutionary Battle of the Masses

Some of the AGIS leaflets are produced in an apartment at Waitzstrasse 2. Cato Bontjes van Beek lives here. At twenty, she is among the youngest members of Rittmeister Kreis. Her ambition is to be a pilot. A sprinkling of freckles dot her nose and cheeks. Before joining Rittmeister Kreis, Cato smuggled food to Jews in hiding. One day she watched SS officers drag her Jewish neighbors — a young mother, father, and their five-year-old son — out of their apartment. She never saw them again.

Now Cato stays up late at night duplicating leaflets using gelatin pads and paper that Harro brings to her apartment. She goes from post office to post office, buying only twenty stamps at a time (buying more could invite suspicion), and mails the leaflets to strangers. She slides the leaflets into stacks of newspapers at kiosks. She smuggles them into U-Bahn stations.

Some of the AGIS leaflets are produced in Annie Krauss's apartment. Annie used to be a journalist; now she is a fortune-teller. The Germans who show up at her door with palms outstretched include military officers. She traces the lines of their palms with her finger-tip, murmuring predictions. Some officers long for a lover. Some are worried about the war. She coaxes them to tell her where they will be stationed, what they plan to do. The officers don't know that Annie has stashed two mimeograph machines in the apartment or that the details they disclose will find their way into the leaflets that she will reproduce on the machines.

4.

On February 15, 1942, the Fourth Division of Reich Central Security receives numerous telegrams from police stations about a certain leaflet. A Nazi officer writes a detailed report stating that the leaflet was mailed to "representatives of the press, the Catholic Church and the intelligentsia." Employees of Goebbels's Ministry of Public Enlightenment and Propaganda are also among the recipients. The officer describes the leaflet. It's not just one piece of paper—there are six single-spaced pages. Across the top are the words "The People Are Troubled About Germany's Future." It begins "Time and again, Minister Goebbels attempts in vain to scatter new sand in our eyes" and goes on to denounce the Nazi regime.

> The most disgraceful tortures and cruelties are being perpetrated on civilians and prisoners in the name of the Reich. Never in history has one man been as despised as Adolf Hitler. The hate of this tormented humanity burdens the entire German nation.... Read the newspaper, watch the weekly newsreel with your wits! Bear in mind that they are doing everything to give you a tainted view of the situation. Protest more and more loudly when you have to line up anywhere and everywhere! Stop putting up with everything. Do not be intimidated anymore!

> The final page is signed *AGIS*.

GG-Mitteilung III
Nro. Zgt. Nr. 9/42/i
17. 8.42

Die Sorge um Deutschlands Zukunft geht durch das Volk. *I.-5.* 8.42

Vergeblich müht sich Minister Goebbels, uns immer neuen Sand in die Augen zu streuen. Die Tatsachen sprechen eine harte, warnende Sprache. Niemand kann mehr leugnen, daß sich unsere Lage von Monat zu Monat verschlechtert. Niemand kann noch länger die Augen verschließen vor der Ungeheuerlichkeit des Geschehens, vor der uns alle bedrohenden Katastrophe der nationalsozialistischen Politik.

Die grossen militärischen Erfolge der ersten Kriegsjahre haben kein entscheidendes Ergebnis gezeitigt. Die meisten deutschen Armeen befinden sich zur Zeit im Rückzug. Allen Fälschungen des OKW zum Trotz steigt die Zahl der Kriegsopfer in die Millionen. In fast jedem deutschen Haus herrscht Trauer. Die Werktätigen sind immer ärgerer Antreiberei und Überanstrengung ausgesetzt. Die letzten Reserven werden aus dem Volkskörper herausgepreßt. Es gibt kaum noch etwas zu kaufen. Das Gold verliert seinen Wert. Immer neue Hunderttausende schluckt die Armee. Industrie und Landwirtschaft leiden empfindlich unter dem Mangel an Arbeitskräften. Zehntausende von Betrieben brechen unter der Last der Kriegsverhältnisse zusammen. Früchte jahrzehntelangen Fleißes gehen verloren. Die Frauen trauern dem entschwundenen Familien- und Liebesglück nach. Der häusliche Frieden ist zerrüttet. Die Tage vergehen freudlos, ohne daß dem Menschen ein eine Hoffnung winkt. Zeit und Nervenkraft gehen verloren mit der immer knapperen Rationen, die die Regierung dem Volk noch zugesteht. Die Allgemeinheit leidet zudem unter den Unverschämtheiten und Schikanen der Behörden und Parteistellen. Die staatliche Bürokratie in ihrer infamen Dummheit ist kaum noch imstande, die ihr zufallenden Aufgaben zu erfüllen. Die Korruption in der Verwaltung, im Wirtschaftsleben, in der SS macht, vor allem aber innerhalb der Gliederungen der Partei hat ein unheiltes Ausmaß erreicht. Während der Arbeitnehmer gezwungen wird, zu immer schlechteren Bedingungen seine Arbeitskraft zu verkaufen, und oft fernab von den Seinen ein graues Dasein als Arbeitssklave zu führen, gibt es immer noch genug Bonzen und Kriegsgewinnler, die ihre Aufgabe darin sehen, die Massen mit den staatlich vorgeschriebenen Lügen zu füttern. Damit auch nur keiner in Versuchung kommt, selbständig nachzudenken, wird auch noch die Freizeit der Werktätigen dem braunen Zwang unterworfen. Eine volksentfremdete Schicht von albernen, aber schädlichen Schwindlern und Angebern spielt heute die erste Rolle im Leben des Volkes. In schwerster Notzeit der Nation kommen diese Leute recht gut auf ihre Kosten. Das Gewissen aller wahren Patrioten aber bäumt sich auf gegen die ganze derzeitige Form deutscher Machtausübung in Europa. Alle, die sich den Sinn für echte Werte bewahrten, sehen schaudernd, wie der deutsche Name im Zeichen des Hakenkreuzes immer mehr in Verruf gerät. In allen Ländern werden heute täglich Hunderte, oft tausende von Menschen standrechtlich und willkürlich erschossen oder gehenkt, Menschen, denen man nichts anderes vorzuwerfen hat, als daß sie ihrem Lande die Treue halten, wie das ehedem in Deutschland Männer wie Hofer, Schill und Palm auch taten. Im Namen des Reiches werden die scheußlichsten Quälereien und Grausamkeiten an Zivilpersonen und Gefangenen begangen. Noch nie in der Geschichte ist ein Mann so gehaßt worden wie Adolf Hitler. Der Hass der gequälten Menschheit belastet das ganze deutsche Volk.

Sind wir schwach und kleinmütig, machen wir uns zu Unrecht Sorgen, lassen wir die Führung charakterlos im Stich? Es ist ganz natürlich, daß man sich Gedanken macht. Die Millionen, die in Augenblick der Machtergreifung durch die NSDAP in der Opposition standen und denen seitdem mit den Mitteln des Terrors der Mund verschlossen wurde, sie haben nichts abgestrichen von ... tiefwurzelnden Verdacht, daß hinter allen völkischen Phrasen der Wille zum imperialistischen Krieg, zu einem neuen Weltkrieg im Interesse einer Clique stünde, die sich die Ausplünderung anderer Völker zur bequemen Richtschnur ihres Handelns machte.

5.

Members of Gegner Kreis get jobs that penetrate Goebbels's Ministry of Public Enlightenment and Propaganda.

Writer Günther Weisenborn gets a job at Grossdeutscher Rundfunk, a German broadcasting network. In a memoir, he describes how he "took home copies of the speeches of foreign statesmen

which we received in the Broadcasting Company as secret material."
He and his wife, Joy, copy the speeches in the evening using two
typewriters. In the morning, another member of Gegner Kreis picks
up the typed pages, which are then transformed into leaflets.

Libertas Schulze-Boysen is hired for a position at the film center
Kulturfilm, where her duties include deciding which films will be
censored. Her job gives her access to photographs that document the
atrocities on the battlefields of Europe. When she walks out the door
of Kulturfilm at the end of the day, she smuggles them out to be
reproduced in leaflets.

6.

Members of the Circle, Tat Kreis, and Gegner Kreis produce an
underground newspaper called *Der innere Front* (the Internal Front).
They write articles that expose I. G. Farben as a war profiteer,
describe the abysmal conditions endured by workers in armament
factories, and urge Germans to engage in active resistance. They
encourage workers in German armament factories to sabotage the
production of bombs and ammunition.

Der innere Front is an attempt by these three resistance groups to
reach beyond Germany's borders. Members translate the German
articles into French, Polish, Italian, Czech, and Russian and distribute the translated issues of the newspaper to soldiers, factory workers, and forced laborers.

7.

Open Letters to the Eastern Front is another series of leaflets. The
eighth in the series features a gruesome photograph of a two-year-
old Russian girl who was murdered on her family's farm along with
her mother, father, six-year-old brother, and infant sister. Libertas
found the photograph at Kulturfilm and hopes it will move readers
to denounce the atrocities committed by German soldiers invading
the Soviet Union. She also interviewed German soldiers on leave

who admit to witnessing war crimes; their statements are incorporated in the text of the leaflet.

8.

"Sometimes we went out at night on 'poster actions,' pasting up on walls and buildings posters calling for the end of the war," Günther Weisenborn remembered. One of the largest poster actions that Weisenborn participates in is in the spring of 1942. Joining him are several dozen coconspirators, including Hans and Hilde Coppi, who head out the front door of their apartment with brushes and pots of paste.

Goebbels has mounted a garish exhibition at the Lustgarten, a park in the center of Berlin where Nazi rallies are frequently staged. Harro Schulze-Boysen meets them on a street corner with others from Gegner Kreis and Rittmeister Kreis. Under cover of night, they paste over Nazi posters advertising the exhibition with posters of their own:

Permanent Exhibition

THE NAZI PARADISE

War, Hunger, Lies, Gestapo

How much longer?

The next night another underground resistance group meets at the Lustgarten. Nearly all the members of Baum Gruppe are Jewish. They will carry out an even bolder act of resistance. They have brought explosives.

Zoya Ivanovna Rybkina's Eleven-Page Table

1941

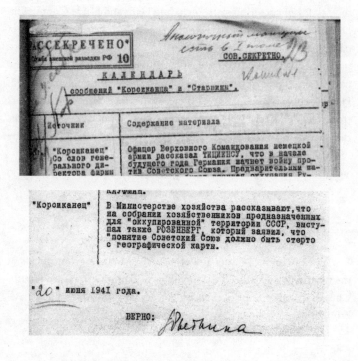

1.

Moscow Center requires Arvid to name the sources who give him the information that ends up in his intelligence reports. During the first few months of 1941, one of Arvid's best sources is Harro Schulze-Boysen. To protect his identity, Moscow Center gives Harro a code name: Starshina.

Two of Arvid's other sources don't have code names: Otto Donner, who heads the Research Bureau for the War Economy under the Four-Year Plan, and Colonel Blau, in the high command of the armed forces. This is a risk. If German intelligence agents in the Abwehr intercept Arvid's transmissions to Moscow Center, Donner and Blau could be arrested. Notices of their executions would be posted outside the courthouse, a warning to any German who might entertain the thought of committing treason.

2.

From January to April 1941, Moscow Center receives an intelligence report from Arvid nearly every week. A woman named Zoya Ivanovna Rybkina analyzes the report and types up a table that summarizes key points and sources.

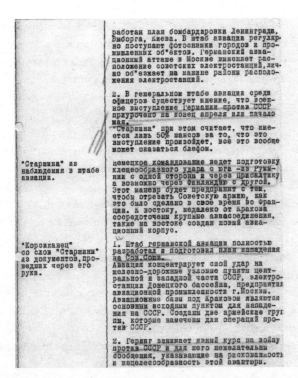

	работан план бомбардировки Ленинграда, Выборга, Киева. В штаб авиации регулярно поступают фотоснимки городов и промышленных об"ектов. Германский авиационный атташе в Москве выясняет расположение советских электростанций, лично об"езжает на машине районы расположения электростанций.
	2. В генеральном штабе авиации среди офицеров существует мнение, что военное выступление Германии против СССР приурочено на конец апреля или начало мая. "Старшина" при этом считает, что имеется лишь 50% шансов за то, что это выступление произойдет, все это вообще может оказаться блефом.
"Старшина" из наблюдения в штабе авиации.	немецкое командование ведет подготовку клещеобразного удара с юга –из Румынии с одной стороны и через Прибалтику, а возможно через Финляндию с другой. Этот маневр будет предпринят с тем, чтобы отрезать Советскую армию, как это было сделано в свое время во Франции. К востоку, недалеко от Кракова сосредоточены крупные авиасоединения, также на востоке создан новый авиационный корпус.
"Корсиканец" со слов "Старшины" из документов, прошедших через его руки.	1. Штаб германской авиации полностью разработал и подготовил план нападения на Сов.Союз. Авиация концентрирует свой удар на железно-дорожные узловые пункты центральной и западной части СССР, электростанции Донецкого бассейна, предприятия авиационной промышленности г.Москвы. Авиационные базы под Краковом являются основным исходным пунктом для нападения на СССР. Созданы две армейские группы, которые намечены для операций против СССР.
	2. Геринг занимает явный курс на войну против СССР и для него нежелательны сообщения, указывающие на рискованность и нецелесообразность этой авантюры.

In the January column, Zoya types:

> In the German Air Force General Staff an order has been issued
> to commence reconnaissance flights over Soviet territory on a
> large scale.
> Source: Corsican, according to oral information provided
> by Starshina.

In the February column, she types:

> A German attack of the Balkans is forthcoming.
> Source: Corsican, according to oral information provided
> by OKW Blau.

In the March column, she types:

> The Four-Year Plan Committee has completed its calculation
> of the economic efficiency of an anti-Soviet action.
> Source: Corsican, according to oral information provided
> by 4-year plan committee official Donner, Otto.

3.

Moscow Center is pleased with Arvid's reports. On March 15, 1941,
Korotkov receives instructions to establish direct contact with
Arvid's source Starshina.

A week later, Korotkov and Harro Schulze-Boysen shake hands.

Their meeting is a success. Harro has numerous sources of his
own who whisper German military secrets into his ear, including a
liaison officer for Göring, a senior counterintelligence chief in the
Reich Air Ministry, and an army captain who is an aide-de-camp
to Wilhelm von List, a field marshal who commanded the Twelfth
Army in the invasion of France (later this spring, he will march his
troops into Yugoslavia and Greece).

Korotkov promptly sends an enciphered message to Moscow
Center:

Starshina gives the impression that he is fully prepared to tell me everything he knows. He answered my questions without evasion....Moreover, he had prepared for the meeting and had put down on a piece of paper certain points to pass over to us.

4.

Now that Korotkov has established direct contact with Harro, he sets his sights on other members of Arvid's network.

He arranges a meeting with Adam Kuckhoff, who he discovers has a number of contacts that extend beyond Tat Kreis to other underground resistance groups. The connections among them are an intricate webbing across Berlin. Arvid's and Adam's mutual friend Adolf Grimme knows a man named John Sieg, who knows a man named Wilhelm Guddorf, who knows a man named Franz Jacob, who knows a man named Julius Leber, who knows a man named Helmuth James Graf von Moltke. In this way, the webbing connects the Circle to Tat Kreis to the Bästlein-Jacob-Abshagen Gruppe to Kreisau Kreis.

Adam Kuckhoff is assigned the code name Old Man.

5.

Korotkov is grooming Arvid to become an illegal *rezident* for the NKVD, though Arvid doesn't know this yet. This is a designation for a deep-cover spy, one who isn't working under diplomatic cover as an official member of a foreign embassy and so cannot claim immunity from prosecution if arrested. The instructions he gives Arvid constitute an introduction to the operational techniques—the tradecraft—of a spy.

Arvid knows he has been summoned to a secret meeting when he finds a copy of the newspaper *Börsen-Zeitung* in his mailbox. The meeting is scheduled to take place seven days after the newspaper's date. A red line over the newspaper's date would have meant that the meeting was urgent, on the very same day. The meeting time and location are always the same: 8:00 p.m. at the Tiergarten S-Bahn station.

Arvid stands by the exit and waits.

Soon, a stranger will approach him and ask, *Can you tell me how to get to Woyrschstrasse?* The stranger is a cutout, espionage jargon for an intermediary. Arvid will surreptitiously slip his intelligence report to the cutout. Later, the cutout will deliver the report to Korotkov, who will encipher it and give it to a radio operator at the Soviet embassy in Berlin. The radio operator will send the enciphered report by Morse code to Moscow Center.

Sometimes Arvid uses a dead drop, leaving an intelligence report in the glove box of an automobile. Sometimes Arvid uses a courier, giving an intelligence report to a trusted member of the Circle, who delivers it to a cutout.

6.

In April 1941, Germany, Italy, and Hungary invade Yugoslavia, where hastily mobilized soldiers don't stand a chance against the Blitzkrieg. The Luftwaffe rains bombs on Belgrade, reducing the capital city to rubble. Yugoslavia surrenders just eleven days later. Greece is next.

The same month, Moscow Center instructs Korotkov to complete Arvid's training. No longer will Korotkov be involved in delivering Arvid's intelligence reports. Arvid must send the reports to Moscow Center himself, using a wireless radio transmitter, a codebook, and a cipher table. The memo is dated April 12:

> Corsican will become our "illegal" *rezident*. . . . The assignment
> is urgent.

Arvid agonizes over the decision. He's a German anti-fascist, not a spy for Stalin. Still, if he is too dogmatic—a conclusion others in the Circle have previously reached—he may end up undermining his own objective. Refusing to send the intelligence reports himself means they may not reach Moscow Center. There is a war going on, after all, and his interactions with Korotkov through cutouts might be abruptly severed. Korotkov could be evacuated, or promoted, or killed. Arvid knows his intelligence reports are vitally important, now more than ever. Hitler seems unstoppable. By the end of April, Athens falls. By the first week of May, Crete is on the verge of collapse.

Finally, and with great reluctance, Arvid relents. Korotkov slips him a bundle of banknotes.

7.

A line has been crossed.

Since 1935, Arvid has insisted to his Soviet handlers that he's a German anti-fascist, not an agent. He will engage in espionage only when it helps him achieve his aims in defeating Hitler. Never before has he accepted money from Moscow Center.

There's no denying it now. Arvid's conversion is complete: he is officially a spy.

Back home at Woyrschstrasse 16 Arvid counts the banknotes: 13,500 Reichsmark. He makes four piles. Three are for immediate disbursement. He will give thirty-five hundred to Greta and Adam Kuckhoff, five thousand to Karl Behrens, and three thousand to Karl's friend Leo Skrzypezinski, who has recently joined the Circle. In the last pile, he sets aside the remaining two thousand.

8.

Moscow Center sends two radio transmitters to Berlin. One is small and portable and powered by a battery; the other has to be plugged into an electrical outlet and is so large and clunky that it must be carried in a suitcase.

Greta Kuckhoff agrees to pick up one of the transmitters. She arrives at the Thielplatz U-Bahn station wearing a bright yellow raincoat.

Many years later, Greta will admit in her memoir that she'd agonized about the wisdom of wearing such a thing. She was about to meet a spy, after all, which required subtlety. A dark raincoat, she knew, would enable her to blend into the crowd, but Greta decided

to employ reverse psychology: Perhaps the best way to avoid attracting Gestapo attention was to appear as if you were *not* trying to
avoid attracting Gestapo attention. Hence the bright yellow
raincoat.

A dark-haired young man gripping a suitcase approaches her.
Greta understands who he is: Korotkov. They walk side by side for
a while. He pretends they're good friends, not perfect strangers. She
does her best to play along. The train station is bustling with people,
many of them uniformed men with swastikas on their armbands.
Greta feels her heart race, a frantic thudding.

Korotkov drops the suitcase.

Drops it. Greta is aghast.

Korotkov recovers smoothly, taking hold of the handle once
again and striding forward, though she can't stop thinking about
what's inside: a transmitter with plugs and tubes and numerous other
parts that are easily damaged.

After a few blocks he sets the suitcase down, this time gently.
Greta picks it up. It's heavier than she expected.

9.

Two men volunteer to operate the radio transmitters: Mildred's
BAG recruit Karl Behrens (code name Worker) and a sculptor in
Gegner Kreis named Kurt Schumacher (Tenor). They get a crash
course in radio-transmitter operation while Arvid and Harro receive
cipher pads and a crash course in enciphering.

Within a few weeks, Kurt is drafted into the German army.

A young man offers to take his place, a member of Gegner Kreis
who has eagerly joined a number of leaflet and poster campaigns.
His name is Hans Coppi (code name Clean).

10.

The transmitter doesn't work.

When Greta is safe inside her apartment she opens the suitcase, uncoils a long, thick cord, and plugs the metal prongs into the wall socket. No blinking lights, no electronic chirps. Nothing.

What should she do? What *can* she do?

Korotkov should be immediately notified that the transmitter is broken, but *how?* Greta doesn't know the proper procedure; she has no training in espionage. The urgency of her dilemma makes her head spin, and there are other obligations that are just as pressing: Ule needs to be fed, and soothed, and tucked into bed.

11.

Spring brings to Moscow Center a slew of intelligence reports that Hitler is planning to invade the Soviet Union. Zoya Ivanovna Rybkina's table includes summaries of Harro's reports in addition to Arvid's, both of which must be carefully analyzed. Zoya Ivanovna Rybkina collaborates with several analysts who assess the reliability of the intelligence and the trustworthiness of the sources. Zoya began working at the tender age of fourteen, when she landed a job as a librarian at the Cheka, the Soviet secret police agency that was the precursor of the OGPU. She is thirty-three now. She has spent her adolescence and the entirety of her adult professional life among secrets in a roomful of men.

She analyzes the reports sentence by sentence, word by word. Her workroom is filled with files stuffed with old intelligence reports that she repeatedly consults, verifying whether they accurately predicted events or were proven false.

The reports Arvid and Harro submit by mid-June have accumulated into a stack. Zoya Ivanovna Rybkina's table condenses the stack into eleven pithy pages. Years later, she will recall, "We were at pains to ensure that only thoroughly sifted out and measured facts would stay."

Stalin's Obscenity

1941

1.

In the six months before Germany attacks the Soviet Union, Stalin is deluged with warnings from Arvid and Harro, such as:

> Plans for bombing the most important objectives are being drawn up. The plans for raiding Leningrad, Vyborg, and Kiev have just been completed. Photographs of cities and industrial targets are being regularly processed by the Luftwaffe staff. The German air attaché in Moscow scouts the location of the Soviet electric power station personally in his car by driving around the area where the generating stations are located.

And

> The German Air Force General Staff has completed preparations for the air attack plan against the Soviet Union. The Luftwaffe is to concentrate its attack on railroad junctions in the central and western part of the USSR, on the electric power stations in the Donetsk coalfields, on aviation factories in Moscow.

And

> It is necessary to warn Moscow seriously that the question of an attack on the Soviet Union is a settled one. The attack is planned for the immediate future. In the German Air Force General Staff, the preparations for operations against the USSR

are being carried out at great speed. In conversations with staff officers, 20 May is often cited as the date for the beginning of war. Others predict that the attack is planned for June.

Stalin ignores the warnings, dismissing Arvid's and Harro's reports as disinformation.

Stalin receives other warnings, from Britain, the United States, and a Soviet spy in Tokyo named Richard Sorge (code name Ramsay), but he's convinced that Western democracies are slyly trying to sow discord between dictatorships and goad him into distrusting Hitler.

By late spring of 1941, Stalin's paranoia reaches epic proportions. While German panzer divisions and warplanes prepare to invade his country, Stalin greets every scrap of intelligence Moscow Center sends him as false, the fantastical construction of liars, double agents, or enemies conspiring to defeat him. Remarkably, the only person the Russian dictator trusts is Germany's dictator. The nonaggression and trade pacts have strengthened their bond. Stalin can't believe Hitler would break it.

2.

One day the Soviet embassy in Berlin receives a package from a secret source in Germany. Whether Arvid Harnack and Harro Schulze-Boysen have anything to do with it remains unknown. Inside is a phrase book that is being distributed to German soldiers to prepare them for an upcoming invasion, with phonetic translations for Russian phrases like:

Hands up!

And

I'll shoot!

And

Are you a Communist?

3.

On June 17, 1941, Stalin summons Pavel Fitin, the head of NKVD foreign intelligence, into his office. Years later, Fitin will describe the encounter in a memoir. A long rectangular table commands the center of the room. Fitin watches Stalin pace its length, fuming, sucking on the stem of his pipe. Now and then he spews a cloud of gray smoke.

"Explain," Stalin says at last, "how does your source obtain information?" The report in his hand is dated June 16, 1941. The sources for this report are Arvid Harnack and Harro Schulze-Boysen. The intelligence they have passed on to Moscow Center is the most urgent and compelling evidence yet that Hitler will attack the Soviet Union very soon, in just a few days.

Fitin does his best to explain, but Stalin is unmoved. He is particularly fixated on intelligence from Harro about a Luftwaffe order of battle. His fury stirs him to obscenity. Stalin scrawls across the report: "You can send your 'source' from the staff of the German air force to fuck his mother."

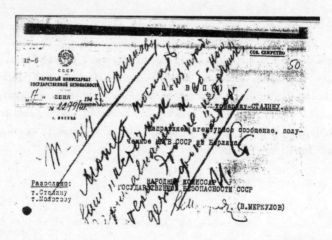

4.

Six days later, on June 22, 1941, Hitler invades the Soviet Union.

Hans Coppi's First Message

1941

1.

At 3:00 a.m. on June 22, 1941, three million German troops attack the Soviet Union over a thousand-mile stretch of land, from the Baltic Sea to the Black Sea. Code-named Operation Barbarossa, the invasion will come to be known as one of the most savage and deadly in history.

The surprise attack gives Germany a tremendous tactical advantage. The Soviet air force—the largest in the world right now—is so unprepared that their pilots are still in bed, asleep, when the Luftwaffe drops the first incendiary bomb. Within forty-eight hours, the Luftwaffe decimates two thousand Soviet warplanes, most of them in hangars or on hardstands, their engines cold. German panzer divisions push relentlessly forward, spraying bullets. Within a week, more than six hundred thousand Red Army troops are captured or killed—mostly killed. As one German soldier puts it, "The Russian is a tough opponent. We take hardly any prisoners, and shoot them all instead."

SS commando units called Einsatzgruppen follow the frontline troops. They have been given the same orders they received in 1939 when Germany invaded Poland: identify and kill as many Jews as possible. Within several months, an Einsatzgruppen commander sends his first battlefield report to Berlin, boasting that his men have murdered 229,052 Russian Jews. Two reports follow in quick succession: an additional 140,467 have been eliminated. Among them are 34,000 men, women, and children from Kiev who are marched to a beautiful ravine called Babi Yar, ordered to strip off their clothing, and shot. The Babi Yar massacre prefigures what is to come.

2.

Operation Barbarossa comes as such a shock to Stalin that three hours after the invasion begins he persists in believing that Hitler had nothing to do with it. He still thinks that their trade agreement is in full force. Trainloads of Russian rubber, iron, and other raw materials chug toward Germany as German troops slaughter Russians.

When the morning sun rises over Berlin, the Soviet embassy is surrounded by the SS. The smell of smoke fills the sumptuously furnished rooms while panicked Russian diplomats fiddle with matches, setting fire to cipher tables and top-secret documents.

A week later, after an SS officer accepts a bribe, Korotkov is on a train heading south, toward Turkey. Perhaps Korotkov finds some small consolation in this: he delivered two radio transmitters to his Berlin network just in the nick of time.

3.

Hans Coppi is bent over a radio transmitter, trying to send a test message to Moscow Center. It's the second transmitter he has used. The first was smaller and battery-powered, its signal not nearly strong enough to reach Moscow. After a series of bewildering transactions with Russian-speaking strangers—couriers, cutouts, operatives, and agents are indistinguishable to Hans—he waited at a train station in Deutschlandhalle for a Russian to give him a transmitter in a suitcase that had traveled from Greta and Adam Kuckhoff's apartment to a shed in Spandau, where it had presumably been repaired. The transmitter is a perplexing, bulky contraption.

Hans Coppi is twenty-five and makes a living as a lathe operator in a factory. When he was seventeen, a month or so after Hitler took power, he and his friends wrote *Down with Hitler* on hundreds of cigarette papers, then ran around the streets of Berlin throwing the papers like confetti. He was promptly arrested and served a one-year prison term. Shortly after his release, he was thrown into a concentration camp for distributing leaflets. His prison record has made it difficult for him to find a job. Just twelve days ago, he married his girlfriend, Hilde Rake, a clerk at the Reich Insurance Institute for Clerical Workers.

At last, exactly four days after Operation Barbarossa begins, Hans Coppi succeeds in sending a test message—and it's an exuberant one, perhaps because he's a newlywed in love: "A thousand greetings to all friends."

Anatoly Gurevich, aka Kent, aka Vincente Sierra, aka Victor Sukolov

1941

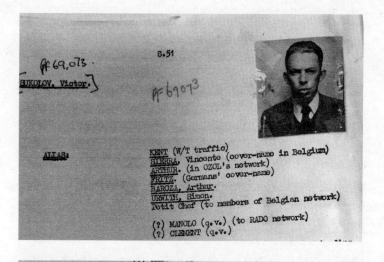

B.51

AF 69.073

SUKOLOV, Victor.

AF 69073

ALIAS:
KENT (W/T traffic)
SIERRA, Vincente (cover-name in Belgium)
ARTHUR. (in OZOL's network)
FRITZ. (Germans' cover-name)
BARCZA, Arthur.
URWITH, Simon.
Petit Chef (to members of Belgian network)

(?) MANOLO (q.v.) (to RADO network)
(?) CLEMENT (q.v.)

ESPIONAGE:
Red Army intelligence agent of long standing.
Leader of group in Belgium 1940-1941 and in
Marseilles 1942.
Had received intensive training in Leningrad
in subjects including W/T, secret writing and
sabotage.

(?) September
1941:
Visited Germany, where gave W/T set to HARNACK
group, a cypher to Ilse STOEBE for von

1.

Then nothing. Moscow Center issues instructions to Soviet embassies in London and Stockholm to tune in to the designated frequency, but all they hear is silence too.

2.

A dot and a dash—the language of Morse code is deceptively simple. If Hans Coppi taps a dash instead of a dot or a dot-dot-dash instead of a dash–dash–dot, the word will lose meaning. Even a virtuoso will make mistakes. Hans does his best to tap the dashes and dots in the right combination, employing the same kind of dexterity and precision that is required of him as a lathe operator on the factory floor.

It's the transmission schedule that causes the most confusion.

Hans Coppi has been hastily trained. He knows that he must send his messages to Moscow Center using a specific call sign and wavelength that change according to a predetermined schedule. But the nameless Russian who gave him a list of six wavelengths to use in combination with thirty call signs—one for each day of the month—didn't explain what to do if the month has thirty-one days. Or perhaps he did explain, but Hans was too exhausted by his ten-hour shift on the factory floor or too anxious about working with the NKVD or too terrified that the Gestapo would track him down to take it all in.

On July 31, 1941, Hans uses the first call sign on the list. This is a mistake. He was supposed to skip that day and begin again on August 1. The wavelength he uses is wrong, and Moscow Center can't pick up the signal. Neither can London or Stockholm. The enciphered report Hans Coppi taps out in Morse code is lost in the ether, a meaningless series of dashes and dots.

3.

Moscow Center has assigned station numbers to both transmitters in Berlin. Hans Coppi's is station D6. There is a second transmitter, station D5, presumably operated by Karl Behrens, but it, too, remains silent. Moscow Center can't pick up a single signal.

Pavel Fitin is frantic. The head of NKVD foreign intelligence knows full well what happens when Stalin is displeased. The director Fitin replaced was shot in the head.

One man can help, an agent who is regarded as "absolutely reliable" and "trusted." He isn't NKVD; he works for Red Army intelligence, otherwise known as the GRU. In other circumstances, Fitin might shy away from asking a favor from a rival—in the fiercely competitive, often murderous atmosphere of Stalin's intelligence bureaucracy, the NKVD and the GRU are frequently pitted against each other—but Fitin overcomes whatever reluctance he may have felt and submits a formal request. On September 11, 1941, the NKVD and the GRU sign an order sanctioning a coordinated effort to reestablish contact with station D5 and D6 by sending to Berlin a twenty-eight-year-old GRU agent with the code name Kent.

4.

At the age of eighteen, Anatoly Markovich Gurevich read Soviet writer N. G. Smirnov's espionage thriller *Diary of a Spy* and resolved to follow in the footsteps of its fearless and nimble protagonist, a British agent named Edward Kent. When Gurevich joined the ranks of Soviet intelligence, he signed all his secret cables with the code name Kent. He is a spy who has named himself after a fictional spy.

Gurevich works under multiple aliases (Vincente Sierra, Arthur Barcza, Simon Urwith, Victor Sukolov) and holds at least four false passports, masquerading as a Mexican tourist and a Uruguayan student, among other identities. He has been in Belgium since 1939, when he began working undercover at Foreign Excellent Trench Coats. As an illegal *rezident,* he runs a network of agents. He has a prodigious appetite and a taste for luxury. At a restaurant he orders "the meat course two or three times" and vodka "by the half bottle or more," according to a fellow spy. The large closet in his spacious apartment accommodates "forty or fifty" elegant suits. Another closet holds five thousand cigars.

Foreign Excellent Trench Coats is no more; a new import-export company has sprouted up as a cover. Simexco, located on 101 rue des Atrébates, is where Gurevich masquerades as a businessman. On August 26, 1941, Gurevich receives an enciphered memo from Moscow Center.

> To Kent. Report immediately Berlin three addresses indicated and determine the causes for failures in radio link. If disruptions continue, undertake transmissions personally. Efforts three Berlin groups and transmission information vitally important.

The addresses that follow belong to Arvid Harnack, Harro Schulze-Boysen, and Adam Kuckhoff. Their real names appear in the memo, not their code names.

The memo originates from Pavel Fitin's office. The young director of NKVD foreign intelligence has already shown himself to be far less experienced than many of his comrades who were murdered in Stalin's bloody purges. A number of the agents he runs—agents like Korotkov—have shown lapses in tradecraft, but the memo he sends Gurevich on August 26, 1941, is a mistake so massive that it threatens to eclipse all the others. Indeed, Fitin's memo will go down in history as one of the most significant espionage blunders of the Second World War.

5.

Gurevich follows Fitin's instructions and travels to Berlin. He meets with Arvid, Harro, and Adam. All of the transmitters Moscow Center has sent this group of German anti-fascists are broken. He stays in Berlin two weeks, tries unsuccessfully to fix the radio transmitters, and returns to Brussels with a stack of intelligence reports from Arvid and Harro. Locked in his office at Simexco, Gurevich takes another week to encipher the reports, which a well-trained Soviet intelligence agent named Mikhail Makarov sends to Moscow Center using a radio transmitter that is fully operational.

Gurevich issues an order for Moscow Center to send more transmitters to Berlin. In the middle of a savage war, the only way this can be done is by parachute.

Code Red

1941

0218

~~TOP SECRET~~

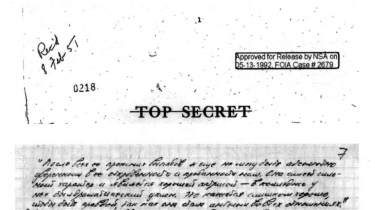

1.

In the months before Gurevich's arrival in Berlin, both the old and newly delivered radio transmitters make the rounds. They are fragile and require constant maintenance. When the transformer in Hans Coppi's transmitter blows, a typist named Erika von Brockdorff volunteers to hide it in her apartment until someone can repair it. Another woman volunteers to hide a transmitter—the dancer Oda Schottmüller, who stashes it in her studio. For a while, Mildred and Arvid hide one in their apartment. Moving a transmitter is a dangerous undertaking. Courage and ingenuity are essential. Women in the Circle walk down the sidewalks of Berlin in broad daylight, pushing transmitters in baby carriages beneath blankets and toys.

Arvid asks his nephew to hide one. Wolfgang Havemann cuts a hole in the hollow wall of his attic and stashes the radio transmitter inside.

Wolfgang has been drafted, just as Arvid predicted he would be so many years ago at Hitler's torchlight parade. He works in naval intelligence. His office is near Mildred and Arvid's apartment, five minutes away. Sometimes he walks there after work, and the three of them sit around the Blaupunkt and listen to foreign broadcasts for news about the Eastern Front. The news is nearly always the same: one victory after another for Hitler. Minsk, Kiev; Moscow is next.

Mildred and Arvid invite Wolfgang on a Sunday hike in the Grunewald forest. It's a beautiful fall day. They reach a lake in the middle of the forest. The Schlachtensee is a deep blue and sparkles in the muted sunshine.

Arvid turns to Wolfgang. "Are you prepared to help defeat Hitler?"

Wolfgang is a father now. Last year, he turned twenty-six and married his girlfriend, Ursel, who has just given birth to their daughter. He has already hidden a typewriter and a transmitter. What more does Arvid want?

2.

Karl Behrens has decided he doesn't want to operate a radio transmitter.

He volunteers to be a courier instead. He picks up the enciphered reports from Woyrschstrasse 16 and delivers them to Hans Coppi, who spends hours hunched over a radio transmitter, tapping away.

Then Karl Behrens is drafted into the German army. If he refuses to report to duty, he will be court-martialed. While he's away, someone needs to take over as a courier.

Rose Schlösinger volunteers to do it.

Rose joined the Circle just a few years ago, after she married Mildred's BAG recruit Bodo Schlösinger. Rose lives alone with their baby now—Bodo has been drafted—and works during the day as a secretary in a factory. At night, after she puts her baby to bed, she enciphers intelligence reports.

3.

Harro, Mildred, and Arvid do most of the enciphering, a complicated and time-consuming process.

The Soviet code is based on a checkerboard pattern.

	1	2	3	4	5
1	a	b	c	d	e
2	f	g	h	ij	k
3	l	m	n	o	p
4	q	r	s	t	u
5	v	w	x	y	z

Each letter of the alphabet is represented by a number from the vertical column (1, 2, 3, 4, 5) and a number from the horizontal column (1, 2, 3, 4, 5). For example, the letter R is 42, the letter E is 15, and the letter D is 14. The word *red* is a set of three two-digit numbers: 42-15-14.

Then a key word is used.

If, for example, the key word *Paris* is used to encipher the word *warning,* both words are turned into two-digit numbers, then the numbers are added together to produce the sequence 87-22-84-57-67-68-33.

Original text	w	a	r	n	i	n	g
Chessboard	52	11	42	33	24	33	22
Key word	35	11	42	24	43	35	11
Encoded text	87	22	84	57	67	68	33

This is the simplified version of a more complex series of computations involving five-digit numbers that Mildred performs using a cipher pad and a set of key words obtained from an obscure novel. The result is a string of numbers that Hans Coppi converts into Morse code and taps into his transmitter.

A Single Error

1941

therefore undoubtedly belonging to the enemy. We knew the radio peculiar-
ities and style of the English radio transmitters and thus deduced that the
new radio transmitters must be working for Moscow. The unknown radio links
were monitored and the messages recorded without, in the beginning, being
able to decode them.

1.

At 3:58 a.m. on June 26, 1941, Abwehr agents based in Cranz, a
coastal town north of Königsberg, intercept an enciphered message
sent from a shortwave radio transmitter. The agents forward the
message to the Funkabwehr, the signals-intelligence branch of the
Abwehr dedicated to monitoring illicit broadcasts and deciphering
signals from the Allies. The Funkabwehr agents, who work in a
building only a few blocks from Mildred and Arvid's apartment,
can't determine where the message originated or who the intended
recipient is.

Two months later, on August 26, 1941, the Funkabwehr inter-
cepts a second message.

To Kent. Report immediately Berlin three addresses indicated
and determine the causes for failures in radio link. If disrup-

tions continue, undertake transmissions personally. Efforts three Berlin groups and transmission information vitally important.

This message is followed by another:

On your visit already planned to Berlin go to Adam Kuckhoff or his wife at the address of 18 Wilhelmstrasse, telephone 83-62-61, the second staircase to the left, on the upper floor, and announce that you have been sent by a friend of Arvid. Remind Kuckhoff of a book which he gave to Erdberg as a present not long before the war and of his play *Till Eulenspiegel*. Suggest that Kuckhoff arrange your meeting with Arvid and Harro, and, if that is impossible, ask Kuckhoff: When will communication begin and what has happened? Where and in what position are all the friends?—in particular those known to Arvid: Italian, Strahlman, Leon, Karo, and others. Receive detailed information for relay to Erdberg. Suggest sending a man for personal contact to Istanbul or one who can personally make contact with the trade representative in Stockholm at the [Soviet] consulate to prepare a [safe] house for receiving people. In the event that Kuckhoff is absent, go to Harro's wife Libertas Schulze-Boysen, at her address 19 Altenburger Allee, telephone 99-58-47.

These messages are also enciphered; what the Funkabwehr agents see right now is the Morse code, a chaos of dots and dashes.

2.

Funkabwehr cryptologists are assigned to decipher the messages. Overseeing them is a middle-aged mathematician named Wilhelm Vauck who has been drafted into the high command of the armed forces and assigned the rank of first lieutenant. Vauck's team is composed of fifteen young mathematicians and philologists who have also been drafted into the war. They look like soldiers, though they will never see combat or touch a weapon. Hour after hour, day after day, month after month, fifteen men in full uniform sit in a room staring at the enciphered messages and scribbling probability calculations based on letters that occur most frequently in German. The frequency of the letter *e* is 18.7 percent; *n* is 11.3 percent; *i* is 7.9 percent. The messages remain a mystery. The Soviets are renowned for their nearly impenetrable ciphers, and the chaos of dots and dashes fails to form any recognizable pattern.

Still, there is a vulnerability in this cipher. If they can discover the key word or the obscure novel that the key word is located in, they can crack the cipher.

3.

So far, Operation Barbarossa is a rousing success for Hitler. In the fall, German troops push through the Ukraine and capture the port city Rostov-on-Don, opening up access to the Caucasus, a region rich in oil. It is a monumental victory. Hitler plans to obliterate Russia's capital city before the onset of winter.

Moscow is seized by panic. Stalin orders the government to evacuate to Kuibyshev, five hundred miles east of Moscow. The Kazan train station is mobbed. Sidewalks swarm with people desperate to escape, their belongings strapped to their backs. Looters smash the windows of deserted stores. Dogs abandoned by their owners howl into the night.

Moscow Center prepares to join the evacuation. A roomful of Soviet cryptologists have been waiting in vain for Hans Coppi's transmissions from Berlin. "A thousand greetings to all friends" is still the only message they have received.

Gollnow

1941

16.) Herbert G o l l n o w,
Beamtenanwärter bei der Reichsbahn,
Konsulatssekretär im Auswärtigen Amt,
Studium an der Auslandswissenschaftlichen
Fakultät der Universität Berlin,
Oberleutnant der Luftwaffe,
Referent für Luftlande-Truppen und Fall-
schirmspringer beim OKW -Abwehrabteilung-.

1.

On November 20, 1941, Mildred receives her PhD.

She has been a graduate student in Germany for over a decade, writing her dissertation in fits and starts, dizzied by all that swirls around her. The title of her dissertation is "The Development of Contemporary American Literature in Some of the Main Exponents of the Novel and Short Story."

2.

Mildred returns to the University of Berlin. She's teaching here again, this time in a different department. The administration has set up a foreign studies department catering to SS and military officers who want to learn English.

The first day of class she strides to the lectern, gripping her leather satchel. So much has changed since she taught here last. What does she think now, seeing rows of Nazis staring at her?

One of them is Herbert Gollnow, a thirty-one-year-old lieutenant in the Abwehr. In many ways, he is Arvid's opposite. His hair is dark; his eyes too. He's not married. Maybe he makes sure Mildred knows this.

Does he sit in the front row or the second or the third? Does he take notes with a pencil or a pen? Perhaps he sits there with his hands folded, silent, watching Mildred lecture, letting the sound of her words wash over him.

3.

Two years ago, Herbert Gollnow started taking private English lessons from Mildred's niece Jane, who placed an ad in a Berlin newspaper, hoping to pick up some extra money. In 1941 Mildred asked Jane to stop teaching Gollnow and suggested he take lessons from her instead. Jane offered no protest.

4.

Jane and Otto Donner recently celebrated their second anniversary. Jane is pregnant with their second child; she gave birth to their first in the dark, during an air raid. Mildred arrived with an enormous bouquet of pink roses, white lilies, and cyclamen with petals that fluttered "like butterflies."

Jane is beginning to suspect that Mildred is keeping a secret from her. One morning while nursing her infant son, Jane asks Otto whether he thinks Mildred is some sort of spy.

Otto purses his lips and, in a theatrical performance of skepticism, resolutely shakes his head.

5.

Gollnow hadn't wanted to switch teachers, but Jane was adamant. So Gollnow enrolled in Mildred's class at the University of Berlin.

After a few classes, Gollnow began showing up at Woyrschstrasse 16 for private lessons.

Mildred makes a pot of peppermint tea, just as she used to do for Don. The little boy who sat on her sofa and stuttered his way through his first lesson is a teenager now. And here on the sofa, taking Don's place, is a grown man.

6.

Mildred misses Don.

The Heaths left Berlin in June, right before Operation Barbarossa. There was no warning. One morning Don showed up for a lesson and said it would be his last. He hugged her hard. Mildred rocked him back and forth. Perhaps she hoped to console herself as much as the thirteen-year-old boy sobbing in her arms.

Later that afternoon, Mildred stood on the platform of the Anhalter Bahnhof, moments before the Heaths boarded their train. Louise told her that the State Department was sending Donald to Chile. She didn't explain why he was being transferred so abruptly, so far from Germany.

Mildred gave Louise an envelope. Inside was a farewell letter and a poem.

The poem was for Don.

One Pain Among So Many

1941–1942

1.

Gollnow is nothing like Mildred's students from the BAG. He has a mediocre mind and a boastful soul, but Mildred can use both qualities to her advantage. Gollnow's position in the Abwehr gives him access to top-secret intelligence about Germany's military tactics in the Soviet Union.

How easy it is to fill his cup with peppermint tea and ask him, under the guise of an English lesson, to talk about himself. To say:

Tell me what you do.

Tell me how you do it.

Tell me, in English.

2.

The Battle of Moscow begins auspiciously for Germany. But with the temperature plummeting below zero, German troops soon falter. Everything freezes—the ground they stand on, the guns they hold, and the bread they eat, which they cut into with hacksaws. Roads smothered in snow prevent vehicles carrying ammunition and supplies from reaching them. Soldiers without jackboots or gloves suffer from frostbite. Frostbite gives way to gangrene. Field surgeons amputate limbs. A good number of the immobilized choose to shoot themselves. An icy wind cuts through to the bones of soldiers trudging eastward, who collapse from hunger and exhaustion.

On December 4, 1941, the temperature plummets to twenty-two

degrees below zero. The next day, the Red Army launches a counterattack.

The Soviets are prepared for arctic conditions. They camouflage themselves in white. Their jackets are padded. The weapons they carry have lubricants that prevent them from freezing up. The tanks they drive have broad tracks and powerful diesel engines that propel them over snowdrifts. The warplanes they fly are also built to withstand freezing conditions. The Luftwaffe is grounded. For the first time since the launch of Operation Barbarossa, the Soviet Union gains an advantage over Germany.

Harro Schulze-Boysen is stationed at a military base on the Havel River, near Potsdam. The weight of responsibilities he bears as a senior lieutenant has increased, threatening to crush him as the Luftwaffe begins to suffer heavy losses. In an intelligence report, Harro explains how both fuel and morale are running low:

> The fuel supply which the German army now has at its disposal is only sufficient to last until February or March next year.... The German air force has had serious losses and now has only about 2,500 aircraft fit for action. Confidence in a quick German victory has evaporated. This loss of confidence has hit the more senior section of the officer corps especially hard.

Harro has no time for enciphering now.

3.

Mildred works late into the night enciphering intelligence reports. Money is running so low she is accustoming herself to hunger pangs.

On December 3, 1941, she writes to Arvid's mother, Clara Harnack.

> *Could you send us potatoes. It is a disturbing feeling not to know whether hunger weakens to a large extent. We eat potatoes now each evening. This evening we had a costly small potato—it tastes like a miracle after chestnuts.*

4.

The weakness worsens. The pain in her abdomen sharpens.

This isn't hunger, she realizes.

Mildred undergoes an emergency surgical procedure. She was alone when she walked into the clinic, and she is alone when she awakens from anesthesia. A nurse informs her that she had been pregnant but it was an ectopic pregnancy. The surgical procedure has long-lasting consequences: thick scar tissue in her fallopian tube will prevent her from ever having a baby.

5.

At 7:55 a.m. on December 7, 1941, a dive-bomber explodes through clouds clustered above the Hawaiian island of Oahu, followed by hundreds more, all bearing on their wings bloodred circles. Among them are Nakajima bombers, Aichi dive-bombers, torpedo planes, and Zero fighters. Every pilot wears the same circle on his headband, a symbol of the rising sun.

For one hour and fifteen minutes, the Imperial Japanese Navy Air Service attacks Pearl Harbor. While the oil fires are still burning— it would take two weeks to extinguish the flames—President Roosevelt asks Congress to declare war on Japan, calling December 7 "a date which will live in infamy." The six-minute speech is broadcast live on the radio. Over 81 percent of households across the United States listen, the largest audience in American broadcasting history.

After two years of bloodshed in Europe, the United States enters the Second World War.

6.

Six weeks later, on January 20, 1942, Reinhard Heydrich arrives at a lakeside villa in Wannsee. The Einsatzgruppen death squads he oversees continue to send him reports about how many Jews they have gunned down in the Soviet Union; the number has now reached seven hundred thousand. Today at noon, he is chairing a conference. Heydrich's guests are fifteen high-ranking SS officers and government officials who have come to the villa to hear the thirty-seven-year-old Nazi present his "Final Solution to the Jewish Question."

Heydrich is tall and slender with blond hair and close-set ice-blue eyes. The son of an opera singer and a composer, he is an accomplished violinist and has been known to weep when he plays a sonata. In other spheres of life he keeps his emotion in check. He follows a strict daily routine. His wife, Lina, describes him as "a man of few words," but he is verbose at today's meeting, which will come to be known as the Wannsee Conference.

He fires off some country-specific statistics. In the Soviet Union, there are 5,000,000 Jews; in France, 750,000; in England, 330,000. Heydrich wants the men in the room to help him achieve his goal: the systematic extermination of all Jews in Europe.

There is a discussion of logistics. A stenographer in the room follows it closely, her fingers flying over the keyboard. When it is over, she has filled fifteen pages.

Heydrich's boss, Himmler, isn't here today. He is occupied with numerous wartime tasks, including the development of a mobile gas van that can asphyxiate up to forty people at a time. While the Wannsee Conference is under way, the Einsatzgruppen are driving these vans through Russian villages, hunting for Jews.

Oil in the Caucasus

1942

1.

American troops in Europe present a formidable challenge for the Germans. Now more than ever, Hitler needs to capture the Caucasus oil fields in Russia. "If I do not," he tells one of his generals, "then I must end this war." General Paulus commands the Sixth Army. This summer, he will lead his troops into the city of Stalingrad. It's Hitler's hope—and Paulus's too—that Stalingrad will be easy to demolish, paving the way toward the Caucasus, where they can seize all the oil they need to fuel Hitler's war machine.

2.

How many private tutoring sessions Mildred has with Herbert Gollnow is not known. What is known is that during a string of them in the spring of 1942, Gollnow tells Mildred all about Hitler's preparations to invade the Caucasus and capture its oil wells.

3.

A Gestapo raid in Brussels turns up a cipher pad and paper covered with code. The paper is singed—a spy had attempted to burn it during the raid—but enough is legible, long sequences of numbers. Under interrogation, the housekeeper spills secrets. Among them is the name of the obscure novel that was used to encipher the messages: *Le Miracle du Professeur Wolmar,* by Guy de Téramond. In 1910, it was offered as a gift to subscribers of *Le Monde Illustré.* A German agent finds a copy in a used-book store in Paris.

4.

The very next day, the book is in the possession of Dr. Vauck and his team of Funkabwehr cryptologists, who use a key word they discover in it—the name *Proctor*—to chip away at the cipher.

By the end of the week, they have deciphered three words.

On July 14, 1942, they crack the cipher wide open.

5.

The Gestapo has three addresses now.

Arvid and Mildred Harnack's.
Adam and Greta Kuckhoff's.
Harro and Libertas Schulze-Boysen's.

6.

In a postwar interrogation, a Gestapo officer says:

Through the police department of Berlin we obtained photographs of these persons and ordered them to be kept under careful visual observation, which showed that these individuals were in contact with one another.

Do Mildred and Arvid suspect they are under surveillance?

The final letter Mildred writes to her family is dated August 14, 1942. Otto Donner smuggles it from Germany to Switzerland, where he posts it to Chevy Chase, Maryland.

The envelope Harriette opens bears a Swiss postmark. The letter is carefully worded:

May we all remain as healthy as possible so that we may see each other again with great happiness. Despite our being separated, let's not be worried and anxious.

Two weeks later, Mildred and Arvid flee Germany.

7.

On September 5, 1942, Mildred and Arvid arrive in Preila, a town on the Curonian Spit in Nazi-occupied Lithuania. Their plan: to escape by boat to Sweden.

A friend of theirs, a historian named Egmont Zechlin, will later write about the two days he and his wife, Anneliese, spent with Mildred and Arvid in Preila.

X

Fragment

Questionnaire
Plötzensee Prison, Berlin
February 16, 1943

What serious illnesses have you suffered? Ectopic pregnancy

Have you experienced any adverse consequences? Yes: weakness, pains, qualms

Arrest

1942

which was on the rear side of the hut, to the front side above
the garden. On opening the door of Harnack's room after a
short knock with the word;"After these exciting events we
will......" I saw both of them packing among three men. Harnack approached me and calmly said:"We shall accompany the
gentlemen to Berlin. I am needed there by my ministry"......

1.

She walks the dunes that night, Arvid by her side, Egmont and Anneliese Zechlin a few steps behind. The dunes stretch along the coastline as far as she can see. No sign of German troops. Panzer tanks thunder down the streets of Klaipeda on the Lithuanian mainland. Mercifully, they leave the dunes alone.

Much has changed since Hitler invaded fourteen months ago. At first, the Lithuanians welcomed German soldiers marching in lockstep through their streets, viewing them as liberators. No longer. The Lithuanians see now that Germany's chancellor is as murderous as their Soviet oppressor. Hitler freed them from Stalin's stranglehold, then tightened his own noose.

The Baltic Sea is most beautiful during a slender margin of time, the breath between dusk and night. Mildred kicks off her sandals and heads toward a dune. This delights Arvid. He rolls up his trousers and races after her.

Egmont says they are crazy. Anneliese shakes her head in a pantomime of disapproval, then flings an arm around Egmont's shoulder and in good humor trudges up the dune.

They reach the top.

The Baltic Sea is cold and majestic, its color a rich purple so dark it is nearly black.

Tomorrow, a fishing boat will take Mildred and Arvid to Sweden. The Harnacks know several people who have escaped this way. It is a dangerous journey. German vessels patrol the Baltic Sea. Even if their small boat manages to evade them, there are air patrols to worry about. But she and Arvid will take their chances. They cannot go back to Berlin. The Gestapo is closing in on them.

Six days ago, on August 31, Harro Schulze-Boysen was arrested. Libertas warned as many as she could.

The smell of rain. It mixes with the brackish tang that comes in great gusts over the water. Anneliese says they should head back immediately or they'll get soaked.

A flash of lightning. A thunderclap.

The rain comes down in sheets, soaking them to the bone. The four of them scramble down the dune and run to the Zechlins' cottage, laughing.

2.

"He seemed to have something special on his mind," Egmont Zechlin wrote, remembering Arvid's demeanor that night.

Egmont is a history professor at the University of Marburg, where, in 1931, Mildred delivered one of her first lectures. She devoted one half to Carl Sandburg, the other to Theodore Dreiser and Sinclair Lewis, weaving together themes of the windswept Midwestern prairie and the unjust political and social forces working against the common man. Her lecture, threaded gently with defiance, impressed him.

Since then, Egmont and his wife, Anneliese, have become Mildred and Arvid's good friends.

"How wonderful to be so free in nature, free at last from all the intrigues," Arvid told Egmont on the dunes. "I am looking forward to the days ahead."

Egmont Zechlin's essay is the only eyewitness account of Mildred and Arvid's arrest. Zechlin focuses most of his attention in the essay on Arvid, recording what he said, how he said it, going so far as to imagine what Arvid was thinking. We are left to imagine what Mildred was thinking.

3.

It's the next morning now, and several men are standing outside the cottage. Mildred sees them from the bedroom window. One, two, three, four.

Should she raise the window sash? No. This would make noise, and she does not want to make noise. Not while Arvid is speaking to the men, who have arranged themselves in a loose circle around him, arms folded across their chests. One, two, three, four. As if they are dancers. As if, at any moment, they will join hands. *Step to the left. Step to the right.* And Arvid still in the center, speaking to them.

What is he saying?

He's in short sleeves though it's September, the breeze carrying a whiff of fish and frost. It blew in from the north, across the Baltic Sea. The men wear wool coats. Three black coats, and one the color of raw charcoal. But no badges. No medals. No armbands.

Arvid keeps talking. Perhaps the man in the charcoal coat nods and purses his lips, as if readying for a kiss, though his eyes on Arvid gleam with contempt.

The men tighten their circle around Arvid almost in unison. One, two, three, four. Perhaps she thinks of dancers again. Gestapo officers in tutus performing a grim choreography. A moment of perversity. Of hysteria.

No. It's important to stay calm.

Arvid's expression remains placid. Behind round-rimmed spectacles, his eyes rest easily on the man questioning him. Now and then he nods or tips his head gently to the side, allowing his interlocutors to see how thoughtfully he considers the questions posed to him.

Arvid presses his palms together, explaining something to the man in the charcoal coat, who seems to be in charge. Arvid speaks evenly, patiently, evincing a professorial ease, as if he were behind a lectern, Herr Professor Harnack holding forth before a quartet of students. Students who are widening the circle now, allowing Arvid to step out of its center, his pace neither quick nor slow. Perhaps she tries to read his expression, which is neither calm nor anxious. Inscrutable.

The four men exchange several words, appear to reach some sort of agreement, and disperse. Two men walk along the south side of the cottage, through Anneliese's garden. Another walks around the north side. The man in the charcoal coat stuffs his hands into his pockets, watching Arvid ascend the porch stairs.

Then, with cold deliberation, the man advances, following Arvid into the cottage.

4.

Seaside air makes the wallpaper buckle. Above the window sash, a flowered strip curls down. Mildred doesn't notice. Perhaps it's the bedroom door that catches her attention.

The door is ajar.

Mildred lowers her body to the floor. Quickly—she does not have a second to waste—she crawls under the windowsill to the bedroom door and shuts it just as Arvid swings open the front door.

Arvid's voice. "Hallo!"

Footsteps from the rear of the cottage. Anneliese and Egmont calling out, "Hallo! Hallo!"

Another set of footsteps: the heavy tread of the man in charge.

Egmont says something to Arvid, sounding confused. The man in the charcoal coat says something to Egmont, interrupting him.

"I'll get my ID card," says Egmont quickly.

"Remain here."

"It is no trouble," says Egmont.

"Remain here, Herr Zechlin."

Boot stomps on the floorboards. The other men are coming in now, one through the front door and two through the rear door.

"The gentleman has informed me that I must go to Berlin," says Arvid, keeping his voice steady.

"Why?" demands Egmont, flustered.

"I am needed at the Ministry of Economics."

"But they only had to send a telegram!" says Anneliese, sounding a note of panic. The man in the charcoal coat hasn't formally introduced himself, nor have the others, but Anneliese doesn't require an introduction. She knows they're Gestapo.

So does Egmont.

He speaks too loudly. "But Arvid has not had his breakfast! You must not leave yet! Anneliese will prepare something to eat; you all must eat before you leave! Anneliese?"

"Yes?"

"Coffee for the gentlemen and—"

"Coffee, yes, we have plenty of coffee."

"And something to eat for—"

"Of course, yes, yes."

Behind the bedroom's closed door, Mildred finds a pencil stub on the nightstand. She rifles through the dresser drawers, searching for paper. She wants to write a message to Egmont and Anneliese.

No paper.

She flings open the closet door. Two coats. She plunges her hand into the pockets. There must be a ticket, a handbill—*something* she can write on.

No paper.

The trash basket is empty. The hatbox is filled with feathers. She falls to her knees and crawls under the bed, finds nothing but dust. She crawls out, coughing.

And then she sees. Above the window sash: a strip of flowered wallpaper curling down. She could tear it off and write a note.

But it's too late—much too late.

The Gestapo Album

1942

1.

Mildred and Arvid are locked in a vehicle that speeds south from Preila to Berlin, a five-hundred-mile trip. By the time they arrive at Gestapo headquarters at Prinz-Albrecht-Strasse 8, it is night.

Mildred has never set a single foot into this building. Flanked by the Gestapo officers, she and Arvid are led down a flight of stairs to the basement. Arvid is shoved into one cell, Mildred into another. In each, there is an iron bed, a tin bowl, a tin spoon. A scattering of small dirty windows near the ceiling offers meager glimpses of the prison yard.

A week goes by.

The basement is cold and damp and resonant with the sharp heel-clicks of patrolling prison guards. It is a "dark catacomb," one of Mildred's coconspirators will recall. Mildred lies on the iron bed and awakens at six a.m. when a guard raps on the bars with a truncheon while striding up and down a narrow corridor that stretches between two long lines of solitary cells. Mildred rises, setting one bare foot, then the other, on the concrete floor. The difference between morning and night is nearly indistinguishable here in the basement, but if it were suddenly bathed in light, she would see the faces of all her friends.

2.

Harro and Libertas Schulze-Boysen are here. Greta and Adam Kuckhoff are here. Hans and Hilde Coppi are here. So are Mildred's

BAG recruits Karl Behrens and Wilhelm Utech. All the links in the chain connecting the Circle, Gegner Kreis, Tat Kreis, and Rittmeister Kreis are here, including Rose Schlösinger, Elisabeth Schumacher, Cato Bontjes van Beek, Erika von Brockdorff, Oda Schottmüller, and Elfriede Paul. Some of the women Mildred has never met face-to-face; she knows them by their deeds alone—the one who hid a radio transmitter in her apartment, the one who was a courier, the one who enciphered intelligence reports, the one who held meetings in her clinic after hours, the one who made leaflets, the one who distributed them.

Late in October, a Nazi is shoved into a cell. Mildred knows him well; he is Herbert Gollnow, the Abwehr lieutenant who whispered military secrets into her ear.

3.

Mildred enters a dark room.

She sees three things: a box camera on a tripod, a stool, a metal rod. A prison official instructs her to sit down and hold still. The rod will keep her upright, in case she feels like slouching. He shoves it against the back of her skull.

He takes three photographs:

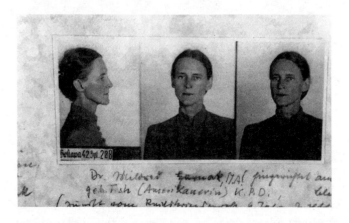

They are assembled in an album.

Over the next few months, Nazi officials will use the Gestapo Album to keep track of everyone the Gestapo arrests in the resistance. Notes scrawled in black ink under Mildred's photographs identify her as an American, a Communist, a wife.

4.

The same procedure is followed for every prisoner. A Gestapo official rolls the prisoner's fingertips, one by one, onto an ink-soaked sponge, then presses them against paper with methodical precision. Another prison official takes the prisoner's photograph.

Some prisoners stare into the camera with barely concealed expressions of grief.

Some, like Hilde Coppi, stare into the camera with defiance. Hilde is seven months pregnant.

5.

Gestapo headquarters used to be the School of Industrial Arts and Crafts. The basement was filled with rows of students pounding clay and dipping paintbrushes into watercolor pigments. The school flourished in the heyday of the Weimar Republic. Now, there are thirty-eight solitary cells here, plus one communal cell that accommodates up to twenty prisoners.

The interrogation rooms are located on the building's upper floors.

When Greta Kuckhoff is led in handcuffs into an interrogation room, she is surprised by how ordinary it looks, "like any other government office." She sees a table and three chairs: one for her interrogator, one for a typist, and one for her. The interrogator already knows about the radio transmitter Korotkov gave her at the U-Bahn station, though Greta can't imagine how.

The typist's fingers are poised on the keys. All Greta has to do is confess to her crime and name a few names.

She refuses.

The interrogator is visibly displeased. "Since your husband and Arvid Harnack have contributed nothing toward clearing up this case, we have now employed the necessary methods to loosen their tongues."

"Are they still alive?" Greta asks.

The interrogator nods, and she is flooded with relief.

What he says next is cryptic—"It depends on you"—but she understands exactly what he means.

6.

Every day the Gestapo casts its net wider, and soon one hundred nineteen are arrested. There isn't enough space for them all, so arrangements are made for other prisons to accept the spillover. The men are sent to men's prisons, the women to women's prisons.

Greta is sent to a prison called Alexanderplatz. Each morning, a green police wagon transports her in handcuffs to Gestapo head-quarters for an interrogation. Transportation of prisoners is strictly regulated by Himmler, who requires prison administrators to submit

a claim form, made out in duplicate.... The top sheet of the claim form must bear the official seal of the appropriate sec-tion, with signature. Claim forms for prisoners who are to be picked up with the initial transport on the day in question must be submitted to the Gestapo the previous day, during weekdays by 4:30 p.m. at the latest, and on Sundays or holidays latest by 11 a.m.

After her first interrogation—it lasts thirteen hours—Greta is dispatched back to Alexanderplatz, where she collapses in her cell. The ceiling is riddled with cracks. In the morning light, Greta sees there are words on the ceiling. A former prisoner has scratched a message: *Geduld ist die Haupttugend eines Revolutionärs* (Patience is the highest virtue of the revolutionary).

7.

A guard shoves Greta into the police wagon. As it rattles toward Gestapo headquarters, her thoughts turn to Mildred. She plans to tell her interrogator that they are simply "good friends" who "read Shakespeare together" at the University of Wisconsin and are entirely uninterested in politics. She will construct an image of Mildred as an American who often "missed her mother" and "her graceful home" in Milwaukee. If the interrogator asks why Mildred visits Greta so often, she will tell him that Mildred has no child of her own and loves to "joke away with our Ule."

Greta is certain that Mildred will say nothing to implicate her. But she worries about the others—especially Libertas.

"Libertas's nerves worried me," Greta admitted in her memoir.

8.

Preparations for a mass trial are under way, and confessions extracted during interrogations will be admitted as evidence, but neither Greta nor anyone else knows this right now.

Hitler has put two high-ranking SS officers in charge: Obersturmbannführer Friedrich Panzinger and Hauptsturmführer Horst Kopkow—the military equivalent of a lieutenant colonel and a captain. Panzinger oversees the entire investigation and Kopkow oversees the prisoners' daily interrogations. Their boss is Gestapo chief Heinrich Müller, who reports directly to Himmler.

Kopkow is thirty-two and nimble on his feet. He has distinguished himself as a Nazi who approaches his work with diligence and zeal, going out of his way to personally arrest Harro Schulze-Boysen, Libertas Schulze-Boysen, Arvid Harnack, and Mildred Harnack. Harro was in his office at the Luftwaffe military base near Potsdam when he heard Kopkow's knock at the door. Libertas was fleeing Berlin on a crowded train when she spotted Kopkow, a good-looking, dark-haired young man, in her carriage; a moment later, he was striding toward her. And Kopkow was so intent on personally handcuffing Mildred and Arvid that he traveled with a trio of Gestapo men nearly eight hundred miles, crossing Poland, to track them down in Lithuania.

Panzinger carries out his duties with comparable devotion. He is known among his Nazi colleagues as an expert in ferreting out resistance networks that have gone underground. Among his triumphs is the liquidation of the German Communist Party. Panzinger, a former police officer in Bavaria with a night-school law degree, was eager to prove himself at the Reich Main Security Office, where he was installed in 1939 and oversaw the arrest of Communists and other political enemies. He arranged for some to be incarcerated and murdered in concentration camps and slyly let others go free to serve as bait. German Communists, he discovered, were easy to catch. Most of them had no idea how to carry on their oppositional work in a clandestine manner. They talked freely on the telephone, unaware that the lines were tapped. They wrote incriminating letters that they dropped in regular mailboxes. Few could keep their mouths shut under Gestapo interrogation.

In the current investigation, Panzinger has made considerable progress in a short time. Now that Kopkow has arrested the Harnacks and the Schulze-Boysens and the Gestapo have arrested the rest, all that remains to be done is to wrap up the prisoners' interrogations and march them into court. Panzinger aims to foster the appearance of a fair trial. A panel of judges will hear each case. Evidence supporting a prisoner's conviction includes a confession and a signed affidavit from two fellow prisoners acquired during their own interrogations.

Panzinger keeps tabs on the interrogations with daily briefings from Kopkow. So far, with just a few exceptions, the interrogators have succeeded in obtaining confessions and have a stack of signed affidavits to boot.

9.

Some blurt out their friends' names at their very first interrogation.

Some break down after their second, or fifth, or tenth interrogation.

Some refuse to name names. For such cases, Himmler has granted Kopkow permission to employ more persuasive tactics than intimidation, lies, threats, and blackmail, sanctioning the use of *verschärfte Vernehmung*—severe interrogation.

Kopkow has installed five interrogators on the upper floors of Gestapo headquarters. The most feared is Walter Habecker, a bald Nazi with a bulbous nose and a mustache that matches Hitler's: a black, sinister smudge. Habecker is known for his agility with whips, and is especially fond of thumbscrews.

Stories about Habecker circulate in the basement of Gestapo headquarters. As prisoners walk up the stairs, they pass a large window. Some jump out the window to their deaths, choosing suicide over Habecker's sadism.

10.

Nine days after she is arrested, Mildred spends her fortieth birthday in the basement of Gestapo headquarters.

Every cell here has a number. Mildred is in cell 25.

11.

A prisoner named Marie Luise von Scheliha is in the prison yard with two dozen other women who shuffle around the perimeter "like withered leaves."

Prison guards stationed around the area watch the women, eagle-eyed. Talking is prohibited. They move silently, in groups of four. For ten precious minutes a day, they are permitted to see daylight.

"Some women lift their arms as if drowning," Marie Luise remembered. Some "spread their arms like dancers in the fresh air."

One moves swiftly toward Marie Luise. Her hair is pulled back in a bun the color of dirty straw. Her gaze is arresting.

"I'm in cell 25," she whispers. "Don't forget me when you get out."

What is your name? Marie Luise wants to ask, but Mildred is already gone, lost among the others.

12.

Arvid's cousin Axel doesn't know why he has been summoned to Gestapo headquarters. He approaches Prinz-Albrecht-Strasse 8 "with some distaste."

When Axel is inside, a Nazi leads him into an elegantly furnished office and politely asks him to take a seat. The stripes, pins, and patches that embellish the Nazi's black uniform announce him as a high-ranking SS officer. Above the brim of his cap, a tiny eagle clutches a swastika in its talons. He wears delicate, wire-framed glasses that are nearly identical to Himmler's. He introduces himself as SS Obersturmbannführer Friedrich Panzinger and poses a simple question. Does Axel know why he has been summoned here?

Axel von Harnack leads a tame, relatively uneventful life as a historian at the Berlin State Library. He shakes his head.

Panzinger asks Axel if he has "a relative who is active politically."

Axel immediately thinks of his brother Ernst von Harnack and "is seized by some uneasiness." But as Panzinger continues his unnervingly gentle interrogation, it dawns on Axel that the relative in question is his cousin Arvid.

"I am telling you now: he is with us," Panzinger says softly, almost tenderly.

As Axel absorbs this news, Panzinger informs him that the charges against Arvid must be kept "absolutely secret." If Axel or anyone else in the family breathes a word about Arvid's arrest, they, too, will be arrested.

Alarmed, Axel pledges he and his family will say nothing, absolutely nothing about it. But what should they tell friends? And what about Arvid's colleagues at work? Surely everyone will notice that Arvid has gone missing and wonder where he is.

Panzinger gives a thoughtful nod. The explanation, he says, is simple. Arvid is on "an official trip to foreign countries of indefinite duration." The same explanation must be given to the landlord at Woyrschstrasse 16.

It's then that Axel realizes Mildred was arrested too.

Axel sees Mildred fairly frequently. She loves to ensconce herself in the Berlin State Library and work on her dissertation. Sometimes they have lunch together in the library cafeteria. He thinks of her "clear, radiant eyes," the way she fixes her gaze on him, listening intently. He conjures an image of how she carries herself, striding into a room with an air of "noble" purpose.

It pains him to imagine Mildred in prison.

13.

Between October and December, Axel von Harnack reports to Prinz-Albrecht-Strasse 8 nearly every week. A Gestapo officer stationed at the door notes the "exact time" he enters the building. Walking down a carpeted corridor to SS Obersturmbannführer Panzinger's office, Axel notices "complicated telephone fixtures" and numerous doors. Black-uniformed SS officers pass by, eyeing him, and Axel feels a flutter of fear. It does not diminish when he opens Panzinger's door.

Once seated, he lets his gaze drift from the polished hardwood floors to the fine rugs to the sumptuous drapes to the ring on Panzinger's left hand: a silver band ornamented with oak leaves and a grinning skull. A *Totenkopf* ring. Himmler wears one too.

Panzinger fixes him with a cold stare and demands that Axel tell him the truth about Arvid and Mildred. The gentleness is gone.

Axel steadies himself. He hopes to convince Panzinger to drop the charges against Arvid and Mildred or at the very least persuade him to make sure they are treated reasonably well during their incarceration.

The truth, he says, is that Arvid and Mildred are "worthy people" with "independent minds."

Panzinger, Axel notices, seems to be "amenable to such thoughts."

Panzinger tells Axel that he personally interrogated Arvid a number of times, and admits that he "carried on long political discussions with Dr. Harnack" that kindled "a certain feeling of respect for him."

By the third visit, Axel believes he has made some headway. He brings parcels of books and food for Mildred and Arvid. Later, he will learn that the parcels are delivered only to Arvid. Mildred receives nothing. When Axel asks why, Panzinger refuses to explain, though his contempt for Arvid's American wife is unmistakable. Weeks later, Panzinger says that Mildred "has been lying a great deal."

14.

A prisoner in handcuffs sits in a large room on an upper floor, waiting to be interrogated. Her name is Maria Grimme. She and her husband, Adolf, are members of Tat Kreis.

The door of an interrogation room swings open. Two Gestapo officers emerge carrying a pale, emaciated woman on a stretcher. Her eyes are sunken in their sockets, glassy with agony. Years later, Maria will describe the "remarkable expression" in them.

The Gestapo officers set the stretcher on the floor and leave. Maria gazes at the woman, immobilized by horror. The woman on the stretcher doesn't move either. She is "hardly breathing." Maria wonders whether she is dead.

The Gestapo officers return. One is especially cheerful and cruel. He grasps the unconscious woman's wrists and yanks her upright.

"So, Frau Harnack," he shouts, "feeling better?"

Knock-Knock

1942

1.

At five a.m. on September 26, a Saturday, Günther and Joy Weisenborn are awakened by a knock on the door.

Günther opens it and sees four men wearing dark coats. They don't look like Gestapo. They don't wear uniforms or badges. They stand there—"ominously," Günther remembered years later—with their hands stuffed in their pockets.

"You are both to come with us," one of them says. "Pack a bag; you may be gone some time."

Joy finds a bag and throws into it a few blouses and Günther's trousers, reaching into drawers with trembling hands.

"Do you think you'll share a cell?" the officer scoffs. "Pack two."

Günther spends the night shivering in his cell. The next day he is led up a staircase in handcuffs and shoved into a room. A bald man sits behind a desk "sharpening a pencil to a pin point." His name is Habecker. His complexion is "gray" and his nose is "sweaty." Most revolting is his "Hitler mustache."

"Now tell me," Habecker begins, "what sort of company do you keep?"

Sometimes the interrogation room is ice cold. Sometimes it's blazing hot. Sometimes Günther is tortured.

2.

John Sieg, a member of Gegner Kreis, enters Habecker's interrogation room determined not to name a single name. Habecker tortures him without mercy.

Later, in his prison cell, John Sieg hangs himself.

His friend Herbert Grasse throws himself out a fifth-floor window.

News of the suicides spreads through the basement of Gestapo headquarters, where prisoners locked in solitary cells wait in dread for their interrogations. They are forbidden to talk to one another, so they devise other ways of communicating.

3.

Late at night, Günther Weisenborn taps at the wall of his prison cell with the end of a pencil. He's trying to communicate with his friend Kurt Schumacher, who's in the cell next to his.

"The odds were piling up against me," Günther wrote in his memoir.

Recently, a member of Gegner Kreis signed a confession that incriminated Günther. Today he found out that Kurt blurted his name while being tortured by Habecker. If Kurt doesn't retract his statement, Günther will face execution.

> I began to tap at regular intervals. Kurt repeated my taps exactly. The sounds were faint as if very distant. I knocked once for a, twice for b, three times for c. He knocked back irregularly. He didn't understand. I repeated. He didn't understand. I repeated. He didn't understand. I repeated a hundred times. He didn't understand. I wiped off the sweat, and tried to master my despair.... We were helpless. He emphasized some tones, softened others. Was it Morse? I did not know Morse.

"I was knocking on the wall for my life," Günther remembered. "Lying on the cot covered by the wool blanket, I tapped...then I lay still. At any moment the light might go on and the guard could look in at me."

At two a.m., Günther gives up, exhausted, and falls into a fitful sleep.

In the morning and all through the day, he's in a fugue state of despair. He has already contemplated suicide. Last week, with a pair of stolen scissors, he cut two narrow strips from his bedsheet. He can wrap the strips around his neck and hang himself. He would rather die than let the Nazis execute him.

But the next night I heard it...twenty-two even knocks. I counted with him. That was the letter v. Then five knocks. After that an r, which I counted breathlessly with precision. Then an s, a t, an e, an h, an e: *"verstehe."* Understand! I lay under the wool blanket, limp and happy....I was wet with sweat.

Later, Günther knocks:

You...must...take...back...your...statement.

Kurt knocks:

Why?

Günther knocks:

Is...second...statement...against...me...means...death.

4.

Other prisoners overhear the knocks. Some learn Günther's knock language. Some develop their own.

They knock to pass on information about their interrogations. They knock to warn about prison guards and stool pigeons. They knock to share news about the world, report battles won and lost. They knock to defy their captors, tell a joke, make a friend, pick a fight, howl their anguish. They knock to hear another human being knock.

Late at night, a symphony of knocks can be heard.

Falk Does His Best

1942

1.

Falk Harnack has been drafted into the German army and is stationed one hundred fifty miles south of Berlin, in Chemnitz. The last time he saw his older brother, Arvid, was August 24, 1942, the day after the Luftwaffe started carpet-bombing the city of Stalingrad.

Arvid had seemed profoundly agitated. He wanted to have a serious discussion with Falk, but first, he stalked around the apartment, peering under furniture, prodding the wires sprouting from lamps. When he was sufficiently reassured that Woyrschstrasse 16 wasn't bugged, he drew Falk close. In a voice barely above a whisper, he unburdened his heart.

He was stuck in a terrible bind. Remaining in Germany seemed both imperative and suicidal. He considered moving the Circle to another country, but doing so would accomplish little. He needed to bear witness to what was happening in Germany; how could he do this from a distance? Then there was the matter of the Circle's reach. He wondered whether a better name might broaden its appeal.

Falk is in a resistance group with a more evocative name: the Weisse Rose — White Rose. At the center of the group are Sophie and Hans Scholl, who, like Falk, attended the University of Munich.

The White Rose produced its first series of leaflets in June 1942. Falk has been active in the resistance since 1934. The advice Falk gave the Scholls — to target a wide spectrum of Germans, from

Communists and Social Democrats to conservative aristocrats—
might as well have come from Arvid.

2.

In mid-October 1942, Falk walks through the grand, arched
entrance of Gestapo headquarters to visit Arvid, who meets him in
a small room on an upper floor of the building and embraces him
"tightly and tenderly." Falk notes that his brother looks much older
than he did in August.

They sit on opposite sides of a wooden table. A prison guard
stands nearby monitoring their conversation, which is strained.
Arvid says he's spending his time behind bars productively—he has
begun writing a new book—and wants to know how their mother
is coping. Falk assures him that Clara Harnack is "healthy and
brave." Arvid says nothing about the interrogations he has endured.

A month later, Falk is granted a second visit.

This time, Arvid tells him more. He describes his prison cell
(there is a "bit of sky" that he can glimpse through the small, barred
window if he stands on a chair) and the bread that constitutes his
morning and evening meals (dry as chalk). When the prison guard
who's monitoring their conversation turns toward a commotion on
the far side of the room, Arvid leans forward and quickly whispers,
"They have tortured me."

3.

Arvid's torturer is Habecker, the same man who has been torturing
Mildred.

Habecker will go on to torture many others in the resistance.
Nearly all of them will be executed. One of the rare firsthand
accounts of Habecker's methods was provided by Fabian von
Schlabrendorff, a legal scholar who conspired with Arvid's cousins
Hans von Dohnányi and Dietrich Bonhoeffer to assassinate Hitler.
The torture proceeds in four stages:

During the first stage, my hands were tied behind my back. Then some contraption was fixed over both of my hands in such a way that it enclosed each of my fingers separately. On the inside of this device were iron spines that pressed on the base of the fingers. The entire machinery could be tightened by means of a screw in such a way that the spines dug into my fingers.

The second stage was like this: I was tied down on top of a contraption that resembled a bedstead, face down. A blanket was thrown over my head and then a sort of stovepipe was placed around each of my bare legs. On the inside of these two pipes were nails. Here, too, the walls of the pipes could be screwed tight by means of a special mechanism so that the nails bored into my thighs and calves.

The "bedstead" also served as the main device for the third stage. I was tied to it, as before, with my head covered by a blanket. Then, by means of some mechanism, the "bedstead" was pulled apart either abruptly or slowly so that my body, bound as it was, was compelled to follow the motions of this procrustean bed.

During the fourth stage I was bound in a twisted fashion by means of a special shackling process such that my body could move neither backward nor sideways. Then the detective sergeant and the lance corporal beat me with heavy clubs from behind so that I fell forward with each blow; and as my hands were tied behind my back, my face and head hit the ground with full force. During this procedure all participants expressed their enjoyment in the form of derisive shouts. The first round of torture ended in a fainting spell. None of the violent measures described here induced me either to confess anything, or to betray any of my like-minded friends.

The next day I was unable to get up, so I could not even change my underwear, which was soaked with blood. Although I had always been perfectly healthy up to then I suffered a serious heart attack later in the day.

4.

Arvid asks Falk whether he has news of Mildred.

Falk has none.

Arvid asks him for a photograph of Mildred. Smuggle it past the prison guards, he says.

Falk says he'll do his best. So far, every attempt he has made to send something to Mildred has failed.

5.

Mildred is in strict solitary confinement.

Arvid is given pencils and paper. He is allowed to write and receive letters. Axel sends him works by Plato, Hegel, and Adam Smith. He is writing a new book, one that puts forth an economic theory that synthesizes all his previous theories.

Mildred is given none of these privileges: no pencils, no paper, no letters, no books.

Arvid's cousin Axel pleads with a prison official to let him visit Mildred. The official refuses. "No one ever received permission to talk to Mildred Harnack," Axel will write later. "Also my repeated requests to allow a female family member to speak [to her] were denied."

Falk tries too—and fails.

6.

Falk tries to find a lawyer. He knows four excellent lawyers in his extended family: Klaus Bonhoeffer, Ernst von Harnack, Justus Delbrück, and Hans von Dohnányi.

But lawyers from the family can't go to court and defend Arvid and Mildred. They're in the resistance too—and just as vulnerable to persecution.

7.

Hans von Dohnányi, Justus Delbrück, and Dietrich Bonhoeffer have gotten positions at the Abwehr, putting them at the red-hot center of German military intelligence. Ernst von Harnack and Klaus Bonhoeffer are working closely with them.

Within the Abwehr, a plot to assassinate Hitler is taking shape. The plot doesn't have a name yet. A former mayor of Leipzig, Carl Goerdeler, is involved in it. So are a number of high-ranking military officers, including Colonel General Ludwig Beck, Major General Hans Oster, and Admiral Wilhelm Canaris.

Admiral Canaris is chief of the Abwehr, and Major General Oster is his second in command. The coup both men tried to organize in 1938 — known as the Oster conspiracy — failed in part because Prime Minister Neville Chamberlain embraced a policy of appeasing Hitler. This time, they hope to gain strong support from Britain's new prime minister, Winston Churchill.

On June 1, 1942, Canaris sent Dietrich Bonhoeffer on a secret mission to alert Britain that the German high command was plotting to assassinate Hitler. Dietrich met with the bishop of Chichester, George Bell, a member of the House of Lords. Dietrich had met Bishop Bell a decade before, during his stint as a pastor in London, and the two had forged a deep and abiding friendship.

Bishop Bell told Dietrich he would do whatever he could to support his mission. He composed a long letter to Foreign Secretary Anthony Eden, whom many regarded as Prime Minister Churchill's closest political ally and confidant. "If there are men in Germany also ready to wage war against the monstrous tyranny of the Nazis from within," Bishop Bell wrote, "is it right to discourage or ignore them?"

Eden sharply rebuked him. The opposition in Germany, he insisted, had "given little evidence of their existence."

Wolfgang's Seventh Interrogation

1942

1.

Wolfgang Havemann is stationed in Flensburg, a port town border-
ing Denmark—so far north that the Gestapo has to travel nearly
three hundred miles to arrest him. They explain nothing to the
senior lieutenant in his naval intelligence unit. They merely let it be
known that Wolfgang's presence is required in Berlin; the war will
have to carry on without him.

At Gestapo headquarters, Wolfgang is photographed, finger-
printed, and shoved into a basement cell.

At his first interrogation, he is questioned about Uncle Arvid.

At his second, he is questioned about Aunt Mildred.

At his third, he is questioned about the rest of the Circle.

Wolfgang feigns ignorance.

"You needn't cover for your uncle," the interrogator tells him.
"He is already so incriminated that you can't save a single hair on
his head."

2.

At Wolfgang's fourth interrogation, a different man enters the room.
He is bald, visibly older than the previous interrogator, about fifty.
He has a meager mustache. His eyes are a dull blue. He produces a
knife and cuts a cigarette in two.

Habecker.

On the table is an album of photographs. Habecker flips the pages casually, as if the Gestapo Album is a compendium of snapshots of people on vacation. He wants to know whether Wolfgang recognizes any of them.

Wolfgang knows nearly everyone Habecker points to. The typist who sits across from him waits, her fingers poised over the keys, for his response.

Wolfgang shakes his head.

3.

Habecker conducts Wolfgang's fifth and sixth interrogations.

At the fifth, Wolfgang endures more questions about Arvid.

At the sixth, Wolfgang puts on an even bigger show than he did at the fourth, bursting "into tears of moral indignation."

4.

At Wolfgang's seventh interrogation, Habecker is gone, replaced by the interrogator who conducted the first three. He adopts a gentle demeanor, suggesting that Wolfgang join him in a walk outside.

It's the first time Wolfgang has been outdoors since his arrest.

His interrogator leads him along a path that cuts through a well-tended garden of winter blooms. Wolfgang, dazzled by sunlight, fills his lungs with the fragrant air as he walks beside this Nazi—his name, he learns, is Büchert—who has the power to determine whether he lives or dies.

Büchert affects a casual tone. He tells Wolfgang he has never been assigned a case like this. It would "make a wonderful novel," he says, "if it weren't so sad."

Kassiber

1942

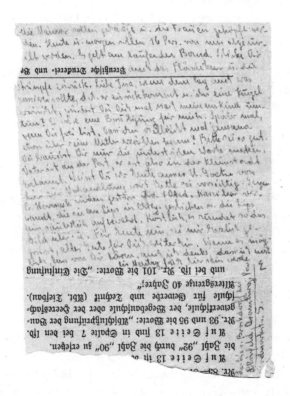

1.

"Always inspect the seams of my pajamas," Cato Bontjes van Beek whispers to her mother. They sit on opposite sides of a table in a room on an upper floor of Gestapo headquarters.

Cato is twenty-one. On November 14, 1942, she will turn twenty-two. She has spent weeks handcuffed in the dark gloom of the basement. Near the ceiling of her cell, a small window provides a glimpse of the prison yard, where men and women are granted ten minutes to walk in a circle. Some of them Cato recognizes, some she doesn't. It doesn't matter. Many are in the underground resistance, the connections between them as strong as the bars on the window. Every day Cato stands on the small table beside her bed and peeks out the window, singing to them as they shuffle past.

A guard is moved by Cato's singing. It's for this reason that Cato's mother, Olga, has been granted a visit. She's lucky; other mothers are granted none.

The visit isn't long. Olga walks out the grand, arched doorway of Gestapo headquarters with Cato's whisper in her ear and an armload of laundry. Some families of prisoners are permitted to do the prisoners' laundry. Other prisons in Berlin adopt this policy as well. Decisions regarding which families are permitted to do a prisoner's laundry are made according to the whims of a prison's administration.

The hems of laundered clothing quickly become hiding places for secret notes passed between prisoners and their families. Secret notes of this kind are known as *Kassiber.*

Sometimes prisoners slip *Kassiber* to each other during their daily walk in the prison yard. Sometimes they hide *Kassiber* in the broken mortar between bricks or in the cracks and fissures of walls for other prisoners to find.

2.

Mildred and Libertas are transferred from the basement prison at Gestapo headquarters to the Charlottenburg women's prison, where they are handcuffed in separate solitary cells. The red-brick building is concealed behind a walled courtyard on Kantstrasse; Berliners walking past the prison may not even know it's there.

Mildred and Libertas slip *Kassiber* to each other.

Every morning they are transported in a police wagon to Gestapo headquarters for their interrogations. Libertas's interrogator isn't Habecker; she's questioned by a police officer who refrains from torturing her. Libertas is lucky. Still, she doesn't understand why, given her family connection to Göring, the officer doesn't unlock her shackles and set her free.

3.

Göring is apoplectic.

He was a guest at Libertas and Harro's wedding. He oversaw Harro's promotion to *Oberleutnant*—the highest lieutenant officer rank in the Luftwaffe—and he is painfully aware that he granted Harro access to highly confidential military intelligence.

An admiral who serves as one of Hitler's aides observes that Göring feels "humiliated" by the whole ordeal. It's beyond Göring's comprehension that an underground resistance group in Germany includes "officers and aristocrats."

Hitler, too, is shocked that the members of this resistance group include "the elite."

4.

Libertas tries to save herself. One afternoon when her interrogator leaves the room, she strikes up a conversation with the typist, a woman named Miss Breiter. Libertas lets it be known that she is the granddaughter of Philipp Friedrich Alexander, prince of Eulenburg and Hertefeld and count of Sandels, and feigns interest in Miss Breiter's background. She wonders how Miss Breiter has ended up here, typing for a police officer at Gestapo headquarters. Then she steers the conversation toward her own predicament.

"I have only one favor to ask you," Libertas says.

5.

That afternoon, Libertas whispers a single name into Miss Breiter's ear: Hans Coppi.

The next afternoon, she whispers another name.

The third afternoon, another.

During a total of twenty-five interrogations, Libertas whispers the names of everyone she knows in the Circle, Gegner Kreis, Tat Kreis, and Rittmeister Kreis. Miss Breiter dutifully dashes up to the third floor and reports the names to SS Hauptsturmführer Kopkow, admitting later that she "was all excited."

Kopkow is astonished. Many of these names he's never heard before. He promptly reports the news to Göring, who sees to it that Miss Breiter receives five thousand Reichsmark and a personal thank-you note from Himmler.

Kopkow receives an even larger reward from Göring: thirty thousand Reichsmark.

6.

Sometime later, the granddaughter of Philipp Friedrich Alexander, prince of Eulenburg and Hertefeld and count of Sandels, sits down in her prison cell to compose a letter to her mother.

"I," Libertas writes, "out of selfishness, have betrayed friends."

The Red Orchestra Is Neither All Red nor Particularly Musical

1942

1.

News of Libertas's betrayals blazes through the women's prisons. In a *Kassiber*, Rose Schlösinger writes:

> *The new arrests are said to be due to Libertas. . . . She is a born princess of Schulenburg or Eulenburg or so and related or known to Göring. Her husband was protected by G. and was probably the head of this whole thing.*

Oda Schottmüller writes a *Kassiber* about the "eleventh-hour panic" that drove Libertas to become "an informer."

Erika von Brockdorff writes a *Kassiber* about the blabbermouth "Lips," who committed a fresh betrayal by showing up at an interrogation with at least a dozen *Kassiber,* all written by Mildred.

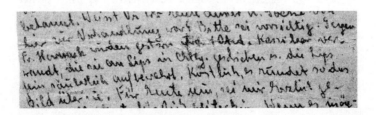

2.

Gestapo officials compile confiscated *Kassiber* and transcripts of interrogations in binders to be used as evidence against the prisoners in court.

By December 1942 there are thirty bulging binders. Nineteen separate trials are planned for a group of seventy-five Germans and one American woman.

3.

The group has a name now: the Rote Kapelle—Red Orchestra. It's not a name they give themselves. The name has its origins in the jargon of German intelligence. The Abwehr uses the word meaning "orchestra" to describe any enemy espionage network. Radio transmitters are "pianos"; their operators are "pianists." When the Abwehr discovered in 1941 that German "pianists" were sending their messages to Moscow, they dubbed the orchestra "Red."

The Abwehr, the Gestapo, and Hitler himself are under the impression that the Red Orchestra is a large, unified network of seasoned spies in Moscow, Paris, Geneva, Brussels, and Berlin.

It is not.

Many of the prisoners in the basement of Gestapo headquarters are mystified when they learn they are defendants in a mass trial intended to prosecute a Soviet spy ring.

4.

The trial will be held at the highest military court in Nazi Germany, the Reichskriegsgericht—Reich Court-Martial. A panel of five judges will hear each case. Defense attorneys will represent the prisoners, and a prosecutor will represent the Reich.

These details are conveyed to Falk Harnack by the prosecutor himself, who prepares at Göring's request an eight-hundred-page indictment.

5.

Falk calls a family meeting.

The Harnacks still haven't found a defense attorney. It's imperative that they hire someone courageous enough to stand up to a prosecutor who takes his orders directly from Göring. So far, all the lawyers they have contacted flatly refuse to have anything to do with Mildred and Arvid. Privately, they convey their sympathies, but they're much too afraid to stick their necks out and publicly defend anyone in the resistance.

Finally, just two weeks before the trial, Arvid's sister Inge finds someone who's willing to take on the case.

6.

It's a bitterly cold morning in December when Falk and his cousins Axel and Ernst von Harnack pay a visit to the lawyer in his cramped, book-strewn office in Berlin. He introduces himself as Herr Schwarz and gives them genial handshakes.

Once they're all seated, Schwarz lets them know that he has been granted no more than a cursory glance at the eight-hundred-page indictment. The Nazi authorities refused to give him a copy of the pages that pertain to Mildred and Arvid. In fact, he wasn't allowed to jot down a single note.

Falk, Axel, and Ernst exchange glances, aghast. How can Schwarz defend Mildred and Arvid with any degree of competence if he doesn't have a firm grasp of the charges against them?

Ernst von Harnack rises to his feet. As a seasoned lawyer and former mayor of Merseburg, he has grappled with the principles of jurisprudence for the better part of two decades, and in recent years he has encountered Nazi corruption with dizzying frequency. He attempts to demonstrate how Schwarz might approach the case, delivering a speech about Arvid's political aims and his commitment to creating a just, humane world.

Schwarz thanks him. It's anyone's guess whether he will follow

Ernst's example in the trial. After another round of handshakes, the meeting is over. Ernst walks out into the frigid morning, wondering what else he can do.

He contacts a Gestapo official who is known to be sympathetic to the resistance and implores him to find out something about the indictment. The official won't, or can't. All he can share is that "it is a very extensive investigation against a vast circle of people shrouded in deep secrecy and that those involved are in danger of losing their lives."

7.

"Still no news from M.," Falk writes in a letter to his mother, Clara.

The date of the letter is December 7, 1942. In eight days, the trial will begin.

8.

Rumors start to spread about Mildred.

In a *Kassiber,* Rose Schlösinger writes:

> *I hear Mildred is in Charlottenburg. She supposedly has really deteriorated mentally lately—has a sort of persecutory delusion.*

Someone swears that Mildred is suicidal and has tried at least twice to swallow a handful of pins.

Someone else sees Mildred get into a tussle with a prison guard. It is rumored that she injured him.

9.

Mildred is permitted to write a single letter.

She hasn't held a pencil in months. She has contracted tuberculosis but says nothing about her illness in the letter, which she addresses to Axel, Falk, and Clara Harnack.

She asks them to send her a "gray suit" that's still at the dry cleaner's on Tauentzienstrasse near the Kaiser Wilhelm Memorial Church. The suit will give her a more polished appearance when she testifies at the trial. She needs to prepare herself, to look as strong and healthy as possible.

She asks for "vitamins and yeast." The bottles, she explains, may be found at Woyrschstrasse 16, "at the top of the pantry" and "in the dresser (bottom) in the hallway near the door."

Mildred doesn't know that the Gestapo raided Woyrschstrasse 16 several days ago and confiscated all their belongings or that an SS officer will soon move in to their former home with his wife and children.

Anneliese and Witch Bones

1942–1943

1.

Morning. Mildred opens her eyes. Weak sunlight filters through a barred window near the ceiling of her cell. She knows it as well as she knows the palm of her hand: the slim cracks cutting through smooth planes, the small pits like constellations. One moment gives way to another, and another, and by slow accretion, time passes. The number of hours she has stared at the ceiling is incalculable. The neat divisions that once ordered her days have collapsed into an end-less expanse of nothingness resonant with the bright jangle of keys, the violent clang of a cell door slammed shut. There are no lectures to prepare, no classes to teach, no meetings to hold. She marks the hours by the tray that arrives three times a day. A prison guard sets it down with a smack.

Breakfast is a hunk of dry bread, a cup of lukewarm water the color of dirt—what passes for coffee here, made from boiled grain. She chews and swallows and coughs. Her lungs are sore from all the coughing.

The mattress is stuffed with wood chips and straw.

Bedbugs and lice crawl over her skin and scalp. Mice scamper across the stone floor.

There is no toilet, just a bucket in the corner of her cell. The stench of it.

One morning she will open her eyes, and something will change. She will rise from the mattress and put on her gray suit and walk out of this solitary cell. Outside, an idling police wagon will be ready to transport her from Charlottenburg prison to a courtroom. Her wrists will be handcuffed. Still, it will be a kind of freedom.

2.

Rose Schlösinger, locked in her cell, writes another *Kassiber*. Her heart is broken: Bodo is dead. She heard about his death the day before the anniversary of their engagement, the news traveling in furtive whispers from the Eastern Front to the corridors of the Alexanderplatz prison.

> *I unfortunately can't even explain what thoughts and feelings this news elicited in me. . . . So much misfortune is piling up on me that I have to numb my heart so that I can bear it all.*

Bodo Schlösinger didn't die in battle; he died by his own hand. Shortly after he heard that the Gestapo had arrested everyone in the Circle, including Rose, he walked into a farmhouse in the Russian countryside and shot himself.

3.

Elfriede Paul is sewing a blouse, locked in a community cell with a group of other prisoners. She is engaged in forced labor; a guard watches over them. Until now, the only sewing she did was suturing wounds at her clinic in Berlin. She wore a watch then; now, her wrist is bare. She knows nine hours have passed when a guard hollers, "Scissors in the hole!"

Elfriede and the other prisoners slip their scissors through a hole in the wall by the heating pipe. They have nicknamed it "the Hot Hole."

Back in her cell, Elfriede writes a *Kassiber:*

> *I feel miserable. And I don't want to be alone.*

Fortunately, she's not. She shares a cell with Erika von Brock-dorff, who has a wicked sense of humor. "I get along well with Erika," Elfriede writes.

> *In the evenings we tell each other bits from our lives, mostly our experiences with men.*

When Elfriede is hungry, Erika "cooks" for her, describing in mouthwatering detail a lavish dinner with a bottle of wine to share. "Then we sleep wonderfully," she writes.

When Elfriede feels melancholy, Erika whistles or sings racy songs or cracks dirty jokes until she smiles. Erika calls herself a *Eulenspiegel*—"joker."

4.

Erika von Brockdorff writes a *Kassiber*—

> *I've never lived life as intensely as in the past year . . . I want to write about the dream I had*

—and slips it to a prison guard.

5.

The guard is Anneliese Kuehn, who will give a statement after the war about her encounters with these women.

At first, Anneliese isn't sure what to think of them. Anneliese shows up to work to earn a paycheck, nothing more. *Kassiber* are prohibited at the Alexanderplatz prison. Any prisoner caught passing one is severely punished. She and the other guards are required to scour the prisoners' cells and perform body searches several times a day. They receive five Reichsmark for each *Kassiber* they confiscate.

One day during a body search, Erika von Brockdorff tells Anneliese that an SS guard attempted to rape her. Hearing this, Anneliese is stung by compassion.

She begins to watch Erika and her friends in the resistance more closely, noticing that they "did everything in their power to stay in communication." Sometimes they throw *Kassiber* out the window to prisoners in the yard. Sometimes they pass *Kassiber* to each other through a ventilation flap.

"I realized with deep respect that these resistance fighters did not give up their struggle even under the very hard conditions of their imprisonment," Anneliese remembered.

6.

During an air raid, Oda Schottmüller sneaks out of her cell and races down the corridor. Behind one of the doors there's a toilet. The stinking bucket in her cell is an indignity she can finally escape, if only just this once.

She flings open the door, yanks up her skirt, and urinates into the toilet, a luxury she hasn't enjoyed in months.

Her joy is short-lived.

A prison guard she detests barges in and scolds her: "Such shamelessness!"

"You know you're *meshugge*," Oda snaps back.

"I'm reporting you!"

Oda knows full well that she will be punished for calling a guard crazy in Yiddish, but she doesn't care. In a *Kassiber,* she describes the episode, nicknaming the guard "Witch Bones."

7.

Witch Bones is nothing like Anneliese Kuehn.

Witch Bones scolds prisoners who say they're starving and want more bread. "Well, well," she sneers, "isn't that our glutton." She surely feels no sympathy for the women she guards.

But Anneliese Kuehn does. She starts smuggling in pencils, paper, candles, matches, and slips them to prisoners when she searches their cells. Instead of confiscating their *Kassiber,* she delivers them to their intended recipients, both inside the walls of the prison and in town.

During air raids she lets them crawl out of their own cells and into their neighbors' to talk with one another.

8.

In the community cell, Elfriede Paul turns fabric into flowers. A prison official demonstrates how to sew it efficiently. It cannot be any old flower. It must be a sweet pea.

"Today," Elfriede writes in a *Kassiber,*

> we're making flowers again and we'll do 37 boxes with 60 flowers each = 2220 pieces. Recently light sweet pea colors, today screaming bright colors.

"Today," she writes in another *Kassiber,*

> two doves sat on the roof of Building II. I saw them very near and large and their beautiful colorful feathers shimmered in the evening sun.

Elfriede has an eye for beauty. She admires a "long icicle on my window flap that sparkles and glistens in the midday sun."

It's the kind of observation Mildred might have made in a *Kassiber,* had she been permitted to have a pencil and paper. After the single letter she wrote to Clara, Falk, and Axel, the guard took away her pencil. At Charlottenburg, there are no guards like Anneliese Kuehn.

9.

Morning. Mildred opens her eyes. Nothing has changed. The bars on the window, the ceiling with its cracks and pits, the bedbugs and lice and mice.

No. Today will be different.

Mildred rises from bed, sets her bare feet on the stone floor. This morning she will cast off her prison garb and put on her gray suit. She will walk out of her cell, out of the prison.

Out of here.

She can't predict what will happen in the courtroom. But she knows this: Arvid will be there.

Hitler's Bloodhound

1942–1943

1.

The Reich Court-Martial is an organ of the high command of the armed forces. Three high-ranking military officers and two civilian judges determine the guilt or innocence of the defendants who stand before them, typically soldiers charged with desertion or generals charged with insubordination for disobeying Göring's decrees.

Mildred Harnack and her coconspirators are charged with treason.

German criminal law recognizes two types of treason: treason against the government (*Hochverrat*) and treason against the country (*Landesverrat*). A defendant found guilty of treason against the government is usually punished with a prison sentence of three to five years. A defendant convicted of treason against the country is punished with death.

The prosecutor Göring has handpicked for the mass trial is Manfred Roeder, a forty-two-year-old lawyer with a colonel's rank—*Oberstkriegsgerichtsrat*. Roeder has proved himself over the years to be an infantile, boorish loudmouth with a mediocre grasp of the law. When assigned by the Luftwaffe to investigate the suicide of stunt pilot Ernst Udet, Roeder ordered the arrest of everyone who had a connection to Udet, however remote, as well as numerous others who didn't. A disapproving colleague later quipped, "We must keep Roeder out of this case; he is quite capable of arresting the Pope." Roeder has undergone numerous disciplinary proceedings and is not particularly admired by his colleagues. One judge believes that

Roeder "does not possess the normal man's sympathy for the sufferings of others." Another thinks that Roeder is "insensitive and biased." The judge who says this is Alexander Kraell, president of the Second Chamber of the Reich Court-Martial, who happens to be the chief judge in Mildred's trial.

Judge Kraell may have a poor opinion of the prosecutor who has earned the nickname "Hitler's Bloodhound," but the two men share a common belief: both Kraell and Roeder regard opposition to Hitler as a horrific crime, especially in wartime. German citizens have a legal obligation to be loyal, in their view, even if Germany has transformed from a parliamentary democracy into a fascist dictatorship. Even if the fascist dictator is murdering millions who fall into a category the Führer considers undesirable.

2.

In the mass trial of the Red Orchestra, Hitler's Bloodhound has a single objective: to sentence every one of the accused to death.

Somewhere within Manfred Roeder's thirty bulging binders are transcripts of the numerous interrogations each of them endured during their imprisonment. Whatever they blurted out under torture will be presented as evidence against them. Roeder is also fortunate that Libertas Schulze-Boysen has voluntarily betrayed a bunch of her friends and provided a wealth of incriminating information about them. Roeder will put it all to good use.

Twelve men and women are scheduled to appear before the court on the morning of December 15, 1942. Among them are Mildred and Arvid Harnack and Libertas and Harro Schulze-Boysen. The mass trial will resume in early January 1943 and continue until all seventy-six defendants are prosecuted.

Hitler will receive daily reports. For the first time in history, the judges of the Reich Court-Martial won't have the final word. All verdicts and sentencing must be approved by the Führer.

3.

Mildred's coconspirators will write about Manfred Roeder in *Kassiber*. In this way, news about their prosecutor spreads from cell to cell, prison to prison. He is known for strutting and crowing during a defendant's testimony. Oda Schottmüller will describe him as "an indescribably conceited rooster." Erika von Brockdorff will call the mass trial a "witch hunt."

4.

There are no *Kassiber* documenting Mildred's impressions of Manfred Roeder. Locked in solitary confinement, forbidden to write or speak, she could not communicate her thoughts to anyone.

The First of Many Trials

1942

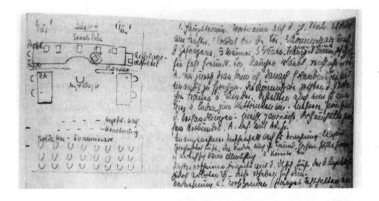

1.

Shortly before nine a.m. on December 15, 1942, Mildred walks into a courtroom. Moments ago, in the hallway, she met her lawyer, Schwarz, for the first time. He says he's prohibited from advising her about anything. He can't even sit near her.

A guard leads Mildred to the back of the room, where wooden chairs are arranged in three orderly rows, and instructs her to sit.

She's wearing her gray suit. Her hair is pulled back in a bun. She has tried to make herself presentable, but the suit doesn't fit as it once did. It hangs shapelessly over her emaciated body, as if she borrowed it from a healthier woman.

One by one, the other defendants enter, flanked by guards.

Arvid walks in. Harro and Libertas Schulze-Boysen walk in.

Hans Coppi walks in. The Abwehr lieutenant Herbert Gollnow, Mildred's former pupil, walks in. Perhaps she's surprised to see him; perhaps not. Six others — two women and four men — walk in, several of whom she has never set eyes on before. It's likely her eyes don't linger long on any of them.

It's likely she's staring at Arvid.

2.

Mildred and Arvid can't speak a single word to each other, much less fall into each other's arms. The rules set forth for the mass trial at the Reich Court-Martial forbid communication between defendants. After three months of ceaseless isolation and intermittent torture, all Mildred and Arvid can do is gaze at each other.

3.

Five judges enter the courtroom and sit in chairs positioned on a raised platform. Judge Kraell calls out the names of the twelve defendants. Glowering on the wall behind him, rendered huge and misshapen by an inexpert sculptor's hands, is a bas-relief of Hitler's face.

Within these walls, a parody of justice will be enacted.

Manfred Roeder calls the defendants to the stand, one by one. His performance is theatrical and ghastly. He sneers and bellows, struts and crows.

When it's Mildred's turn, she rises from the wooden chair and approaches the stand. He hammers her with questions.

She fixes him with a level gaze and lies. No, she can't name names or point fingers. No, she doesn't know anything about acts of espionage. No, the meetings she held weren't treasonous; they were strictly focused on the discussion of American novels.

4.

The trial lasts four days. On December 19, the sentences are handed down.

Axel von Harnack sends a telegram to Falk:

BOOK OUT OF STOCK BUT SIX PICTURES

Book means Arvid; *out of stock* means death sentence; *picture* means Mildred.

The coded message tells Falk that Arvid received a death sentence and Mildred received six years' imprisonment.

5.

Harro and Libertas Schulze-Boysen receive death sentences.

Hans Coppi receives a death sentence.

In the trials to come, nearly all members of the Circle, Gegner Kreis, Tat Kreis, and Rittmeister Kreis will receive death sentences.

Mildred's Cellmate

1942–1943

1.

It's snowing when Gertrud Klapputh arrives at Charlottenburg prison.

She is twenty-nine years old. She grew up in Leopoldshall, a destitute village where her father worked in the salt mines. She has been in the underground resistance since she was twenty-one, when she renounced Nazi Germany and declared herself an exile. In 1934, she went to Moscow. In 1935, she went to Paris. In 1938, she went to Brussels, where she "lived illegally with a Dutchwoman," according to her Gestapo file.

The six pages of the file present a dry, meticulous recitation of offenses. She distributed illegal leaflets. She consorted with Communists. She was a member of the Communist prisoners' aid group Rote Hilfe—Red Aid—and participated in treasonous activities under the alias "Hertha."

In 1940, the Gestapo hauled her back to Berlin and threw her in prison for six months. Ten months after her release, the Gestapo arrested her again.

Gertrud has no idea how long she will be incarcerated this time. So far she has spent a year and three months behind bars, first at Moabit, then at Alexanderplatz, and now here, at Charlottenburg, where she shares a cell with twenty other women.

2.

The first time Gertrud Klapputh sees Mildred in the Charlottenburg prison yard is on December 10, 1942. Snow falls in wet clumps from a colorless sky. Prisoners are required to walk the perimeter after lunch for exactly thirty minutes. They walk in pairs, side by side, in a large circle. They are forbidden to speak. "The Bear Dance," the prisoners inexplicably call it. Gertrud is a new arrival; she's still learning the lingo.

Rumors spread from cell to cell in whispers. This is how she learns that Mildred is an American anti-fascist in strict solitary confinement. Gertrud is intrigued. Every day during the Bear Dance, she scans the circle of women, looking for Mildred. Now and then, their eyes meet.

"We could only exchange glances," Gertrud wrote.

3.

On December 20, 1942, the head guard informs Gertrud that she is being transferred to a smaller cell. When Gertrud walks in, she locks eyes with the prisoner sitting there.

It's Mildred.

After the cell door slams shut and the guard is gone, they "spontaneously fall into each other's arms," Gertrud remembered. "So great was our mutual affection, which until then we could only express with our eyes."

4.

Mildred is a suicide risk. This is why, after three months of solitary confinement, she was given a cellmate.

"Mildred possessed a great treasure," Gertrud remembered, "a pencil." At some point during her four-day trial, Mildred spotted this treasure and snatched it. She tells Gertrud she has been sentenced to six years' hard labor. Soon she will be transferred to a work camp. Until then, she wants to make the best use of her time.

"After we got up in the morning we did exercises, as much as the extremely narrow room allowed," Gertrud wrote.

> Then we washed up until the meager breakfast, a piece of dry bread and a cup of "coffee," came.

It is watery and tasteless, but she's used to it; they both are.

> Then we studied or told each other stories until lunch.

The "studying" Mildred and Gertrud do is an improvisation. They have no books. But Gertrud gets her hands on a scrap of paper, and Mildred joyfully retrieves her pencil from the hole where she's hidden it. "She wrote down Goethe verses for me," Gertrud remembered.

> I also learned American songs from her.... She learned songs and poems from me as well. She loved to hear best: "Oh valleys wide, oh heights!"

They hear a jangle of keys. The cell door swings open. A guard sets down a lunch tray with a clatter. Another meager meal. And afterward: the Bear Dance. And so it goes.

> Mildred unfortunately got no mail, neither from her husband nor from anyone else in the family. She cried sometimes when she spoke about Arvid.... I comforted her as best I could. She worried a lot about how she would survive the six years of labor camp.

5.

The last glimpse Mildred had of Arvid was in the courtroom after their sentences were pronounced.

Arvid caught her eye and "beamed," elated that her life had been spared. She held his gaze as long as she could, expressing with her eyes her anguished love.

Mildred still holds on to the hope that they will be reunited.

Perhaps Arvid's verdict will be appealed, she tells Gertrud. Perhaps another, more capable lawyer will replace Schwarz and argue convincingly for a stay of execution. Perhaps the war will end before Arvid's execution is carried out. Perhaps the resistance will succeed in assassinating Hitler. Mildred convinces herself that these possibilities, however remote, are worth clinging to.

But sometimes Mildred loses hope. Sometimes she is "sad and sometimes close to despair."

6.

It's January 1943. The second or third day of the new year — Gertrud can't be sure — a guard appears. Mildred has been summoned by her lawyer.

Mildred doesn't understand. She has already received her sentence. There must be some sort of mix-up.

Mildred rises to her feet. A jangle of keys, the cell door swings open and shuts. Another jangle of keys. And she is gone.

Later, when Mildred returns, she has terrible news. For some reason, the verdict has been overturned. Mildred's lawyer told her she should "expect a stiffer sentence."

Gertrud tries to console Mildred, but she is inconsolable. Schwarz told her something else.

Arvid is dead.

Shortly before eight p.m. on December 22, 1942, Arvid was hanged, along with six other men in the Red Orchestra case, including Harro Schulze-Boysen, Hans Coppi, and Kurt Schumacher. Arvid spent the last hour of his life in his prison cell writing a letter to Mildred. She has the letter now; Schwarz gave it to her. She has read it countless times, and still she can't quite believe Arvid is dead. It's not possible. She can't be a widow.

Harro and Hans and Kurt can't be dead.

And she can't go back into that courtroom again.

7.

But she must.

Göring "exploded" when he learned that Mildred wasn't given a death sentence. The word *imprisonment* drove him into an apoplectic fit, a court officer recalled in a postwar interrogation. He screamed that he "had been commissioned by the Führer" to "cauterize this abscess," and swore that Hitler would overturn her sentence.

The next day, Hitler swiftly rejected Mildred's verdict and ordered her execution. To preserve the appearance of judicial propriety, he assigned a different panel of judges to hear her case.

The Greatest Bit of Bad Luck

1943

1.

On January 13, 1943, Mildred walks into the Reich Court-Martial, once again wearing her gray suit. In her pocket is Arvid's farewell letter. The courtroom is so much emptier than it was the last time she was here.

There is a new panel of judges, she sees. But the prosecutor is the same.

Today, Manfred Roeder calls to the witness stand Mildred's pupil Herbert Gollnow.

The Abwehr officer testifies that he told Mildred military secrets last spring—specifically, about Hitler's preparations to invade the Caucasus and capture its oil wells and "about twelve" Abwehr sabotage missions behind Soviet lines.

Why did you tell her these secrets? Hitler's Bloodhound asks him.

Gollnow says Mildred forced him to.

What was the nature of your relationship with Arvid Harnack's wife?

Herbert Gollnow characterizes their relationship as one of "sexual bondage."

Gollnow's salacious testimony is presented as evidence to support a new sentence for Mildred: death.

2.

"Then came the greatest bit of bad luck," Gertrud remembered.

I had to leave Mildred....I had come to care for Mildred so, like a very dear good sister. And she needed me right then most urgently.

On January 15, 1943, Gertrud is transferred out of Charlottenburg. She doesn't know where she's going. Mildred asks her to smuggle out Arvid's farewell letter.

Gertrud says she'll try. If she ends up in another prison, it might be possible. If she ends up in a concentration camp, it might not.

And then she is gone. Mildred is alone again.

3.

But not for long. The next morning another prisoner is shoved into Mildred's cell. She is in her late teens or early twenties. Her name remains unknown; other prisoners refer to her as "the new one."

The Armband She Wore

1943

1.

The Bear Dance.

On February 12, 1943, a prisoner named Irmgard Kamlah joins the others in the prison yard as they walk in pairs around its perimeter. Years later, she wrote about this day in a letter.

> I heard the officer accompanying us say to the supervising guard, with a glance at Mildred, "You know, no talking and she has to walk alone."

Mildred wears a gray cape with a hood. "I couldn't see her hair," Irmgard wrote, "since she pulled the hood down pretty far." Mildred also wears an armband stamped with two black letters: *TK,* short for *Todeskandidatin*—death candidate.

Now and then, the prisoners dart glances at Mildred. "We always left room for her with a certain timidity so she wouldn't be suspected of speaking with one of us," Irmgard wrote. Today, Mildred looks

> shockingly frail and miserable, as though she had trouble holding herself up. Yet she raced like she was being hunted, with big steps, from one corner of the yard to the other, looking past us with a vacant expression.

She is the first TK Irmgard has seen.

2.

Late at night Irmgard hears footsteps. She's lying on a cot under a thin blanket, shivering. She's not alone; several other shivering women share her cell. In the dark she makes out the shadowy form of a guard and a girl. The girl is "half naked and crying very hard." The guard shoves the girl in the cell.

The women lie in their cots, silent, listening to the girl sob. This can only mean one thing. Mildred has been taken away.

After a long while, we then talked in whispers to the "new one" who had been Mildred's cellmate until she had been picked up for her execution.

3.

In the months to come, Irmgard will meet other TKs on the prison yard. During the Bear Dance, she will see a woman walking alone, hiding her face under a hood. Her days are numbered. It never takes long.

In her cell, Irmgard lies shivering in the dark, hearing the prison gate swinging open, the grumble of an engine.

I learned what it meant when a vehicle drove into the deadly quiet prison yard at nine o'clock at night and drove out again a quarter hour later.

The vehicle is headed for Plötzensee Prison, where women are decapitated.

The Mannhardt Guillotine

1943

1.

In the mid-1800s, a clockmaker in Munich named Johann Mannhardt sought to improve on an apparatus the French had built half a century earlier to murder people efficiently.

The French guillotine stood fourteen feet tall and weighed over a ton, a formidable instrument that had decapitated an estimated seventeen thousand people in a single year during the French Revolution. The mechanism that drove a massive blade to the top crossbar and down again was rudimentary and brutish, far simpler than the delicate arrangement of hanging weights, pulleys, and pendulums that operated Johann's turret clocks. The French guillotine was made entirely of wood; Johann constructed his version with iron and steel. The French guillotine had a thick hemp rope and a pulley; Johann's version used a durable steel cable and a ratcheted hand crank. The French guillotine required an executioner to cut the rope with his sword to release the blade; an executioner operating Johann's version activated a blade-release mechanism by pressing a single button.

The Johann Mannhardt Company produced six guillotines by 1860. One ended up at Bruchsal Prison in southwest Germany, near the town of Karlsruhe, though it fell quickly into disuse, as did the others. A Mannhardt guillotine may have been more efficient at murdering people than a French guillotine, but there was not much demand for such a device at that moment in history. Johann returned to clockmaking. He died in 1878.

2.

Over half a century later, the number of executions in Germany rose exponentially. Judges became so efficient at handing out death sentences to traitors, saboteurs, and other political criminals that the prisons were filled to capacity. This presented a problem. Executions by hanging were time-consuming. Executions by ax were cumbersome. Most pressing, there were only three properly trained executioners in the whole of Germany.

On December 28, 1936, Hitler's minister of justice issued a new set of guidelines that he hoped would maximize efficiency. He divided Germany into three execution regions and assigned one region to each executioner. Eleven prisons in Germany would serve as execution sites. He dispensed with scaffolds and axes, tools of the past. From then on, executions would be conducted exclusively by guillotine.

The prison in Berlin didn't have a guillotine, which posed a problem, but the minister of justice devised a quick, simple solution. Rather than build a new guillotine, he would find an underutilized one at a smaller prison and transport it to Berlin.

3.

On February 8, 1937, a team of men at Bruchsal Prison dismantled the Mannhardt guillotine, distributed the parts into an assortment of wooden crates, and loaded them onto a truck bound for Berlin.

The truck trundled northeast.

It passed the Rhine River, where Mildred loved to swim when the weather was warm.

It passed Jena, where Mildred spent her first year in Germany, sequestering herself for hours in the university library to research her dissertation.

It passed the Thuringian Forest and the Harz Mountains, where Mildred hiked with Arvid on Sundays, their rucksacks stuffed with sandwiches and books.

Some of the roads were blanketed with snow, some slick with ice. When at last the truck arrived at Plötzensee Prison, it was late at night. The truck parked alongside a cellblock called Gefängnis III. This was where prisoners awaiting execution were shackled.

In the morning, a group of guards unpacked the crates under the supervision of the director of Plötzensee Prison, a man named Paul Vacano. An envelope inside one of the crates contained detailed instructions for reassembling the Mannhardt guillotine. The director decided that an empty shed behind Gefängnis III would be an ideal spot for the contraption, "quite spacious and suitable."

4.

Paul Vacano has devoted a considerable amount of thought to the question of how the executions should be carried out. In a long memo, he expressed his concern that a prisoner might resist being strapped to the guillotine, causing trouble for the executioner and wasting time. He concluded that a black curtain should conceal the guillotine until the very last second. "This would ensure a smooth flow," he wrote.

All the Frequent Troubles
of Our Days

1943

1.

Harald Poelchau was hired to be a prison chaplain on April 1, 1933.
He was twenty-nine, the son of a pastor. A year later, he witnessed
his first execution.

> I had already experienced sleepless nights leading up to the
> dreaded day.... Before I knew it, the executioner threw the
> prisoner to the ground, pressed his neck against a block of
> wood and immediately beheaded him with a hand ax. I did not
> look. I was overcome with nausea and tried desperately to
> regain control of myself.

He was so horrified by the "blasphemy" that he considered resign-
ing from his post. After anguished deliberation, he decided to stay.

In his official capacity at Plötzensee Prison, Chaplain Poelchau
provides spiritual counsel to men and women shortly before their
executions. He is permitted to roam the grounds of the prison as he
wishes. Prison guards greet him as he walks past, unlocking whatever gates and doors he would like opened. He enters cells with the
full approval of prison director Paul Vacano, who has not the slightest idea that Chaplain Poelchau, who works under the auspices of
the Ministry of Justice, is a member of the resistance.

Poelchau smuggles notes to prisoners, acting as a courier between members of their families as well as others in the resistance. He attends secret meetings held by the Kreisau Circle, whose members include Helmuth James Graf von Moltke and Adam von Trott zu Solz. Moltke and Trott zu Solz are among the conspirators who will be executed—along with Ernst von Harnack, Hans von Dohnányi, Dietrich Bonhoeffer, Klaus Bonhoeffer, and Justus Delbrück—for their participation in the Valkyrie plot to assassinate Hitler.

2.

On February 16, 1943, Chaplain Harald Poelchau enters Gefängnis III and finds Mildred shackled in her cell, bent over a book.

Axel von Harnack finally persuaded a prison official to smuggle the book in to her. Arvid's sister Inge asked Chaplain Poelchau to smuggle in an orange and a photograph. It's absolutely forbidden for a pastor to act as a courier for the condemned prisoner's family, but Harald Poelchau takes the risk.

The book, he sees, is a volume of Goethe's poems. In her hand is a pencil stub. She's translating the poems into English. The margins of the book are filled with her handwriting. On page 74, Mildred has written:

> In all the frequent troubles of our days
> A God gave compensation—more his praise
> In looking sky- and heavenward as duty
> In sunshine and in virtue and in beauty.

The evidence of her suffering is plain. Her hair has thinned to wisps. She is emaciated. Her breathing is labored, her lungs ravaged by tuberculosis. Her shoulders hunch forward, her spine following the curve of a question mark.

Chaplain Poelchau sits down beside her.

From the pocket of his robe he withdraws the orange and the photograph. It's a picture of Georgina Fish.

Mildred peers at it wordlessly. She finds her pencil stub and writes a note on the back:

The face of my mother expresses everything that I want to say at this moment. This face was with me all through these last months.

Soon, a prison guard will ask Poelchau to leave. Another man will enter the cell and search Mildred's mouth for gold fillings, cut her hair. He will slip onto her bare feet a pair of wooden clogs. Flanked by two wardens, Mildred will walk to the execution shed, hearing the hollow clap of the clogs against concrete. She will place her head on a block.

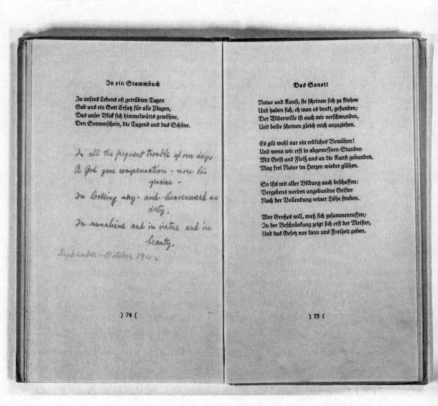

Stieve's List

1943–1945

Lfd.Nr.	Name	Alterin J.	Geburts-datum	Sterbe-datum
1	Juhnemann			
2	Schröter			8. 7.
3	Witzke *August*	21	28.5.15	28. 7.36
4	Groger, *Marie*		11.5.96	25. 5.37
5	Kneup, *Katharina*	39	7. 7.99	4.10.38
6	Kuhlmann	23	26.10.14	19. 7.38
7	Seyferth, *Annie*	36	24.11.02	12.11.38
8	Schweitzer *Georg Schweitzer*		1.8.03	15. 4.38
9	Schweitzer *Anna*	41	8. 1.97	15. 6.38
10	Glssner	40	16.11.99	7.12.39
11	Gose *Arthur*	19	13. 2.20	2. 3.39
12	Diecker, Marie	33	29.7.06	29. 7.48
13	Martyn, Janine	20	15.5.21	21. 8.41
14	Puschewski	41	13. 4.99	21. 3.41
15	Schubert, Ruth	20	22.11.20	1. 2.41
16	Augustiniok, Veronika	42	30.11.99	15. 8.42
17	Ball	61	24. 4.80	19. 3.42
18	Baum, Marianne	30	9.2.12	18. 8.42
19	Buoaoh, Else	30	3. 7.11	17. 5.42
20	Czubokowska, Bronislawa	29	9.7.18	15. 8.42
21	Fiedermann	23	3. 9.18	20. 6.42
22	Götze, Ursula	26	29. 3.16	5. 8.42
23	Golombiowski, Sophie	35	8. 2.07	7. 8.42
24	Großvogel	42		6. 7.42
25	Harnaoh, Erika	22	25. 4.20	17. 7.42
26	Jadanowitz, Hildegard	26	11.6.16	15. 8.42
27	Kaescheli, Juliette	21	20.11.20	2.10.42
28	Koohmann, Sara	30	7.6.12	18. 8.42
29	Korsing, Frieda	53	17. 4.89	5. 6.42
30	Lambert, Elisabeth	45	15.10.97	14.12.42
31	Lastech, Ulla	31	22. 8.10	7. 7.42

1.

Margarete von Zahn-Harnack is a young woman studying to be a physician at the University of Berlin. One day a professor summons her into his office. Why, she has no idea. She is accustomed to seeing Dr. Hermann Stieve, chairman of the Anatomical Department, in a lecture hall. Professor Stieve is known for delivering rigorous lectures with theatrical gusto. He wears a black gown with billowing sleeves. An imposing figure of authority, he holds forth on subjects like the function of the adrenal glands in the human endocrine system. Apparently ambidextrous, Professor Stieve punctuates his lectures with drawings on the blackboard, both chalk-dusted hands impressively engaged in rendering the follicular epithelial cells of the ovary. He is impressive even now, seated behind a massive desk, a wall of medical books behind him. He gestures at a chair and instructs Margarete to sit.

Bewildered, she sits.

Arvid's niece doesn't always do as she is told. Growing up, Margarete von Zahn-Harnack was taught that "it is worthwhile to rebel." Members of her family emphasized by their own example the importance of challenging dogma and calcified social norms. Her grandfather Adolf von Harnack won as many admirers as detractors in the Lutheran Church for his unorthodox views on scripture. Her mother, Agnes von Zahn-Harnack, a women's rights activist, was the first woman to attend the University of Berlin (Margarete knows the date of her enrollment— 1908—as well as she does her own birthday). Nearly four decades later, Margarete sits in lecture halls still jammed mostly with men.

Dr. Stieve tells Margarete he has something he would like to return to her family. He places on the desk a vase.

Margarete thanks him, takes the vase. How her anatomy professor came to possess something that belongs to her family is a mystery. She is baffled until she realizes that the object in her hands isn't a vase. It's an urn. Inside are Mildred Harnack's ashes.

"I have saved her," Stieve says, "from being dissected."

2.

Margarete rambles around campus in a daze, the urn in her hands.

There's so much more she wants to know. How did Professor Stieve know that Mildred was in her family? Why and how had he saved her from dissection?

Nine members of her family have recently been executed for opposing Hitler's regime. Margarete adored Mildred; her beheading was unspeakably horrific. The urn is a gift, an act of generosity that provides the Harnacks a small measure of comfort. Now at least Mildred can have a proper burial.

After receiving her medical degree, Dr. Margarete von Zahn–Harnack opens a clinic in Berlin where she goes on to treat patients for over thirty years. During this time she will speak of her former professor in glowing terms, believing that he had "put his life in danger" by saving Mildred from dissection. Margarete won't know until the late 1980s that Dr. Hermann Stieve lied to her. He didn't save anyone from dissection.

3.

Dr. Stieve keeps a list of all the women he dissects.

The list is 182 names long. Next to each name is the age of the woman at her death.

Number 84 is Mildred Harnack, age 40.

Number 37 is Libertas Schulze-Boysen, age 29.

Number 103 is Erika von Brockdorff, age 32.

Number 102 is Rose Schlösinger, age 36.

Number 104 is Oda Schottmüller, age 38.

Number 44 is Cato Bontjes van Beek, age 22.

And so on.

Women in the resistance provide a steady supply of bodies. When speaking to students and lab assistants, Dr. Stieve refers to them as "bodies of criminals." He has negotiated a special arrangement with the director of Plötzensee Prison, who accommodates his request for the bodies of executed women to be delivered straight to his laboratory.

4.

"It is extremely difficult to find ovaries from really healthy girls," Dr. Stieve commented in 1931 when he was immersed in research on the effects of stress on reproductive organs. Back then, his female subjects were limited to hens.

After Hitler became chancellor, the number of death sentences doled out in courtrooms rose sharply. Between 1933 and 1944, judges ordered 17,383 executions, the overwhelming majority of which were punishments for political crimes, including treason. Exactly how many bodies were delivered to anatomical departments in Germany's universities remains unknown.

The number of medical journals that publish Dr. Stieve's research increases as his supply of bodies increases. He becomes a recognized authority on *plötzlich Tod*—sudden death—and how the extreme stress brought on by imprisonment and execution affects the female reproductive tract. In his laboratory he has a large collection of human uteri preserved in jars, some in various stages of pregnancy.

In 1943, Dr. Stieve receives the decapitated body of a woman who recently gave birth at a delivery ward inside Barnimstrasse prison.

She is Hilde Coppi, number 53, age 34.

5.

Hilde named her baby Hans, after his father, who was permitted a single visit before he was hanged at Plötzensee Prison. Hilde nursed her baby in her cell until the day a guard arrived to take Hans Coppi Jr. away.

The next day, Hilde was decapitated.

6.

Greta Kuckhoff is not on Stieve's list. She has been sent to a concentration camp in Waldheim.

She will survive and become Hans Coppi Jr.'s godmother.

The Final Solution

1943–1945

1.

In 1943, the number of prisoners in concentration camps skyrockets.

Two years ago, there were fifty-three thousand. Last year, there were eighty thousand. By the winter of 1943, there are three hundred and fifteen thousand prisoners. Auschwitz has the largest number of prisoners, over eighty-five thousand. Dachau, Buchenwald, Sachsenhausen, Mauthausen, and Ravensbrück have between twenty-four thousand and thirty-seven thousand prisoners. Eleven other main camps each have approximately six thousand prisoners.

Some are forced-labor camps. Some are extermination camps. Some are both forced-labor and extermination camps.

2.

People with mental illness or physical impairments are gassed. Sinti and Roma—given the derogatory name "Gypsies"—are gassed. Forced laborers from Poland, the Soviet Union, and other countries who can no longer work due to frailty or sickness are gassed.

3.

At Auschwitz, the systematic extermination of Jews is carried out using the poison gas Zyklon B, produced by the chemical conglomerate I. G. Farben. Between 1943 and 1944, an estimated six thousand Jews are murdered each day at Auschwitz.

An accurate tally of the deaths at concentration camps is impossible. Available evidence indicates that two-thirds of the Jewish population in Europe—or six million Jews—were murdered.

Gertrud

1943–1945

1.

The prisoners at the concentration camp wear striped smocks with felt triangles sewn onto their left shoulders. At a glance, the SS guards know why you're here. Red triangles are for Communists, Social Democrats, and other political enemies; green are for common criminals; lilac are for Jehovah's Witnesses; and black are for so-called asocials—lesbians and prostitutes. Yellow triangles are for Jews, who are divided into subcategories. If you are a Jew who is also a Communist, you wear a yellow triangle over a red background. If you are a Jew who is also a lesbian, you wear a yellow triangle over a black background.

2.

Form a line. Take off your clothes. Your underthings.

Gertrud Klapputh obeys the guards, peeling off a dirty dress. She is naked now, and cold. Snow cakes the ground outside, icicles hang from rafters in mid-drip.

Widen your legs.

Gertrud does as she's told. The shavers are here now, rummaging through everyone's pubic hair, looking for lice. She feels this stranger's fingers probing her vagina, then the nape of her neck, behind her ears. Gertrud's hair is raven black. Lice would be easy to spot. The shavers drag razors over the skin and scalps of lice-ridden women. *Ravensbrück is a clean camp; filth won't be tolerated.* This is a lie. For her feet, she receives a filthy pair of wooden clogs. To clean herself, a nugget of soap. She is assigned to cellblock 1, which houses women arrested for opposing Hitler—the "political" prisoners. She is given a needle and thread and told to sew a red triangle on her smock. She is prisoner number 16277.

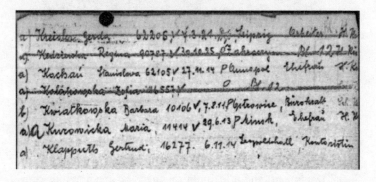

She is twenty-nine years old. Will she survive to see thirty? Thirty-one? She doesn't know whether she'll survive until morning. She has smuggled Arvid's letter in here and stashed it somewhere she hopes the guards won't look. She promised Mildred she'd keep the letter safe. She will go to great lengths to keep a promise.

3.

Ravensbrück is the only concentration camp built exclusively for women.

It is located fifty miles north of Berlin, nestled deep in a forest. Three pristine lakes dot the countryside. Himmler selected this site for its beauty. He believes that the purification of German blood is best achieved in nature. Amid the orchards, flower gardens, and gooseberry bushes that beautify Ravensbrück, a crematorium is erected.

The first women sent here are Germans arrested for opposing Hitler. A bevy of prostitutes, lesbians, criminals, Jehovah's Witnesses, and Sinti and Roma join them. As the war progresses, women from Nazi-occupied countries—including Poland, France, Czechoslovakia, and the Soviet Union—begin to fill the cellblocks. In 1944, twelve thousand Jewish women arrive, many of them members of the Polish underground resistance.

4.

Every morning promptly at four o'clock, Gertrud reports to roll call—the *Appell*. It lasts three hours, sometimes four. There are thousands of women here, and they must all be accounted for before being sent off to work.

A Siemens factory nearby employs Ravensbrück prisoners to manufacture electrical components for weapons. Twelve hours a day, they wind bright copper wire around spools. Only young women with good eyesight are selected to be spool-winders. They must have "smooth dry skin and lean straight fingers." The women receive no wages for their work; Siemens pays the SS directly, about forty pfennigs an hour for each spool-winder. There are incentives as well as disincentives built into the system. If a spool-winder winds more spools than her daily quota, she receives a coupon, as good as money, which she can spend at the Ravensbrück prisoners' shop. If she winds fewer spools than her daily quota, she is whipped—twenty-five lashes.

An SS enterprise called the Company for Textile and Leather Utilization (Texled) also capitalizes on free labor from Ravensbrück and does a booming business in military uniforms and prisoner garments. Here, too, there are daily quotas. A single shirt must be produced in two and a half minutes. To ensure both quality and productivity, a thick-necked Austrian swaggers past rows of prisoners hunched over sewing machines, pausing when he spots a crooked stitch, a sluggish hand. He holds a stopwatch. If a woman doesn't finish a shirt in time, he flogs her. If he is especially displeased, he throws a shoe bristling with needles in her face. In just eight months, Ravensbrück prisoners make seventy-three thousand shirts.

Women who aren't selected to be spool-winders or seamstresses endure twelve hours of manual labor, digging ditches, shoveling coal, building barracks. Women who lack the physical strength for manual labor are made to dig through a mountain of uniforms belonging to dead or captured Russian soldiers and separate them into piles. The uniforms are caked with dried blood and crawl with lice.

Women who are "pretty, with good teeth" are bused to brothels at Dachau, Buchenwald, Mauthausen, and Flossenbürg, where they are paraded before thousands of emaciated male prisoners, offered as prizes to a select few. In a letter to a Nazi colleague, Himmler expresses his hope that the women will "encourage the men to work better."

Women are also subjected to sadistic experiments.

5.

Rabbits are everywhere. You can spot them by the scars on their legs, the way they limp. Some are missing legs. Rabbits are dragged into locked rooms, strapped down, sliced open. Their fibulae and tibiae are removed. The muscles of their calves are cut out. Their wounds are stuffed with glass fragments and wood splinters. They are injected with mysterious liquids.

Rabbits are predominantly women in the Polish resistance. They can't walk. They can only hop.

The team of SS physicians who conduct these experiments work under the guidance of Dr. Karl Gebhardt, Himmler's personal physician. Dr. Gebhardt is not considered a psychopath or a quack in the medical community. He is chair of the department of orthopedic surgery at the University of Berlin and runs a prestigious hospital called Hohenlychen, where he established the very first sports medicine clinic in Germany. Dr. Gebhardt is president of the German Red Cross.

"I felt great pain," remembered a woman named Wladislawa, one of the very few who survived the experiments.

For weeks, Wladislawa lies in a strange room. Beneath the plaster cast, her calf swells monstrously, turning purple. She doesn't know that SS physicians are testing the efficacy of sulfanilamides in treating gas gangrene, an infection that's currently wiping out German soldiers on the Eastern Front. The physicians inserted cloth fibers and dirt along with glass fragments and wood splinters into the incisions in her calf, simulating the debris on a battlefield.

Sometimes a rabbit awakens in a strange room with a leg missing. She is unaware that SS physicians are conducting a bone-grafting experiment, the amputated leg "carefully wrapped up in sterile gauze" and swiftly transported to Hohenlychen hospital, where another team of SS physicians endeavor to attach it to a legless German soldier.

"Everyone was shocked by these experiments," a Ravensbrück survivor remembered, "and terrified the same might happen to them."

6.

Gertrud knows many rabbits in Ravensbrück, and she doesn't want to become one. Nor is she selected to be a spool-winder, a seamstress, a ditch-digger, a coal-shoveler, or a barrack-builder.

What she becomes is a secretary to an SS officer. She knows shorthand and can type. She is required to wear a green armband, which marks her as a *Kapo*.

Every concentration camp depends on *Kapos* to provide free labor in its day-to-day operations. Some *Kapos* are assigned to monitor prisoners in the cellblocks—they are known as "Blockovas"—and are encouraged to be as vicious as the SS guards. Some, like Gertrud, are given administrative tasks.

Every morning after the *Appell,* Gertrud and eleven other women are picked up in a truck that transports them outside the barbed wire to an office. Gertrud is given an extra nugget of soap for her labors, and the SS officer she works for, a man named Artur Conrad, doesn't beat her.

It is likely that Gertrud inspires deep resentment among the prisoners at Ravensbrück who aren't *Kapos* and have none of these privileges.

The *Kapo* system is a way to contain costs by exploiting prisoners for free labor, but it serves a more insidious function as well. As the Nazi who oversaw Auschwitz, SS Obersturmbannführer Rudolf Höss, put it:

> The more there are rivalries, the more battles between the prisoners, the easier it is to control the camp. Divide and rule — that is the principle not only of high politics but also in a concentration camp.

7.

Dorothea Binz arrives on a bicycle, her black cape billowing like a sail. A honey blonde with a perky nose, the new head guard is twenty-two and carries a whip. Her dog—a German shepherd— trots obediently by her side at the four a.m. *Appell.* Now and then, Dorothea orders her dog to attack a prisoner. She's also fond of stomping on fingers, punching heads, whipping backs, kicking stomachs.

But these are superficial injuries. Women die every day at Ravensbrück, many during the *Appell.* Those who survive the *Appell* face the possibility of being dragged before an execution squad.

To her horror, Gertrud discovers that the SS officer she works for is on the squad. Artur Conrad boasts about his skill in killing women with a 7.65 mm pistol.

8.

Ravensbrück was originally designed to hold three thousand women; by 1942 it holds eighteen thousand, and more trucks stuffed with prisoners arrive every week. One day, there are no more striped smocks. A meeting is held; the problem is resolved. The striped smock will be abandoned. From now on, the women at Ravensbrück will wear the clothes of the dead. In the summer of 1943, trucks stuffed with clothes begin to arrive from Auschwitz.

Dorothea Binz tours the grounds on her bicycle, her black cape aflutter. The prisoners know she arrived at Ravensbrück just a few years ago, when she was nineteen, and worked briefly as a maid. Her sadism was especially valued, and she was swiftly promoted to her current position.

One of the prisoners at Ravensbrück writes a poem:

> "A beautiful blonde"
> You are so beautiful,
> With shining eyes and locks of hair,
> But if we could, we would tear the insides of your soul
> And strangle your bloodthirsty heart.
> Do you remember the girl you were whipping, Jacque-
> line?
> How you stomped on Wanda, the Polish girl?
> How you tortured the Russian girl Veronicka? You and
> the dog.

Dorothea's dog dies in 1944. She buries it beside a cellblock. Later, several prisoners steal the flowers she lays on its grave.

In February 1945, a gas chamber is constructed at Ravensbrück.

9.

And now it is spring, though Gertrud doesn't know it. She has stopped thinking about what day it is.

10.

Germany will surrender this spring.

As Allied forces advance into Germany, SS officers and camp guards at Ravensbrück start fleeing. Some round up prisoners and send them south to the Mauthausen concentration camp or west to the Bergen-Belsen concentration camp. In late April, SS officers force twenty thousand women in ragged prison garb to march north toward the town of Mecklenburg.

In the midst of the chaos, some prisoners hide, huddling behind doors, crawling under beds. One prisoner scrambles into a large empty crate, followed by her friend. She remembered, "We could hear the SS shouting *'Raus raus, schnell schnell'*" ("Out, out, quick, quick").

> Then they left, but one man came back with his dog and my ear was squashed against my friend's chest and I could hear her heart going *boom boom* and I thought, my God, the whole world can hear this, but then he left, leaving us and all the sick behind. We waited several hours and we could hear the sick women calling out for water in every language.

11.

On April 30, 1945, the day Hitler commits suicide, a patrol unit from the Red Army reaches Ravensbrück.

At first the Russian soldiers don't know what they're looking at. They've spotted a wall stretching a distance in both directions topped by a snarl of barbed wire. One soldier leaps off his motorcycle and touches the wire. It's electrified. The shock knocks him to the ground.

A few minutes later, a tank rolls up. Inside is Colonel Mikhail Stakhanov. Behind him are more tanks. "We drove over the barbed wire in our tanks and broke the camp gates," Colonel Stakhanov remembered.

And then we stopped. It was impossible to move further as the human mass surrounded the tanks; women got under our tanks and on top of them, they shouted and they cried. There was no end to them. They looked awful, wearing overalls, skinny; they didn't look like human beings.

The patrol unit forges ahead, assuring the women that the units behind them will bring food and medical supplies. While the women wait they hang a red banner over the wall to welcome their rescuers.

The Red Army units that arrive are nothing like the men in the patrol unit. They roll into Ravensbrück in their jeeps and tanks, drunk. "And then it began," a prisoner named Ilse remembered.

I had only one thought at that time—to die, because I was little more than a corpse.

There are no official estimates of how many women were raped in the liberation of Ravensbrück. Many didn't survive long enough to tell anyone. Those who did survive were reluctant to talk.

12.

Gertrud and several other women hide in the forest for two days. In an essay Gertrud writes decades after the war, when she is seventy-two, she doesn't mention the rapes.

13.

Approximately 130,000 women were imprisoned at Ravensbrück between 1939 and 1945. The number who died there is estimated to be between 30,000 and 90,000. Women were shot, starved, poisoned, and flogged to death. Nearly all who were subjected to medical experiments died. Roughly 6,000 were gassed.

An accurate tally is impossible.

Days before the camp was liberated, SS officers emptied wagon-loads of documents into the crematorium and incinerated the evidence.

14.

Toward the end of 1945, Gertrud Klapputh walks through the war-torn streets of Berlin, knocking on doors, searching for friends and family. Most apartments and houses are heaps of rubble.

Eventually, she finds a place to live. She has no possessions, not a single cup. She left Ravensbrück with nothing except the soiled dress on her back and two folded pieces of paper: Arvid's last letter to Mildred.

XI

Harriette's Rage

1942–1945

Continued on Page 3,

Maryland Girl, 3 Bal

With U.S. 3d Army, April 19 [By Radio]—Mrs. Jane Donner, formerly of Chevy Chase, and her three small sons, who fled across central Germany by horse and wagon from Mecklenburg to Bavaria, where they were picked up by American troops, are temporarily domiciled in a hotel at the town of Hof, while American military authorities make up their minds how to handle the case.

Mrs. Donner, wife of a German professor at the University of Berlin, and her three children are living on German civilian rations which the town burgomeister has been ordered to provide.

By LEE McCARDELL
[Sunpapers War Correspondent]

With U.S. 90th Division Near Czech Border, April 18 [By Radio]. A former Maryland girl and her three small children, the youngest a year-old baby, are sleeping in a small town here tonight, after a 300-mile flight by horse and wagon across central Germany, through the lines of the retreating German Army into the territory occupied by American troops of the 90th Infantry Division.

She is Mrs. Jane Donner, aged 29, daughter of Fred Esch, United terday when she entered

1.

Harriette hasn't heard a word from her sister.

For all she knows, a post office in Berlin has a heap of Mildred's letters stashed in a sack somewhere, and they will find their way across the Atlantic to her mailbox in Chevy Chase once the fighting calms down. But as Christmas comes and goes, Harriette grows alarmed.

A letter from a stranger arrives. Franziska Heberle lives in Baton Rouge; she fled Germany in 1938. She wants to know where her friend Mildred is. She praises Mildred as "a courageous Anti-Nazi."

The letter irks Harriette.

My sister's whereabouts are uncertain, Harriette replies, and she leaves it at that.

2.

The Red Cross is no help. Harriette writes the organization countless times, but she doesn't receive a single response.

Another Christmas comes and goes.

3.

On May 15, 1943, the *New York Times* publishes an article with the headline NAZIS CONFISCATE ESTATE: AMERICAN-BORN WIFE OF HANGED AIDE ACCUSED OF COMMUNISM. The article states that Arvid was "one of a dozen or more Germans reported to have been hanged for treason earlier this year." Harriette searches the article for news about Mildred and finds none. Just that she's "implicated in a sensational conspiracy that still awaits clarification."

The next day, an article in Mildred's hometown newspaper, the *Milwaukee Journal,* also reports that Mildred is involved in "a sensational conspiracy." That same day, Harriette's sister Marion writes a letter:

> *This morning while I was making the Sunday pancakes, one of our*
> *neighbors came in and I knew by the looks of her face that something*

*was just not right. She had the Milwaukee Journal with her and
showed us the enclosed article written about Mildred. It is too bad that
Arvid is no more, and I am wondering what has become of Mildred.*

4.

The last letter Harriette received from Mildred was dated August
14, 1942; the envelope has a Swiss postmark. Harriette doesn't consider herself a sentimental type, but now and then she indulges in
the ritual of slipping the letter out of the envelope and reading it,
her eyes resting on the last line:

Despite our being separated, let's not be worried and anxious.

Harriette is worried and anxious, no doubt about it, but what
overtakes her these days is rage.

Rage at Mildred for running off to Germany.

Rage at Jane for following in her footsteps.

In 1944, Jane goes missing. She is somewhere in Germany—in
enemy territory—with her three little boys. Harriette tries to fathom
what has happened and imagines the worst. She writes letter after
letter—to the Red Cross; to Jane's husband, Otto; to Otto's
family—but hears nothing. Not a word.

Harriette has lost her own daughter, not to mention three grand-
children, and it's all Mildred's fault. All of it.

5.

A stark black-and-white photograph shows Mildred wearing loose-
fitting pants and an oversize white button-down shirt rolled up at
the sleeves. A man's clothes. Her long, honey-colored hair? Gone.
She'd cut it all off, or most of it, anyway. A man's haircut.

In the photograph, Mildred, head tilted, chin lifted, stares straight
into the camera as if daring whoever's taking the picture to stop her
from doing what she wants to do. *Go ahead,* she seems to be saying.
Just try.

The photograph was taken in 1927. Mildred was a newlywed in her mid-twenties then, dazzled by abundant possibilities just waiting for her, ripe and ready to be plucked like plums. She talked of becoming a citizen of the world and traveling with Arvid from country to country to advocate for the working poor. They planned to go to Mexico and urge everyone laboring on sun-scorched farms for untold hours to band together and form unions. They never ended up going to Mexico. But in a surge of idealism, the newly-weds hitchhiked from Madison to a small town in Colorado where a strike of unprecedented proportions was in full force. Coal miners marched in picket lines—across the state, over eight thousand were on strike—to protest mistreatment and poor pay. Mildred and Arvid joined the picket line outside the town's mine and visited the town jail to talk with strikers who'd been locked up. They hitch-hiked back to Madison energized, radicalized, and dressed, in Harriette's estimation, "like tramps."

Harriette feels her rage freshen, thinking about it all.

6.

A reporter for the *Baltimore Sun* stationed with the U.S. Army near the Czech border encounters Jane on April 18, 1945, and writes a story under the headline MARYLAND GIRL, 3 BABIES FLEE REICH, REACH YANKS.

A former Maryland girl and her three small children, the youngest a year-old baby, are sleeping in a small town here tonight, after a 300-mile flight by horse and wagon across central Germany, through the lines of the retreating German Army into the territory occupied by American troops of the 90th Infantry Division.

"I came to Germany to visit my mother's sister, Mrs. Mildred Harnack," Jane tells the reporter.

Harriette reads the article at the breakfast table, sipping tea.

So—Jane is safe. The absurdity of finding that out from the *Baltimore Sun* is not lost on Harriette.

7.

A few weeks later, on June 10, 1945, a letter arrives from the Red Cross. *At last.* Harriette opens the envelope. It's addressed to her husband, even though Fred hadn't written any of the letters to the Red Cross.

"Dear Sir," it begins. The letter goes on to describe what happened to Mildred. Harriette is so overcome by emotion that she can barely make it past the first paragraph.

Harriette's rage is as all-encompassing as her grief.

She orders the family to get rid of Mildred's letters, photographs, and anything else they have in their possession that might remind them of her. It is imperative, she tells her brother, that "any documentation relative to that particular era be destroyed in its entirety since the sooner that sad episode be put behind us & forgotten once & for all, the better for all concerned." When Christmas comes again, Harriette knows this much: she has once more found her strength.

Harriette dies in 1987 at the age of ninety-four, blissfully unaware that roughly fifty years earlier, her own mother, Georgina Fish, had stashed a bundle of Mildred's letters in the attic.

Valkyrie

1942–1945

1.

The United States and Britain won't help the German resistance.

CIA director Allen Dulles would later observe that resistance groups in France and other German-occupied countries

> received large-scale support from powerful allies. Arms and supplies were smuggled to them, they maintained more or less organized liaison with foreign powers, or with their own governments in exile, which could give them assistance, help them organize, inform them, instruct them, render them financial aid, and last but most important, give them the hope and moral support that kept alive their faith in ultimate deliverance.

Dulles admitted, "The West did not take too seriously the pleas of those anti-Nazi Germans who tried to enlighten it."

2.

Dietrich Bonhoeffer has held on to the hope that securing support would be possible. Now, he's not so sure. After his appeal to the British government through Bishop George Bell fails, Dietrich decides that he has little choice but to continue conspiring within the Abwehr.

Sometimes, Dietrich passes his brother-in-law Hans von

Dohnányi in the corridors of the Abwehr headquarters, located in a massive building complex near the Tiergarten. Hans is finding it increasingly difficult to feign complicity with the Nazi regime while working secretly to undermine it, and he confides his anguish to Dietrich.

Dietrich is also agonized by the moral and spiritual accommodations he must make to walk through the doors of the Abwehr every morning. As a theologian, he has pondered deeply whether he is committing a sin by assisting a conspiracy to assassinate Hitler. He has, he decides, a "clear conscience." He must consider "how the coming generation is to live." At Christmas, Dietrich composes an essay that he gives to Hans von Dohnányi and their coconspirator within the Abwehr, Major General Hans Oster:

> We have been silent witnesses of evil deeds; we have been drenched by many storms; we have learned the arts of equivocation and pretense; experience has made us suspicious of others and kept us from being truthful and open; intolerable conflicts have worn us down and even made us cynical.... Will our inward power of resistance be strong enough?

3.

On March 12, 1943, Hans von Dohnányi and Abwehr chief Admiral Canaris board a plane to Smolensk, a city west of Moscow, where Hitler is scheduled to give a rallying speech to troops.

Hans stashes a small bomb under his seat.

After the plane touches down, he slips the bomb to his coconspirator Colonel Henning von Tresckow, who hands it off to Lieutenant Fabian von Schlabrendorff. Schlabrendorff activates the detonator and smuggles the bomb, disguised as a gift box containing two bottles of Cointreau, onto the plane Hitler takes back to Germany. Half an hour after takeoff, the bomb should explode.

It doesn't.

The plane lands safely, and Hitler emerges unscathed.

4.

Three weeks later, Dietrich Bonhoeffer and Hans von Dohnányi are arrested.

The Gestapo knows nothing about the assassination attempt. Bonhoeffer and Dohnányi have come under suspicion as possible traitors, perhaps because of their family connection to the Harnack brothers. Arvid Harnack is now a notorious case of a high-ranking ministry official who was hanged for treason. Falk Harnack is known to the Gestapo as a member of the White Rose. He, too, has been arrested, and he faces a trial in the People's Court in just a few weeks.

Dietrich Bonhoeffer and Hans von Dohnányi are held in separate prisons and subjected to interrogations by none other than Manfred Roeder, chief prosecutor of the Red Orchestra trial.

5.

While incarcerated, Dietrich and Hans manage to communicate through smuggled notes with their coconspirators in the Abwehr as well as with family.

Dietrich slyly sends messages in a thick book written by the German theologian Karl Holl. Beginning at the back of the book, he makes a faint pencil mark under a single letter every ten pages. When the Bonhoeffer family receives the book, they spend hours poring over the pages to reconstruct the message.

Emmi Bonhoeffer hides messages "in the double-layered lid of a yogurt container" that she sends to one of Dietrich's imprisoned coconspirators. When she needs to summon Ernst von Harnack to her home for a secret meeting with her husband, Klaus, she calls him on the telephone and tells him he's invited to a "musical party." She reminds him to bring "his flute."

Some messages Dietrich sends in the book are for the Abwehr chief, Admiral Canaris. Another assassination plot is taking shape.

6.

On the morning of July 20, 1944, Colonel Claus von Stauffenberg arrives at Hitler's headquarters on the Eastern Front, steals into an empty room, and attempts to activate two plastic explosives in a briefcase. Using pliers, he crushes a glass capsule at the end of a slim, pencil-shaped detonator attached to the first explosive, releasing acid that slowly erodes a taut wire connected to a spring-loaded striker. The thickness of the wire determines when the bomb will explode; in this case, approximately thirty minutes after Stauffenberg crushes the glass with the pliers. It is a difficult, delicate task for Stauffenberg, who was recently wounded in battle, leaving him with one eye and a single, three-fingered hand. His right arm is a stump.

An officer raps on the door and orders Stauffenberg to hurry to a briefing that Hitler has already begun.

Panicked, Stauffenberg activates only one bomb.

He enters the bunker and sets the briefcase near Hitler. Two dozen officers surround him, studying a map of the Eastern Front.

A few minutes later, Stauffenberg slips out of the room. At 12:42 p.m., the bomb explodes, killing three officers and a stenographer. Hitler suffers minor cuts and a perforated eardrum.

7.

On April 9, 1945, Dietrich Bonhoeffer and Hans von Dohnányi are hanged.

Klaus Bonhoeffer is shot.

Ernst von Harnack is hanged.

Justus Delbrück dies in prison.

Tresckow commits suicide. Canaris, Oster, Stauffenberg, and roughly five thousand others—including the families of the plotters and people with the remotest connections to them—are executed.

8.

Falk Harnack narrowly escapes death.

He stands trial for his involvement with the White Rose and is released. Hans Scholl, Sophie Scholl, and four others in the group are executed in 1943. Falk suspects that his life has been spared for a nefarious purpose; perhaps the Gestapo plans to keep him under surveillance, hoping he will lead them to more Germans in the resistance.

Falk is ordered to put on a Wehrmacht uniform and fight in Greece, where he deserts his unit and joins the Greek People's Liberation Army. He and a friend establish a resistance organization called the Antifaschistische Komitee Freies Deutschland—the Anti-Fascist Committee for a Free Germany—that recruits German soldiers defecting from their units.

When the war is over, Falk Harnack returns to Germany on foot.

Recruited

1945–1948

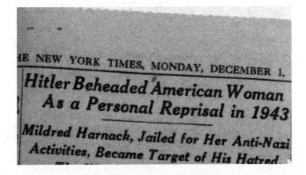

IE NEW YORK TIMES, MONDAY, DECEMBER 1,

Hitler Beheaded American Woman
As a Personal Reprisal in 1943

Mildred Harnack, Jailed for Her Anti-Nazi Activities, Became Target of His Hatred

that Mildred HARNACK was in fact deeply involved in underground activities aimed to overthrow the government of
Germany; that the trial (although secret), was conducted
before five judges of the highest state military court
and that this court, in view of the activities in which
she had been engaged, was justified in imposing the
sentence which was imposed.

1.

Men guilty of war crimes in Hitler's regime are not prosecuted at
the Nuremberg Trials; they are courted by Allied intelligence.

2.

On May 29, 1945, a month after Hitler commits suicide, British
troops capture Horst Kopkow, the Nazi who personally arrested
Mildred Harnack and presided over her torture. During a lengthy

series of top-secret interrogations by British intelligence agents, Kopkow boasts that as an SS *Hauptsturmführer,* he eradicated the Red Orchestra under the direction of Heinrich Himmler, the architect of the concentration-camp system. Himmler is dead—he recently swallowed a cyanide capsule while in British custody—but thirty-four-year-old Kopkow is very much alive and wishes to stay that way. Kopkow convinces his British captors that he can deliver to them valuable information about Soviet espionage, including "Russian plots against British interests." MI6 agents fake Kopkow's death—hypoxia due to a bad case of pneumonia—and give the Nazi a new identity as the manager of a textile factory, christening him "Peter Cordes."

The War Crimes Commission in London drops its case against Kopkow after receiving from an MI6 agent a phony death certificate paper-clipped to a letter explaining that Kopkow "was found to be running a temperature and after two days was sent to hospital, where we regret to say he died of Bronchopneumonia before any information was obtained from him."

3.

The same month that Kopkow is taken into British custody, U.S. troops capture Manfred Roeder. The chief prosecutor of the Red Orchestra trial is on the verge of being indicted as a war criminal when agents at the U.S. Army Counter Intelligence Corps (CIC) intervene, whisking Roeder away to a top-secret location and disguising his identity with the code name Othello. CIC Special Agent Benjamin Gorby is convinced that Roeder possesses "a wealth of information" that could be valuable to the United States, which faces a new enemy now that the Allies have defeated Germany: the Soviet Union.

Roeder positions himself as an expert on Communist conspiracies, feeding the CIC whatever lies he thinks will get him off the hook at Nuremberg. Hitler's Bloodhound insists that he isn't a criminal. The criminals are Mildred Harnack and the other members of the Red Orchestra, a sprawling Communist network that is "still alive and active" in numerous countries—including the United States.

Special Agent Gorby wants names. *Who, in particular, is still alive and active?*

Roeder rattles off a list that includes Greta Kuckhoff.

Greta and her nine-year-old son, Ule, occupy a small apartment in Berlin at Wilhelmshöherstrasse 18. Two CIC agents posing as "strong leftists" knock on her door.

She informs them that her husband, Adam, has been executed by the Nazis.

The agents feign sympathy and urge Greta to tell them all about her friends in the underground resistance who so valiantly fought the Nazi regime. Greta's "confidence was soon obtained," one of the agents later reported.

The CIC produces a quantity of paperwork about the German widow they hope will lead them to a sprawling network of Communist spies, tapping her phone and dispatching agents to shadow Greta around Berlin when she takes Ule to school or goes to work.

Manfred Roeder continues to spin tales of subversion, insisting that the Red Orchestra poses a dangerous threat to democracy.

The authorities overseeing the Nuremberg Trials are astonished by what the CIC has done. Manfred Roeder "could well qualify as Public Enemy No. 1 in any German democracy," observes the deputy director of the Evidence Division, castigating the U.S. intelligence agency for recruiting a "notorious, unscrupulous, opportunistic Nazi."

4.

The War Crimes Group of the U.S. Army drops Mildred Harnack's case.

"Mildred Harnack was in fact deeply involved in underground activities aimed to overthrow the government of Germany," an officer writes in a memo. He concludes that her execution was "justified."

By Chance

1952

1.

It takes Gertrud many years to write to Clara Harnack. She doesn't want to think about the horrors she survived.

On October 8, 1952, she decides it's time. By now, Gertrud Klapputh is Gertrud Lichtenstein. In 1946, she married a journalist named Kurt Lichtenstein, the son of a Jewish shoemaker. Kurt's parents and his sister died in Auschwitz. Gertrud and Kurt have two daughters, born in 1946 and 1948, and a son, born in 1947.

2.

"Very dear and honorable Mrs. Harnack," Gertrud writes.

> *I learned through an article in the newspaper Die Tat that you, Arvid Harnack's mother, are still alive.*

She goes on to explain that she was a prisoner at Charlottenburg in December 1942. "By chance — or was it not chance? — I was placed in Mildred's cell." She tells Clara about the letter Arvid wrote to Mildred and how Mildred had asked her to keep it safe. She tells Clara that the "beautiful and difficult hours that I spent with Mildred make it almost impossible even today for me to write about it."

The letter is half a page long.

A month later, on November 9, 1952, Gertrud writes another

letter. She stops after a page and a half, then returns to it again after mustering her strength.

She describes the time she shared with Mildred. Sometimes Mildred sang songs. American songs — Gertrud still remembers some of the words. Sometimes Mildred recited poetry. Sometimes she talked about Arvid,

> *who was an inexhaustible topic for her, about their time at university, about the work in Germany, about the fear that she constantly had for him, about how she came to be involved with illegal work, and finally we spoke of God and the world.*

At the end of the letter, she asks Clara to send her a photograph of Mildred.

> *When my children are older one day, I will tell them about this time in my life.*

She folds the letter and slips it into an envelope. She also slips in Arvid's farewell letter.

3.

The photograph of Mildred hasn't survived. But Arvid's letter has.

Arvid's Letter

1942

My dear beloved heart,

If in the last months I found the strength to be inwardly calm and composed, it is because I feel a strong attachment to all that is good and beautiful in this world, a feeling that sings out of the poet Whitman. Those who are close to me embody this feeling. Especially you.

Despite the pain, I look back gladly on my life. The bright outshone the dark. And our marriage is to the greatest degree the reason for this. Last night I let many of the wonderful moments of our marriage go through my head, and the more I thought about them, the more memories came. It was as if I looked at a starry sky in which the numbers of stars increase the more meticulously one looks.

Can you remember Picnic Point, when we got engaged? Early morning at the club I sang for happiness. And before that our first serious talk at lunch in the restaurant on State Street? That talk became my guiding star and has remained so. How often in the following sixteen years we laid our heads on each other's shoulders, at night, when life had made us tired, either yours on mine or mine on yours; and then everything was fine. I did this in my mind over these last weeks, and will keep doing so. I have also thought of you and all my loved ones at eight o'clock in the morning and nine o'clock at night. Do this as well, so our love will merge in the world.

Our taxing work did not make our life easy, and the danger of being overwhelmed was not small, but despite this we remained lively *people. I realized this when we visited Grossglockner, and in September when we saw the huge elk appear before us.*

You are in my heart. You shall be in there forever. My greatest wish is that you are happy when you think of me. I am when I think of you.

Many, many kisses. Hugging you tight—

Your
A.

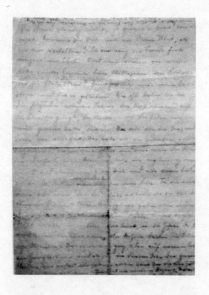

The Boy
XII

Don Goes Back

1946

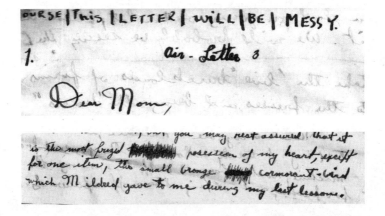

OURSE|This |LETTER| WiLL|BE | MESSY.

1.   *Air - Letter* 8

Dear Mom,

is the most prized ~~████~~ possession of my heart, except
for one item, the small bronze ~~████~~ cormorant-bird
which Mildred gave to me during my last lesson.

1.

Don is eighteen when he returns to Berlin.

He stands taller now, and not only because he has just received his high-school diploma. He has grown. He's taller than his father.

He's not sure what pulls him back here. He doesn't know how to disentangle it all.

He remembers standing on the street while someone's mother sobbed. Her husband was dead. A British bomb had exploded on the house. An ambulance appeared and two men jumped out and took a boy away to an orphanage. Pladik.

What happened to Achim, Peter, and Siggy? What happened to Mole?

2.

Don walks alone through Berlin. Rubble. So much of it. What he sees is an assault on his memory. He walks around trying to remember what the buildings looked like.

Mole's neighborhood—bombed.

Innsbrücker Strasse 44: bombed.

The American School, the American Church: bombed to rubble too.

He gets on the U-Bahn. He gets off at Nollendorfplatz, walks to Woyrschstrasse 16.

He stands on the sidewalk for a long time, his hands stuffed in his pockets, looking at the apartment building where Mildred once lived, following the ghost of each floor with his eyes—one, two, three.

The fourth floor, where he once had lessons. Where he once sat on a sofa with wooden armrests next to Mildred.

He remembers telling her about the *Fram*, a ship built for exploring Antarctica. *Fram* means "forward" in Norwegian. Built at the end of the nineteenth century, it is said to be the strongest wooden ship in the world.

Tell me more, Mildred said.

Don went on, recounting all the details. The *Fram* was designed to withstand the harsh, frigid conditions of the Antarctic. The sailors on the *Fram* ate dogs. *Dogs!* This was how they were able to make a two-year expedition.

You have a good memory, Mildred said. She often said this.

Once, he forgot to do his reading assignment. *You've got a brain in there,* she said, *and you've got to use it, or it will turn into a rotten apple.* Her voice was kind but stern. He felt ashamed, looking down at the open book. His eyes moistened; the words swam on the page.

Don't forget, she told him.

Die gottgedachte Spur, die sich erhalten!
Ein Blick, der mich an jenes Meer entrückte,
Das flutend strömt gesteigerte Gestalten.
Geheim Gefäß, Orakelsprüche spendend!
Wie bin ich wert, dich in der Hand zu halten,
Dich höchsten Schatz aus Moder fromm entwendend
Und in die freie Luft, zu freiem Sinnen,
Zum Sonnenlicht andächtig hin mich wendend?
Was kann der Mensch im Leben mehr gewinnen,
Als daß sich Gott=Natur ihm offenbare?
Wie sie das Feste läßt zu Geist verrinnen,
Wie sie das Geisterzeugte fest bewahre.

Vermächtnis

Kein Wesen kann zu nichts zerfallen!
Das Ew'ge regt sich fort in allen,
Am Sein erhalte dich beglückt!
Das Sein ist ewig; denn Gesetze
Bewahren die lebend'gen Schätze,
Aus welchen sich das All geschmückt.

Das Wahre war schon längst gefunden,
Hat edle Geisterschaft verbunden,
Das alte Wahre, fass' es an!
Verdank' es, Erdensohn, dem Weisen,
Der ihr, die Sonne zu umkreisen,
Und dem Geschwister wies die Bahn.

Sofort nun wende dich nach innen,
Das Zentrum findest du da drinnen,
Woran kein Edler zweifeln mag.
Wirst keine Regel da vermissen,
Denn das selbständige Gewissen
Ist Sonne deinem Sittentag.

Den Sinnen hast du dann zu trauen,
Kein Falsches lassen sie dich schauen,
Wenn dein Verstand dich wach erhält.

) 81 (

Acknowledgments

The recognition that many Germans supported Hitler often leaves little room for stories about those who opposed him. For assistance in telling Mildred Harnack's story, and the stories of Germans who joined her in the resistance, I am grateful to Dr. Johannes Tuchel at the German Resistance Memorial Center (Gedenkstätte Deutscher Widerstand) and especially to Dr. Hans Coppi, director of the Red Orchestra Collection. Dr. Coppi was an infant when his parents, Hans and Hilde Coppi, were executed for their participation in the resistance. I benefited greatly from Dr. Coppi's expertise and abiding faith in this book from the first day I met him.

In 2018 and 2019, I was a biography fellow at the Leon Levy Center for Biography, which provided significant research support and funded transcriptions of my interviews with sources. Thanks to Kai Bird and Thad Ziolkowski for their mentorship and to my excellent fellows Stephen Heyman, Jennifer Homans, and Samanth Subramanian, all of whom read early chapters. The Women Writing Women's Lives Biography Seminar at the City University of New York merits a special mention for inviting me into their community of outstanding biographers and for providing both inspiration and professional support.

The Corporation of Yaddo twice gave me the time and space to write, and the Ucross Foundation also awarded residencies — one when I began writing this book and another when I was finishing the final draft. For making me feel welcome, I am grateful to Elaina Richardson and Candace Wait at Yaddo and to Sharon Dynak, Tracey Kikut, and Ruthie Salvatore at Ucross.

Over five years I consulted with archivists in the United States, England, and Germany; my book would not have been possible

without them. Ulf Rathje swiftly located significant documents at the
Bundesarchiv in Berlin, even during a global pandemic. At the National
Archives, Wanda Williams kindly attended to my Freedom of Information Act appeals, and Paul Brown and Cate Brennan responded to
numerous document requests with patience and alacrity. The phenom-
enal staff at the Arolsen Archives and the International Tracing Service
tracked down World War II–era and postwar records about Gertrud
Klapputh. I would also like to gratefully acknowledge Susan Evans at
the United States Holocaust Memorial Museum, Holocaust Survivors
and Victims Resource Center; Carol Leadenham and Sarah Patton at
the Hoover Institution Archives; Aleksandra Pawliczek at the Humboldt University of Berlin archives; Olaf Schneider at the Justus Liebig
University of Giessen archives; Torsten Zarwel at the Bundesarchiv of
Berlin-Lichterfelde; Antje Schröpfer at the Niedersächsisches Landesarchiv; Bastian Fillner at the Landesarchiv Nordrhein-Westfalen; Paul
Friedman at the New York Public Library; David Null at the University of Wisconsin archives; Kevin Abing at the Milwaukee County
Historical Center; and Lee Christopher Grady, Laura Hemming, and
Jonathan Nelson at the Wisconsin Historical Society.

I am grateful to Sarah Helm for providing key information about
Mildred's cellmate Gertrud Klapputh, and to Dr. Joanne Sayner for
advice and encouragement. Christian Grüner and staff at the Peter A.
Silbermann Schule (formerly the Berliner Städtisches Abendgymnasium für Erwachsene) hosted me for a memorable afternoon and
permitted me to photograph pages from the 1934 school handbook.
Andreas Sander, former curator at the Topographie des Terrors in
Berlin, helped me to understand a prisoner's experience in the basement cells of Gestapo headquarters.

I could not have achieved either depth or nuance in passages
concerning Soviet espionage without the superlative contributions
of Dr. Svetlana Chervonnaya, who conducted extensive archival
research in Moscow, translated numerous documents, fact-checked
early drafts, and met my barrage of questions with good humor and
meticulous responses. I am likewise indebted to the peerless Dr.
Robert G. Waite, a research historian at the German Resistance
Memorial Center with a two-decade tenure as a senior historian at

the U.S. Department of Justice, whom I interviewed in Berlin about his current project, a two-volume history of Plötzensee Prison. Dr. Waite was unfailingly generous in giving me incisive feedback on several drafts of my manuscript, sharing his original research with me, guiding my research, and cheering me on.

I am immeasurably grateful to Jude Vachon, who made significant contributions to this book as translator and research assistant. She helped me sort through thousands of pages of German documents, translated fragile, nearly illegible postwar testimonies, and read numerous drafts. Her passion for this story has sustained me through years of writing. CUNY doctoral student Kathryn Kelley tracked down articles and book reviews in German periodicals, Erica Brisson assisted with early research, and Dr. Irena Fliter and Dr. Jennifer Petzen accompanied me on trips to German archives.

I would also like to acknowledge Shareen Blair Brysac for publishing the first biography about Mildred Harnack two decades ago. Brysac's research and interviews with sources who have since passed away were valuable to me when I was beginning my own research. My book has benefited from the work of historians Thomas Childers, Peter Hoffmann, Claudia Koonz, Dónal O'Sullivan, Corina Petrescu, and Nikolaus Wachsmann.

For crucial early support, I am grateful to Michael Cunningham, Ruth Franklin, David Gates, Jonathan Lethem, David Means, David Remnick, Dr. Susanne Rohr, Dani Shapiro, and James Wood.

Thanks to the photographer Beowulf Sheehan for documenting my interviews with key sources. I would also like to thank Cami Anderson, Robert Baertsch, Michael Bilton, Alethea Black, Jill Blakeway, Charles Bock, Amy Braunschweiger, Eric Carlson, Rammonn Clarke, Dana Czapnik, Ann-Kristin Grimm, Sharon Guskin, Arthur Heitzer, Bokyun Kim, Adrian Kinloch, Gerd Klamandt, Stephan Krannich, Jan Kucharzewski, Vanessa Manko, Michèle Menzies-Abrash, Robin Morgan, Claudia Mustafa, Katrin Reichelt, Janelle Robinson, Adrien Schriel, Cindy Spiegel, Elizabeth Thompson, and Wendy Weisman.

Thanks to my literary agent, Jim Rutman, for championing this book and encouraging me to remain true to my artistic convictions. I am grateful to another early champion, Lee Boudreaux, who acquired this book for Little, Brown when it was just a prologue and two chapters. Asya Muchnick inherited the book and adopted it as her own, bringing to these pages compassion, coherence, and precision; I could not have wished for a more ideal match. Thanks to Asya's colleagues at Little, Brown: Evan Hansen-Bundy, Jayne Yaffe Kemp, Alyssa Persons, and Tracy Roe. Allison Saltzman transformed a chaos of archival documents and images into a superb jacket. I am lucky to have in my court the magnificent Kimberly Burns at Broadside.

This book is as much about family found as family lost. Arvid Harnack's great-niece Jilly Allenby-Ryan kindly offered to put me up in her home while I was conducting research at the National Archives in London and shared recollections of Harnack family members; I remain grateful for Jilly's gracious hospitality. In Düsseldorf, Juergen Havemann answered all my questions about his father, Wolfgang, with sensitivity and insight. I am grateful to Rainer von Harnack for sharing his memories of Falk Harnack, to Robin Esch for sharing his memories of Mildred Harnack and Harriette Esch, and to Neal Donner for providing copies of family letters.

I owe a special debt of gratitude to Mildred's niece, Jane Donner Sweeney. Jane is my grandmother. Several years before she passed away, she gave me copies of Mildred's letters and told me that an American boy, the son of a diplomat at the U.S. embassy in Berlin, had been Mildred's courier. His name, she said, was Don.

When I finally tracked him down in Northern California, Don Heath was eighty-nine. He still possessed a vivid memory of his childhood. In his book-crammed living room, he recounted all his memories of Mildred. I remain profoundly grateful to him.

After Don passed away, his wife, Julie Heath, permitted me to review the contents of twelve steamer trunks packed with letters, diaries, datebooks, unfinished memoirs, and photographs. Don's nephew Richard Brown painstakingly sorted through it all and set up Dropbox files for me to access containing what amounted to thousands of pages. Richard has been a splendid correspondent, offering memories, newly unearthed documents, and encouragement. To the Heath family, I express heartfelt gratitude.

Notes

~~~

Sources

I conducted a series of interviews with Donald Heath Jr. in November and December of 2016; they are cited in the endnotes that follow as "Author interviews with Donald Heath Jr."

The Heath family granted me permission to review the contents of twelve steamer trunks that contained primary-source materials from 1937 to 1946, including family letters, photographs, Louise Heath's diaries and datebooks, and Donald R. Heath Sr.'s correspondence with Secretary of the Treasury Henry Morgenthau Jr. and other colleagues at the U.S. State Department. I also reviewed an unpublished memoir, letters, and e-mail correspondence written by Donald Heath Jr. (ca. 1981–2006); notes and recollections written by his sister, Sue Heath Brown (ca. 1985–1989); and an unpublished memoir written by Donald R. Heath Sr. These materials are in the process of being archived at the Hoover Institution.

I relied on Donald Heath Jr.'s recollections in our interviews and on these primary-source documents to tell the story of his boyhood in Berlin and reconstruct Mildred Harnack's encounters with him, Louise Heath, and Donald Heath Sr., as well as their interactions with each other.

I relied on Jane Donner's recollections to reconstruct Mildred's childhood and a section of the book that chronicles the time Jane lived with Mildred and Arvid in Berlin.

Mildred Harnack's letters furnished me with factual details and descriptions that I used throughout this book to tell her story and the Heath family's story. Not all her letters survived. After Mildred's execution, her sister Harriette Esch urged family to destroy letters, photographs, and any other documentation about her. Many years later, Jane Donner discovered a cache of letters that have since been bequeathed to the Wisconsin Historical Society.

In addition to these interviews, recollections, letters, diaries, and unpublished memoirs, I drew on a wide range of primary-source materials at archives and institutions in the United States, Germany, the United Kingdom, and Russia.

Archives

United Kingdom

TNA	The National Archives, Kew

Germany

BArch	Bundesarchiv, Berlin
BADH	Bundesarchiv, Dahlwitz-Hoppegarten
GDW	Gedenkstätte Deutscher Widerstand, Berlin
JLU	Justus Liebig Universität, Giessen
HU	Universitätsarchiv der Humboldt-Universität zu Berlin, Berlin
LAV NRW	Landesarchiv, Nordrhein-Westfalen
NLB	Niedersächsische Landesbibliothek, Hannover

Russia

APRF	Archive of the President of the Russian Federation
GARF	State Archive of the Russian Federation
RGASPI	Russian State Archive of Social and Political History

| SVRA | Archive of the Foreign Intelligence Service of the Russian Federation |
| TsAMO | Central Archive of the Ministry of Defense of the Russian Federation |

United States

DEL	University of Delaware, Special Collections, Newark, DE
FDRL	Franklin D. Roosevelt Presidential Library, Hyde Park, NY
HUA	Harvard University Archives, Cambridge, MA
HIA	Hoover Institution Archives, Stanford, CA
LOC	Library of Congress, Washington, DC
MHC	Milwaukee County Historical Center, Milwaukee, WI
NARA	National Archives and Records Administration, College Park, MD
NYPL	New York Public Library Archives, New York, NY
USHMM	United States Holocaust Memorial Museum, Washington, DC
UWA	University of Wisconsin Archives, Madison, WI
WHS	Wisconsin Historical Society, Madison, WI
YUA	Yale University Archives, New Haven, CT

Private Collections

Donner family (papers of Mildred Harnack, Jane Donner)
Heath family (papers of Donald Heath Sr., Louise Heath, Donald Heath Jr., Sue Heath Brown)

Author's Note

"Her utterances were sparse": Ingeborg Havemann, "Mildred Harnack: A Remembrance," 1950, Falk Harnack collection, GDW.

"She listened quietly": Martha Dodd, "In Memory," Martha Dodd papers, box 13, LOC.

FRAGMENT

Questionnaire: Plötzensee Prison, Berlin, February 16, 1943, Mildred Harnack papers, SGY/4, BArch.

Introduction

She was at the harrowing center: Petrescu, *Against All Odds,* 194; Gestapo final report, RG 319, ZA 020253, NARA. It is important to note that historians writing about the Rote Kapelle frequently ignore Mildred Harnack or mention her merely as Arvid Harnack's wife. Richard J. Evans (*The Third Reich at War*) states that "women played a particularly prominent role" in the Red Orchestra, "notably Harnack's American wife Mildred Harnack-Fish," then goes on to ignore her contribution entirely. David Dallin (*Soviet Espionage*) describes Mildred as "a nonpolitical person interested only in literature and languages." Heinz Höhne (*Codeword: Direktor*) also describes Mildred as "non-political." See also Guillaume Bourgeois, *La Véritable Histoire de L'Orchestre Rouge*, and Gilles Perrault, *The Red Orchestra*. In "Choice and Courage," Claudia Koonz observes, "Most histories of the resistance have ignored or underplayed women's participation. Accounts of the Red Orchestra...pass over Mildred Harnack."

Armless, Beamer, Worker: Brysac, *Resisting Hitler,* 272.

the largest underground resistance group in Berlin: After the Gestapo rounded up and executed nearly all the members of Mildred's group (referred to historically as the Harnack-Schulze-Boysen group), the Saefkow-Jacob-Bästlein group formed in Berlin; it grew to roughly five hundred members.

"Hitler's Bloodhound": Breitman et al., *U.S. Intelligence and the Nazis,* 298.

real whoppers: Haase, *Das Reichskriegsgericht,* 109–10. Transcripts of the trials were allegedly burned in 1945 by Heinz Pannwitz, the SS officer who led the German counterintelligence operation against the Red Orchestra. The sentencing documents survived; see Höhne, *Codeword: Direktor,* xviii–xix. The trial is also described by an eyewitness, Axel von Harnack (cousin of Arvid Harnack), in the article "Arvid und Mildred Harnack."

"Mildred Harnack's actions are laudable": D. P. Hervey to Lt. Col. Bruton, February 21, 1946, RG 153, file 12-2262, NARA.

"It is quite possible": A. R. Perry Jr. to Captain Sloan, November 21, 1946, ibid.

"This case is classified S/R": Lt. Col. Ellis to Lt. Col. Herte, January 15, 1947, ibid.

HITLER BEHEADED AMERICAN WOMAN AS A PERSONAL REPRISAL IN 1943: *New York Times,* December 1, 1947.

"one of the leaders in the underground": Charles Yarbrough, "Victim of Nazi Ax Lived Here," *Washington Post,* December 3, 1947.

lack of documentary evidence: Höhne, *Codeword: Direktor,* xviii.

East German archive: In 1990, sentencing documents for the Rote Kapelle trials were discovered in the archives of the Institut für Marxismus-Leninismus, located in the former German Democratic Republic.

Russia permitted historians a peek: Costello and Tsarev, *Deadly Illusions,* vi–vii.

began to release records: Records were declassified by the Nazi War Crimes Interagency Working Group (IWG); see Breitman et al., *U.S. Intelligence and the Nazis,* 293.

thick as your wrist: Documents produced by British intelligence, U.S. intelligence (U.S. Army Counter Intelligence Corps, CIA, FBI), and Soviet intelligence (NKVD, GRU). Most German counterintelligence files were seized by Allied intelligence in 1945. British counterintelligence conducted the most thorough investigation of the Red Orchestra, producing three lengthy reports between 1945 and 1949; see Breitman et al., *U.S. Intelligence and the Nazis,* 293–94.

The Boy with the Blue Knapsack (1939)

Pay attention: Author interviews with Donald Heath Jr.

ALL BRITISH AIR ATTACKS ARE DOOMED TO FAIL: "Alle englischen Luftangriffe," *Der Führer,* December 20, 1939; "Judenplage in Belgien," *Deutsches Nachrichtenbüro,* December 12, 1939; "Der Sieg ist uns gewiβ!," *Rheinsberger Zeitung,* December 23, 1939.

a man in the foreign service: H. Merle Cochran, a U.S. State Department Consular and Financial Secretary in Europe from 1927 to 1941.

An important job: Author interviews with Donald Heath Jr.

U.S. embassy in Berlin: Donald Heath Sr. was first secretary at the U.S. Embassy in Berlin, a position that was announced in *American Foreign Service Journal* 732, December 12, 1937. He was also "Morgenthau's Man," a confidential arrangement between Secretary of the Treasury Henry Morgenthau, Assistant Secretary of State George Messersmith, and Undersecretary of State Sumner Welles. Between January 1938 and June 1941, Heath worked in Berlin as an ad hoc intelligence agent for the U.S. government, occupying a territory in the nexus between the Treasury Department, the State Department, and the soon-to-be-formed Office of the Coordinator of Information (COI), an intelligence agency run by William "Wild Bill" Donovan, who modeled it after the British Secret Intelligence Service (MI6). Heath received payment as an officer of the COI. In June 1942, the COI underwent an organizational overhaul and was rechristened the Office of Strategic Services (OSS), forerunner of the Central Intelligence Agency.

Help how: Author interviews with Donald Heath Jr.

Make sure no one follows you: Ibid.

Tell me what this book is about: Ibid.

We Must Change This Situation as Soon as Possible (1932)

University of Berlin: The university was also known as the Friedrich-Wilhelms-Universität. In 1949 the university was renamed Humboldt-Universität zu Berlin (Humboldt University of Berlin).

she has lectured: Mildred Harnack to Georgina Fish, March 15, 1931.

"Germany is going through": Mildred Harnack to Georgina Fish, February 14, 1932, Donner family papers.

"a great increase of misery and oppression": Mildred Harnack to Georgina Fish, April 2, 1932, Donner family papers.

"There is a large group": Mildred Harnack to Georgina Fish, October 18, 1932, Donner family papers.

a petition: In a letter, Mildred writes that "nearly a hundred" students at the University of Berlin signed it. Mildred Harnack to Georgina Fish, May 8, 1921, Donner family papers.

It's so high I can't see your faces: Paraphrase of Mildred's description of the joke she made to her students; she also mentioned the lavender and golden blooms. Mildred Harnack to Georgina Fish, August 8, 1932, Donner family papers.

a Nazi fraternity: The fraternity was the Nationalsozialistischer Deutscher Studentenbund (National Socialist German Students Union). Members of the union in an estimated thirty-four towns across Germany participated in the book burning on May 19, 1933.

"un-German": Rabinbach and Gilman, The Third Reich Sourcebook, 449.

Left-wing politicians outnumber Nazis: Kershaw, Hitler, 370.

"Work! Freedom! Bread!": Arbeit! Freiheit! Brot! Political campaign poster, 1932. Exhibited at the U.S. Holocaust Memorial Museum, Washington, DC, 2008–2009; Nazi Propaganda, Prints and Photographs Division, LOC.

Nazi Party gets 37 percent of the vote: Die Ergebnisse der Reichstagwahl in Senstenberger Anzeiger, 59 Jrg. August 1, 1932; Volksmehrheit gegen Diktatur in: Vossische Zeitung, no. 366, Abend-Ausgabe, August 1, 1932.

"Radical Middle Party": Kerwin, "The German Reichstag Elections," 921–22.

An English translation: The first abridged English translation of Mein Kampf was published in 1933; the first full English translation was published in 1939.

"completely finished": Frankfurter Zeitung und Handelsblatt, November 11, 1925.

"fuzzy mind": "Hitler's Abrechnung," Neue Zürcher Zeitung, November 8, 1925.

"illogical ranting": Deutsche Zeitung, September 9, 1925.

"One seeks ingenuity": Neue Preussliche Zeitung, October 1, 1925.

"O how modest": "O mein!," Das Bayerische Vaterland, July 29, 1925.

a derisive front-page caricature: Simplicissimus 30, no. 22 (August 31, 1925).

His oratorical style: Kershaw, Hitler, 145.

"Our motto": Ibid., 146.

3,300 members by the end of 1921: Ibid., 149.

a new title: The Nazi Party had previously been run by a chairman who oversaw a committee. As its new leader, Hitler drafted a new party constitution granting himself dictatorial powers.

A cartoon in 1930 lampooned: The caption reads: "Isn't that strange that you can make such a lot of trouble with so little stuff?" *Simplicissimus* 35, no. 33 (November 10, 1930): 388.

Another showed two policemen: *Simplicissimus* 35, no. 2 (April 7, 1930): 13.

"has no secrets from us": "Hitler Gegen Die Münchener Post," *Münchener Post,* December 7, 1921; see Rosenbaum, *Explaining Hitler,* 40.

"It makes no difference": Kershaw, *Hitler,* 147.

THE JEWS IN THE THIRD REICH: *Münchener Post,* December 9, 1931; see Rosenbaum, *Explaining Hitler,* 42.

"Cell G": "The Tsechka in the Brown House," *Münchener Post,* April 8, 12, 19, 1932; see Rosenbaum, *Explaining Hitler,* 42.

"We are hungry": Mildred Harnack to Georgina Fish, January 23, 1932, Donner family papers.

400,000: Siemens, *Stormtroopers,* 142. By April 1934, the number of Storm Troopers increased to four million.

Many of the unemployed; They eat potatoes; The situation grows steadily; standing on the street-corner: Mildred Harnack to Georgina Fish, January 23, 1932; February 13, 1932; July 3, 1932; Mildred Harnack to Jane Donner, February 1, 1932, Donner family papers.

Good Morning, Sunshine (1932)

the apartment has wide windows: Details in this chapter are derived from Mildred's descriptions in letters to Georgina Fish in 1932. Mildred described the "two tattered rugs" in response to a question about her assets in the lengthy questionnaire she was required to fill out at Plötzensee Prison prior to her execution; SGY/4, BArch.

the wrong lecture hall: Arvid's serendipitous error was to confuse two nearly adjacent buildings on the University of Wisconsin campus, Sterling Hall and Bascom Hall.

"A great bunch of thick, white odorous flowers": This scene is reconstructed from an unpublished autobiographical story by Mildred Harnack called "Prothalamion," box 2.4, signature 30, HU. All dialogue is reproduced verbatim.

"Men from the North Sea": Ibid.

"the greatest of all the lakes": Ibid.

"We were so happy": Mildred Harnack to Georgina Fish, December 3, 1931, Donner family papers.

(ARPLAN): The headquarters of ARPLAN was in Berlin, which was also the site of the organization's first conference, held January 3 and 4, 1932. In a letter, Mildred informed her mother about the conference; Mildred Harnack to Georgina Fish, January 1, 1932, Donner family papers.

"Most of the exercises": Mildred Harnack to Georgina Fish, November 22, 1931, Donner family papers.

crossroads of Europe: Large, *Berlin,* 20–22.

Censorship is forbidden: Stackelberg and Winkle, *Nazi Germany Sourcebook,* 62.

Weimar Constitution: Ibid., 61–62.

crammed with Germans: In a letter, Mildred writes about the experience: "All
    around me are people reading newspapers or books. I often see men and
    women reading classical literature, philosophy." Mildred Harnack to
    Georgina Fish, April 16, 1931, Donner family papers.

four thousand seven hundred weeklies and dailies: "Propaganda: Writing the
    News," Holocaust Encyclopedia, USHMM.

Ullstein: "The Press in the Third Reich," Holocaust Encyclopedia, USHMM.

"Life seemed more free": Shirer, *Berlin Diary,* 118. Shirer would go on to write
    The Rise and Fall of the Third Reich.

"For many of my friends and for myself": Stephen Spender, *The Temple* (London:
    Faber and Faber, 1987), x. Spender and his friends W. H. Auden and
    Christopher Isherwood would come to be known as the Oxford poets.

"In the streets of Berlin": Isenberg, "Voluptuous Panic," 1. The writer is Siegfried
    Krazauer, who made this observation in a 1926 article.

The BAG (1932–1933)

The BAG: Students at the BAG attended classes from 7:00 to 10:00 p.m. Monday
    through Friday; they took four classes, each of which lasted forty-five
    minutes. The BAG handbook from 1934 features comparative enrollment
    statistics from 1931 to 1934; see *Handbuch des Berliner Abend Gymnasiums,* 82.
    Descriptions of Mildred's lectures and syllabi are obtained from this source
    and from her letters.

"have come hoping to win": Mildred Harnack to Georgina Fish, May 2, 1933,
    Donner family papers.

"You never heard her coming": Beck, "Erinnerungen an Mildred Harnack," 6.

"Hitler soll Kanzler werden?": Samson Knoll's diary, Mildred Harnack papers, file
    3, signature 41, HU.

"a stream of little lights": Mildred Harnack to Georgina Fish, May 23, 1932,
    Donner family papers.

focus of the English club: *Handbuch des Berliner Abend Gymnasiums,* 110. Mildred
    writes about Consul General George Messersmith's lecture in a letter to
    Georgina Fish, January 23, 1932.

"With few exceptions": Messersmith to Undersecretary of State Phillips, June 26,
    1933, Messersmith papers.

"Clementine": Mildred Harnack to Georgina Fish, October 29, 1932, and
    November 6, 1932, Donner family papers.

"embarrassed": Beck, "Erinnerungen an Mildred Harnack," 6.

"tender respect": Ibid.

Otto Harnack: "On the one hand, he loved Goethe so much," Arvid wrote in a
    letter, "on the other, he was, in his private life, in some ways a 'professor' in
    the negative sense." Arvid Harnack to Clara Harnack, February 20,
    1929, Falk Harnack collection, GDW.

There's so much to work for: Mildred Harnack to Georgina Fish, January 29, 1933,
    Donner family papers.

Chancellor Hitler (1933)

"like cast bronze": Fromm, *Blood and Banquets,* 76.

"beside himself with excitement": Shirer, *The Rise and Fall of the Third Reich,* 5. In his diary, Goebbels also wrote that Hitler's eyes were "full of tears." See Goebbels, *Vom Kaiserhof zur Reichskanzlei,* 252.

"Butchers": Wolfgang Havemann, "Über die notwendige Einheit von Theorie und Praxis bei der Anwendung des Marxismus-Leninismus (Erinnerungen an Arvid Harnack aus den Jahren 1931–1942)," March 2, 1983, Rote Kapelle collection, GDW.

"too soft and sensuous": Hass, *Forbidden Music,* 209.

"With their torches": Havemann, "Über die notwendige Einheit," Rote Kapelle collection, GDW.

"An ominous night": Fromm, *Blood and Banquets,* 76.

"Germany has awakened": Goebbels, *Vom Kaiserhof zur Reichskanzlei,* 358.

"steep roofs": Mildred Harnack to Georgina Fish, February 1, 1933, Donner family papers.

lookout: She has already written about the big, arched window in previous letters. Now, calling it a lookout brings her a step closer to telling her mother the truth.

"leader" and a "misleader": Leader (*Führer*) and misleader (*verführer*). The title of his speech is "Changes in the Concept of the Leader in the Younger Generation." See Sifton and Stern, *No Ordinary Men,* 35; Bethge, *Dietrich Bonhoeffer,* 259–60; Hoffmann, *Behind Valkyrie,* 13–19.

Two Nazi Ministers (1933)

first cabinet meeting: The minutes of this meeting and a list of the attendees remained secret until after the Second World War, when captured German documents were submitted to the Nuremberg Trials.

"polite and calm": This won't last. In April 1933, Hitler will begin to exhibit his authoritarianism in cabinet meetings. See Schwerin von Krosigk, *Staatsbankrott,* 185.

coalition with the DNVP: In 1931, the DNVP attempted to form a short-lived coalition with the Nazis that would come to be known as the "Harzburg Front."

"We might": *Trial of the Major War Criminals,* vol. 2, 187.

"I've just committed": Ritter, *Carl Goerdeler,* 60. Some scholars question whether the quotation is apocryphal; see Jones, " 'The Greatest Stupidity of My Life,' " 81.

"The cabinet is really Alfred Hugenberg's": Kershaw, *Hitler,* 432. The Social Democrat is Kurt Schumacher, who was arrested by the Gestapo in 1933 and spent the next ten years in concentration camps.

"If Hitler sits in the saddle": Jones, " 'The Greatest Stupidity of My Life,' " 71. The diarist is Reinhold Quaatz, a DNVP politician and Hugenberg's close confidant, who served in the Reichstag from 1924 to 1933. Diary entry dated January 17, 1933.

"the foxy capitalist": The *Berliner Tageblatt* article is quoted in "Nationalists to Dominate in Government Led by National Socialist," *New York Times,* January 31, 1933.

"has never concealed": "Sees Hitler Facing Fall: *Le Temps* Believes Responsibility May Bare His Weaknesses," *New York Times,* February 1, 1933.

"twice rejected": "Nationalists to Dominate in Government."

"Dissension and hatred": The full text of Hitler's radio address can be found in Domarus, *Hitler Reden und Proklamationen,* 191–94.

in just six months: Shirer, *The Rise and Fall of the Third Reich,* 188.

A Whisper, a Nod (1933)

the Circle: While the Circle was a private nickname Mildred and Arvid used to describe their group, it should be noted that *Circle* was used by many in the resistance to designate their coconspirators and is now used by historians: Kreisau Circle, Bonhoeffer Circle, Goerdeler Circle, et cetera. See von Klemperer, *German Resistance Against Hitler,* 52.

"searching look": Kuckhoff, *Vom Rosenkranz zur Roten Kapelle,* 200.

"crumbling heroes": Ibid., 201.

"Exceptionally pretty": Ibid.

"It was not friendship": Ibid., 54.

"To me": Kuckhoff papers, 200, BArch.

"I had to force myself": Ibid., 201.

"awkward in all practical things": Ibid.

"Have you read": Ibid.

"Follow Your Nose": Kuckhoff, *Vom Rosenkranz zur Roten Kapelle,* 54.

Later, she will wonder: Ibid., 124.

"circle of acquaintances": Ibid.

"a small rowhouse": Ibid., 132.

The People's Radio (1933–1934)

he needs to hold on to it: Hitler's slogan was "Give me four years' time" (*"Gebt mir vier Jahre Zeit"*); see Lochner, *What About Germany?,* 25.

Reich Ministry of Public Enlightenment and Propaganda: At a press conference, Goebbels assured journalists that the ministry would "unite" Germans. "This government is in the truest sense of the word a people's government. It arose out of the people and will always execute the will of the people. I reject most passionately the idea that this government stands for reactionary aims, that we are reactionaries." See Joseph Goebbels, "Two Speeches on the Tasks of the Reich Ministry for Popular Entertainment and Propaganda," March 15 and March 25, 1933, GHDI.

wrote a novel: Irving, *Goebbels,* 18–19.

a "genius": Goebbels's diary, April 13, 1926, in Shirer, *The Rise and Fall of the Third Reich,* 129.

Goebbels wastes no time: The Reich Chamber of Culture (Reichskulturkammer) is established on September 22, 1933.

Germany's museums are purged of art: Over the next few years, more than twenty thousand works of art will be removed from Germany's museums. In 1937, the defamatory show *Degenerate Art* was held in Munich to "educate" the public on the "art of decay"; see Childers, *The Third Reich*, 295.

"unparalleled and inimitable": Shirer, *The Rise and Fall of the Third Reich*, 244.

Six million units: By 1938, there were more than nine million People's Radios, approximately one for every two households in Germany. By 1941, the number increased to fifteen million. The model number of the People's Radio, or Volksempfänger, was VE 301 (301 being January 30 in the European style). See "Propaganda," Holocaust Encyclopedia, USHMM.

"It would not have been possible": Goebbels, "Radio as the Eighth Great Power," speech delivered on August 18, 1933, published in *Signale der neuen Zeit: 25 ausgewählte Reden von Dr. Joseph Goebbels* (Munich: Zentralverlag der NSDAP, 1938), 197–207.

this is what Mildred believes: Petrescu, *Against All Odds*, 196.

The Reichstag Fire (1933)

"Now it will be easy": Shirer, *The Rise and Fall of the Third Reich*, 189.

"Private enterprise cannot be maintained": *Law Reports of Trials of War Criminals*, vol. 7, 558.

"This is not impossible": Ibid., 561.

three million Reichsmark: Shirer, *The Rise and Fall of the Third Reich*, 190.

"naked from the waist upwards": Hett, *Burning the Reichstag*, 14.

"through the big corridors": Rudolf Diels, head of the Prussian Political Police, on the Reichstag fire of February 27, 1933 (retrospective account, 1949), GHDI.

"high leather boots": Schacht, *Confessions of "the Old Wizard,"* 336.

"the beginning of a Communist revolution": Shirer, *The Rise and Fall of the Third Reich*, 192.

"There will be no mercy": Hett, *Burning the Reichstag*, 16.

More than four thousand: Evans, *The Third Reich in Power*, 11; *Völkischer Beobachter*, Berliner Ausgabe, February 28, 1933.

"Decree of the Reich President for the Protection of the People and State": This is a salient excerpt from the law, which is divided into six sections; *Reichsgesetzblatt* 1, no. 17 (1933): 83.

"Radio and press are at our disposal": Shirer, *The Rise and Fall of the Third Reich*, 189.

"terrorist acts": Ibid., 195.

89 percent: Hoffmann, *The History of the German Resistance*, 4.

44 percent: Childers, *The Third Reich*, 248. Forty-one percent of the vote went to the Social Democratic Party (18 percent), the Communist Party (12 percent), and the Catholic Center Party (11 percent). The remaining 15 percent was divvied up among ten other political parties. Although the Nazi

Party did not achieve an absolute majority, Goebbels boasted, "We are the masters of the Reich...Everything else shrinks to insignificance." See Goebbels, *Vom Kaiserhof zur Reichskanzlei*, 140.

"scarred bully faces": Shirer, *The Rise and Fall of the Third Reich*, 198.

"quietly and with great dignity": Ibid., 199.

441 in favor: Ibid.

"Law to Remove the Distress of People and State": Stackelberg and Winkle, *Nazi Germany Sourcebook*, 142–43.

An Act of Sabotage (1933–1934)

"A fundamental change": Rabinbach and Gilman, *The Third Reich Sourcebook*, 317.

Contraception was readily available: By 1928, the condom manufacturer Fromm sold 144,000 condoms a day; see Usborne, *The Politics of the Body*, 112.

"her husband, her family": Adolf Hitler, speech to the NS-Frauenschaft, September 8, 1934; see Rabinbach and Gilman, *The Third Reich Sourcebook*, 311–14.

nineteen thousand: Koonz, *Mothers in the Fatherland*, 145.

Women lawyers: By 1935, women physicians in Germany could not receive payments from publicly funded health-care insurance, and by 1936, German women were barred from serving as judges or public prosecutors. See Koonz, *Mothers in the Fatherland*, 145.

Restaurant owners are threatened: Kirkpatrick, "Recent Changes in the Status of Women," 656.

double-earners: Evans, *The Third Reich in Power*, 331.

10 percent: Mouton, "From Adventure to Advancement," 948.

plummets to 5,447: Said, "Zur Situation der Lehrerinnen," 110.

The single goal: Rabinbach and Gilman, *The Third Reich Sourcebook*, 313.

the new Mother's Day: Koonz, *Mothers in the Fatherland*, 186.

Agnes von Zahn-Harnack: The *von* that precedes her last name used to signify nobility back when Germany was ruled by a monarchy; now it signifies the achievements of her father, Adolf von Harnack. Her siblings are Ernst von Harnack and Axel von Harnack. After her marriage Agnes hyphenated her name, putting her maiden name after her husband's. Inspired by Agnes, Mildred often referred to herself as "Mildred Harnack-Fish."

whom she adores: In a letter, Mildred wrote about one of her first encounters with Agnes von Zahn-Harnack at the Harnack House, where they had supper together; she described her as "good-hearted" and "capable" and "clever." Mildred Harnack to Georgina Fish, January 25, 1930, Donner family papers.

five hundred thousand members: Koonz, *Mothers in the Fatherland*, 143. In 1933, President Agnes von Zahn-Harnack terminated the Bund Deutscher Frauenvereine to protest Nazi attempts to take over the organization.

"fallen into men's hands": Zahn-Harnack, "Frauenbewegung und Nationale Revolution."

a pipe dream: Koonz, *Mothers in the Fatherland*, 145.

"No more Paris models": Fromm, *Blood and Banquets*, 118.

"German men want real German women": Rosen, *Das ABC des Nationalsozialismus,*
   199. First published in January 1933, the 288-page handbook was in its fifth
   edition in September 1933.
"the German woman of the future": Guenther, *Nazi Chic?,* 132.
Law for the Encouragement of Marriage: Koonz, *Mothers in the Fatherland,* 185–86.
   By the end of 1933, an estimated 100,000 marriage loans are granted, increasing
   to 700,000 by 1937. See Baerwald, "How Germany Reduced Unemployment,"
   627; Kirkpatrick, "Recent Changes in the Status of Women," 653.
one-fifth: Koonz, *Mothers in the Fatherland,* 149.
"immediately leave": Baerwald, "How Germany Reduced Unemployment," 627.
60 percent: Koonz, *Mothers in the Fatherland,* 186.
"I am grateful": Mildred Harnack to Georgina Fish, August 1, 1933. It is unknown
   whether Mildred told Arvid.

Mildred's Recruits (1933–1934)

about a dozen members: There are no reliable estimates of the number of members
   during this time. A confidential CIA document (dated June 23, 1967,
   subsequently declassified) states there were eventually 283 members of the
   Berlin group (the Circle) and 600 members of Harro Schulze-Boysen's group
   (Gegner Kreis), which merged with the Circle in 1940.
"English tutoring session": Wilhelm Utech, Protokoll, Rote Kapelle collection,
   GDW.
number 35: *Handbuch des Berliner Abend Gymnasiums,* 69.
Bodo Schlösinger: Griebel, Coburger, and Scheel, *Erfasst?,* 136–37.
They can't meet: Wilhelm Utech, Protokoll, Rote Kapelle collection, GDW.
Karl Behrens: Griebel, Coburger, and Scheel, *Erfasst?,* 166–67; Juchler, *Mildred
   Harnack,* 111–21.
At eighteen, he became a Storm Trooper: In 1926, Karl was one of roughly five
   thousand boys who marched in Hitler's rallies. By the end of 1933, Hitler
   Youth membership reached over two million. Three years later, on December
   1, 1936, all boys between the ages of ten and eighteen were required by law
   to join Hitler Youth.
"The object": Wilhelm Utech, Protokoll, Rote Kapelle collection, GDW.
"I threw her out of the front door": The recipient of West's letter was Allen
   Dulles, who had recently retired from his job as director of the CIA; see
   West, *Selected Letters,* 395.

Tumbling Like Dominoes (1933)

Law for the Restoration of the Professional Civil Service: Rabinbach and Gilman,
   The Third Reich Sourcebook, 53.
Law Against Overcrowding in Schools and Universities: *Reichsgesetzblatt* 1, no. 43
   (1933): 225. In 1933, 75 percent of Jewish students in Germany were enrolled
   in public schools; see "Law Limits Jews in Public Schools," Holocaust
   Encyclopedia, USHMM.

Germans are sterilized: The law was passed in 1933, and forced sterilization began in January 1934. See "Forced Sterilization," Holocaust Encyclopedia, USHMM.

Even a joke: Boehm, *We Survived,* xii. "The remark 'I shall live to see the end of Hitler's thousand-year Reich' was enough to send one to trial or straight to concentration camp," remembered the Jewish writer Eric Boehm, who fled Germany at the age of sixteen and moved in with relatives in Youngstown, Ohio.

"loyal attitude": *Simplicissimus* 38 (April 1, 1933), insert; *Simplicissimus* 38 (April 16, 1933): 26. This new editorial stance was not embraced by Franz Schoenberner, who had edited the magazine since 1929. In April 1933, Schoenberner fled to Switzerland.

Münchener Post: Rosenbaum, *Explaining Hitler,* 53.

Protective custody: Hoffmann, *German Resistance to Hitler,* 25.

nichts dagegen zu machen: Mayer, *They Thought They Were Free,* 75.

"The majority tumbled like dominoes": Meding, *Courageous Hearts,* 8. Emmi was the daughter of Hans Delbrück. Among her siblings was Justus Delbrück, who was involved in the Valkyrie plot to assassinate Hitler.

an essay criticizing church leaders: Bethge, *Dietrich Bonhoeffer,* 273–75.

Rabbi Stephen Wise: Ibid., 267.

"I shall buy my butter": Ibid.; Meding, *Courageous Hearts,* 9.

Requirements are strict: "Like a nursery gardener trying to reproduce a good old strain which has been adulterated and debased, we started from the principles of plant selection and then proceeded quite unashamedly to weed out the men whom we did not think we could use," Himmler said. With his poor eyesight and poor health, Himmler would not have met the standards he set for the elite SS. Pringle, *The Master Plan,* 41.

one hundred twenty: Wachsmann, *KL,* 4. Most of these prisoners were Communists arrested in Munich.

inappropriate to let them go free: See "The Former Gunpowder Factory in Dachau."

concentration camp: The acronym used to denote a concentration camp was KL, for *Konzentrationslager;* see Wachsmann, *KL,* 5.

An estimated forty thousand: Ibid. An accurate estimate of how many people were imprisoned and died at Dachau is impossible to determine, as the records were incomplete and many were destroyed prior to the liberation of the camp in 1945. Twenty-two ledger books at Dachau labeled "Entry Registers" put the number at about thirty-three thousand. See "Concentration Camp Dachau Entry Registers (*Zugangsbücher*), 1933–1945," publication no. M1938, 2004, RG 238, NARA.

"Nazi torture dens": Wachsmann, *KL,* 36. The available evidence indicates that deaths while in custody were still relatively infrequent, a marked contrast to the mass murder in concentration camps during the Second World War.

170 makeshift camps: Ibid., 36.

Sachsenhausen: Ibid., 187. By 1939, these six main camps collectively hold 21,400 prisoners.

Over eleven hundred satellite camps: Ibid., 5.

a six-week stretch: Ibid., 56. The period is April 12 to May 26, 1933.

shot while trying to escape: Ibid.

two hundred thousand: Ibid., 31. The figure is an estimate of the total number of political prisoners detained throughout 1933. While some prisoners are prominent figures, like KPD leader Ernst Thälmann, most are young, working-class men, the foundation of the Communist movement in Germany.

Torched (1933)

"The age of extreme Jewish intellectualism": "The Book Burning: Report by Louis P. Lochner, Head of the Berlin Bureau of the Associated Press," May 10, 1933, GHDI.

"which had not been witnessed": Shirer, *The Rise and Fall of the Third Reich,* 241.

twenty-five thousand: "Book Burning," Holocaust Encyclopedia, USHMM.

Volk: Hitler's attempt to define the word takes up seven pages of *Mein Kampf.* According to William Shirer, "The German word *Volk* cannot be translated accurately into English. Usually it is rendered as 'nation' or 'people,' but in German there is a deeper and somewhat different meaning that connotes a primitive, tribal community." See Shirer, *The Rise and Fall of the Third Reich,* 88.

poster lists twelve decrees: Sauder, *Die Bücherverbrennung,* 93–94. The twelve decrees were a deliberate evocation of Martin Luther's ninety-five theses. The poster was headlined "Down with the Un-German Spirit."

"All anti-Semitic students are assholes": Ibid., 94–95. For the full English translation of the twelve decrees on both posters, see Rabinbach and Gilman, *The Third Reich Sourcebook,* 449–51.

Dietrich Does Battle with the Aryan Clause (1933–1934)

international ecumenical conference: The conference was hosted by the World Alliance for Promoting International Friendship through the Churches, an organization founded in Germany in 1914.

Aryan clause: The law stipulates that government employees "who are not of Aryan descent" must be fired. Rabinbach and Gilman, *The Third Reich Sourcebook,* 53.

"We especially deplore": Bethge, *Dietrich Bonhoeffer,* 315.

leaflets to trees: Ibid., 319. The leaflets are addressed "To the National Synod."

Eighteen pastors: Evans, *The Third Reich in Power,* 229.

grants moral legitimacy to Hitler: The implications of the concordat are a matter of heated historical debate, as is Pope Pius XII's response to Nazism and the Holocaust. Documentation pertaining to Pope Pius XII's tenure remained sealed at the Vatican Archives until March 2, 2020.

nailed his ninety-five theses: Contemporary historians dispute whether Luther actually did nail his theses to the church door. See Peter Marshall, *1517: Martin Luther and the Invention of the Reformation* (Oxford: Oxford University Press, 2017).

"The Lord has called us": "Pastors Protest Nazi Domination," *New York Times,* September 28, 1933.

"I feel that in some way": Bethge, *Dietrich Bonhoeffer,* 325–26.

Arvid Burns His Own Book (1933–1934)

"very careful": Brysac, *Resisting Hitler,* 128–29. After Ewart Turner's death in 1987, Martha Turner threw away Arvid's manuscript. Ewart Turner's replacement at the American Church in Berlin was Stewart Herman, who was pastor from 1936 to 1941. In a self-published memoir, Herman describes the Germans and Americans who attended church-sponsored events: "Even within the American colony, whom the church purported to serve, there were pro-Nazis, anti-Nazis, and those—and the Embassy, for example—who endeavored to keep themselves appropriately cloaked in diplomatic neutrality." Herman, *American Church in Berlin,* 56–57.

American in Berlin (1938–1939)

Stadtpark: After the Second World War, the Stadtpark U-Bahn stop was renamed Rathaus Schöneberg.

the American Church: From 1938 to 1943, the congregation included Ambassador Hugh Wilson, Chargé d'Affaires Alexander Kirk, and a slew of other wealthy diplomats. Journalists Sigrid Schultz, Louis Lochner, and William Shirer were frequent attendees. Don wrote an essay about his experience at the American Church in Berlin; descriptions here are derived from his essay "The American Church in Berlin" and author interviews.

"the student should be made": Reichsministerium für Wissenschaft, Erziehung, und Volksbildung, *Erziehung und Unterricht in der Höheren Schule,* 52, 137.

"Very satisfactory": American School in Berlin, Donald Heath Jr. report card, Donald R. Heath Papers, HIA.

"Verboten in Germany": Ziemer, *Two Thousand and Ten Days of Hitler,* 58–60. In 1939, the Ziemers fled Berlin and settled in Lake City, Minnesota. A year later, twelve-year-old Patsy Ziemer published a memoir about her experience in Berlin. The "Verboten" and "Uniforms" lists are quite long; I have abridged them here.

instructs Don not to tell: Author interviews with Donald Heath Jr.

a Berlin court issues an order: "American School in Berlin Dispossession from Building Owned by Jewess," Jewish Telegraphic Agency, July 5, 1938.

Trenck's Panduren: The name refers to a scrappy group of soldiers headed by the German-speaking nobleman Baron Franz von der Trenck who fought on behalf of the Habsburg monarchy in the War of the Austrian Succession (1740–1748). In 1747 Baron Trenck published a memoir exhaustively titled *Memoirs of the Life of the Illustrious Francis Baron Trenck: Sometime Lord of the Bed-Chamber to Her Majesty the Queen of Hungary and Bohemia. And Colonel of a Body of Pandours, and Sclavonian Hussars. Containing a Compleat Account of His Several Campaigns in Muscovy, Silesia, Austria, Bavaria, and Other Parts of the Empire, Together with Divers Entertaining Anecdotes Relating to His Secret History. Written by Himself, and Done from the Original German into English.*

Don't Dawdle (1939)

one of Goebbels's many mistresses: Fromm, *Blood and Banquets,* 114.

The Proper Care of Cactus Plants (1933–1935)

"a thousand years": September 5, 1934, at a Nazi rally in Nuremberg; see Shirer,
　The Rise and Fall of the Third Reich, 5.
agitators produce leaflets: Merson, *Communist Resistance in Nazi Germany,* 118–21.
printer in Solingen-Ohligs: Ibid., 115. The printer's full name was Georg Haberer.
　Although his newspapers were confiscated by the Gestapo he managed to
　evade arrest and fled Germany.
a million leaflets: Merson, *Communist Resistance in Nazi Germany,* 115.
"green reports": Peukert, *Inside Nazi Germany,* 49.
Transportkolonne Otto: Its leader was Willi Bohn. See Bohn, *Transportkolonne
　Otto.*
In 1934, the Gestapo seizes: Duhnke, *Die KPD,* 117.
Cookery Book with 70 Approved Recipes: Merson, *Communist Resistance in Nazi
　Germany,* 115, 120.

Fair Bright Transparent (1933–1934)

"fair bright transparent": Martha Dodd, untitled essay, Martha Dodd papers, box
　13, LOC. Another version of this essay is titled "In Memory."
"ambiguous": Ibid.
"is very poor": Martha Dodd to Thornton Wilder, December 14, 1933, Wilder
　Papers, YUA.
"worn to spiderwebs": Mildred Harnack to Georgina Fish, July 27, 1934, Donner
　family papers.
"Please excuse me": Mildred Harnack to Georgina Fish, November 12, 1933,
　Donner family papers.
"It is lousy": Martha Dodd to Thornton Wilder, September 25, 1933, Wilder
　Papers, YUA.
they had a torrid love affair: Carl Sandburg's free-verse poems to Martha included
　this line: "I love you past telling I love you with Shenandoah shouts and dim
　blue rain whispers." See Larson, *In the Garden of Beasts,* 26.
"Mother," she writes: Mildred Harnack to Georgina Fish, December 11, 1933,
　Donner family papers.

Two Kinds of Parties (1933–1935)

"sense or nonsense": Martha Dodd to Thornton Wilder, December 14, 1933,
　Wilder Papers, YUA.
"I produced": Ibid.
The snow is soft: Ibid.
"he had the most sinister": Dodd, *Through Embassy Eyes,* 52.

Bugged (1933–1935)

"intrigues": Dodd, *Through Embassy Eyes,* 53.

"placed against the wall": Ibid., 56.

difficult to wire: Ibid., 277.

"Do you like beer": Mildred Harnack to Martha Dodd, May 14, 1934, Martha Dodd papers, box 13, LOC. Whether they took the trip Mildred proposed remains unknown.

Esthonia, and Other Imaginary Women (1934–1935)

The invitations: Donner family papers.

"Jews Are Not Wanted Here": Evans, *The Third Reich in Power,* 540.

Since then the group: Mildred Harnack to Georgina Fish, undated, probably April 1934, Donner family papers.

How beautiful it was: Mildred Harnack to Georgina Fish, May 2, 1933, Donner family papers.

How is Esthonia: Ibid.

uses codes to communicate: Boehm, *We Survived,* xiii; Meding, *Courageous Hearts,* 15.

Tiny bits of paper: Sifton and Stern, *No Ordinary Men,* 53–54.

Arvid Gets a Job (1934–1935)

"How often do I have to tell you": This scene is reconstructed from an unpublished autobiographical story by Mildred Harnack called "The New Apartment," box 2.4, signature 29, HU. All dialogue is reproduced verbatim.

Unfortunately we are: Helm, *Ravensbrück,* 12–13.

ousted from his job: Chancellor Franz von Papen ejected Ernst von Harnack on July 20, 1932.

aid the resistance: In 1937 Otto John was hired as assistant legal counsel at Lufthansa; several years later, he joined Klaus Bonhoeffer and others in the Valkyrie plot to assassinate Hitler.

hopelessly behind on her dissertation: Mildred finished her dissertation ("The Development of Contemporary American Literature in Some of the Main Exponents of the Novel and Short Story") in 1941 and was awarded a PhD on November 20, 1941.

Thieves, Forgers, Liars, Traitors (1934–1935)

"Many in the group": Boehm, *We Survived,* 193. Weisenborn had to publish under the pseudonyms W. Bohr, Christian Munk, and Eberhard Förste. After the war, Weisenborn cowrote a film called *The Plot to Assassinate Hitler,* directed and cowritten by Arvid's brother, Falk Harnack.

Rudolf Ditzen, aka Hans Fallada (1934)

faced with a decision: Williams, *More Lives Than One,* 144.

"ridiculous, grotesque": Ibid., 154.

"swallow the bitter pill": Ibid., 154–55.

second category: Nearly all Germany's internationally famous writers had fled and were in exile. Many tried to warn the rest of the world about Hitler in works of fiction. See Bertolt Brecht, *The Resistible Rise of Arturo Ui;* Lion Feuchtwanger, *The Oppermanns;* Arnold Zweig, *The Axe of Wandsbek;* Evans, *The Third Reich in Power,* 152.

"In order to be published": Kesten, *Thomas Mann Diaries,* 201.

Boris Vinogradov: In published accounts, Boris's last name has been transliterated into English in four ways: Vinogradov, Winogradov, Winogradow, and Vinogradow.

"It must be difficult": This scene is reconstructed from Metcalfe, *1933,* 194; Crepon, *Leben und Tode,* 200–201.

His face turned scarlet: Martha Dodd, "In Memory," Martha Dodd papers, box 13, LOC.

The Night of the Long Knives (1934)

more than 50 percent: Between January 1933 and June 1934, unemployment fell from 6 million to 2.5 million (Baerwald, "How Germany Reduced Unemployment," 621). The improvement in unemployment was "hailed as a miracle" (Shirer, *The Rise and Fall of the Third Reich,* 258).

The vice-chancellor's press secretary: The speechwriter is Edgar Jung; the friend is Erich Klausener.

one hundred fifty: Shirer, *The Rise and Fall of the Third Reich,* 223.

Over a thousand: Historians have not been able to make an accurate estimate of the number of arrests and murders. In a speech to the Reichstag on July 13, 1934, Hitler claimed that 1,000 were arrested and 74 were shot (Evans, *The Third Reich in Power,* 39). A book published in Paris by German émigrés (*The White Book of the Purge*) states that 401 were murdered (Shirer, *The Rise and Fall of the Third Reich,* 223).

"The Reich Government Has Enacted": *Reichsgesetzblatt* 1, no. 71 (1934): 529.

"Let it be known": Domarus, *Hitler Reden und Proklamationen,* 409.

signed it with her own initials: "Brief Reviews," *Berlin Topics,* February 18, 1934.

Mildred writes a note: Undated, probably summer of 1934, Martha Dodd papers, LOC.

A Molekül and Other Small Things (1939)

a photograph of Mole: Donald R. Heath Papers, HIA.

Kansas Jack Gang: Author interviews with Donald Heath Jr.

The Kansas Jack Gang (1939)

"The wolf was certain": Heath, "Remembering Arvid and Mildred Harnack," 7, Donald R. Heath Papers, HIA.

FRAGMENT

Questionnaire: Plötzensee Prison, Berlin, February 16, 1943, SGY/4, BArch.

A New Strategy (1935)

Hjalmar Schacht: After Schacht was ousted from his position in 1937, Arvid
    reported to Schacht's successor, Walther Funk. Schacht's full name was
    Horace Greeley Hjalmar Schacht; his father reportedly named him after the
    New-York Tribune editor Horace Greeley, whom he admired (Smith, *Paper
    Money*, 74).
"almost bored": Wolfgang Havemann, Protokoll, Falk Harnack collection, GDW.
"who formed his free judgment": Bethge, *Dietrich Bonhoeffer*, 139.

Bye-Bye, Treaty of Versailles (1935)

The Treaty of Versailles: The treaty was signed on June 28, 1919. In 1920, the
    British economist John Maynard Keynes wrote: "I believe that the campaign
    for securing out of Germany the general costs of the war was one of the most
    serious acts of political unwisdom for which our statesmen have ever been
    responsible" (Keynes, *Economic Consequences*, 146).
"peaceful and happy": Domarus, *Hitler Reden und Proklamationen*, 563, 571.
Two thousand printing presses: Ferguson, *When Money Dies*, 167.
Inflation skyrocketed: In 1914, the German mark was equivalent in value to the
    British shilling, the French franc, and the Italian lira, all exchanged at about
    four or five to the dollar. In 1921, 75 Marks was worth one dollar. In 1922,
    400 Marks equaled one dollar. At the beginning of 1923, it was 18,000
    Marks, by August it was one million, and by November it was one trillion.
    Shirer, *The Rise and Fall of the Third Reich*, 61; Smith, *Paper Money*, 67–68.
    In 1924, the Mark was replaced by the Reichsmark.
a cup of coffee: Smith, *Paper Money*, 71.
"When you go shopping": Fromm, *Blood and Banquets*, 13. The diary entry is
    dated November 15, 1923.
Suicides escalated: For women, suicide rates were highest in fifteen- to thirty-
    year-olds; for men, in thirty- to sixty-year-olds. See Goeschel, *Suicide in
    Nazi Germany*, 15.
"There is not much to add": Friedrich Korner, "Überreizte Nerven," *Berliner
    Illustrierte Zeitung*, August 26, 1923. Published by Ullstein, *Berliner Illustrierte
    Zeitung* pioneered the newsmagazine format, featuring drawings, photo-
    graphs, and photo essays. In 1934 the publication was "Aryanized" and
    became a major instrument of Nazi propaganda.
Käthe Kollwitz: Kollwitz produced a series of six prints titled *Weaver's Revolt*,
    inspired by a group of peasant weavers who had revolted in 1844 to protest
    low factory wages. This work, exhibited in 1898, was "so well received it
    immediately established Kollwitz as one of the foremost artists in Germany,"
    but it did not win the gold medal at the Great Berlin Art Exhibition, possibly
    because Kaiser Wilhelm II remarked, "I beg you gentlemen, a medal for a

woman, that would really be going too far...Orders and medals of honor belong on the breasts of worthy men!" See Knafo, "The Dead Mother," 27.

"Never Again War": Käthe Kollwitz created the lithograph in 1924.

degenerate: Kollwitz's work was included in the "Degenerate Art" exhibition held in Munich from July 19 to November 30, 1937.

tycoons amassed even larger fortunes: Shirer, *The Rise and Fall of the Third Reich,* 282; Evans, *The Third Reich in Power,* 371.

Tommy (1935)

Mrs. Harnack: Kennedy and Reeves, *The Notebooks of Thomas Wolfe,* 748.

"I haven't dared": All dialogue appears in Mildred's article; see Mildred Harnack-Fish, "One of the Greatest of Younger American Authors in Berlin," *Continental Post,* May 12, 1935.

"the embodiment": Ledig-Rowohlt, "Thomas Wolfe in Berlin," 192.

It is such an event: Martha Dodd to Thomas Wolfe, William B. Wisdom Collection, bMS Am 1883.1, Houghton Library, HUA.

guest list: Mildred invited "about 40 people, writers, poets, publishers and magazine editors" (Dodd, *Through Embassy Eyes,* 85).

"showed very clearly": Ledig-Rowohlt, "Thomas Wolfe in Berlin," 197.

"standing around drinking": Dodd, *Through Embassy Eyes,* 86.

"with as many guests": Kuckhoff, *Vom Rosenkranz zur Roten Kapelle,* 189–90.

Who Goes Nazi: Thompson, "Who Goes Nazi?" Thompson was an American journalist who wrote the book *I Saw Hitler!,* published in 1932, based on an interview she'd had with Hitler the year before.

"I don't trust him": Tau, *Das Land das ich verlassen musste,* 251.

two articles: Harnack-Fish, "One of the Greatest of Younger American Authors"; Harnack-Fish, "Thomas Wolfe," *Berliner Tageblatt.*

"a butterfly": Kennedy and Reeves, *The Notebooks of Thomas Wolfe,* 749.

a more lengthy, serious talk: Martha Dodd notes in her memoir that Mildred had worked to "develop Wolfe's later political understanding."

"Perkins cable": Kennedy and Reeves, *The Notebooks of Thomas Wolfe,* 748–49.

"six hundred or so": Shirer, *Berlin Diary,* 37.

"Germany wants peace": William Shirer writes about this speech in both *Berlin Diary* (37–39) and *The Rise and Fall of the Third Reich* (285–88).

"turns out to be reasonable": Shirer, *The Rise and Fall of the Third Reich,* 287.

"the solid magnificence": Kennedy and Reeves, *The Notebooks of Thomas Wolfe,* 747.

he won't remember a word: After Thomas Wolfe's second trip to Berlin, he began to see things differently. In a section of his novel *You Can't Go Home Again,* he wrote about his changed attitude. In 1937, the section was excerpted in the *New Republic* under the title "I Have a Thing to Tell You." Heinrich Ledig-Rowohlt wrote about this transformation in Thomas Wolfe and cited an excerpt from the book: "It was the creeping paralysis of mistrust that crippled and infected all relations between men and peoples...It was a poison against which there was no antidote, and from which no salvation was to be found" (Ledig-Rowohlt, "Thomas Wolfe in Berlin," 198).

Monkey Business (1935)

Geist described her indiscretions: Raymond Geist to Wilbur Carr, June 5, 1933, Wilbur Carr Papers, box 12, LOC.

Ernst Hanfstaengl: Martha and everyone else call Ernst by his nickname "Putzi." Hanfstaengl fled Germany after the Spanish Civil War and worked for FDR's S-Project, providing information on approximately four hundred Nazis. Hanfstaengl introduced Martha to Hitler at a tea, a meeting she wrote about in her memoir; see Dodd, *Through Embassy Eyes,* 53–54.

"undesirable": George Messersmith to Jay Pierrepont Moffat, June 13, 1934, George S. Messersmith papers, box 4, F24, DEL.

his English is awful: On a Communist Party member form he signed and dated June 22, 1936, Boris Vinogradov wrote that he "has command of German, French (somewhat weaker)." (Boris Dmitrievich Vinogradov, fond 17, op. 97, file 258, p. 6, RGASPI). Evidently, Boris and Martha spoke a kind of pidgin German because her grasp of the language was so weak, not his. Martha wrote in her memoir that "I knew very little German" (Dodd, *Through Embassy Eyes,* 64).

at Sigrid Schultz's party: This was Martha's recollection at one point, but Sigrid Schultz disputed it (Martha Dodd to Agnes Knickerbocker, July 16, 1969; Sigrid Schultz to Martha Dodd, March 14, 1970, Martha Dodd papers, box 6, 9, LOC). At another point, Martha wrote that she met Boris at a pub.

"I am in the Soviet embassy": Martha wrote about the encounter in an unpublished autobiographical essay, "Bright Journey into Darkness," Martha Dodd papers, box 14, LOC.

"a near diplomatic scandal": Dodd, *Through Embassy Eyes,* 170.

a polka-dot blouse: Ibid., 199. A photograph of Martha Dodd posing next to the Junkers plane is featured in her memoir.

"They work seven hours a day": Ibid., 173.

"a pretty rosy-faced girl": Ibid., 171.

murder of millions of Ukrainians: Ibid., 179. Known variously as the Soviet Famine of 1932–33, the Terror-Famine, and the Holodomór (translation: "to kill by starvation"), the famine was not limited to Ukraine; it also involved North Caucasus and the lower and middle Volga areas. Bullitt told Martha five million Ukrainians had been murdered. A 2003 United Nations joint statement signed by twenty-five countries estimated the death toll was seven to ten million (United Nations Digital Library, letter from the Permanent Representative of Ukraine to the United Nations Secretary-General, November 7, 2003). Scholars continue to debate this estimate.

"glistening face": Dodd, *Through Embassy Eyes,* 179.

"What pleased me most": Ibid., 176.

"there seemed to be": Ibid., 177.

"To Martha, my wife": Martha Dodd to Agnes Knickerbocker, July 16, 1969, Martha Dodd papers, box 6, LOC. Other guests at the lunch included the American journalist H. R. Knickerbocker and his wife, Agnes.

"Hitler surely couldn't shoot": Dodd, *Through Embassy Eyes,* 144.

Martha: Boris Vinogradov to Martha Dodd, June 7, 1934, box 10, Martha Dodd papers, LOC.

Your three monkeys: Ibid.

abruptly abandoned the plan: Kennedy and Reeves, *The Notebooks of Thomas Wolfe,* 749. Wolfe left Berlin in July 1935.

He is needed in Moscow: According to a document in Boris Vinogradov's file, Boris left Berlin for Bucharest in December 1934; he remained there until June 1936 (Boris Dmitrievich Vinogradov, fond 17, op. 97, file 258, RGASPI).

Rindersteak *Nazi (1935)*

"set the table": Kuckhoff, *Vom Rosenkranz zur Roten Kapelle,* 183.

"financial wizard": "Walther Funk Replaces Schacht as Reich Economics Minister," Jewish Telegraphic Agency, November 28, 1937.

Deutscher Klub: The Deutscher Herrenklub was renamed the Deutscher Klub in 1933.

Rindersteak: The term was also applied to careerist Germans who wanted to keep their civil-service jobs. On January 26, 1937, a new law empowered Nazi officials to fire employees who did not seem sufficiently loyal to the Nazi cause.

NKVD: An acronym for Narodnyi Komissariat Vnutrennykh Del (the People's Commissariat for Internal Affairs), established in 1934.

Artur Artusov: In August 1931, Artusov was named head of the foreign intelligence department of the Joint State Political Directorate (OGPU). In July 1934, Artusov became the head of the foreign intelligence department of the Main Directorate of State Security (GUGB) of the NKVD.

"expedite preparations": Corsican file, no. 34118, vol. 1, 12, cited in Costello and Tsarev, 75. Note that the Corsican file remains classified; all citations are drawn from *Deadly Illusions,* by Costello and Tsarev, who were briefly granted permission to view sections of the file.

An Old Pal from ARPLAN (1935)

Hirschfeld: His surname also appears in the archives as "Girshfel'd" (Гиршфельд). Costello and Tsarev misrepresent Hirschfeld as a "diplomat in Berlin" who "may not have been a professional intelligence officer" (see *Deadly Illusions,* 74–75), when in fact he was a Soviet military intelligence operative working undercover as a diplomat.

Hirschfeld volunteered to help: In a January 13, 1932, memo, Ambassador Lev Khinchuk wrote to VOKS new deputy chairwoman Elena Ossipovna Lerner, cc'ing the NKID, "We have created ARPLAN," suggesting that the Russians' role was not merely advisory (GARF, fond 5283, op. 1a, file 218, 43). David-Fox suggests that Hirschfeld's chief aim was to cultivate Germany's radical right wing with the help of "well-placed assets" like Arvid Harnack. The right wing represented roughly fifteen of approximately fifty members of ARPLAN. See David-Fox, *Showcasing the Great Experiment,* 253–54.

invited Arvid to events at the Soviet embassy: It's probable that Mildred went too.

a hidden agenda: In his own words, Hirschfeld sought to familiarize "the German public...with the Soviet methods of planning" and the "people's economy as a whole" (Hirschfeld to VOKS's Section of Central Europe, August 14, 1931, GARF, fond 5283, op. 1a, file 181, 164). In two memos, Hirschfeld emphasized that ARPLAN must appear "absolutely German to the outside world" and Moscow's influence "must be deeply and reliably concealed behind the scenes" (Hirschfeld to Lerner, November 18, 1932, GARF, fond 5283, op. 1a, file 196, 198; Hirschfeld to Sheinin, October 27, 1932, GARF, fond 5283, op. 1a, file 196, 193). See David-Fox, *Showcasing the Great Experiment,* 253.

handpicked delegation: The so-called study delegation took place between August 20 and September 12, 1932; see David-Fox, *Showcasing the Great Experiment,* 259.

Hirschfeld orchestrated: VOKS was involved in planning the tours and activities for the ARPLAN delegation.

"unite radical intellectuals": Hirschfeld to VOKS chairman Petrov (cc to NKID), February 5, 1932, GARF, fond 5283, op. 1a, file 196, 156.

Arvid promptly joined the BGB: According to Georgi Dimitrov, leader of Comintern from 1934 to 1943, Mildred "also participated in the work of BGB"; see Coppi, Danyel, and Tuchel, *Die Rote Kapelle,* 119.

careful notes: Hirschfeld reported to three agencies—under diplomatic cover to the NKID, under cultural cover to VOKS, and to Soviet military intelligence. I have based this chapter on documents in the APRF and GARF archives. To date, the archives of Soviet military intelligence remain inaccessible.

"ideological influence": Costello and Tsarev, *Deadly Illusions,* 74.

"very close to us": Alexander Hirschfeld to Nickolai Nickolaevich [Krestinsky], NKID, cc to Schumann, March 12, 1932, GARF, fond 5283, op. 1a, file 196, 163–64; Alexander Hirschfeld to the VOKS section of Central Europe, cc to NKID, February 29, 1932, GARF, fond 5283, op. 1a, file 196, 112. The words *at any cost* are underlined in red.

rivalrous as siblings: Both the Red Army and the NKVD "legal" stations operated under the same embassy roof and shared the same cipher room.

The two men: According to Peschersky, spymaster Boris Gordon accompanied Hirschfeld on his first visit to Arvid. Peschersky, "Krasnaia Kapella 1935–1941," 417.

a detailed memo: Corsican file, no. 34118, vol. 1, 9–10, cited in Costello and Tsarev, 75.

Naum Belkin: Belkin was Arvid's control officer from 1935 to 1936. He is misidentified in Brysac, *Resisting Hitler,* and Costello and Tsarev, *Deadly Illusions,* as "Alexander Belkin."

konspiratsia: Peschersky, *"Krasnaia Kapella,"* 17 (page cited from electronic edition).

oath of loyalty: Ibid.

successfully recruited his target: The documents usually produced when a spy is recruited into Soviet intelligence—a report and a signed "obligation" (*obiazatel'stvo*)—do not appear in Arvid's NKVD file, indicating that he succeeded in resisting formal recruitment into Soviet intelligence.

Spies Among Us (1935–1936)

A magnificent train: Martha was upset that the train was not the famous Fliegende Züge (the Flying Hamburger), which she described in her memoir as "the fastest and most expensive" train; Dodd, *Through Embassy Eyes,* 21.

"a steady stream": These and other details of Martha Dodd's arrival in Berlin were obtained from her memoir; see Dodd, *Through Embassy Eyes,* 21–22.

"I am told state secrets": Martha Dodd to Thornton Wilder, September 25, 1933, Wilder Papers, YUA.

"I have heard Schacht": Ibid., November 10, 1934.

a wife and child in Moscow: Boris Vinogradov married Tatiana Vassilievna Izvekova in 1922; they had a daughter. He married his second wife, Vassa Konstantinovna Sneltsova, in 1929; Boris Dmitrievich Vinogradov, fond 17, op. 97, file 258, 7. RGASPI.

(code name Alex): This is the abbreviation that is used in Vassiliev's notebooks — short for "Alexander"; White Notebook # 2, 14, Alexander Vassiliev papers, LOC.

"The situation": Ibid., 15.

Dmitri Bukhartsev: Ibid., 16–17.

He's actually a spy: Dmitri Bukhartsev was indeed a journalist and a scholar — his primary occupations. It may be said that he moonlighted on some assignments for the INO OGPU. In the jargon of Soviet intelligence, Bukhartsev is known as a "cooptee"; Dmitri Bukhartsev, fond 17, op. 171, file 228, 236, 265, RGASPI.

"swinish behavior": White Notebook # 2, 14, Alexander Vassiliev papers, LOC.

"intensively": Ibid. The book is Stalin's *The Problems of Leninism (Voprosy leninizma),* originally published in 1926.

"Harnack": White Notebook # 2, 14, Alexander Vassiliev papers, LOC.

"Martha says": Ibid., 25.

Beheadings Are Back (1935–1936)

forty-seven crimes: Waite, *"Rote Plötze"*; Hollweck, *Die Todesstrafe,* 52–53. The day Hitler took power, the criminal code mandated the death penalty for eight crimes and recommended it for 206 others. Germans convicted of treason — *Landesverrat* — were led to the chopping block with greater frequency than those convicted of other crimes.

wearing a black top hat: In June 1935, the Ministry of Justice questioned Gröpler about his attire. Gröpler explained that the tailcoat was more practical than the standard uniform worn by prison officials, which was "too constricting"; the tailcoat enabled him to swing his ax and chop necks with greater precision (Schreiben des Generalstaatanwalts von Naumburg an den Reichsminister der Justiz vom 12, Juni 1935 zum Vertrag mit dem Scharfrichter, R22/1323, 55–58, BArch).

"Executioner, do your duty": *The State Journal,* "Women Go to Death by Axe Without Show of Emotion," February 19, 1935.

seventy-nine men and nine women: *Zur Anzahl der Todesurteile und der Hinrich-*
  tungen 1934, in: *Kriminalstatistik für die Jahre 1935 und 1936,* 13, 16.

also covered the story: "Nazis Behead Two Women; 'Betrayed Military Secrets,' "
  New York Times, February 19, 1935; "Germany Beheads Woman for Murder
  of Neighbor," *New York Times,* February 24, 1935; "Hitler Beheads Another
  Woman; Third in a Week," *Chicago Daily Tribune,* February 24, 1935;
  "Foreign News: Stoogettes & Neuter," *Time,* March 4, 1935.

"What impressed us most": "Eighteen Witnesses at Execution. Nazis to Behead
  Two Men; Women Faced Axe Calmly," *New York Times,* February 20, 1935.

by guillotine: Men in the resistance were also executed by guillotine, but the
  majority were shot or, in certain cases, hanged. Arvid Harnack, Harro
  Schulze-Boysen, Dietrich Bonhoeffer, Hans von Dohnányi, Wilhelm
  Canaris, and Hans Oster were all hanged.

a letter: Mildred Harnack to Georgina Fish, undated, probably the summer of
  1930, Donner family papers.

"What an historic moment": Dialogue and descriptions derived from an article
  written by Emil Kortmann, "Zusammenarbeit mit Mildred und Arvid
  Harnack," Falk Harnack collection, GDW.

"the new developments": Kuckhoff, *Vom Rosenkranz zur Roten Kapelle,* 200.

Widerstand *(1935–1937)*

"Heil Hitler": Hoffmann, *The History of the German Resistance,* 20.

translates what she's written: Mildred's translations of Churchill's speeches were
  also turned into leaflets; see Dodd, *Through Embassy Eyes,* 279.

Law for the Protection of German Blood and German Honor: Rabinbach and
  Gilman, *The Third Reich Sourcebook,* 209–10.

Nuremberg Laws: The laws came to be known as the Nuremberg Laws because
  they were announced during the annual Nazi Party rally in the city of
  Nuremberg. The Nuremberg Laws were presented as key evidence in the
  Nuremberg Trials. *Reichsgesetzblatt* 1, no. 100 (1935): 1146–47.

Mildred will help Jews escape: Max Tau and Samson Knoll both wrote about
  Mildred's help in getting Jewish family members out of Germany. Tau, *Ein
  Flüchtling findet sein Land,* cited in Brysac, *Resisting Hitler,* 173, 418; Samson
  Knoll, Protokoll, Rote Kapelle collection, GDW. Documentation of other
  attempts Mildred may have made to help Jews flee Germany has not been
  found.

2,197 people in underground resistance groups: Hoffmann, *The History of the
  German Resistance,* 16.

twelve thousand people: Boehm, *We Survived,* viii.

"We kept strict discipline": Ibid., 193, 194.

"To any outsider": Paul, *Ein Sprechzimmer,* 97.

1,643,200: In 1937, the number was 927,430; see Hoffmann, *German Resistance
  to Hitler,* 55.

classification system: Hall, "An Army of Spies?," 255.

"VM": Ibid., 256, 260.

Hitler keeps telling the world: This point is emphasized in *Law Reports of Trials of War Criminals*, which cites numerous speeches Hitler gave between 1933 and 1938 in which he falsely claimed he desired peace. The report concludes that Hitler's "immediate circle of confidants and plotters" knew of Hitler's plans to wage war, but "the evidence failed to show the existence of a common knowledge of Hitler's plans, either with respect to a general plan to wage war, or with respect to the specific plans to attack individual countries, beginning with the invasion of Poland." (*Law Reports of Trials of War Criminals: The I.G. Farben and Krupp Trials,* vol. 10, 14–16.)

"There is not": Domarus, *Hitler Reden und Proklamationen,* 563, 571.

3,300 soldiers: Evans, *The Third Reich in Power,* 635.

"Night after night": Paul, *Ein Sprechzimmer,* 97.

Harro Schulze-Boysen visits Mildred and Arvid's apartment: They met sometime in 1935. The introduction was made through Rudolf Heberle, who attended the University of Wisconsin the same time Mildred and Arvid did. Like Arvid, Heberle was a German exchange student on a Rockefeller scholarship.

his friend's injuries: His friend was Henry Erlanger; see Höhne, *Codeword: Direktor,* 105.

"too dangerous": Brysac, *Resisting Hitler,* 231.

Ernst and Ernst (1935–1937)

"I have put": Salomon, *Fragebogen,* 288.

"smart young men": Ibid., 167.

"smiling attractively": Ibid.

"printed on the most expensive paper": Ibid., 112.

"clear vodka": Ibid.

"What good news": Ibid., 159. This entire encounter was told to Ernst von Salomon by his friend Franz Hessel, who witnessed it.

Bahbiett: Ibid.

"A publishing house": Ibid.

"I have nothing to hide": Williams, *More Lives Than One,* 167.

"I can't write anymore": Ibid., 171.

"I stick flags": Salomon, *Fragebogen,* 289.

"an assured place": Ibid., 288.

"enough of revolutions": Ibid., 289–91.

"the greatest crime": Ibid., 293.

Identity Crisis (1936–1937)

two million: Evans, *The Third Reich in Power,* 108. The number of block wardens in Germany reached two million in 1939.

"You couldn't say anything": Ibid., 109.

merge into one centralized agency: This happened twenty-one days after Hitler launched the Second World War.

I. G. Farben: The company's prominence in Germany's military preparations was so significant that some historians referred to Hitler's Four-Year Plan as the "I. G. Farben Plan"; see "The I. G. Farben Company Presents Its Synthetic Rubber ('Buna')," GHDI.

"The battle we are now approaching": Shirer, *The Rise and Fall of the Third Reich,* 300.

"Just as we are now": *Documents on German Foreign Policy,* Series C (1933–1937), *The Third Reich: First Phase,* vol. 5: March 5–October 31, 1936 (Washington, DC: United States Government Printing Office, 1957–1964).

"valuable documentary materials": Summary of materials received from 1935 to June 1938, Corsican file, no. 34118, vol. 1, 37, cited in Costello and Tsarev, *Deadly Illusions.*

"bold, tall, blue eyes": Corsican file, no. 34118, vol. 2, 77, cited in Costello and Tsarev, *Deadly Illusions.* The memo was written by Martha Dodd under her code name, Liza.

Homecoming (1937)

everyone calls him Bob: As a toddler, Mildred had trouble pronouncing Marbeau, so she called him "Bobbo," and the nickname stuck.

"under surveillance": Bob Fish Jr. to Sue Heath, October 4, 1988, Donald R. Heath Papers, HIA.

Francis Birch: Birch went on to work on the Manhattan Project in Los Alamos, New Mexico, and was awarded the Legion of Merit for his participation in building the Little Boy, the nuclear weapon that was dropped on Hiroshima on August 6, 1945.

"introspective": Brysac, *Resisting Hitler,* 31.

"It was very strange": Ibid., 205.

a biography about Leonard: The project consumed sixty years.

Did I tell you: Clara Leiser to William Ellery Leonard, January 11, 1937, Leiser family papers, cited in Brysac, *Resisting Hitler,* 201.

I envy her: Clara Leiser to William Ellery Leonard, January 18, 1937, Leiser family papers, cited in Brysac, *Resisting Hitler,* 202.

Mildred delivers a lecture: In a letter, the chair of the English Department at New York University praised her for her "extraordinarily illuminating" insights (Oscar Cargill to Mildred Harnack, March 29, 1937, HU).

her own literary ambitions: Clara had published a book about a nineteenth-century Polish tenor titled *Jean de Reszke and the Great Days of Opera* (New York: Minton, Balch, 1934).

"anybody she approaches": Clara Leiser to William Ellery Leonard, January 18, 1937, Leiser family papers.

"extremely frightened": Brysac, *Resisting Hitler,* 203.

"We don't talk about that": Ibid.

"I have the feeling": Ibid.

"kind of strained": Interview conducted by Arthur Heitzer, May 1987, Harriette Esch, Marion Potter, Jane Donner, Donner family papers.

Georgina's Tremors, Big and Small (1937–1938)

"If capitalism keeps": Mildred Harnack to Georgina Fish, June 4, 1931, Donner family papers.

"Ninety-six percent": Mildred Harnack to Georgina Fish, February 13, 1931, Donner family papers.

"In Berlin one never forgets": Ibid., August 15, 1931.

"walked through the streets": Ibid., June 4, 1931.

"old, bourgeois humiliation": *Lenin's Collected Works* (Moscow: Progress Publishers, 1965), 371–72. First published in *Pravda,* February 22, 1920.

"It's good": Ibid., August 8, 1932.

Women are allowed: Ibid., September 3, 1932.

Georgina was in her late sixties: Georgina Fish was born in 1865 and died at the age of seventy-three.

"I am so sorry": Mildred Harnack to Georgina Fish, February 8, 1933, Donner family papers.

"only of the individual": Ibid.

"You are quite right": Ibid., April 28, 1932.

Whatever ailment she suffers from: Jane Donner believed she died from the flu; Bob Fish Jr. speculated that Georgina had Parkinson's disease (Bob Fish Jr. to Sue Heath, October 4, 1988, Donald R. Heath Papers, HIA).

"Surely you are": Mona Wollheim: "Gießen zu Beginn der dreißiger Jahre," in *Hessische Heimat (Heimatbeilage der Gießener Allgemeinen Zeitung)* (1972), 21–22, Hs NF 401, JLU.

Jane in Love (1937–1938)

"See that menu": Jane Esch to Esch family, June 17, 1937, Donner family papers.

"The cows look just like ours": Ibid., June 26, 1937.

"I'm getting expert": Ibid., August 26, 1937.

"A couple of nights ago": Ibid., June 26, 1937.

"tawny fields": Ibid., August 12, 1937.

A week from tomorrow: Ibid., August 13, 1937.

The letter Jane composes: Ibid., August 19, 1937.

When you want: Ibid.

The rooms are hung: Ibid., November 7, 1937.

The picture I am enclosing: Ibid., November 16, 1937.

My Little Girl (1937–1938)

Harriette is furious: The letters Harriette mails to Jane during this time "drip with venom," Jane will recall years later; interview, Jane Donner Sweeney and Sue Heath Brown, Donald R. Heath Papers, HIA.

"My Little Girl": Harriette Esch to Jane Esch, November 27, 1937, Donner family papers.

a fascination with biology: Twenty-five-year-old Max Delbrück was profoundly influenced by Niels Bohr's "Light and Life" lecture, which he delivered in

Copenhagen on August 15, 1932. See "Interview with Max Delbrück," 1979, Caltech Oral Histories, Caltech Institute Archives.

Nobel Prize: Delbrück shared the Nobel Prize in 1969 with Salvador Luria and Alfred Hershey "for their discoveries concerning the replication mechanism and the genetic structure of viruses."

A Circle Within the Circle (1937–1938)

"Everyone knew": Wolfgang Havemann, Protokoll, GDW.

Wolfgang agrees to hide the typewriter: Wolfgang Havemann, Protokoll, GDW.

Beamer: Behrens was assigned the Russian cryptonym *Luchistyi* (in German, *Strahlman*). The Anglicized version of *Luchistyi* is "Beaming."

code name Turk: Hans Rupp is an example of a source who was given a code name to conceal his identity in Arvid's communications with Moscow; Arvid Harnack, Harro Schulze-Boysen, and Adam Kuckhoff were given code names to enable them to communicate directly with a control officer.

ARPLAN days: Baron Wohlzogen-Neuhaus and Arvid were both members of the Bund Geistiger Berufe (BGB).

Boris Gordon has his eye: Gordon is credited with running Arvid and Mildred Harnack. Abramov, *Jevrei v KGB: Palachi izhertvy,* 165; Peschersky, "Krasnaia Kapella 1935–1941," 416–18.

highly desirable: In a CIA document dated June 23, 1967, Mildred is identified as "one of the most prominent American women in Berlin society" ("East German Postage Stamps Honor Rote Kapelle Agents," RG 263, NARA).

"use her": In 2018, the Russian embassy to the United States gave the author an excerpt from this file (housed at SVRA), which notes that Mildred visited Moscow in 1933 and 1934 "to talk with Kuusinen." Otto Kuusinen was a leader of the Comintern who organized the short-lived Socialist Workers Party of Finland.

Japonka: Gladkov, *Lift v razvedku,* 51 (page cited from electronic edition). The English translation is "Japanese."

A Child, Almost (1937–1938)

He even buys a motorcycle: Wilhelm Utech, Protokoll, Rote Kapelle collection, GDW.

"chronicle of shame": Bethge, *Dietrich Bonhoeffer,* 624. The safe is located in an office at a military base in Zossen.

a captain: He is Captain Fritz Wiedemann; ibid., 626.

two generals strongly objected: Hoffmann, *The History of the German Resistance,* 37. According to notes that will later be discovered in War Ministry files, the argument at the meeting between the two generals and Göring was "very sharp." The notes were written by Colonel Friedrich Hossbach and are known as the Hossbach Minutes. The generals are Field Marshal General Werner von Blomberg, who serves in Hitler's cabinet as minister of war, and Colonel-General Werner von Fritsch, who is commander in chief of the army.

"peace for our time": "Neville Chamberlain," Holocaust Encyclopedia, USHMM.
"Unity Front": Hoffmann, *The History of the German Resistance,* 103. Julius Leber, Wilhelm Leuschner, Otto John, and Richard Kuenzer were present.
Hitler's military aid: Hochschild, *Spain in Our Hearts,* 48.
Deutsche Freiheitssender: Palmier, *Weimar in Exile,* 357. German and American authors, including Thomas Mann and Ernest Hemingway, appeared on the radio program as guests. The station invited German listeners to mail letters with information on the political and social climate in Germany to a Paris address.
obtain enough explosives: Martha Utech, Protokoll, Rote Kapelle collection, GDW. It remains unknown whether they succeeded in carrying out plans for sabotage missions of this sort.
"Her sorrow astonished me": Franziska Heberle to Renate Dörner, March 22, 1965, Renate Dörner collection, GDW.
"A. has been away": Mildred Harnack to Marbeau Fish, June 7, 1938, Donner family papers.

Stalin and the Dwarf (1937–1938)

"Darling": Martha Dodd to Boris Vinogradov, January 29, 1937, White Notebook # 2, 30, Alexander Vassiliev papers, LOC.
"the Soviet Government": Martha Dodd to "the Soviet Government," March 14, 1937, White Notebook # 2, 37, Alexander Vassiliev papers, LOC.
"I don't quite understand": March 21, 1937, White Notebook # 2, 45, Alexander Vassiliev papers, LOC.
his current wife: Boris Vinogradov's file does not state explicitly whether he remained married to Vassa Konstantinovna Sneltsova; Boris Dmitrievich Vinogradov, fond 17, op. 97, file 258, 7, RGASPI.
"At present": White Notebook # 2, 39, Alexander Vassiliev papers, LOC.
"TOP SECRET": Ibid., March 29, 1937, 48.
the Dwarf: He was known ex post facto as the "Bloody Dwarf"; see Montefiore, *Stalin,* 168.
sixty thousand: In 2002, evidence of a mass grave was found in a forest outside St. Petersburg; see Ben Aris, "Forest Skulls May Tell Where 30,000 Stalin Victims Lie," *Telegraph,* September 26, 2002.
one thousand murders a day: an estimated 12.5 million people were executed during the Great Purge, also known as the Great Terror; see Sophia Kishkovsky, "Moscow Ceremony Remembers People Killed in Soviet Purge," *New York Times,* October 29, 2007.
Moscow Show Trials: The trials featured twenty-one defendants, nineteen of whom were executed.
mercury-tainted curtains: Montefiore, *Stalin,* 218.
"If you have reason": Agnes Knickerbocker to Martha Dodd, July 29, 1969, LOC.
"a brief summary": White Notebook # 2, 34, Alexander Vassiliev papers, LOC.
"200 American dollars": Ibid.
A memo in her file: Ibid., 33.
mass-execution site: It is called Kommunarka.

Boris's Last Letter (1937–1938)

"rarely demonstrative": Martha Dodd, "In Memory," Martha Dodd papers, box 13, LOC.

Dodd knows he is unpopular: Dallek, *Democrat and Diplomat,* 313.

"sad years": William E. Dodd to Franklin D. Roosevelt, August 26, 1937, President's Secretary's File (PSF), Safe Files, State Department, 1941, Franklin D. Roosevelt Presidential Library and Museum Digital Archives.

"greeted by his daughter": "Dodd Back, Bitter on Dictatorships," *New York Times,* January 7, 1938.

"We are informing you": Moscow Center to Jung, January 8, 1938, White Notebook # 2, 52, Alexander Vassiliev papers, LOC.

"She lives in a rich": Weinstein and Vassiliev, *The Haunted Wood,* 61.

"It was a sad": Martha Dodd to Ilya Ehrenburg, October 29, 1957, Martha Dodd papers, box 5, LOC.

"She is very keen": Weinstein and Vassiliev, *The Haunted Wood,* 61.

"We, all of us": Martha Dodd, untitled essay, Martha Dodd papers, box 13, LOC.

Seeking Allies (1938–1939)

The Dwarf presides over thousands of executions: Yezhov insisted on witnessing many of the executions. He was arrested on April 10, 1939, in the office of his successor, Lavrenty Beria. On February 3, 1940, Yezhov was sentenced to death; the following day he was shot in the back of his head by an executioner named Blokhin.

"New people came to fill": O'Sullivan, *Dealing with the Devil,* 21.

"the man who has pulled": Larson, *In the Garden of Beasts,* 355.

"Best wishes": The notes were sent as telegrams and featured in two issues of the Russian newspaper *Pravda* (December 23 and 25, 1939). Stalin's note to Foreign Minister Ribbentrop is erroneously described by William Shirer as a note he wrote to Hitler in Shirer, *The Rise and Fall of the Third Reich,* 670.

Morgenthau's Man (1937–1939)

Get up off the ground: Author interviews with Donald Heath Jr.

"style, grace, poise": Weil, *A Pretty Good Club,* 47.

"the most-talked-of diplomat": Harold Hinton, "Welles: Our Man of the Hour in Cuba," *New York Times,* August 20, 1933.

A colleague of mine: Details in this account not otherwise cited are from author interviews with Donald Heath Jr.

"Donald R. Heath of Topeka, Kansas": *American Foreign Service Journal,* December 1937.

typically jammed with meetings: "Morgenthau Correspondence: Appointments of HM Jr. [1937–1938]," box 14, Henry Morgenthau Jr. papers, FDRL.

William "Wild Bill" Donovan: "The Legend of Wild Bill: How Donovan Got His Nickname," Central Intelligence Agency, November 11, 2020, http://cia.gov.

"to strangle this unwanted newcomer": Smith, *OSS,* 19.

"Roosevelt's folly": MacDonald, "The OSS and Its Records," 83.

Two agencies followed: The Central Intelligence Group (CIG) created an operational unit called the Office of Special Operations (OSO) in July 1946, giving it jurisdiction over foreign intelligence.

"We may be headed": Messersmith labeled the letter *personal and confidential* and sent it to Consul Gilbert on October 25, 1937. The next day, Messersmith sent a copy of the personal and confidential letter to First Secretary Raymond Geist. The attached note begins: "I am sending you herewith for your private and confidential information a letter which I have addressed to Gilbert... Perhaps it is better that you not let him know that I have sent you a copy of the letter" (George Messersmith to Prentiss Gilbert, October 25, 1937, box 8, F57; George Messersmith to Raymond Geist, October 26, 1937, box 8, F57, George S. Messersmith papers, DEL).

"Morgenthau's Man": Hugh Wilson to George Messersmith, June 20, 1938, RG 59, confidential file 123, H 353/217, NARA; George Messersmith to Raymond Geist, April 15, 1938, George S. Messersmith papers, box 9, F61, DEL.

Schacht cannot be trusted: George Messersmith to Secretary of State [Cordell Hull], Undersecretary of State [Sumner Welles], January 14, 1939, George S. Messersmith papers, box 21, F168, DEL. Messersmith observes, "Dr. Schacht is so complex a character that any real analysis of the part which he has played would have to be quite lengthy... I may add that there is further ample evidence of his complete unscrupulousness."

carefully worded letter of protest: Messersmith wrote a letter to Wilson in response and secretly sent a copy to two State Department colleagues. In an attached note, Messersmith told his colleagues that Wilson's letter "seems to indicate that he did not have as fully, as we thought, the background of the assignment of Heath to the Embassy and the financial reporting in which we are interested in this Department and which he is doing for Treasury" (George Messersmith to Mr. Shaw, Dr. Feis, June 10, 1938, George S. Messersmith papers, box 20, F154, DEL).

"From Heath to Treasury": Henry Morgenthau Jr. papers, State Department cables, boxes 521–23, FDRL.

The most confidential information: Donald Heath Sr. and his colleagues at the U.S. embassy were exceedingly careful to hold their conversations outside the office (Hugh Wilson to George Messersmith, March 17, 1938, George S. Messersmith papers, box 20, F154, DEL).

"principally on business": "Foreign Service Officers," *American Foreign Service Journal.*

Joy Ride (1938)

It will be: Author interviews with Donald Heath Jr.

Goodbye, boys: Ibid.

Will you take: Ibid.

Lunch Before Kristallnacht (1938)

October 24, 1938: Louise Heath diary, Donald R. Heath Papers, HIA.

"The greatest wave": Lochner, "Nazis Burn, Pillage."

"In Berlin an American": Schultz, "Homes Burned."

"The policeman threw my wife": Childers, *The Third Reich,* 364.

Ninety-one Jews: Ibid., 365; Shirer, *The Rise and Fall of the Third Reich,* 431;
     "Kristallnacht," Holocaust Encyclopedia, USHMM. Police records also
     document a spike in suicides among Jews during this time. According to
     recent scholarship, the number of Jews who died may have reached several
     hundred.

It is the first time: "Kristallnacht," Holocaust Encyclopedia, USHMM.

"systematically trained": Shirer, *The Rise and Fall of the Third Reich,* 430.

"recalled for consultations": Ibid., 433.

"Refugees were to be found": Russell, *Berlin Embassy,* 23.

Getting to Be Pretty Good (1938–1939)

meticulously transcribed: Morgenthau makes sure all his morning meetings are
     transcribed for the entirety of his term as U.S. treasury secretary. Intent on
     establishing his legacy, he hired the team of transcribers himself.

"I don't know whether": In 1948, Harry White was accused of spying for the Soviet
     Union, which he denied. Decades later, the discovery of secret cables through
     a U.S. counterintelligence program (the Venona Project) suggested that he had
     (December 13, 1938, Henry Morgenthau Jr. papers, diaries, vol. 156, FDRL).

a telegram: Telegram number 21, Cordell Hull to American Embassy, Berlin,
     Germany, February 4, 1939, Henry Morgenthau Jr. papers, State Department
     cables, box 521, FDRL.

"Heath has all the stuff": Meeting transcript, February 27, 1939, Henry
     Morgenthau Jr. papers, diaries, vol. 166, FDRL.

"an unmistakable firm stand": Donald R. Heath to Henry Morgenthau Jr., May
     2, 1939, Henry Morgenthau Jr. papers, diaries, vol. 187, FDRL.

Germany's reserves: Donald Heath to William C. Bullitt, April 8, 1939, Donald
     R. Heath Papers, HIA. As with other written correspondence, Heath is
     careful to conceal Arvid's identity. See Brysac, *Resisting Hitler,* 249–50.

"The Embassy has received": Heath to Treasury, April 24, 1939, Henry
     Morgenthau Jr. papers, State Department cables, box 522, FDRL.

As early as 1937: Hoffmann, *The History of the German Resistance,* 55, 104–10;
     Dulles, *Germany's Underground,* 22. These emissaries include Carl Goerdeler,
     who met with Churchill in May 1939; Adam Trott zu Solz, who met with
     Chamberlain and members of the House of Lords in June 1939; and Fabian
     von Schlabrendorff and Helmuth James Graf von Moltke, who in the summer
     of 1939 also met with members of the House of Lords.

"Are the stories": June 8, 1944, Public Record Office, London, FO 371/39087/
     C8865/180/18. For a more detailed discussion of this point, see von
     Klemperer, *German Resistance Against Hitler,* and Hoffmann, *The History of
     the German Resistance.*

"Nazi military aggression": Unpublished memoir, Donald Heath Sr., Donald R. Heath Papers, HIA.

"so funny singing": Louise Heath diary, August 26, 1939, Donald R. Heath Papers, HIA.

"operatic register": Miscellaneous notes, undated, Sue Heath Brown, Donald R. Heath Papers, HIA. Sue planned to write a book about Mildred Harnack and amassed boxes of research. She died before she could begin the manuscript.

A Fateful Decision (1939)

A boy Don nicknames Boobie: Details in this chapter are obtained from Don's letter to his parents (Don Heath Jr. to Louise Heath and Don Heath Sr., July 7, 1939, Donald R. Heath Papers, HIA).

"with faint painting": Louise Heath diary, August 29, 1939, Donald R. Heath Papers, HIA.

"horrible bombings": Ibid., Louise Heath diary, September 5, 14, 24, 29, 1939.

"nothing but repetition": Ibid., November 4, 1939.

"Mad rush": Ibid.

"the idea of hope": Ibid., November 15, 1939.

At nite; Couldn't keep; Early at: Ibid., November 19, 20, 21, 1939.

"I feel really as tho": Ibid., November 22, 1939.

Air Raid (1940)

Don likes: Author interviews with Donald Heath Jr.

Don misses: Ibid.

Dear Louise: Ibid.

Now they've buried: Ibid.

If you want coal: Russell, *Berlin Embassy,* 138.

"At the Embassy": Ibid.

"one roll": Louise Heath diary, November 8, 1939, Donald R. Heath Papers, HIA.

"was supposed to suffice": Russell, *Berlin Embassy,* 139.

One-pot Sundays: Ibid., 138.

"unlimited supplies": Ibid., 146.

"What's the difference": Ibid., 140.

air raid: Author interviews with Donald Heath Jr.

a wild, exuberant thumping: Ibid.

"For reasons of national": Murrow famously ends the broadcast with the words "Good night, and good luck." "Murrow, the Blitz, and the Race to War," NPR, May 22, 2006.

"Are the Roosevelts Jews?": Russell, *Berlin Embassy,* 151.

"crashed through the double window": Shirer, *Berlin Diary,* 504. *Berlin Diary* was published in 1941, nineteen years before the publication of his mammoth tome *The Rise and Fall of the Third Reich.*

"For three weeks": Klemperer, *I Will Bear Witness,* 355. Victor Klemperer kept a diary from 1933 to 1945.

Louise Heath's Diary (1940)

his name appears twice: Louise Heath's datebook, January 1, 1940, Donald R.
    Heath Papers, HIA.

"twilight zone": Mayers, "Neither War nor Peace," 60.

"Mr. Kirk's residence here": Louise Heath, undated postcard, Donald R. Heath
    Papers, HIA. The hotel that she refers to is most likely the Hotel Adlon.

Mamzelle and Mildred and Mole (1940)

"a weekly shipment": Russell, *Berlin Embassy,* 138.

You're very lucky...Did anyone try: Author interviews with Donald Heath Jr.

Who are your mother's: Ibid.

Tell me how you got here: Ibid.

Where does your teacher: In an interview Don's sister, Sue, conducted in 1987, Don
    explained he was "well schooled and never mentioned any names...[and]
    would pretend to be not listening." Sue Heath Brown interview of Donald
    Heath Jr., September 4, 1987, Donald R. Heath Papers, HIA.

a lady from Leipzig: Author interviews with Donald Heath Jr. Through Arvid's
    cousin Ernst von Harnack, the Circle had ties to Carl Goerdeler, the mayor
    of Leipzig from 1930 to 1937. Goerdeler was one of the conspirators in the
    July 1944 plot to assassinate Hitler. Don speculated during the interview that
    "the lady from Leipzig" was connected to Goerdeler; her identity cannot be
    verified with available documentation.

he shoots him: Author interviews with Donald Heath Jr.

Fragment

Questionnaire: Plötzensee Prison, Berlin, February 16, 1943, SGY/4, BArch.

Foreign Excellent Trench Coats (1940)

606,600 tons: Fond 500, op. 12463, file 190, 40, TsAMO. According to Soviet
    records, Stalin sent 267,500 tons in the first half of 1941. Romanian oil also
    fueled the German war machine.

mass graves in Moscow and its outskirts: The Donskoye cemetery, located in
    central Moscow, had a crematorium. The Butovo and the Kommunarka
    mass-execution sites were located southwest of Moscow.

Foreign Excellent Trench Coats: Trepper, *The Great Game,* 97.

Corsican Drops a Bombshell (1940)

Mildred has traveled alone: It's unknown what the purpose of the trip was.
    Mildred sent a postcard to Clara Harnack while she was there.

We need your help: Corsican file, no. 34118, vol. 1, 108, cited in Costello and
    Tsarev, 79. In his report to Moscow Center, Korotkov notes that Arvid
    regarded him with tremendous suspicion.

"carefully selecting": Ibid.

two hundred hastily trained: O'Sullivan, *Dealing with the Devil,* 38.

"an honest person": Corsican file, no. 34118, vol. 1, 112, cited in Brysac, *Resisting Hitler,* 264.

"a very careful treatment": Corsican file, no. 34118, vol. 1, 63, cited in Costello and Tsarev, 81.

"has told Corsican": Corsican file, no. 34118, vol. 1, 62, cited in Costello and Tsarev, 82.

Libs and Mildred Among the Cups and Spoons (1940)

"It was so rare": Kuckhoff, *Vom Rosenkranz zur Roten Kapelle,* 278.

"protected from all eyes and ears": Ibid., 232.

"I needed to hold": Ibid.

AGIS and Other Agitations (1940–1942)

"fervent": Korotkov report to Moscow Center, March 31, 1941, Corsican file, no. 34118, vol. 1, 217, cited in Costello and Tsarev, 84.

"humanist": Friedman, "The Red Orchestra," 156.

"Call for Resistance": R 58/4105, BADH.

"What Is a Majority": Petrescu, *Against All Odds,* 199–200; Friedman, "The Red Orchestra," 156–57. Petrescu states that the writers of the AGIS leaflets were Arvid Harnack, Harro Schulze-Boysen, Adam Kuckhoff, Wilhelm Guddorf, and John Sieg. Friedman suggests that women were also involved in writing the leaflets and describes an episode when Harro Schulze-Boysen orders Cato Bontjes van Beek to write a leaflet urging sabotage. The available information on the writers of the leaflets is limited to what members of these resistance groups confessed to during Gestapo interrogations. It remains unknown whether Mildred Harnack participated in producing the AGIS leaflets. During his trial, Arvid Harnack tried to save her life by minimizing her involvement in the resistance and lying about her participation in espionage, among other activities.

Waitzstrasse 2: This is the address of Cato Bontjes van Beek's apartment. Höhne refers to Cato as another member's "girlfriend" and states that the leaflets were produced in Harro's apartment (not Cato's). Höhne describes Eva-Maria Buch, who translated the leaflets into French for distribution to the French resistance, as another member's "mistress." Höhne suggests that only Harro and John Rittmeister authored the leaflets; see Höhne, *Codeword: Direktor,* 134.

mails the leaflets: All details from Friedman, "The Red Orchestra," 153–56.

Annie Krauss's: Krauss works with her neighbor John Graudenz to produce the leaflets. Both are members of Gegner Kreis.

among the recipients: By May 20, 1942, the number of leaflets that the office receives reaches 260; see Petrescu, *Against All Odds,* 219–20.

"The People Are Troubled": R 58/4105, BADH.

Grossdeutscher Rundfunk: In 1939 the Reichs-Rundfunk-Gesellschaft (RRG) was renamed Grossdeutscher Rundfunk.

"took home copies": Boehm, *We Survived,* 195.

Members translate: Petrescu, *Against All Odds,* 215–17.

Open Letters: Ibid., 217–19; Sieg, *Einer von Millionen,* 131–40; R 3018/NJ 2, BADH.

"Sometimes we went out": Boehm, *We Survived,* 194.

a garish exhibition: The anti-Soviet exhibition "The Soviet Paradise" opened at the Lustgarten on May 8, 1942.

"Permanent Exhibition": "Meldungwichtiger staatspolizeilicher Ereignisse Nr. 9 vom 20 Mai 1942," *Gestapo-Berichte über den antifaschistischen Widerstandskampf der KPD 1933–1943,* hrsg. Margot Pikarski und Elke Warning, bd. 2 (Berlin: Karl Dietz Verlag, 1989–1990), 227.

Baum Gruppe: The explosives that the Baum Group set off at the exhibition failed to burn it down. The Gestapo arrested nearly thirty of its members. Herbert Baum committed suicide in Moabit prison in June 1942. Marianne Baum was executed in August 1942.

Zoya Ivanovna Rybkina's Eleven-Page Table (1941)

Zoya Ivanovna Rybkina: After retiring in 1956, she became a popular writer of books for children under her maiden name, Voskresenskaya. She wrote a memoir of her intelligence work, *Now I Can Tell the Truth,* that was published after her death.

types up a table: Corsican file, no. 34118, vol. 2, 23–33, cited in Costello and Tsarev, 85, 390–93.

an aide-de-camp: Ibid. This source's name remains unknown; his code name was Schwed.

"Starshina gives the impression": Corsican file, no. 34118, vol. 1, 217, cited in Costello and Tsarev, 83.

a meeting with Adam Kuckhoff: Corsican file, no. 34118, vol. 1, 327, cited in Costello and Tsarev, 84. The meeting is on April 19, 1941.

"Corsican will become": Corsican file, no. 34118, vol. 1, 249, cited in Costello and Tsarev, 394.

too dogmatic: Kuckhoff, *Vom Rosenkranz zur Roten Kapelle,* 130–31.

13,500 Reichsmark: Brysac, *Resisting Hitler,* 290.

Greta Kuckhoff agrees to pick up: Kuckhoff, *Vom Rosenkranz zur Roten Kapelle,* 281.

Kurt Schumacher: Kurt's wife is Elisabeth Schumacher, also a member of Gegner Kreis.

Clean: Costello and Tsarev, *Deadly Illusions,* 396.

What should she do: Greta finally decides to contact Arvid, who arranges for the transmitter to be taken to Spandau, where friends hid it in a shed.

"We were at pains": Peschersky, "Krasnaia Kapella 1935–1941," 452.

Stalin's Obscenity (1941)

"Plans for bombing": These are among the reports that Zoya Ivanovna Rybkina included in her eleven-page table (Corsican file, no. 34118, vol. 2, 25, 26, 30, cited in Costello and Tsarev, *Deadly Illusions*).

disinformation: O'Sullivan, *Dealing with the Devil,* 38.

other warnings: Childers, *The Third Reich,* 481.

"Hands up": Beevor, *The Second World War,* 188.

"Explain": Peschersky, "Krasnaia Kapella 1935–1941," 493. The conversation was mostly between Stalin and Fitin. Also present at the meeting was People's Commissar of State Security Vsevolod Merkulov.

"You can send your 'source'": V. Merkulov to comrade Stalin, June 17, 1941, Fond 3, op. 50, file 45, p. 50, APRF; cited in Dmitry Volkogonov Papers, reel 19, box 29, folder 15, Manuscript Division, LOC.

Hans Coppi's First Message (1941)

the most savage and deadly: Childers, *The Third Reich,* 481.

"The Russian": Beevor, *The Second World War,* 195.

reports follow in quick succession: Childers, *The Third Reich,* 483.

he persists in believing: Beevor, *The Second World War,* 191. According to Shevyakov, the last train holding Soviet grain crossed the Western Bug River one hour and fifteen minutes before Germany attacked the Soviet Union. See A. A. Shevyakov, "Sovetsko-germanskie economicheskie svyazi v predvoennye gody," *Sotsiologicheskie issledovaniia* 5 (1995): 13–25.

Down with Hitler: Finck report, CIA, declassified 2004/2006, 27.

"A thousand greetings": Costello and Tsarev, *Deadly Illusions,* 396.

Anatoly Gurevich, aka Kent, aka Vincente Sierra, aka Victor Sukolov (1941)

D6: Costello and Tsarev, *Deadly Illusions,* 396.

"absolutely reliable": Ibid.

prodigious appetite: A CIA file notes: "[Gurevich] stocked up to the point of making himself ludicrous on leather shoes and cigarettes when he first arrived in the West because he was convinced that these articles were available only on the day he saw them in a store. This was a typical Soviet reaction, i.e. to buy as much as possible when the wares were available" (Heinz Pannwitz, vol. 2, RG 263, 14, NARA).

"forty or fifty": Perrault, *The Red Orchestra,* 44.

August 26, 1941: Sources are conflicted on the date. Costello and Tsarev (397) state that "according to a GRU postwar report" the date the message was radioed to Kent was October 10, 1941, "with an additional cryptogram" that included details about what Kent should find out from Arvid, Harro, and Adam.

"To Kent": O'Sullivan, *Dealing with the Devil,* 251. The memo is signed by both GRU Commissar Ilyichev and General Panfilov, head of foreign intelligence

of the Red Army General Staff, with an endorsement by NKVD intelligence
chief Pavel Fitin.

significant espionage blunders: O'Sullivan, *Dealing with the Devil,* 251.

Code Red (1941)

Arvid asks his nephew: Wolfgang Havemann, Protokoll, GDW. Brysac
    erroneously states that Wolfgang Havemann refused to keep one in his
    apartment; see Brysac, *Resisting Hitler,* 295.

"Are you prepared": Wolfgang Havemann, Protokoll, GDW.

enciphers intelligence reports: The Rote Kapelle (Finck Study), RG 319,
    66, NARA.

do most of the enciphering: Gestapo final report, RG 319, 22, NARA.

checkerboard pattern: Some elements of this description are derived from Höhne,
    Codeword: Direktor, 87–88, and Tarrant, *The Red Orchestra,* 53–55. This is a
    simplified explanation of an exceedingly complicated code.

simplified version: Soviet intelligence utilized a two-step process: first, encoding
    with a codebook, and second, encryption with a cipher pad (called
    pereshifrovochnye gammy) that corresponded with an identical pad at Moscow
    Center. To add another layer of security, the cipher pad was to be used
    only once.

A Single Error (1941)

"To Kent": Cryptogram from GRU to Kent, September 26, 1941, Corsican file,
    no. 93621, vol. 1, 26, cited in Costello and Tsarev, 397–98.

18.7 percent: Höhne, *Codeword: Direktor,* 88.

a monumental victory: Evans, *The Third Reich at War,* 203.

still the only message: This is disputed in the Gestapo final report, which states
    that five hundred radio messages were sent to Moscow between June 14,
    1941, and August 30, 1942.

Gollnow (1941)

"like butterflies": Arvid Harnack to Clara Harnack, October 12, 1940, Falk
    Harnack collection, GDW.

letter and a poem: Hand-delivered to Louise on June 10, 1941. The poem is a translation
    of a Goethe poem titled "Gegenwart" (Donald R. Heath Papers, HIA).

One Pain Among So Many (1941–1942)

choose to shoot themselves: Beevor, *The Second World War,* 245.

"The fuel supply": Harro hand-delivered this report to Kent during Kent's two-
    week visit. Kent sent the report from Brussels after he returned from Berlin
    to Pavel Fitin at NKVD/GRU temporary headquarters (they evacuated
    Moscow Center headquarters as the Wehrmacht approached Moscow).

Cryptogram, Kent to GRU, November 1941, Corsican file, no. 34118, vol. 2, 64–66, cited in Costello and Tsarev, 399.

Could you send us potatoes: Mildred Harnack to Clara Harnack, December 3, 1941, Falk Harnack collection, GDW.

the largest audience in American broadcasting history: Brown, *Manipulating the Ether,* 118.

seven hundred thousand: Childers, *The Third Reich,* 485.

known to weep: Evans, *The Third Reich in Power,* 53.

"a man of few words": Lina Heydrich to Jean Vaughan, December 12, 1951. See https://spartacus-educational.com/Lina_Heydrich.htm.

country-specific statistics: Shirer, *The Rise and Fall of the Third Reich,* 965.

fifteen pages: Wannsee Protocol, January 20, 1942, *Law Reports of Trials of War Criminals,* vol. 13, 210–19.

Oil in the Caucasus (1942)

"If I do not": Paulus's testimony to the International Military Tribunal at Nuremberg; see Bellamy, *Absolute War,* 497.

the obscure novel: Dr. Vauck and his team of cryptologists were unaware that in addition to *Le Miracle du Professeur Wolmar,* another, less obscure book was used: Balzac's *La Femme de Trente Ans.*

"Through the police department": Brysac, *Resisting Hitler,* 315.

May we all remain: Mildred Harnack to Esch family, August 14, 1942, Donner family papers.

to escape by boat: Numerous books erroneously conjecture that Mildred and Arvid were "on holiday," including Höhne, *Codeword: Direktor,* 158.

FRAGMENT

Questionnaire: Plötzensee Prison, Berlin, February 16, 1943, SGY/4, BArch.

Arrest (1942)

She walks the dunes: This chapter is based on Zechlin's published account of Mildred and Arvid's arrest; all dialogue that appears in quotation marks appears in this primary-source account. See Zechlin, "Erinnerungen," 395–404.

"He seemed to have something special": Ibid.

The Gestapo Album (1942)

"dark catacomb": This is how Georgi Dimitrov, leader of the Comintern, described his solitary cell in the basement of Gestapo headquarters; see Topography of Terror Foundation, *The House Prison,* 43.

thirty-eight solitary cells: In 1933, there were twenty cells; in 1935 a second cellblock was built with eighteen cells and a communal cell. "In front of all cells were walkways, in between a controlled passage, and an air raid shelter which served simultaneously as a guard room" (Rürup, *Topography of Terror*, 89).

"like any other government office": Topography of Terror Foundation, *The House Prison*, 53.

"Since your husband": Quoted in Höhne, *Codeword: Direktor*, 169, and Brysac, *Resisting Hitler*, 337.

one hundred nineteen: Breitman et al., *U.S. Intelligence and the Nazis*, 294.

"a claim form": Rürup, *Topography of Terror*, 85.

Geduld ist die: Kuckhoff, *Vom Rosenkranz zur Roten Kapelle*, 334.

"good friends": Ibid., 333.

"Libertas's nerves": Ibid.

German Communists: Perrault, *The Red Orchestra*, 199.

verschärfte Vernehmung: O'Sullivan, *Dealing with the Devil*, 256.

five interrogators: Captured files reveal that the interrogators were Walter Habecker, Johannes Strübing, K. K. Büchert, Alfred Göpfert, and Hans Henze.

As prisoners walk up the stairs: In 1936, an elevator was installed at Gestapo headquarters to stop this; see Topography of Terror Foundation, *The House Prison*, 50.

"like withered leaves": Marie Luise von Scheliha survived her imprisonment and recalled the encounter in Sahm, *Rudolf von Scheliha*, 197.

"with some distaste": The dialogue and descriptions in this scene are based on an article written by Axel von Harnack. Harnack, "Arvid und Mildred Harnack."

Maria Grimme: Maria was the wife of Adolf Grimme, a member of Tat Kreis. It remains unknown whether she participated in acts of resistance; in archival documents she is referred to only as a "wife" (RG 319/63, interrogation of Alexander Kraell, July 9, 1946, 5).

"remarkable expression": Testimony, Maria Grimme, Lüneberg, vol. 8, NLB; N/2506/68/51, BaRCH.

Knock-Knock (1942)

"ominously": Dialogue and descriptions in this scene obtained from Günther Weisenborn's essay "Reich Secret," published in Boehm, *We Survived*, 192–211.

"Pack two": Ibid.

"Hitler mustache": Ibid., 199.

"Now tell me": Ibid.

"The odds were piling up": Ibid., 200.

"I began to tap": Ibid., 201–2.

Falk Does His Best (1942)

The advice Falk gave the Scholls: Falk Harnack met with Hans Scholl and Alex Schmorell in November 1942 (Dumbach and Newborn, 7).

"tightly and tenderly": Falk Harnack to Clara Harnack and Ansa Harnack, October 26, 1942, Falk Harnack collection, GDW.

"During the first stage": Cited in Topography of Terror Foundation, *The House Prison,* 53.

Arvid asks Falk: Falk's conversations with Arvid are derived from an unpublished essay Falk wrote, "Vom anderen Deutschland," 1947, Falk Harnack collection, GDW.

"No one ever": Harnack, "Arvid und Mildred Harnack."

The coup both men tried to organize: The plan was to storm the Reich Chancellery and either arrest or assassinate Hitler. Reichsbank president Hjalmar Schacht was among the plotters. See Hoffmann, *The History of the German Resistance,* 82–88, 91–93.

"If there are men": George K. A. Bell to Anthony Eden, July 25, 1942, Public Record Office, London, Foreign Office 3471/30/913/C 4425/48/18; Anthony Eden to George K. A. Bell, August 17, 1942, Public Record Office, London, Foreign Office 3471/30/913/C 4425/48/18. The British Foreign Office assumed a patronizing stance toward George Bell, dismissing the UK-born bishop of Chichester as "our good German bishop" (Foreign Office 371/34415/C8903/29/18). See also Metaxas, *Bonhoeffer,* 394–404.

Wolfgang's Seventh Interrogation (1942)

"You needn't cover": Wolfgang Havemann, Protokoll, GDW. Wolfgang was taken prisoner by the Red Army in 1944. This chapter is based on a transcript of his interrogation by his Russian captors, who questioned him about his involvement in the Rote Kapelle. In 1994, Hans Coppi Jr. (son of Hans and Hilde Coppi, born in prison shortly before their execution) discovered the transcript in a Russian archive.

"into tears of moral indignation": Ibid., February 13, 1944.

"make a wonderful novel": Ibid.

Kassiber (1942)

"Always inspect the seams": Friedman, "The Red Orchestra," 158.

A guard is moved: Ibid.

a police officer: His name is Alfred Göpfert.

"humiliated": Testimony, Admiral Karl-Jesko von Puttkamer, September 30, 1948, Lüneberg Trial, vol. 4, NLB.

"the elite": Testimony, Werner Krauss, Lüneberg Trial, vol. 10, NLB.

"I have only one favor": Höhne, *Codeword: Direktor,* 160.

"was all excited": Ibid.

"out of selfishness": Libertas Schulze-Boysen to Thora Eulenburg, December 22, 1942, Renate Dörner collection, GDW. After whispering into the typist's ear the names of dozens of her friends and collaborators in the resistance, Libertas Schulze-Boysen deceitfully claimed that she didn't know the typist would alert the Gestapo. In this letter to her mother, Libertas admits that she "betrayed" her friends "out of selfishness," then puts the blame on the Gestapo typist: "a human being, in whom I had trusted completely, Gertrud Breiter, betrayed me (and you)."

The Red Orchestra Is Neither All Red Nor Particularly Musical (1942)

The new arrests: Kassiber, Rose Schlösinger, Marianne Siderie Heinemann collection, GDW.

"eleventh-hour panic": *Kassiber,* Oda Schottmüller, Rote Kapelle collection, GDW.

"Lips": *Kassiber,* Erika von Brockdorff, Rote Kapelle collection, GDW.

"pianists": O'Sullivan, *Dealing with the Devil,* 252; Höhne, *Codeword: Direktor,* xv.

"it is a very extensive": Harnack, "Arvid und Mildred Harnack," 15–18.

"Still no news from M.": Falk Harnack to Clara Harnack and Ansa Harnack, December 7, 1942, GDW.

I hear Mildred: Kassiber, Rose Schlösinger, Marianne Siderie Heinemann collection, GDW.

It is rumored: Brysac, *Resisting Hitler,* 342.

"vitamins and yeast": Mildred Harnack to Axel von Harnack, Clara Harnack, Falk Harnack, December 7, 1942, Falk Harnack collection, GDW.

Anneliese and Witch Bones (1942–1943)

wood chips and straw: Descriptions of Mildred's cell are based on details her coconspirators record in *Kassiber,* GDW.

I unfortunately: Kassiber, Rose Schlösinger, Marianne Siderie Heinemann collection, GDW.

"Scissors in the hole!": *Kassiber,* Elfriede Paul, Rote Kapelle collection, GDW.

"the Hot Hole": Ibid.

"sleep wonderfully": Ibid.

Eulenspiegel: Kassiber, Erika von Brockdorff, Rote Kapelle collection, GDW.

I've never lived life: Ibid.

"did everything in their power": Anneliese Kuehn, Protokoll, Rote Kapelle collection, GDW.

"I realized with deep respect": Ibid.

"Such shamelessness. . . . Witch Bones": *Kassiber,* Oda Schottmüller, Rote Kapelle collection, GDW.

"Well, well": Ibid.

But Anneliese Kuehn does: Anneliese Kuehn, Protokoll, GDW.

"Today": *Kassiber,* Elfriede Paul, Rote Kapelle collection, GDW.

"a long icicle": Ibid.

Hitler's Bloodhound (1942–1943)

"We must keep Roeder": Höhne, *Codeword: Direktor,* 180.

"does not possess": Ibid., 179.

"insensitive and biased": Ibid.

"Hitler's Bloodhound": Breitman et al., *U.S. Intelligence and the Nazis,* 298.

early January 1943: After prosecuting seventy-six men and women in the Red Orchestra, chief prosecutor Manfred Roeder was replaced by another prosecutor in mid-February; see Höhne, *Codeword: Direktor,* 201, 203.

"an indescribably conceited rooster": *Kassiber*, Oda Schottmüller, Rote Kapelle collection, GDW.

"witch hunt": *Kassiber*, Erika von Brockdorff, Rote Kapelle collection, GDW. Erika von Brockdorff underwent a second trial and was sentenced to death.

The First of Many Trials (1942)

"BOOK OUT OF STOCK": Axel von Harnack to Falk von Harnack, telegram, Falk Harnack collection, GDW.

Mildred's Cellmate (1942–1943)

"lived illegally with a Dutchwoman": Possibly a euphemistic reference to a lesbian relationship. Gestapo file: Gertrud Klapputh, 1942, RW58/21723, LAV NRW.

"The Bear Dance": Gertrud Lichtenstein (née Klapputh) to Clara Harnack, November 9, 1952, Falk Harnack collection, GDW.

"We could only exchange": Ibid.

"spontaneously fall": Ibid.

"Mildred possessed a great treasure": Ibid.

"She wrote down Goethe verses for me": Ibid. Gertrud misremembers the verse as "Edel sei der Mensch und gut"; it is actually "Edel sei der Mensch, hilfreich und gut" (Let man be a noble creature, helpful and good).

"beamed": Harnack, "Arvid und Mildred Harnack." Mildred's lawyer, Leonhard Schwarz, reported this to Axel von Harnack.

"sad and sometimes close to despair": Gertrud Lichtenstein (née Klapputh) to Clara Harnack, November 9, 1952, Falk Harnack collection, GDW.

"expect a stiffer sentence": Ibid.

Arvid is dead: Ibid. Harald Poelchau, the Lutheran minister who saw Mildred the day of her execution, February 16, 1943, believed that he was the first to inform Mildred that Arvid had been executed. Gertrud's letter suggests that Mildred's lawyer, Schwarz, informed her in January 1943.

"exploded": Testimony, Rudolf Lehmann, September 28, 1948, Lüneberg Trial, vol. 12, NLB.

assigned a different panel: Memo regarding Hitler's decision on December 21, 1942, Oberkommando der Wehrmacht, December 23, 1942, BArch. The judges in Mildred's second trial belonged to the Third Chamber of the Reich Court-Martial.

The Greatest Bit of Bad Luck (1943)

"about twelve": Testimony, Karl Schmauser, September 9, 1950, Lüneberg Trial, vol. 12, NLB.

Why did you tell her: SS officer Heinz Pannwitz allegedly burned court records of the trial; sentencing documents from the first trial survived. See Höhne, *Codeword: Direktor,* xviii–xix.

"sexual bondage": Testimony, Johannes Strübing, Lüneberg Trial, vol. 10, NLB. See also David Dallin papers, D papers, NYPL.

"Then came the greatest": Gertrud Lichtenstein (née Klapputh) to Clara Harnack, November 9, 1952, GDW.

"the new one": Irmgard Kamlah to Axel von Harnack, February 14, 1947, Falk Harnack collection, GDW.

The Armband She Wore (1943)

"I heard the officer": Irmgard Kamlah to Axel von Harnack, February 14, 1947, GDW.

"for her execution": Ibid.

"I learned what it meant": Ibid.

The Mannhardt Guillotine (1943)

seventeen thousand: The murders took place from 1793 to 1794.

Judges became: The Volksgerichtshof—People's Court—was established in 1934 to prosecute political crimes, including treason.

a new set of guidelines: Schreiben des Reichsjustizministers vom 12. Januar 1937 an den Generalstaatsanwalt in Karlsruhe zur Vollziehung der Todesstrafe, und, Schreiben an den Generalstaatsanwalt beim Kammgergericht, R22/1314, 217, BArch.

Mildred loved to swim: In a letter to her mother, Mildred wrote about swimming in the Rhine "opposite vine-covered slopes in the brilliant sunshine" (Mildred Harnack to Georgina Fish, August 28, 1930, Donner family papers).

detailed instructions: Schreiben des Reichsministers der Justiz vom 28, Dezember 1936 zur Vollziehung der Todesstrafe. R22/1314, 216, BArch.

"quite spacious": Ibid., 256.

"This would ensure": Ibid.

All the Frequent Troubles of Our Days (1943)

"I had already experienced": Poelchau, *Die letzten Stunden,* 16. The execution was carried out at Tegel Prison on April 17, 1934.

He attends secret meetings: Hoffmann, *German Resistance to Hitler,* 63.

February 16, 1943: Harald Poelchau describes this encounter in a 1949 memoir; see Poelchau, *Die letzten Stunden,* 62–65. Details from this chapter are also based on a 1954 memoir by Mildred's coconspirator Günther Weisenborn, who met with Poelchau in August 1946 and implored him to share his observations of Mildred the hour before her execution. "I came away with this impression from his description of Mildred: Mildred had been physically mistreated by her interrogators. She was suffering from advanced tuberculosis...[and was] 'völlig verwirrt,' which translates politely as 'completely distracted,' but actually means 'quite out of her mind.'" See Weisenborn, *Der lautlose Aufstand,* 211.

"In all the frequent troubles of our days": The title of the poem is "In Ein Stammbuch"; it appears in the book *Das Göttliche: Gedichte,* by Johann

Wolfgang von Goethe. The book with Mildred's handwritten translations is at GDW.

The evidence of her suffering: Harald Poelchau writes about the encounter in a 1949 memoir; see Poelchau, *Die letzten Stunden,* 62–65.

orange and the photograph: Falk Harnack, Protokoll, Falk Harnack collection, GDW.

The face of my mother: Photograph of Georgina Fish, Red Orchestra collection, GDW.

place her head on a block: Mildred Harnack was executed at 6:57 p.m. on February 16, 1943. Errors abound in a multiplicity of books about the date and manner of Mildred Harnack's execution, most recently *Bohemians* by Norman Ohler, who fetishizes Mildred as "the once radiant blond woman" who "climbs the scaffold" and is hanged (220).

Stieve's List (1943–1945)

"it is worthwhile": All quotations and other details about Margarete von Zahn's encounter with Dr. Hermann Stieve are based on a radio interview she gave in 2005, when she was eighty-five years old (Wonschik, *Mildreds Asche,* 2005). See also Wulfert, "Margarete von Zahn."

Dr. Stieve keeps a list: Hildebrandt, *The Anatomy of Murder,* 18–21. For a copy of Stieve's list, see DP1/6490, BArch.

"bodies of criminals": Ibid., 152.

a special arrangement: On the medical research of Stieve, see the recent study by Tuchel, *Hinrichtungen im Strafgefängnis.*

"It is extremely difficult": Wonschik, *Mildreds Asche,* 2005.

17,383 executions: Hildebrandt, *The Anatomy of Murder,* 16.

Exactly how many bodies: Ibid., 187. A conservative estimate is 35,000 to 40,000; the proportion of political dissidents among them is unknown.

plötzlich Tod: Winkelmann and Schagen, "Hermann Stieve's Clinical-Anatomical Research," 163–71.

he has a large collection: See H. Stieve, *Der Einfluss des Nervensystems auf Bau und Tätigkeit der Geschlechtsorgane des Menschen* (Stuttgart: Thieme, 1952).

The Final Solution (1943–1945)

number of prisoners: Wachsmann, *KL,* 192, 415.

six thousand Jews: "Gassing Operations," Holocaust Encyclopedia, USHMM.

two-thirds: "Final Solution," ibid.

Gertrud (1943–1945)

prisoner number 16277: Ravensbrück registry, 1.1.35.1 / 3768233, Klapputh— Blockbuch Block 1 KZ Ravensbrück, Arolsen archive. Many details about Gertrud Klapputh's experience at Ravensbrück are obtained from her postwar recollection: Gertrud Klapputh Lichtenstein, "So war mein leben! So wurde ich Antifaschistin," Falk Harnack collection, GDW.

He believes: Helm, *Ravensbrück,* 20.

twelve thousand: Megargee, *Encyclopedia of Camps and Ghettos,* 1188.

"smooth dry skin": Helm, *Ravensbrück,* 241.

seventy-three thousand shirts: The time period is July 1940 to March 1941 (Wachsmann, *KL,* 227).

crawl with lice: A member of the French resistance who was a Ravensbrück survivor recalled in a 1945 interview that many women who were made to sort these lice-ridden uniforms contracted typhus; see Flanner, "Letter from Paris," 52.

"pretty, with good teeth": Affidavit, Dr. Gerhard Schiedlausky, August 7, 1945, cited in Helm, *Ravensbrück,* 198.

a select few: The brothel at Buchenwald, for example, saw an average of fifty-three daily visitors in October 1943 (see Wachsmann, *KL,* 413).

"encourage the men": Heinrich Himmler to Oswald Pohl, March 23, 1942, BArch, cited in Helm, *Ravensbrück,* 198.

sadistic experiments: *Law Reports of Trials of War Criminals,* vol. 1, 367–76, 381–87, 391–417. See also Bagatur, "Nazi Medicine," 1899–1905.

"I felt great pain": Testimony, Wladislawa Karolewska, Mitscherlich and Mielke, *Medizin ohne Menschlichkeit,* 182–83, cited in Helm, *Ravensbrück,* 12–13.

"carefully wrapped up": Deposition, Dr. Zdenka Nedvedova-Nejedla, Nuremberg Trials, September 6, 1946, RG 238, NARA.

"Everyone was shocked": Helm, *Ravensbrück,* 225.

"Blockovas": Ibid., 34.

administrative tasks: Gertrud was one of twelve women who worked as secretaries for SS officers at Ravensbrück. Gertrud may have also worked as a Blockova, although documentation is scant. Helm observes, "The SS burned all documents about the appointment of Kapos and other prisoner staff" (Helm, *Ravensbrück,* 57).

"The more there are rivalries": Ibid., 51. At the Nuremberg Trials, Rudolf Höss was convicted as a war criminal and sentenced to death by hanging. At the request of the Polish authorities, Höss wrote a memoir before he was hanged.

eighteen thousand: Ibid., 278.

"A beautiful blonde": Ibid., 282.

a gas chamber: The gas chamber was a wooden structure that was erected near the crematorium. Gertrud wrote about the smell of burning bodies and the "constant meters-high flame" emerging from the high chimney of the crematorium, which was built in 1943 (Lichtenstein, "So was mein leben!"). Some Ravensbrück survivors refused to talk about the gas chamber or the crematorium (Flanner, "Letter from Paris," 55).

"We could hear the SS shouting": Helm, *Ravensbrück,* 617. The prisoner's name was Maria Bielicka.

"And then we stopped": Ibid., 622.

"And then it began": Ibid., 624.

an essay Gertrud writes: Lichtenstein, "So was mein leben!"

30,000 and 90,000: Helm, *Ravensbrück,* xviii.

6,000 were gassed: Rydén, "When Bereaved of Everything," 514.

Harriette's Rage (1942–1945)

"courageous Anti-Nazi": The letter was addressed to Mildred's mother; Franziska was unaware that Georgina Fish had died (Franziska Heberle to Mrs. Fish, December 21, 1943, Mildred Harnack papers, MHC).

"a sensational conspiracy": "Nazis Seized Estate, Word: Former Milwaukeean's Goods Confiscated, Husband Hanged, Report," *Milwaukee Journal,* May 16, 1943.

This morning: Marion Carlson to Harriette Esch, May 16, 1943, Donner family papers. In an article that appeared in the *Milwaukee Journal* on October 6, 1943 ("Woman Dead, a Nazi Victim: Native of Milwaukee"), Mildred's death is announced without a shred of evidence. Mildred's brother-in-law Albert Carlson speculated that Mildred died "in a concentration camp." Harriette speculated, "looks like a Gestapo job."

A stark black-and-white photograph: Donner family papers.

"like tramps": Memoir, Harriette Esch, ibid.

Baltimore Sun: "Maryland Girl, 3 Babies Flee Reich, Reach Yanks," *Baltimore Sun,* April 19, 1945.

"Dear Sir": John Schwertman, field director of the American Red Cross, to Fred Esch, June 10, 1945, Mildred Harnack papers, MHC.

"any documentation relative to that particular era": Bob Fish to Sue Heath, October 14, 1988, Donald R. Heath Papers, HIA. Bob Fish is the son of Marbeau "Bob" Fish.

Valkyrie (1942–1945)

"received large-scale": Dulles, *Germany's Underground,* 22.

"clear conscience": Bethge, *Dietrich Bonhoeffer,* 791, 797.

"We have been silent witnesses": Ibid., 796. Dietrich Bonhoeffer titled the essay "After Ten Years." His parents stashed a copy of the essay under the roof beams of their house at Marienburger Allee 43 in Berlin.

Dietrich slyly sends messages: For examples of these messages, see ibid., 812.

"in the double-layered lid": Meding, *Courageous Hearts,* 12. Emmi Bonhoeffer sends the messages in the winter of 1944 to Hans John. Both Hans John and his brother Otto John were deeply involved in the Valkyrie plot.

"musical party": Ibid., 15.

Justus Delbrück dies in prison: Delbrück was imprisoned but was liberated by the Allies. Several days later, he was taken prisoner by the Soviet secret police. He died in a Soviet prison camp in October 1945.

Recruited (1945–1948)

"Russian plots": O'Sullivan, *Dealing with the Devil,* 271.

"was found to be running": Sarah Helm, "The Gestapo Killer Who Lived Twice," *Sunday Times,* August 7, 2005.

"a wealth of information": Memo, Benjamin Gorby, Special Agent, CIC, to Lt. Kirkpatrick, December 31, 1947, RG 319, NARA.

"confidence was soon obtained": Memo, Major Earl S. Browning, CIC, May 20, 1948, in ibid.

to shadow Greta: Greta Kuckhoff was president of Deutsche Notenbank from 1950 to 1958 and had the distinction of being the first woman ever to run a German state bank.

"notorious, unscrupulous, opportunistic Nazi": Benno Selke, deputy director, Evidence Division, to commanding general, Office of the Deputy Director for Intelligence, August 4, 1948, RG 319, NARA.

"Mildred Harnack was in fact": Memo, Albert R. Perry Jr. to Captain H. H. Sloane, RG 152, NARA.

By Chance (1952)

"Very dear and honorable": Gertrud Lichtenstein (née Klapputh) to Clara Harnack, October 8, 1952, GDW.

who was an inexhaustible topic: Ibid., November 9, 1952.

Arvid's Letter (1942)

My dear beloved heart: Arvid Harnack to Mildred Harnack, December 22, 1942, Falk Harnack collection, GDW.

Don Goes Back (1946)

He remembers standing on the street: Details and descriptions in this chapter are based on author interviews with Donald Heath Jr.

What happened to Mole: Don later learned that Mole was killed when a building collapsed on him sometime in 1945.

You've got a brain in there: Author interviews with Donald Heath Jr.

Bibliography

―∾∾∾―

Unpublished Material

Brown, Sue Heath. "Autobiography." Donald R. Heath Papers, HIA.
Harnack, Mildred. "The New Apartment." HU.
―――. "Prothalamion." HU.
Heath, Donald, Jr. "The American Church in Berlin: January 1938–June 1941." Donald R. Heath Papers, HIA.
―――. "Remembering Arvid and Mildred Harnack." Donald R. Heath Papers, HIA.
―――. "Walking with Janey." Donald R. Heath Papers, HIA.
Heath, Donald R., Sr. "Education of a Foreign Service Officer." Donald R. Heath Papers, HIA.
Heath, Louise. Datebooks, 1938–1941. Donald R. Heath Papers, HIA.
―――. Diaries, 1938–1941. Donald R. Heath Papers, HIA.

Books and Articles

Abramov, Vadim. *Jevrei v KGB: Palachi izhertvy.* Moskva: Jauza, EKSMO, 2005.
"All British Air Attacks Are Doomed to Fail" [*"Alle englischen Luftangriffe waren zum Scheitern veruteilt"*]. *Der Führer,* December 20, 1939.
Baerwald, Friedrich. "How Germany Reduced Unemployment." *American Economic Review* 24, no. 4 (December 1934).
Bagatur, Erdem. "Nazi Medicine—Part 1: Musculoskeletal Experimentation on Concentration Camp Prisoners During World War II." *Clinical Orthopaedics and Related Research* 476 (2018).
Beck, Maria-Dorothea. "Erinnerungen an Mildred Harnack." *Die Andere Zeitung,* September 14, 1967.
Beevor, Antony. *The Second World War.* Boston: Little, Brown, 2012.
Bellamy, Chris. *Absolute War: Soviet Russia in the Second World War.* New York: Vintage, 2008.
Bethge, Eberhard. *Dietrich Bonhoeffer: A Biography.* Translated by Eric Mosbacher, Peter and Betty Ross, Frank Clarke, and William Glen-Doepel. Rev. ed. Minneapolis: Fortress Press, 2000.

Boehm, Eric H. *We Survived: The Stories of Fourteen of the Hidden and Hunted of Nazi Germany.* New Haven, CT: Yale University Press, 1949.

Bohn, Willi. *Transportkolonne Otto: Bibliothek des Widerstandes.* Frankfurt: Röderberg-Verlag, 1970.

Bourgeois, Guillaume. *La Véritable Histoire de L'Orchestre Rouge.* Paris: Nouveau Monde, 2015.

Breitman, Richard, Norman J. W. Goda, Timothy Naftali, and Robert Wolfe. *U.S. Intelligence and the Nazis.* Cambridge: Cambridge University Press, 2005.

Brown, Robert J. *Manipulating the Ether: The Power of Broadcast Radio in Thirties America.* Jefferson, NC: McFarland, 1998.

Brüning, Eberhard. *Mildred Harnack-Fish: Variationen über das Thema Amerika: Studien zur Literatur der USA.* Berlin: Aufbau-Verlag, 1988.

Brysac, Shareen Blair. *Resisting Hitler: Mildred Harnack and the Red Orchestra.* New York: Oxford University Press, 2000.

Buchanan, Andrew. *World War II in Global Perspective, 1931–1952.* New York: John Wiley, 2019.

Central Intelligence Agency. *The Rote Kapelle: The CIA's History of Soviet Intelligence and Espionage Networks in Western Europe, 1936–1945.* Washington, DC: University Publications of America, 1979.

Childers, Thomas. *The Third Reich: A History of Nazi Germany.* New York: Simon and Schuster, 2017.

Coppi, Hans. *Harro Schulze-Boysen— Wege in den Widerstand.* Koblenz, Germany: Fölbach, 1995.

Coppi, Hans, Jürgen Danyel, and Johannes Tuchel, eds. *Die Rote Kapelle im Widerstand gegen den Nationalsozialismus.* Berlin: Gedenkstätte Deutscher Widerstand, 1994.

Costello, John, and Oleg Tsarev. *Deadly Illusions: The KGB Orlov Dossier Reveals Stalin's Master Spy.* New York: Crown, 1993.

Crepon, Tom. *Leben und Tode des Hans Fallada: Eine Biographie.* Halle, Germany: Mitteldeutscher Verlag, 1992.

Dallek, Robert. *Democrat and Diplomat: The Life of William E. Dodd.* New York: Oxford University Press, 1968.

Dallin, David J. *Soviet Espionage.* New Haven, CT: Yale University Press, 1955.

David-Fox, Michael. *Showcasing the Great Experiment: Cultural Diplomacy and Western Visitors to the Soviet Union 1921–1941.* New York: Oxford University Press, 2012.

Dodd, Martha. *Through Embassy Eyes.* New York: Harcourt, Brace, 1939.

Domarus, Max, ed. *Hitler Reden und Proklamationen 1932 bis 1945.* Loenburg, 1998.

Duhnke, Horst. *Die KPD von 1933 bis 1945.* Cologne: Kiepenheuer and Witsch, 1972.

Dulles, Allen Welsh. *Germany's Underground: The Anti-Nazi Resistance.* New York: Da Capo Press, 2000.

Dumbach, Annette E., and Jud Newborn. *Shattering the German Night: The Story of the White Rose.* Boston: Little, Brown, 1986.

Evans, Jedidiah. *Look Abroad, Angel: Thomas Wolfe and the Geographies of Longing.* Athens: University of Georgia Press, 2020.

Evans, Richard J. *The Coming of the Third Reich.* New York: Penguin, 2004.

―――. *The Third Reich in Power, 1933–1939.* New York: Penguin, 2005.

―――. *The Third Reich at War.* New York: Penguin, 2008.

Ferguson, Adam. *When Money Dies: The Nightmare of Deficit Spending, Devaluation, and Hyperinflation in Weimar Germany.* New York: PublicAffairs, 2010.

Flanner, Janet. "Letter from Paris." *The New Yorker,* May 5, 1945.

"Foreign Service Changes." *American Foreign Service Journal* 14, no. 12 (December 1937).

"Foreign Service Officers." *American Foreign Service Journal* 16, no. 4 (April 1939).

Friedman, Ina. "The Red Orchestra and Cato Bontjes van Beek." In: *Confront! Resistance in Nazi Germany,* edited by John J. Michalczyk. New York: Peter Lang, 2004.

Fromm, Bella. *Blood and Banquets: A Berlin Social Diary.* New York: Birch Lane, 1990.

Gladkov, Teodor Kirillovich. *Lift v razvedku. "Korol Nelegalov". Aleksandr Korotkov.* Moscow: Tsentrpolygraph, 2002.

Goebbels, Joseph. *Vom Kaiserhof zur Reichskanzlei: eine historische Darstellung in Tagebuchblättern.* Munich: Franz Eher Nachf, 1942.

Goeschel, Christian. *Suicide in Nazi Germany.* New York: Oxford University Press, 2009.

Griebel, Regina, Marlies Coburger, and Heinrich Scheel. *Erfasst? Das Gestapo-Album zur Roten Kapelle.* Halle, Germany: Audioscop, 1992.

Grimme, Adolf. *Briefe.* Heidelberg: Schneider, 1967.

Guenther, Irene. *Nazi Chic? Fashioning Women in the Third Reich.* Oxford: Berg, 2004.

Haase, Norbert. *Das Reichskriegsgericht und der Widerstand gegen die nationalsozialistische Herrschaft.* Berlin: Gedenkstätte Deutscher Widerstand, 1993.

Hall, Claire M. "An Army of Spies? The Gestapo Spy Network 1933–1945." *Journal of Contemporary History* 44, no. 2 (April 2009).

Handbuch des Berliner Abend Gymnasiums. Berlin: Carl Heymanns Verlag, 1934.

Harnack, Axel von. "Arvid und Mildred Harnack: Erinnerungen an ihren Prozess." *Die Gegenwart* 2 (1947): 15–17.

Harnack, Clara. "Unermüdlicher Streiter für die Menschenrechte: Die Mutter Arvid Harnacks über ihren Sogn und die Schwiegertochter Mildred." *Neues Deutschland* (December 1977).

Harnack-Fish, Mildred. "Thomas Wolfe." *Berliner Tageblatt,* May 26, 1935.

Harrprecht, Klaus. *Harald Poelchau: Ein Leben im Widerstand.* Berlin: Rowohlt, 2004.

Hass, Michael. *Forbidden Music: The Jewish Composers Banned by the Nazis.* New Haven, CT: Yale University Press, 2013.

Helm, Sarah. *Ravensbrück: Life and Death in Hitler's Concentration Camp for Women.* New York: Doubleday, 2014.

Herman, Stewart W. *American Church in Berlin: A History.* Rev. ed. Self-published, 2001.

Hett, Benjamin Carter. *Burning the Reichstag: An Investigation into the Third Reich's Enduring Mystery.* New York: Oxford University Press, 2014.

Hildebrandt, Sabine. *The Anatomy of Murder: Ethical Transgressions and Anatomical Science During the Third Reich.* New York: Berghahn, 2016.

Hochschild, Adam. *Spain in Our Hearts: Americans in the Spanish Civil War, 1936–1939.* Boston: Mariner, 2017.

Hoffmann, Peter. *German Resistance to Hitler.* Cambridge, MA: Harvard University Press, 1988.

———. ed. *Behind Valkyrie: German Resistance to Hitler.* Montreal: McGill–Queen's University Press, 2011.

———. *The History of the German Resistance 1933–1945.* Cambridge, MA: MIT Press, 1977.

Höhne, Heinz. *Codeword: Direktor: The Story of the Red Orchestra.* New York: Coward, McCann, and Geoghegan, 1971.

Hollweck, Joseph. *Die Todesstrafe im neuen Reich.* Erlangen, jur. diss., v. 20, 1935.

Irving, David. *Goebbels: Mastermind of the Third Reich.* London: Focal Point, 1996.

Isenberg, Noah. "Voluptuous Panic." *New York Review of Books,* April 28, 2018.

Jones, Larry Eugene. "'The Greatest Stupidity of My Life': Alfred Hugenberg and the Formation of the Hitler Cabinet." *Journal of Contemporary History* 27, no. 1 (January 1992).

Juchler, Ingo. *Mildred Harnack und die Rote Kapelle in Berlin.* Potsdam: Universitätsverlag Potsdam, 2017.

"Judenplage in Belgien." *Deutsches Nachrichtenbüro,* December 12, 1939.

Kennedy, Richard S., and Paschal Reeves, eds. *The Notebooks of Thomas Wolfe.* Vol. 2. Chapel Hill: University of North Carolina Press, 2011.

Kershaw, Ian. *Hitler: 1889–1936 Hubris.* New York: Norton, 1999.

———. *Popular Opinion and Political Dissent in the Third Reich, Bavaria 1933–1945.* New York: Oxford University Press, 1993.

Kerwin, Jerome G. "The German Reichstag Elections of July 31, 1932." *American Political Science Review* 26, no. 5 (October 1932).

Kesten, Hermann, ed. *Thomas Mann Diaries: 1918–1939.* New York: Abrams, 1982.

Keynes, John Maynard. *The Economic Consequences of the Peace.* New York: Harcourt, Brace, and Howe, 1920.

Kirkpatrick, Clifford. "Recent Changes in the Status of Women and the Family in Germany." *American Sociological Review* 2, no. 5 (October 1937).

Klemperer, Klemens von. *German Resistance Against Hitler: The Search for Allies Abroad, 1938–1945.* Oxford: Clarendon, 1992.

Klemperer, Victor. *I Will Bear Witness 1933–1941: A Diary of the Nazi Years.* Translated by Martin Chalmers. New York: Modern Library, 1999.

Knafo, Danielle. "The Dead Mother in Käthe Kollwitz." *Art Criticism* 13 (1998): 24–36.

Koonz, Claudia. "Choice and Courage." In *Contending with Hitler: Varieties of German Resistance in the Third Reich,* edited by David Clay Large. New York: Cambridge University Press, 1991.

———. *Mothers in the Fatherland: Women, the Family, and Nazi Politics.* New York: St. Martin's, 1987.

Kuckhoff, Greta. *Adam Kuckhoff zum Gedenken: Novellen, Gedichte, Briefe.* Berlin: Aufbau-Verlag, 1946.

———. *Vom Rosenkranz zur Roten Kapelle.* Berlin: Verlag Neues Leben, 1972.

Large, David Clay. *Berlin.* New York: Basic Books, 2000.

———. ed. *Contending with Hitler: Varieties of German Resistance in the Third Reich.* New York: Cambridge University Press, 1991.

Larson, Erik. *In the Garden of Beasts: Love, Terror, and an American Family in Hitler's Berlin*. New York: Crown, 2011.

Ledig-Rowohlt, Heinrich. "Thomas Wolfe in Berlin." *American Scholar* 22, no. 2 (Spring 1953).

Lochner, Louis P. "Nazis Burn, Pillage." *Washington Post,* November 11, 1938.

———. *What About Germany?* London: Hodder and Stoughton, 1943.

———. ed. *The Goebbels Diaries*. London: Hamish Hamilton, 1948.

MacDonald, Lawrence H. "The OSS and Its Records." In *The Secrets War: The Office of Strategic Services in World War II.* Edited by George C. Chalou. Washington, DC: National Archives and Records Administration, 2002.

Mayer, Milton. *They Thought They Were Free: The Germans 1933–45.* Chicago: University of Chicago Press, 1955.

Mayers, David. "Neither War nor Peace: FDR's Ambassadors in Embassy Berlin and Policy Toward Germany, 1933–1941." *Diplomacy and Statecraft* 20, no. 1 (2009).

Meding, Dorothee von. *Courageous Hearts: Women and the Anti-Hitler Plot of 1944.* Translated by Michael Balfour and Volker R. Berghahn. New York: Berghahn Books, 1997.

Megargee, Geoffrey P., ed. *Encyclopedia of Camps and Ghettos, 1933–1945.* Vol. 1. Bloomington: Indiana University Press, 2009.

Merson, Allan. *Communist Resistance in Nazi Germany.* London: Lawrence and Wishart, 1985.

Metaxas, Eric. *Bonhoeffer: Pastor, Martyr, Prophet, Spy.* Nashville: Thomas Nelson, 2010.

Metcalfe, Philip. *1933.* Sag Harbor, NY: Permanent Press, 1988.

Mitscherlich, A., and F. Mielke, eds. *Medizin ohne Menschlichkeit. Dokumente des Nürnberger Ärzteprozesses.* Frankfurt: Fischer, 1978.

Montefiore, Simon Sebag. *Stalin: The Court of the Red Tsar.* New York: Vintage, 2005.

Mouton, Michelle. "From Adventure to Advancement to Derailment and Demotion: Effects of Nazi Gender Policy on Women's Careers and Lives." *Journal of Social History* 43, no. 4 (Summer 2010).

Moynahan, Brian. *Leningrad: Siege and Symphony: The Story of the Great City Terrorized by Stalin, Starved by Hitler, Immortalized by Shostakovich.* New York: Atlantic Monthly Press, 2013.

"News from the Department." *American Foreign Service Journal* 17, no. 3 (March 1940).

O'Sullivan, Dónal. *Dealing with the Devil: Anglo-Soviet Intelligence Cooperation During the Second World War.* New York: Peter Lang, 2010.

"Our Victory Is Certain!" ["Der Sieg ist uns gewiβ!"]. *Rheinsberger Zeitung,* December 23, 1939.

Page, Norman. *Auden and Isherwood: The Berlin Years.* New York: St. Martin's, 1998.

Palmier, Jean-Michel. *Weimar in Exile: The Antifascist Emigration in Europe and America.* Translated by David Fernbach. London: Verso, 2017.

Paul, Elfriede. *Ein Sprechzimmer der Roten Kapelle.* Berlin: Militärverlag der DDR, 1981.

Perrault, Gilles. *The Red Orchestra.* New York: Simon and Schuster, 1970.

Peschersky, Vladimir. "Krasnaia Kapella 1935–1941." In: *Ocherki istorii rossiiskoi vneshnei razvedki*, tom 3 (1933–1941). Moskva: Mezhdunarodnye otnosheniia, 2003.

———. *"Krasnaia Kapella": Sovetskaia razvedka protiv abvera i gestapo*. Moskva: Tsentrpoligraf, 2000.

Petrescu, Corina L. *Against All Odds: Models of Subversive Spaces in National Socialist Germany*. Bern, Switzerland: Peter Lang, 2010.

Peukert, Detlev J. K. *Inside Nazi Germany: Conformity, Opposition, and Racism in Everyday Life*. Translated by Richard Deveson. New Haven, CT: Yale University Press, 1987.

Poelchau, Harald. *Die letzten Stunden*. Berlin: Verlag Volk und Welt, 1949.

Pringle, Heather. *The Master Plan: Himmler's Scholars and the Holocaust*. New York: Hyperion, 2006.

Rabinbach, Anson, and Sander Gilman, eds. *The Third Reich Sourcebook*. Berkeley: University of California Press, 2013.

Reichsministerium für Wissenschaft, Erziehung, und Volksbildung. *Erziehung und Unterricht in der Höheren Schule: Amtliche Ausgabe des Reichs und Preuszischen Ministeriums für Wissenschaft, Erziehung, und Volksbildung*. Berlin: Weidmann, 1938.

Ritter, Gerhard. *Carl Goerdeler und die deutsche Widerstandsbewegung*. Stuttgart: Deutsche Verlag-Anstalt, 1954.

Roeder, Manfred. *Die Rote Kapelle*. Hamburg: Verlag Hans Siep, 1952.

Rosen, Curt. *Das ABC des Nationalsozialismus*. Berlin: Schmidt, 1933.

Rosenbaum, Ron. *Explaining Hitler: The Search for the Origins of His Evil*. New York: Da Capo Press, 1998.

Rürup, Reinhard, ed. *Topography of Terror: Gestapo, SS and Reichssicherheitshauptamt on the "Prinz-Albrecht-Terrain": A Documentation*. Translated by Werner T. Angress. Berlin: Verlag Willmuth Arenhövel, 2003.

Russell, William. *Berlin Embassy*. London: Michael Joseph, 1942.

Rydén, Johanna Bergqvist. "When Bereaved of Everything: Objects from the Concentration Camp of Ravensbrück as Expressions of Resistance, Memory, and Identity." *International Journal of Historical Archaeology* 22 (2018).

Sahm, Ulrich. *Rudolf von Scheliha, 1897–1942: Ein deutscher Diplomat gegen Hitler*. Munich: Verlag C. H. Beck.

Said, Erika. "Zur Situation der Lehrerinnen in der Zeit des Nationalsozialimus." In *Frauengruppe Faschismusforschung, Mutterkreuz und Arbeitbuch: Zur Geschichte der Frauen in der Weimarer Republik und im Nationalsozialismus*. Frankfurt: Fischer Taschenbuch Verlag, 1981.

Salomon, Ernst von. *Fragebogen [The Questionnaire]*. Translated by Constantine FitzGibbon. New York: Doubleday, 1955.

Sauder, Gerhard, ed. *Die Bücherverbrennung: Zum 10. Mai 1933*. Munich: Carl Hanser Verlag, 1983.

Sayner, Joanne. *Reframing Antifascism: Memory, Genre, and the Life Writings of Greta Kuckhoff*. New York: Palgrave Macmillan, 2013.

Schacht, Hjalmar. *Confessions of "the Old Wizard": The Autobiography of Hjalmar Horace Greeley Schacht*. Translated by Diana Pyke. Boston: Houghton Mifflin, 1956.

Schultz, Sigrid. "Homes Burned; Stores Looted; Terror Reigns: Mobs Run Wild in German Streets." *Chicago Tribune*, November 11, 1938.

Schwerin von Krosigk, Johann Graf. *Staatsbankrott*. Göttingen: Musterschmidt, 1974.

Shirer, William. *Berlin Diary: The Journal of a Foreign Correspondent, 1934–1941*. New York: Knopf, 1941.

———. *The Rise and Fall of the Third Reich: A History of Nazi Germany*. New York: Simon and Schuster, 1960.

Sieg, John. *Einer von Millionen Spricht: Skizzen, Erzählungen, Reportagen, Flugschriften*. Berlin: Dietz Verlag, 1989.

Siemens, Daniel. *Stormtroopers: A New History of Hitler's Brownshirts*. New Haven, CT: Yale University Press, 2017.

Sifton, Elisabeth, and Fritz Stern. *No Ordinary Men: Dietrich Bonhoeffer and Hans von Dohnanyi, Resisters Against Hitler's Church and State*. New York: New York Review Books, 2013.

Smith, Adam. *Paper Money*. New York: Summit Books, 1981.

Smith, R. Harris. *OSS: The Secret History of America's First Central Intelligence Agency*. Berkeley: University of California Press, 1972.

Speer, Albert. *Inside the Third Reich: Memoirs*. Translated by Richard and Clara Winston. New York: Macmillan, 1970.

Stackelberg, Roderick, and Sally A. Winkle, eds. *The Nazi Germany Sourcebook: An Anthology of Texts*. New York: Routledge, 2002.

Stibbe, Matthew. *Women in the Third Reich*. London: Hodder Education, 2003.

Sudoplatov, Viktor. *Inside Soviet Military Intelligence*. New York: Macmillan, 1984.

Tarrant, V. E. *The Red Orchestra: The Soviet Spy Network Inside Nazi Europe*. London: Arms and Armour, 1995.

Tau, Max. *Das Land das ich verlassen musste*. Hamburg: Hoffmann und Campe, 1961.

———. *Ein Flüchtling findet sein Land*, Gütersloh: Bertelsmann Lesering, 1966.

Thompson, Dorothy. "Who Goes Nazi?" *Harper's*, August 1941.

Topography of Terror Foundation. *The House Prison: At Gestapo Headquarters in Berlin*. Berlin: Stiftung Topographie des Terrors, 2005.

Trepper, Leopold. *The Great Game: Memoirs of the Spy Hitler Couldn't Silence*. New York: McGraw-Hill, 1977.

Trial of the Major War Criminals Before the International Military Tribunal. Nuremberg, Germany, November 14, 1945, to October 1, 1946. 42 vols. LOC.

Tuchel, Johannes. *Hinrichtungen im Strafgefängnis Berlin-Plötzensee 1933 bis 1945 und der Anatom Hermann Stieve*. Berlin: Gedenkstätte Deutscher Widerstand, 2019.

United Nations War Crimes Commission. *Law Reports of Trials of War Criminals*. Vol. 10, *I. G. Farben and Krupp Trials*. London: United Nations War Crimes Commission, 1949.

Usborne, Cornelie. *The Politics of the Body in Weimar Germany: Women's Reproductive Rights and Duties*. London: Palgrave Macmillan, 1992.

Voskresenskaya, Zoya, and Eduard Sharapov. *Taina Zoii Voskresenskoi*. Moskva: Olma Press, 1998.

Wachsmann, Nikolaus. *KL: A History of the Nazi Concentration Camps.* New York: Farrar, Straus and Giroux, 2015.

Waite, Robert G. *"Rote Plötze": Die Geschichte des Strafanstalt Plötzensee* (in press).

Weil, Martin. *A Pretty Good Club: The Founding Fathers of the U.S. Foreign Service.* New York: Norton, 1978.

Weinstein, Allen, and Alexander Vassiliev. *The Haunted Wood: Soviet Espionage in America — the Stalin Era.* New York: Modern Library, 1999.

Weisenborn, Günther. *Der lautlose Aufstand: Bericht über die Widerstandsbewegung des deutschen Volkes 1933–1945.* Hamburg: Rohwolt Verlag, 1954.

———. *Memorial.* Frankfurt: Röderberg-Verlag, 1977.

Welles, Benjamin. *Sumner Welles: FDR's Global Strategist.* New York: St. Martin's, 1997.

West, Rebecca. *Selected Letters of Rebecca West.* Edited by Bonnie Kime Scott. New Haven, CT: Yale University Press, 2000.

Williams, Jenny. *More Lives Than One: A Biography of Hans Fallada.* London: Libris, 1998.

Winkelmann, Andreas, and Udo Schagen. "Hermann Stieve's Clinical-Anatomical Research on Executed Women During the Third Reich." *Clinical Anatomy* 22 (2009): 163–71.

"Wisconsin Girl Beheaded by Hitler, Magazine Says." *Washington Post,* December 2, 1947.

Wulfert, Tatjana. "Margarete von Zahn (Geb. 1924)." *Der Tagesspiegel,* November 18, 2010.

Zahn-Harnack, Agnes von. "Frauenbewegung und Nationale Revolution." *Deutsche Allgemeine Zeitung,* April 30, 1933.

Zechlin, Egmont. "Erinnerungen an Arvid und Mildred Harnack." *Geschichte in Wissenschaft und Unterricht* 33 (1982): 395–404.

Ziemer, Gregor. *Education for Death: The Making of a Nazi.* New York: Oxford University Press, 1941.

Ziemer, Patsy. *Two Thousand and Ten Days of Hitler.* New York: Harper, 1940.

Radio and Film

Wonschik, Helmut. *Mildreds Asche,* Südwestdeutscher Rundfunk, 2005.

Electronic Sources

Central Intelligence Agency (CIA), www.cia.gov

German History in Documents and Images (GHDI), https://ghdi.ghi-dc.org

United States Holocaust Memorial Museum (USHMM), https://www.ushmm.org

Illustration Credits

The author is grateful to the following individuals and institutions for supplying images and for granting permission to publish them in this work:

109, 111, 112, 119, 120	Donald R. Heath Papers, Hoover Institution Archives
125	Reproduced by permission of Gedenkstätte Deutscher Widerstand
130, 140, 160	Courtesy of Library of Congress, Martha Dodd papers, box 13
161, 165	Donald R. Heath Papers, Hoover Institution Archives
180	National Archives and Records Administration
198	State Archive of the Russian Federation, 5283-6-1727-177; 5283-6-1727-197
247 (top, middle)	Courtesy of Donner family
247 (bottom)	National Archives and Records Administration
250 (top)	The Archive of the Foreign Intelligence Service of the Russian Federation
250 (bottom)	National Archives and Records Administration
253	The Archive of the Foreign Intelligence Service of the Russian Federation
273 (top)	Donald R. Heath Papers, Hoover Institution Archives
273 (bottom)	Franklin Delano Roosevelt Presidential Library & Museum, Henry Morgenthau Jr. papers, Morgenthau Correspondence, Appointments of HM Jr (1937–38), box 14
280	National Archives and Records Administration
281	Reproduced with permission of the *American Foreign Service Journal,* Vol. 16, No. 4, April 1939
284, 285, 287, 292	Donald R. Heath Papers, Hoover Institution Archives
293	Franklin Delano Roosevelt Presidential Library & Museum, Henry Morgenthau Jr. papers, Diaries, Book 156 (December 13–December 18, 1938), December 13, 1938, p. 15
296, 297 (top)	Donald R. Heath Papers, Hoover Institution Archives
297 (bottom)	Courtesy of Richard E. Brown

445   Landesarchiv Nordrhein-Westfalen, RW 58/21723
446   ITS Digital Archive, Arolsen Archives, Klap-
               puth—Blockbuch Block 1 KZ Ravensbrück, 1.1.35.1
               / 3768233
457   Permission from Baltimore Sun Media. All Rights
               Reserved.
467 (top)   From the *New York Times* © 1947 The New York Times
               Company. All rights reserved. Used under license.
467 (bottom)   National Archives and Records Administration
474   Reproduced by permission of Gedenkstätte Deutscher
               Widerstand
477   Donald R. Heath Papers, Hoover Institution Archives
480–81   Reproduced by permission of Gedenkstätte Deutscher
               Widerstand

Photo Insert

[p1] All photographs reproduced by permission of Gedenkstätte
      Deutscher Widerstand

[p2] Photograph of Mildred reproduced by permission of Gedenk-
      stätte Deutscher Widerstand; photograph of Mildred and
      Arvid courtesy of Donner family

[p3] Photograph of Mildred courtesy of Donner family; photo-
      graph of Mildred and Arvid reproduced by permission of
      Gedenkstätte Deutscher Widerstand

[p4] All photographs reproduced by permission of Gedenkstätte
      Deutscher Widerstand

[p5] All photographs courtesy of Donald R. Heath Papers, Hoover
      Institution Archives

[p6] All photographs reproduced by permission of the Bundesarchiv,
      R 58 Bild 03191-229; 03191-227; 03191-225; 03191-187;
      03191-179; 03191-175; 03191-228; 03191-215; 03191-181

[p7] All photographs reproduced by permission of the Bundesarchiv,
      R 58 Bild 03191-180; 03191-195; 03191-226; 03191-213;
      03191-173; 03191-178; 03191-196; 03191-210; 03191-230

[p8] All photographs reproduced by permission of Gedenkstätte
      Deutscher Widerstand

Index

~~~~

Page numbers in italic type refer to photographs.